THE POLITICS BOOK

DK

LONDON, NEW YORK, MELBOURNE,
MUNICH, AND DELHI

DK LONDON

PROJECT ART EDITOR
Amy Orsborne

SENIOR EDITOR
Sam Atkinson

MANAGING ART EDITOR
Karen Self

MANAGING EDITOR
Esther Ripley

PUBLISHER
Laura Buller

ART DIRECTOR
Phil Ormerod

ASSOCIATE PUBLISHING DIRECTOR
Liz Wheeler

PUBLISHING DIRECTOR
Jonathan Metcalf

ILLUSTRATIONS
James Graham

PRODUCER, PRE-PRODUCTION
Rachel Ng

SENIOR PRODUCER
Gemma Sharpe

original styling by
STUDIO 8 DESIGN

DK DELHI

SENIOR ART EDITOR
Anjana Nair

ART EDITOR
Nidhi Mehra

ASSISTANT ART EDITORS
Niyati Gosain, Vidit Vashisht,
Namita, Gazal Roongta

MANAGING ART EDITOR
Arunesh Talapatra

DESIGN CONSULTANT
Shefali Upadhyay

SENIOR EDITOR
Monica Saigal

ASSISTANT EDITOR
Archana Ramachandran

MANAGING EDITOR
Pakshalika Jayaprakash

PRODUCTION MANAGER
Pankaj Sharma

DTP MANAGER/CTS
Balwant Singh

DTP DESIGNERS
Arvind Kumar, Rajesh Singh Adhikari,
Syed Md Farhan, Dheeraj Arora,
Bimlesh Tiwary

PICTURE RESEARCHER
Surya Sankash Sarangi

produced for DK by
TALL TREE LTD

MANAGING EDITOR
Rob Colson

ART DIRECTION
Ben Ruocco

SENIOR EDITORS
Richard Gilbert, Camilla Hallinan,
Scarlett O'Hara, Sarah Tomley

First published in Great Britain in
2013 by Dorling Kindersley Limited,
80 Strand, London, WC2R 0RL
Penguin Group (UK)

4 6 8 10 9 7 5
010 - 187978 - Mar/2013

A CIP catalogue record for this
book is available from
the British Library.

ISBN: 978-1-4093-6445-0

Printed and bound in Hong Kong

**Discover more at
www.dk.com**

CONTRIBUTORS

PAUL KELLY, CONSULTANT EDITOR

Paul Kelly is a Pro-Director and Professor of Political Theory at the London School of Economics and Political Science. He is the author, editor, and co-editor of 11 books. His main interests are British political thought and contemporary political philosophy.

ROD DACOMBE

Dr Rod Dacombe is Lecturer in Politics in the Department of Political Economy at King's College, University of London. His research focuses primarily on democratic theory and practice, and on the relationship between the voluntary sector and the state.

JOHN FARNDON

John Farndon is the author of many books on the history of science and ideas and on contemporary issues. He also writes widely on science and environmental issues and has been shortlisted four times for the young Science Book prize.

A.S. HODSON

A.S. Hodson is a writer and former contributing editor of BushWatch.com.

JESPER JOHNSØN

Jesper Stenberg Johnsøn is a political scientist advising on governance and anti-corruption reforms in developing countries. He works at the Chr. Michelsen Institute's U4 Anti-Corruption Resource Centre in Bergen, Norway.

NIALL KISHTAINY

Niall Kishtainy teaches at the London School of Economics, and specializes in economic history and development. He has worked for the World Bank and the United Nations Economic Commission for Africa.

JAMES MEADWAY

James Meadway is Senior Economist at the New Economics Foundation, an independent British think-tank. He has worked as a policy advisor to the UK Treasury, covering regional development, science, and innovation policy.

ANCA PUSCA

Dr Anca Pusca is Senior Lecturer in International Studies at Goldsmiths College, University of London. She is the author of *Revolution, Democratic Transition and Disillusionment: The Case of Romania* and *Walter Benjamin: Aesthetics of Change*.

MARCUS WEEKS

Marcus Weeks studied philosophy and worked as a teacher before embarking on a career as an author. He has contributed to many books on the arts and popular sciences.

CONTENTS

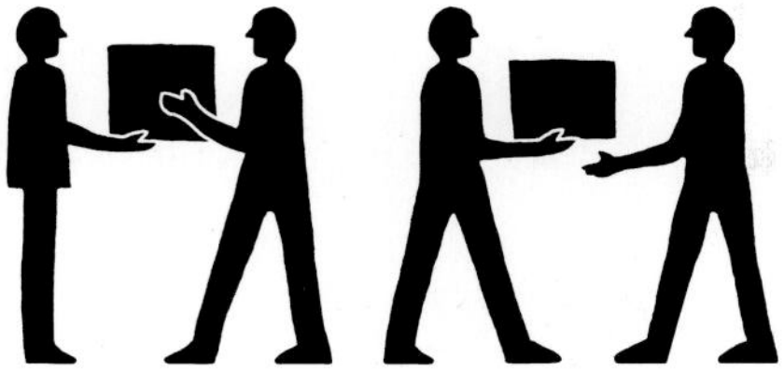

REVOLUTIONARY THOUGHTS
1770–1848

THE RISE OF THE MASSES
1848–1910

THE CLASH OF IDEOLOGIES
1910–1945

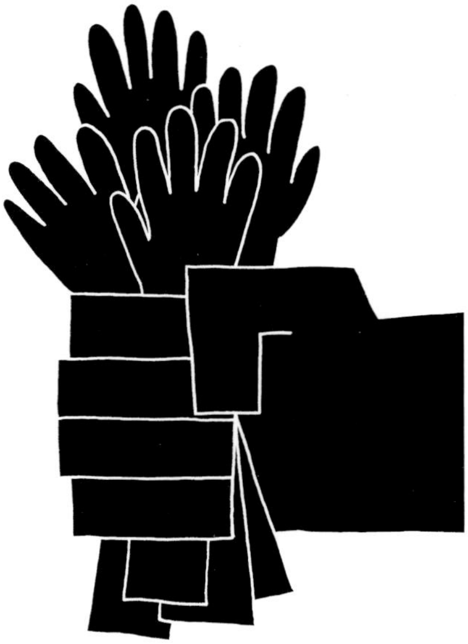

POST-WAR POLITICS
1945–PRESENT

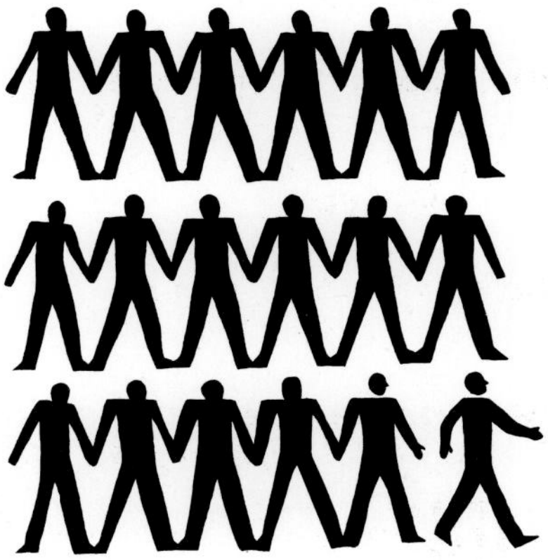

INTRODU

CTION

If everyone could have everything they wanted whenever they wanted, there would be no such thing as politics. Whatever the precise meaning of the complex activity known as politics might be – and, as this book illustrates, it has been understood in many different ways – it is clear that human experience never provides us with everything we want. Instead, we have to compete, struggle, compromise, and sometimes fight for things. In so doing, we develop a language to explain and justify our claims and to challenge, contradict, or answer the claims of others. This might be a language of interests, whether of individuals or groups, or it might be a language of values, such as rights and liberties or fair shares and justice. But central to the activity of politics, from its very beginnings, is the development of political ideas and concepts. These ideas help us to make our claims and to defend our interests.

> Political society exists for the sake of noble actions, and not of mere companionship.
> **Aristotle**

But this picture of politics and the place of political ideas is not the whole story. It suggests that politics can be reduced to the question of who gets what, where, when, and how. Political life is undoubtedly in part a necessary response to the challenges of everyday life and the recognition that collective action is often better than individual action. But another tradition of political thinking is associated with the ancient Greek thinker Aristotle, who said that politics was not merely about the struggle to meet material needs in conditions of scarcity. Once complex societies emerge, different questions arise. Who should rule? What powers should political rulers have, and how do the claims to legitimacy of political rulers compare to other sources of authority, such as that of the family, or the claims of religious authority?

Aristotle said that it is natural for man to live politically, and this is not simply the observation that man is better off in a complex society than abandoned and isolated. It is also the claim that there is something fittingly human about having views on how matters of public concern should be decided. Politics is a noble activity in which men decide the rules they will live by and the goals they will collectively pursue.

Political moralism

Aristotle did not think that all human beings should be allowed to engage in political activity: in his system, women, slaves, and foreigners were explicitly excluded from the right to rule themselves and others. Nevertheless, his basic idea that politics is a unique collective activity that is directed at certain common goals and ends still resonates today. But which ends? Many thinkers and political figures since the ancient world have developed different ideas about the goals that politics can or should achieve. This approach is known as political moralism.

For moralists, political life is a branch of ethics – or moral philosophy – so it is unsurprising that there are many philosophers in the group of moralistic political thinkers. Political moralists argue that politics should be directed

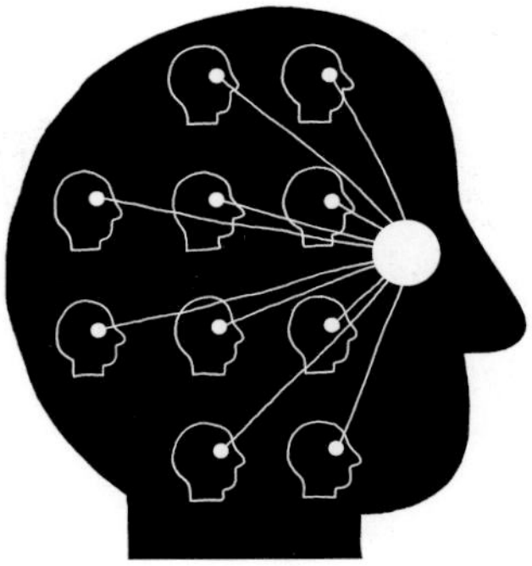

towards achieving substantial goals, or that political arrangements should be organized to protect certain things. Among these things are political values such as justice, equality, liberty, happiness, fraternity, or national self-determination. At its most radical, moralism produces descriptions of ideal political societies known as Utopias, named after English statesman and philosopher Thomas More's book *Utopia*, published in 1516, which imagined an ideal nation. Utopian political thinking dates back to the ancient Greek philosopher Plato's book the *Republic*, but it is still used by modern thinkers such as Robert Nozick to explore ideas. Some theorists consider Utopian political thinking to be a dangerous undertaking, as it has led in the past to justifications of totalitarian violence. However, at its best, Utopian thinking is part of a process of striving towards a better society, and many of the thinkers discussed in this book use it to suggest values to be pursued or protected.

Political realism

Another major tradition of political thinking rejects the idea that politics exists to deliver a moral or ethical value such as happiness or freedom. Instead, they argue that politics is about power. Power is the means by which ends are achieved, enemies are defeated, and compromises sustained. Without the ability to acquire and exercise power, values – however noble they may be – are useless.

The group of thinkers who focus on power as opposed to morality are described as realists. Realists focus their attention on power, conflict, and war, and are often cynical about human motivations. Perhaps the two greatest theorists of power were Italian Niccolò Machiavelli and Englishman Thomas Hobbes, both of whom lived through periods of civil war and disorder, in the 16th and 17th centuries respectively. Machiavelli's view of human nature emphasizes that men are "ungrateful liars" and neither noble nor virtuous. He warns of the dangers of political motives that go beyond concerns with the exercise of power. For Hobbes, the lawless "state of nature" is one of a war of all men against each other. Through a "social contract" with his subjects, a sovereign exercises absolute power to save society from this brutish state. But the concern with power is not unique to early modern Europe. Much 20th-century political thought is concerned with the sources and exercise of power.

> “For forms of Government let fools contest. Whate'er is best administered is best.”
> **Alexander Pope**

Wise counsel

Realism and moralism are grand political visions that try to make sense of the whole of political experience and its relationship with other features of the human condition. Yet not all political thinkers have taken such a wide perspective on events. Alongside the political philosophers, there is an equally ancient tradition that is pragmatic and concerned merely with delivering the best possible outcomes. The problems of war and conflict may never be eradicated, and arguments »

about the relationship between political values such as freedom and equality may also never be resolved, but perhaps we can make progress in constitutional design and policy making, or in ensuring that government officials are as able as possible. Some of the earliest thinking about politics, such as that of Chinese philosopher Confucius, is associated with the skills and virtues of the wise counsellor.

Rise of ideology

One further type of political thinking is often described as ideological. An important strand of ideological thinking emphasizes the ways in which ideas are peculiar to different historical periods. The origins of ideological thinking can be found in the historical philosophies of German philosophers Georg Hegel and Karl Marx. They explain how the ideas of each political epoch differ because the institutions and practices of the societies differ, and the significance of ideas changes across history.

Plato and Aristotle thought of democracy as a dangerous and corrupt system, whereas most people in the modern world see it as the best form of government. Contemporary authoritarian regimes are encouraged to democratize. Similarly, slavery was once thought of as a natural condition that excluded many from any kind of rights, and until the 20th century, most women were not considered citizens.

This raises the question of what causes some ideas to become important, such as equality, and others to fall out of favour, such as slavery or the divine right of kings. Marx accounts for this historical change by arguing that ideas are attached to the interests of social classes such as the workers or the capitalists. These class interests gave rise to the great "isms" of ideological politics, from communism and socialism to conservatism and fascism.

> The philosophers have only interpreted the world… the point is to change it.
> **Karl Marx**

The social classes of Marx are not the only source of ideological politics. Many recent political ideas have also emerged from developments within liberalism, conservatism, socialism, and nationalism.

Ideological political thinking has also been the subject of hostility and criticism. If ideas are merely a reflection of historical processes, critics argue, that must mean that the individuals caught up in those processes are playing an essentially passive role, and that rational deliberation and argument have limited value. Ideological struggle is rather like the competition between football teams. Passion, as opposed to reason, matters in supporting one's team, and winning is ultimately all that counts. Many worry that ideological politics results in the worst excesses of realism, in which the ends are seen to justify brutal or unjust means. Ideological politics appears to be a perpetual struggle or war between rival and irreconcilable camps.

Marx's solution to this problem was the revolutionary triumph of the working class and the technological overcoming of scarcity, which would solve the problem of political conflict. In light of the 20th century,

this approach to politics seems to many to be highly over-optimistic, as revolutionary change has been seen to have replaced one kind of tyranny with another. In this view, Marxism and other ideologies are merely the latest forms of unrealistic Utopian moralism.

A disputed future

According to Georg Hegel, political ideas are an abstraction from the political life of a society, state, culture, or political movement. To make sense of those ideas, and the institutions or movements they explain, involves examining their history and development. That history is always a story of how we got to where we are now. What we cannot do is look forward to see where history is going.

In Roman mythology, the Owl of Minerva was a symbol of wisdom. For Hegel, the Owl only "takes flight at twilight". By this, he means that understanding can only come retrospectively. Hegel is warning against optimism about developing ideas for where to go next. He is also issuing a subtle warning against his other famous claim that the rise of the modern state is the end of history. It is very easy to see ourselves as the most progressive, enlightened, and rational age ever – after all we believe in democracy, human rights, open economies, and constitutional government. But as we shall see in this book, these are by no means simple ideas, and they are not shared by all societies and peoples even today.

The last 80 years of world history have seen the rise of new nation-states as a result of imperial retreat and decolonization. Federations such as Yugoslavia and Czechoslovakia have fragmented into new states, as has the former USSR. The desire for national sovereignty is also strong in places such as Quebec, Catalonia, Kurdistan, and Kashmir. Yet, while peoples have struggled for statehood, states have sought complex federations and political union. The last three decades have seen the rise of the European Union, which aspires to closer political integration, as well as the North American Free Trade area and many other organizations for regional cooperation.

Old ideas of state sovereignty have an awkward role in the new political world of pooled sovereignty, economic cooperation, and globalization. Hegel's point seems very pertinent here – we cannot predict how we will appear to those in the future, nor whether what seems common sense to us will be seen as persuasive by our descendants.

Making sense of the present requires an understanding of the variety of political ideas and theories conceived throughout history. These ideas serve as an explanation of the possibilities of the present, as well as a warning against overconfidence in our own political values, and they remind us that the demands of organizing and governing the collective life of society change in ways that we cannot fully predict. As new possibilities for the exercise of power arise, so will new demands for its control and accountability, and with these will come new political ideas and theories. Politics concerns all of us, so we should all be involved in that debate. ■

> Politics is too serious a matter to be left to the politicians.
> **Charles de Gaulle**

ANCIENT POLITICAL THOUGHT
800 BCE—30 CE

c.770 BCE — The **Spring and Autumn period** begins in China, and the "Hundred Schools of Thought" emerge.

600 BCE — The **Chinese general Sun Tzu** writes his treatise *The Art of War* for King Helü of Wu.

600–500 BCE — Confucius proposes a system of government based on **traditional values**, administered by a class of scholars.

594 BCE — Solon creates a **constitution for Athens** that paves the way for a democratic city-state.

c.510 BCE — The **Roman Republic** is founded.

476–221 BCE — During the **Warring States period**, the seven largest Chinese states vie for supremacy.

c.460 BCE — In Greece, Sophists including Protagoras maintain that political justice is an imposition of **human values**, not a reflection of justice in nature.

399 BCE — After years of **questioning politics and society** in Athens, Socrates is sentenced to death.

Political theory can trace its beginnings to the civilizations of ancient China and Greece. In both places, thinkers emerged who questioned and analysed the world around them in a way we now call philosophy. From around 600 BCE, some of them turned their attention to the way we organize societies. At first, both in China and Greece, these questions were considered part of moral philosophy or ethics. Philosophers examined how society should be structured to ensure not only the happiness and security of the people, but to enable people to live a "good life".

Political thought in China

From around 770 BCE, China experienced a time of prosperity known as the Spring and Autumn period, as various dynasties ruled over the separate states relatively peaceably. Scholarship was highly valued in this period, resulting in the so-called Hundred Schools of Thought. By far the most influential of the philosophers to emerge was Confucius, who combined moral and political philosophy in his proposals for upholding traditional Chinese moral values in a state led by a virtuous ruler, and advised by a class of administrators.

This idea was further refined by Mozi and Mencius to prevent corruption and despotic rule, but as conflict between the states increased in the 3rd century BCE, the Spring and Autumn period came to a close, replaced by the Warring States period and the struggle for control of a unified Chinese empire. It was in this atmosphere that thinkers such as Han Fei Tzu and the Legalist school advocated discipline as the guiding principle of the state, and the military leader Sun Tzu applied the tactics of warfare to ideas of foreign policy and domestic government. These more authoritarian political philosophies brought stability to the new empire, which later reverted to a form of Confucianism.

Greek democracy

At much the same time as these developments in China, Greek civilization was flourishing. Like China, Greece was not a single nation, but a collection of separate city-states under various systems of government. Most were ruled by a monarch or an aristocracy, but Athens had established a form of democracy under a constitution

c.470–391 BCE
Chinese philosopher Mozi proposes a purely **meritocratic class** of ministers and advisors chosen for their virtue and ability.

c.380–360 BCE
In the *Republic*, Plato advocates rule by "**philosopher kings**" who possess the wisdom and knowledge to understand the nature of a good life.

335–323 BCE
In his *Politics*, Aristotle describes various forms of rule of the city-state, and suggests polity – **constitutional government** – as the most practical.

c.370–283 BCE
Chanakya's advice to Chandragupta Maurya helps to establish the **Mauryan empire** in India.

372–289 BCE
Mencius popularizes **Confucian ideas** in China.

300 BCE
In the attempt to unify China, the authoritarian ideas of Shang Yang and Han Fei Tzu are adopted as the **doctrine of Legalism**.

200 BCE
The Han dynasty adopts Confucianism as the **official philosophy** of China.

54–51 BCE
Cicero writes *De republica*, modelled on Plato's *Republic*, but advocating a **more democratic form** of government.

introduced by the statesman Solon in 594 BCE. The city became the cultural centre of Greece, and provided an intellectual space in which philosophers could speculate on what constituted the ideal state, what its purpose was, and how it should be governed. Here, Plato advocated rule by an elite of "philosopher kings", while his pupil Aristotle compared the various possible forms of government. Their theories would form the basis for Western political philosophy.

After Aristotle, the "golden age" of classical Greek philosophy drew to a close, as Alexander the Great embarked on a series of campaigns to extend his empire from Macedon into northern Africa and across Asia as far as the Himalayas. But in India, he met with resistance from an organized opposition. The Indian subcontinent was composed of various separate states, but the emergence of an innovative political theorist, Chanakya, helped to transform it into a unified empire under the rule of his protégé, Chandragupta Maurya. Chanakya believed in a pragmatic approach to political thinking advocating strict discipline, with the aim of securing economic and material security for the state rather than the moral welfare of the people. His realism helped to protect the Mauryan empire from attack, and brought most of India into a unified state that lasted for more than 100 years.

The rise of Rome

Meanwhile, another power was rising in Europe. The Roman Republic had been founded in about 510 BCE with the overthrow of a tyrannical monarchy. A form of representative democracy similar to the Athenian model was established. A constitution evolved, with government led by two consuls elected by the citizens annually, and a senate of representatives to advise them. Under this system, the Republic grew in strength, occupying provinces in most of mainland Europe. However, in the 1st century BCE, civil conflict spread in the Republic as various factions vied for power. Julius Caesar seized control in 48 BCE and effectively became emperor, bringing the Republic to an end. Rome had once again come under a monarchical, dynastic rule, and the new Roman empire was to dominate most of Europe for the next 500 years. ■

IF YOUR DESIRE IS FOR GOOD THE PEOPLE WILL BE GOOD

CONFUCIUS (551–479 BCE)

IN CONTEXT

IDEOLOGY
Confucianism

FOCUS
Paternalist

BEFORE
1045 BCE Under the Zhou dynasty of China, political decisions are justified by the Mandate of Heaven.

8th century BCE The Spring and Autumn period begins, and the "Hundred Schools of Thought" emerge.

AFTER
5th century BCE Mozi proposes an alternative to the potential nepotism and cronyism of Confucianism.

4th century BCE The philosopher Mencius popularizes Confucian ideas.

3rd century BCE The more authoritarian principles of Legalism come to dominate the system of government.

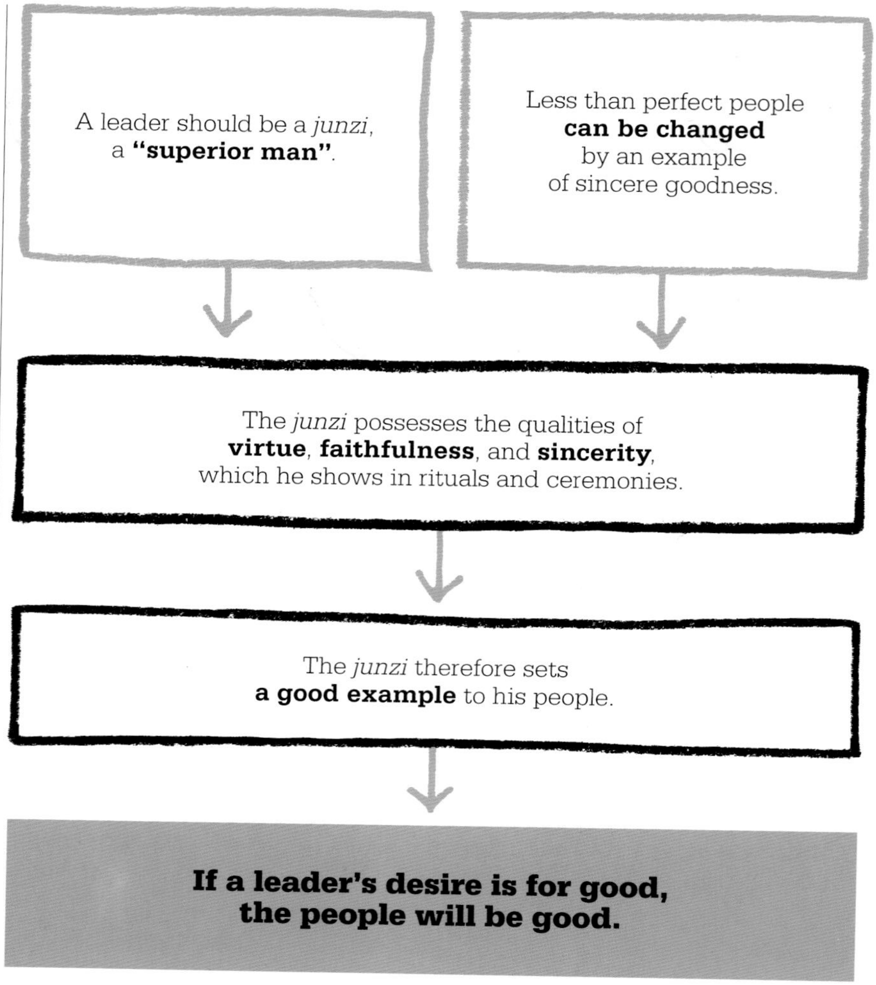

Kong Fuzi ("Master Kong"), who later became known in the West by the Latinized name of Confucius, lived during a turning point in China's political history. He lived at the end of China's Spring and Autumn period – around 300 years of prosperity and stability during which there was a flowering of art, literature, and in particular, philosophy. This gave rise to the so-called Hundred Schools of Thought, in which a wide range of ideas was freely discussed. In the process, a new class of thinkers and scholars emerged, most of them based in the courts of noble families where they were valued advisors.

The influence of these scholars' new ideas inspired a shake-up of the structure of Chinese society. The scholars were appointed on merit rather than due to family connections, and this new meritocratic class of scholars was a challenge to the hereditary rulers, who had previously governed with what they believed was a mandate from Heaven. This caused a series of conflicts as various rulers vied for control over China. During this era, which became known as the Warring States period, it became increasingly clear that a strong system of government was necessary.

The superior man

Like most educated, middle-class young men, Confucius pursued a career as an administrator, and it was in this role that he developed his ideas about the organization of government. Seeing first-hand the relationships between the ruler and his ministers and subjects, and keenly aware of the fragility of the

See also: Sun Tzu 28–31 ▪ Mozi 32–33 ▪ Han Fei Tzu 48 ▪ Sun Yat-Sen 212–13 ▪ Mao Zedong 260–65

political situation of the time, he set about formulating a framework that would enable rulers to govern justly, based on his own system of moral philosophy.

Confucius's moral standpoint was firmly rooted in Chinese convention, and had at its heart the traditional virtues of loyalty, duty, and respect. These values were personified in the *junzi*: the "gentleman" or "superior man", whose virtue would act as an example to others. Every member of society would be encouraged to aspire to the *junzi*'s virtues. In Confucius's view, human nature is not perfect, but it is capable of being changed by the example of sincere virtue. Similarly, society can be transformed by the example of fair and benevolent government.

The notion of reciprocity – the idea that just and generous treatment will be met with a just and generous response – underpins Confucius's moral philosophy, and it is also a cornerstone of his political thinking. For a society to be good, its ruler must be the embodiment of the virtues he wishes to see in his subjects; in turn, the people will be inspired through loyalty and respect to emulate those virtues. In the collection of his teachings and sayings known as the *Analects*, Confucius advises: "If your desire is for good, the people will be good. The moral character of the ruler is the wind; the moral character of those beneath him is the grass. When the wind blows, the grass bends." In order for this idea to work effectively, however, a new structure for society had to be established, creating a hierarchy that took account of the new meritocratic administrative class while respecting the traditional »

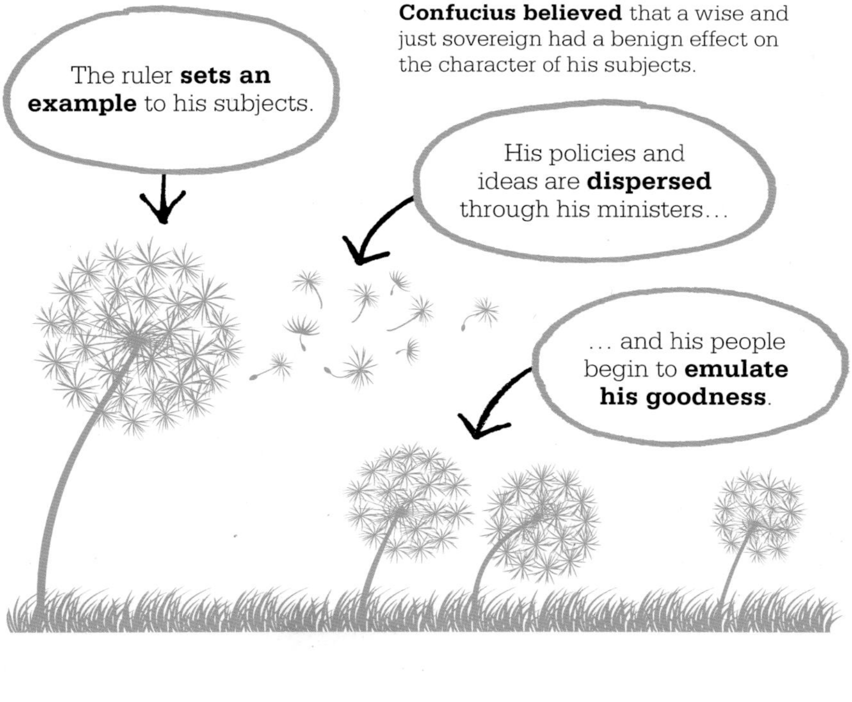

Confucius believed that a wise and just sovereign had a benign effect on the character of his subjects.

Confucius

Despite his importance in Chinese history, little is known of Confucius's life. He is traditionally believed to have been born in 551 BCE, in Qufu in the state of Lu, China. His name was originally Kong Qiu (he earned the honorific title "Kong Fuzi" much later), and his family was both respected and comfortably well off. Nevertheless, as a young man he worked as a servant after his father died in order to support his family, and studied in his spare time to join the civil service. He became an administrator in the Zhou court, where he developed his ideas of how a state should be governed, but his advice was ignored and he resigned from the position. He spent the rest of his life travelling throughout the Chinese empire, teaching his philosophy and theories of government. He eventually returned to Qufu, where he died in 479 BCE.

Key works

Analects
Doctrine of the Mean
The Great Learning
(All assembled during the 12th century by Chinese scholars.)

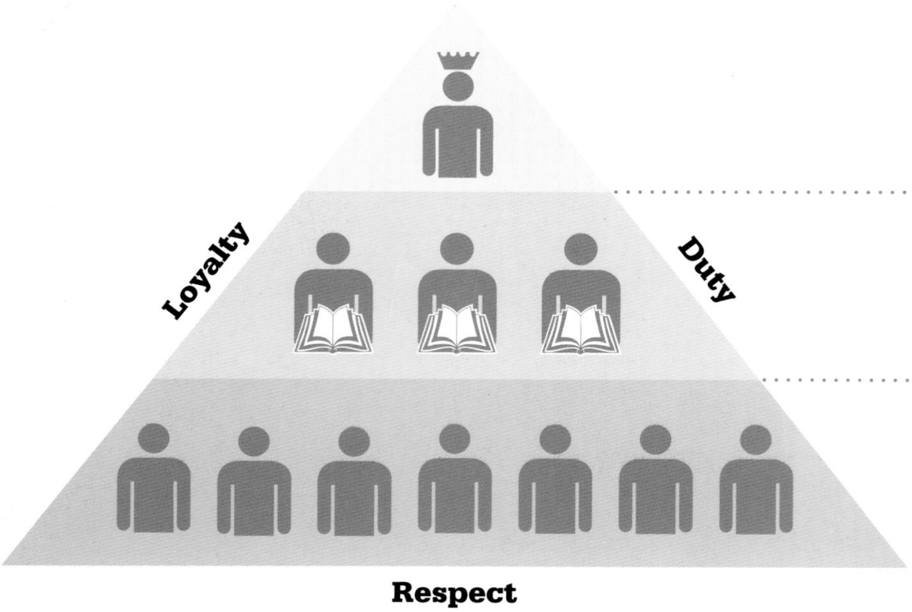

The sovereign was regarded by Confucius as inherently superior. His task was to model perfect behaviour, setting a good example to those below him.

Ministers and advisors played an important role as "middle men" between the sovereign and his subjects. They had a duty of loyalty to both parties.

The people, given a good example to follow and a clear idea of what was expected of them, would behave correctly, according to Confucius.

rule of the noble families. In his proposal for how this might be achieved, Confucius again relied very much on traditional values, modelling society on relationships within the family. For Confucius, the benevolence of the sovereign and the loyalty of his subject mirror the loving father and obedient son relationship (a relationship considered by the Chinese to be of the utmost importance).

Confucius considers that there are five "constant relationships": sovereign/subject, father/son, husband/wife, elder brother/younger brother, and friend/friend. In these relationships, he emphasizes not only the rank of each person according to generation, age, and gender, but the fact that there are duties on both sides, and that the responsibility of the superior to the inferior in any relationship is just as important as that of the junior to the senior. Extending these relationships to the wider society, their reciprocal rights and responsibilities give society its cohesion, creating an atmosphere of loyalty and respect from each social stratum towards the next.

Justifying hereditary rule

At the top of Confucius's hierarchy was the sovereign, who would unquestionably have inherited this status, and in this respect Confucius shows the conservative nature of his political thinking. Just as the family provided a model for the relationships within society, the traditional respect shown to parents (especially fathers) extended also to ancestors, and this justified the hereditary principle. Just as a father was considered the head of the family, the state should naturally be ruled over by a paterfamilias figure – the sovereign.

Nevertheless, the sovereign's position was not unassailable in Confucius's thinking, and an unjust or unwise ruler deserved to be opposed or even removed. However, it was in the next layer of society that Confucius was at his most innovative, advocating a class of scholars to act as ministers, advisors, and administrators to the ruler. Their position between the sovereign and his subjects was crucial, as they had a duty of loyalty both to their ruler and the people. They carried a high degree of responsibility, so it was essential that they be recruited from the most able and educated candidates, and that anybody serving in public

> Good government consists in the ruler being a ruler, the minister being a minister, the father being a father, and the son being a son.
> **Confucius**

office should be of the highest moral character – a *junzi*. These ministers were to be appointed by the sovereign in Confucius's system, so much depended upon the sovereign's own good character. Confucius said: "The administration of government lies in getting proper men. Such men are to be got by means of the ruler's own character. That character is to be cultivated by his treading in the ways of duty. And the treading of those ways of duty is to be cultivated by the cherishing of benevolence."

The role of these public servants was mainly advisory, and ministers were not only expected to be well-versed in the administration and structure of Chinese society, but also to have a thorough knowledge of history, politics, and diplomacy. This was necessary to advise the ruler on matters such as alliances and wars with neighbouring states. However, this new class of civil servants also served an equally important function in preventing the ruler from becoming despotic, because they showed loyalty to their superior, but also benevolence to their inferiors. Like their ruler, they too had to lead by example, inspiring both the sovereign and his subjects by their virtue.

The importance of ritual

Many parts of Confucius's writings read like a handbook of etiquette and protocol, detailing the proper conduct for the *junzi* in various situations, but he also stressed that this should not merely be empty show. The rituals he outlined were not mere social niceties, but served a much deeper purpose, and it was important that the participants behaved with sincerity for the rituals to have any meaning. Public servants not only had to fulfil their duties virtuously, they also had to be seen to be acting virtuously. For this reason, Confucius laid great emphasis on ceremonies and rituals. These also worked to underline the positions of the various members within a society, and Confucius's approval of this illustrates his tendency to conservatism.

The ceremonies and rituals allowed people to manifest their devotion to those above them in the hierarchy and their consideration towards those below them. According to Confucius, these rituals were to permeate the whole of society, from formal royal and state ceremonies right down to everyday social interactions, with participants meticulously observing their respective roles. Only when virtue was sincerely and honestly manifested in this way could the idea of leading by example succeed. For this reason, Confucius held sincerity and honesty to be the most important of virtues, next only to loyalty.

> "The superior man governs men according to their nature, with what is proper to them, and as soon as they change what is wrong, he stops."
> **Confucius**

Many of these rituals and ceremonies had their basis in religious rites, but this aspect was not important to Confucius. His moral philosophy was not founded on religion, and the political system he derived from it simply acknowledged that there was a place for religion in society. In fact, he seldom referred to the gods in his writings, except in terms of a hope that society could be organized and governed in accordance with the Mandate of Heaven, which would help to »

Actors performing a Confucian ritual in Shandong Province, China, convey the importance of restraint and respect to modern visitors unversed in their highly formalized tradition.

unify the states vying for power. Although he firmly believed in rule by a hereditary sovereign, he did not feel the need to justify it as a divine right.

This implicit dismissal of the divine right, combined with a class system based on merit rather than inheritance, showed Confucius at his most radical. While he advocated a hierarchy reinforced by strict rules of etiquette and protocol, so that everybody was very aware of their place in society, this did not mean there should be no social mobility. Those with ability (and good character) could rise through the ranks to the highest levels of government, whatever their family background; and those in positions of power could be removed from office if they failed to show the necessary qualities, no matter how noble the family they were born into. This principle extended even to the sovereign himself. Confucius saw the assassination of a despotic ruler as the necessary removal of a tyrant rather than the murder of a legitimate ruler. He argued that the flexibility of this hierarchy engendered more real respect for it, and that this in turn engendered political consent – a necessary basis for strong and stable government.

Crime and punishment

The principles of Confucius's moral philosophy also extended into the fields of law and punishment. Previously, the legal system had been based on the codes of conduct prescribed by religion, but he advocated a more humanistic approach to replace the divinely ordained laws. As with his social structure, he proposed a system based on reciprocity: if you are treated with respect, you will act with respect. His version of the Golden Rule ("do as you would be done by") was in the negative: "what you do not desire for yourself, do not do to others", moving the emphasis from specific crimes to avoidance of bad behaviour. Once again, this could best be achieved by example as, in his words, "When you meet someone better than yourself, turn your thoughts to becoming his equal. When you meet someone not as good as you are, look within and examine your own self."

> He who governs by means of his virtue is... like the Pole Star: it remains in its place while all the lesser stars do homage to it.
> **Confucius**

Rather than imposing rigid laws and stern punishments, Confucius felt that the best way to deal with crime lay in instilling a sense of shame for bad behaviour. Although people may avoid committing crime if guided by laws and subdued by punishment, they do not learn a real sense of right and wrong, whereas if they are guided by example and subdued by respect, they develop a sense of shame for any misdemeanours and learn to become truly good.

Unpopular ideas

Confucius's moral and political philosophy combined ideas about the innate goodness and sociability of human nature with the rigid,

The Chinese emperor presides over the civil service examinations in this Song dynasty painting. The exams were introduced during Confucius's lifetime and were based on his ideas.

Religious functions were absorbed into Confucianism when it became the official philosophy of China. Confucian temples such as this one in Nanjing sprang up throughout the country.

formal structure of traditional Chinese society. Unsurprisingly, given his position as a court administrator, he found an important place for the new meritocratic class of scholars. However, his ideas were met with suspicion and were not adopted during his lifetime. Members of the royal and noble ruling families were unhappy with his implied dismissal of their divine right to rule, and felt threatened by the power he proposed for their ministers and advisors. The administrators might have enjoyed more control to rein in potentially despotic rulers, but they doubted the idea that the people could be governed by example, and were unwilling to give up their right to exercise power through laws and punishment.

Later political and philosophical thinkers also had their criticisms of Confucianism. Mozi, a Chinese philosopher born shortly after Confucius's death, agreed with his more modern ideas of meritocracy and leading by example, but felt that his emphasis on family relationships would lead to nepotism and cronyism. Around the same time, military thinkers such as Sun Tzu had little time for the moral philosophy underlying Confucius's political theory, and instead took a more practical approach to matters of government, advocating an authoritarian and even ruthless system to ensure the defence of the state. Nevertheless, elements of Confucianism were gradually incorporated into Chinese society in the two centuries following his death. Championed by Mencius (372–289 BCE), they gained some popularity in the 4th century BCE.

> What you know, you know;
> what you don't know,
> you don't know.
> This is true wisdom.
> **Confucius**

The state philosophy

Confucianism may have been adequate to govern in peacetime, but it was felt by many not to be robust enough for the ensuing Warring States period and the struggle to form a unified Chinese empire. During this period, a pragmatic and authoritarian system of government known as Legalism supplanted Confucius's ideas, and continued as the emperor asserted his authority over the new empire. By the 2nd century BCE, however, peace had returned to China, and Confucianism was adopted as the official philosophy of the state under the Han dynasty. It continued to dominate the structure of Chinese society from then on, particularly in the practice of recruiting the most able scholars to the administrative class. The civil service exams introduced in 605 CE were based on classic Confucian texts, and this practice continued into the 20th century and the formation of the Chinese Republic.

Confucianism has not entirely disappeared under China's communist regime, and it had a subtle influence on the structure of society right up to the Cultural Revolution. Today, elements of Confucian thinking, such as those that deal with societal relationships and the notion of filial loyalty, are still deeply ingrained in the Chinese way of life. Confucian ideas are once again being taken seriously as the country shifts from Maoist communism to a Chinese version of a mixed economy. ■

THE ART OF WAR IS OF VITAL IMPORTANCE TO THE STATE

SUN TZU (c.544–c.496 BCE)

IN CONTEXT

IDEOLOGY
Realism

FOCUS
Diplomacy and war

BEFORE
8th century BCE A "golden age" of Chinese philosophy begins, which produces the so-called Hundred Schools of Thought.

6th century BCE Confucius proposes a framework for civil society based on traditional values.

AFTER
4th century BCE Chanakya's advice to Chandragupta Maurya helps to establish the Mauryan empire in India.

1532 Niccolò Machiavelli's *The Prince* is published, five years after his death.

1937 Mao Zedong writes *On Guerrilla Warfare.*

In the late 6th century BCE, China was reaching the end of an era of peaceful prosperity – the so-called Spring and Autumn period – in which philosophers had flourished. Much of the thinking had focused on moral philosophy or ethics, and the political philosophy that followed from this concentrated on the morally correct way that the state should organize its internal affairs. The culmination of this came with Confucius's integration of traditional virtues into a hierarchy led by a sovereign and administered by a bureaucracy of scholars.

Towards the end of the Spring and Autumn period, however, the political stability of the various

See also: Chanakya 44–47 ▪ Han Fei Tzu 48 ▪ Niccolò Machiavelli 74–81 ▪ Mao Zedong 260–65 ▪ Che Guevara 312–13

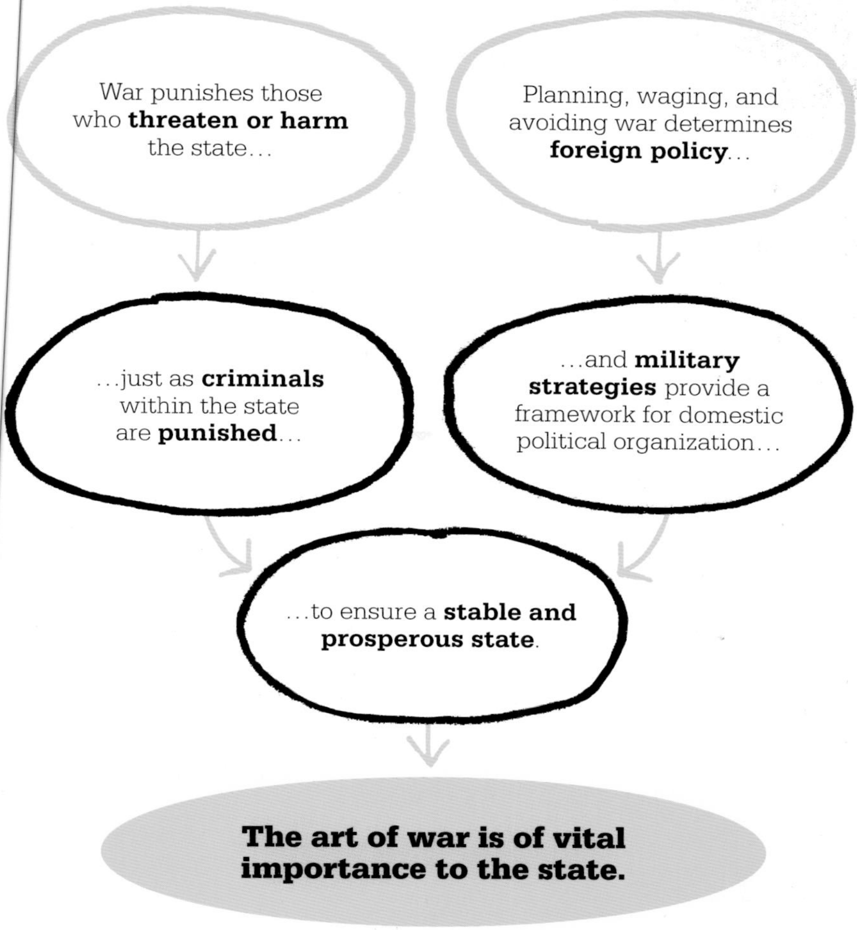

states of China became fragile, and tensions between them increased as the population grew. Rulers of the states not only had to manage their internal affairs, but also to defend themselves against attack from neighbouring states.

Military strategy

In this atmosphere, military advisors became as important as the civil bureaucrats, and military strategy began to inform political thinking. The most influential work on the subject was *The Art of War*, believed to have been written by Sun Tzu, a general in the army of the King of Wu. The opening passage reads: "The art of war is of vital importance to the state. It is a matter of life and death, a road either to safety or to ruin. Hence it is a subject of inquiry which can on no account be neglected." This marked a distinct break from the political philosophy of the time, and Sun Tzu's work was perhaps the first explicit statement that war and military intelligence are critical elements of the business of the state.

A terracotta army was built to line the tomb of Emperor Qin Shi Huang, showing the importance of the military to him. Qin lived 200 years after Sun Tzu, but would have read his works closely.

The Art of War deals with the practicalities of protecting and maintaining the prosperity of the state. Where previous thinkers had concentrated on the structure of civil society, this treatise focuses on international politics, discussing public administration only in connection with the business of planning and waging wars, or the economics of maintaining military and intelligence services.

Sun Tzu's detailed description of the art of war has been seen as providing a framework for political organization of any sort. He gives a list of the "principles of war" that are to be considered when planning a campaign. In addition to practical matters such as weather and terrain, the list includes the moral influence of the ruler, the ability and qualities of the general, and the organization and discipline of the men. Implicit in these principles of war is a hierarchical structure »

The Five Fundamentals of Warfare

The *Dao*, or **the Way**, allows all soldiers to be of one mind with their rulers.

Generals must be aware of **Heaven**, which is Yin and Yang, and the cycle of the seasons.

A strategist must take into account the **Earth**: high and low, near and distant, open and confined.

Command is shown by wisdom, integrity, compassion, and courage.

Organization and the proper chain of command instil **Discipline**.

with a sovereign at its head, taking advice from and giving commands to his generals, who lead and organize their troops.

For Sun Tzu, the role of the sovereign is to provide moral leadership. The people must be convinced that their cause is just before they will give their support, and a ruler should lead by example; this was an idea that Sun Tzu shared with Confucius. Like the bureaucrat of civil society, the general acts as both advisor to the ruler and administrator of his commands.

Unsurprisingly, Sun Tzu places great emphasis on the qualities of the general, describing him as the "bulwark of the state". His training and experience inform the counsel he gives the sovereign, effectively determining policy, but are also vital to the organization of the army. At the head of the chain of command, he controls the logistics, and especially the training and discipline of the men. *The Art of War* recommends that discipline be rigorously enforced with harsh penalties for disobedience, but that this should be tempered by a consistent application of rewards and punishments.

Knowing when to fight

While this description of a military hierarchy mirrored the structure of Chinese society, *The Art of War* was much more innovative in its recommendations for international politics. Like many generals before and since, Sun Tzu believed that the purpose of the military was to protect the state and ensure its welfare, and that war should always be a last resort. A good general should know when to fight and when not to fight, remembering that an enemy's resistance can often be broken without armed conflict. A general should first try to thwart the enemy's plans; failing that, he should defend against attack; only failing that should he launch an offensive.

To avoid the necessity for war, Sun Tzu advocated maintaining a strong defence and forming alliances with neighbouring states. As a costly war is harmful to both sides, it often makes sense to come to a peaceful settlement. Prolonged campaigns, especially tactics such as laying siege to an enemy's city, are such a drain on resources that their cost often outweighs the benefits of victory. The sacrifices that have to be made by the people put a strain on their loyalty to the moral justness of the cause.

Military intelligence

The key to stable international relationships, argues Sun Tzu, is intelligence, which was then the responsibility of the military. Spies provide vital information on a potential enemy's intentions and capabilities, allowing the generals who command the spies to advise the ruler on the likelihood of victory in the event of conflict. Along the same lines, Sun Tzu goes on to explain that the next most important element in this information warfare is deception.

> If you know both yourself and your enemy, you can win a hundred battles without jeopardy.
>
> **Sun Tzu**

> A leader leads by example not by force.
> **Sun Tzu**

The Great Wall of China, begun in the 7th century BCE, acted to fence off newly conquered territories. For Sun Tzu, such defensive measures were as important as attacking force.

By feeding misinformation to the enemy about defences, for example, war can often be averted. He also advised against what he saw as the folly of attempting to destroy an enemy in battle, as this decreased the rewards that could be gained from the victory – both the goodwill of any defeated soldiers and the wealth of any territory gained.

Underlying the very practical advice in *The Art of War* is a traditional cultural foundation based on moral values of justice, appropriateness, and moderation. It states that military tactics, international politics, and war exist to uphold these values and should be conducted in accordance with them. The state exercises its military capability to punish those that harm or threaten it from outside, just as it uses the law to punish criminals within it. When done in a morally justifiable way, the state is rewarded by happier people and the acquisition of territory and wealth. *The Art of War* became an influential text among the rulers, generals, and ministers of the various states in the struggle for a unified Chinese empire. It was later an important influence on the tactics of revolutionaries, including Mao Zedong and Ho Chi Minh. It is now required reading at many military academies, and is often included as a set text in courses on politics, business, and economics. ■

Sun Tzu

Traditionally believed to be the author of the legendary treatise *The Art of War*, Sun Wu (later known as Sun Tzu, "the Master Sun") was probably born in the State of Qi or Wu in China in around 544 BCE. Nothing is known of his early life, but he rose to fame as a general serving the State of Wu in many successful campaigns against the neighbouring State of Chu.

He became an indispensable advisor (equivalent to a contracted military consultant today) to King Helü of Wu on matters of military strategy, writing his famous treatise to be used as a handbook by the ruler. A concise book, made up of 13 short chapters, it was widely read after his death in c.496 BCE, both by state leaders fighting for control of the Chinese empire, and military thinkers in Japan and Korea. It was first translated into a European language, French, in 1782, and may have influenced Napoleon.

Key work

6th century BCE *The Art of War*

PLANS FOR THE COUNTRY ARE ONLY TO BE SHARED WITH THE LEARNED

MOZI (c.470–c.391 BCE)

IN CONTEXT

IDEOLOGY
Mohism

FOCUS
Meritocracy

BEFORE
6th century BCE Chinese philosopher Laozi advocates Daoism – acting in accordance with the Way (*dao*).

5th century BCE Confucius proposes a government system based on traditional values enacted by a class of scholars.

AFTER
4th century BCE The authoritarian ideas of Shang Yang and Han Fei Tzu are adopted in the state of Qin as the doctrine of Legalism.

372–289 BCE The philosopher Mencius advocates a return to a form of Confucianism.

20th century Mozi's ideas influence both Sun Yat-Sen's Republic and the communist People's Republic of China.

Towards the end of the "golden age" of Chinese philosophy that produced the so-called Hundred Schools of Thought between the 8th and the 3rd centuries BCE, thinkers began to apply their ideas of moral philosophy to the practical business of social and political organization. Foremost among these was Confucius, who proposed a hierarchy based on traditional family relationships, reinforced with ceremony and ritual. Within

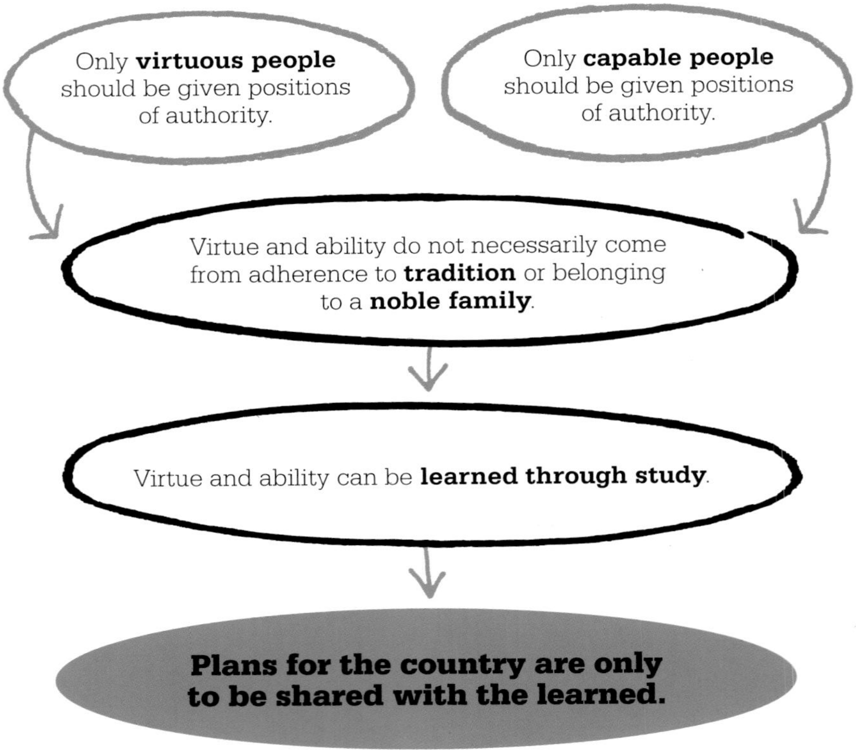

See also: Confucius 20–27 ▪ Plato 34–39 ▪ Han Fei Tzu 48 ▪ Sun Yat-Sen 212–13 ▪ Mao Zedong 260–65

For Mozi, skilled workers such as carpenters could – with training and aptitude – be made into able administrators in government.

this hierarchy, however, he recognized the importance of an administrative class to aid and advise the ruler, an idea that was later developed by Mozi.

Both Confucius and Mozi believed that the wellbeing of the state relied on the competence and dependability of the bureaucratic class, but they differed over the way that administrators should be chosen. To Mozi, Confucius adhered too closely to the conventions of the noble families, which did not necessarily produce the virtue and ability essential to a successful bureaucracy. Mozi felt that the qualities and skills for high office resulted from aptitude and study, regardless of background.

A unifying code

"Elevating the worthy", as Mozi described his meritocratic idea, forms the cornerstone of Mohist political thinking, but it is also linked to other aspects of Mozi's moral philosophy. He believed in the inherent goodness of people, and felt that they should live in an atmosphere of "universal love". At the same time, he recognized the human tendency to act in self-interest. This, he believed, often happened in situations of conflict, which arose not from a lack of morality, but from differing ideas of what is morally correct. It was therefore the task of political leaders to unite the people with a coherent moral code that was enforced by a strong and ethical system of government. This code would be based on what was necessary for the greatest good of society, and formulating it required knowledge and wisdom that was only available to the learned.

Mozi's preference for a ministerial class chosen on merit and ability no doubt stemmed from his own experience of working his way up to high office from humble beginnings. He saw the potential for nepotism and cronyism when the nobility appointed ministers. He also believed that government needed to be run in such a way that it would cultivate the prosperity of the state for the welfare of the people as a whole.

> Exaltation of the virtuous is the root of government.
> **Mozi**

Although Mozi attracted a large group of followers, he was regarded as an idealist and Mohism was not adopted by the Chinese rulers of the time. However, elements of his political thinking were incorporated into later political systems. For example, his emphasis on enforcing a unified moral code was a significant influence on the authoritarian Legalist regimes that arose in the 4th century BCE. In the 20th century, Mozi's notions of equality of opportunity were rediscovered by Chinese leaders Sun Yat-Sen and Mao Zedong. ■

Mozi

It is believed that Mozi was born around the time of Confucius's death, in Tengzhou, Shandong Province, China, into a family of artisans or possibly slaves. Named Mo Di, he was a woodworker and engineer, and worked at the courts of noble families, rising through the civil service to establish a school for officials and advisors. His philosophical and political views gained him a following and the title Mozi ("Master Mo").

Mohists, as his followers were known, lived according to Mozi's principles of simplicity and pacifism during the Warring States period, until the Qin dynasty established its Legalist regime. After his death, Mozi's teachings were collected in *The Mozi*. Mohism disappeared after the unification of China in 221 BCE, but were rediscovered in the early 20th century.

Key works

5th century BCE *The Mozi*

UNTIL PHILOSOPHERS ARE KINGS CITIES WILL NEVER HAVE REST FROM THEIR EVILS

PLATO 427–347 BCE

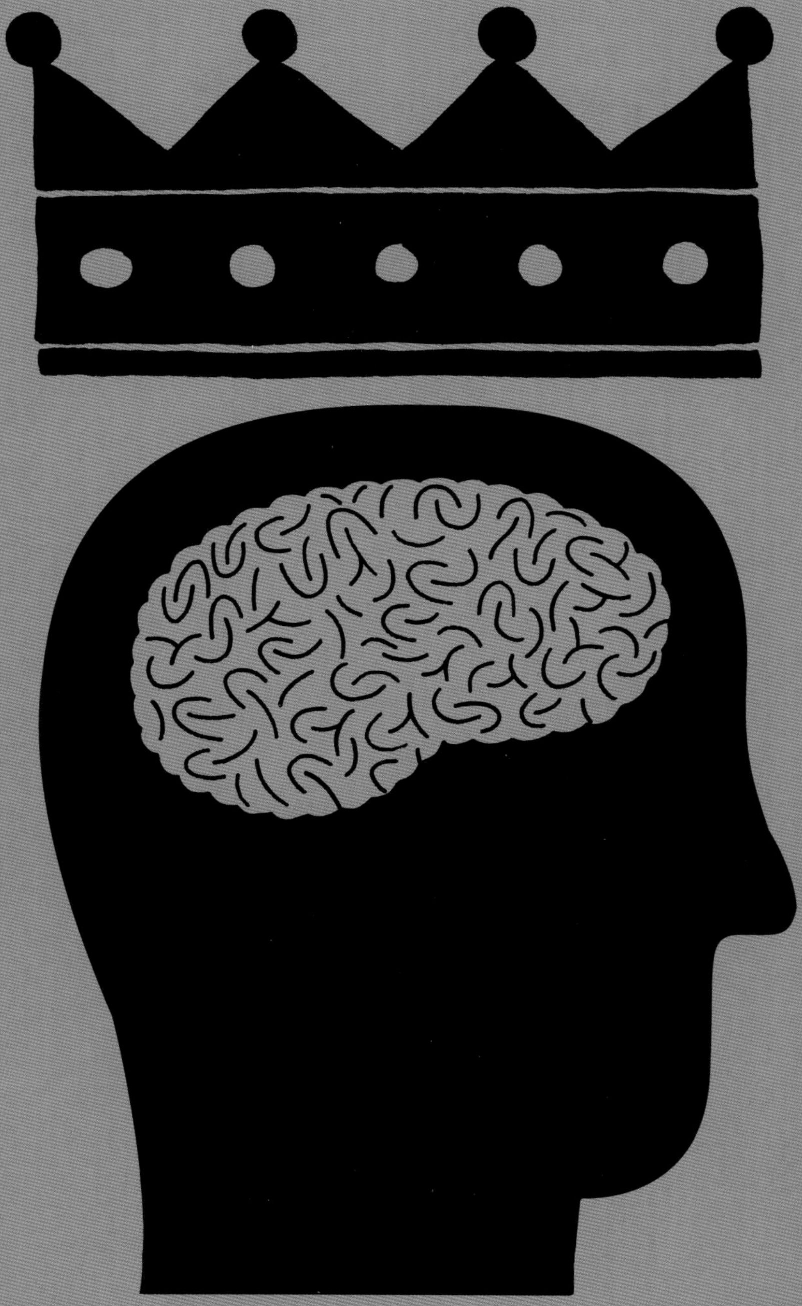

IN CONTEXT

IDEOLOGY
Rationalism

FOCUS
Philosopher kings

BEFORE

594 BCE The Athenian lawmaker Solon lays down laws that act as the foundation for Greek democracy.

c.450 BCE Greek philosopher Protagoras says that political justice is an imposition of human ideas, not a reflection of natural justice.

AFTER

335–323 BCE Aristotle suggests that polity (constitutional government) is the most practical of the better ways to run a state.

54–51 BCE Cicero writes *De republica*, advocating a more democratic form of government than suggested by Plato's *Republic*.

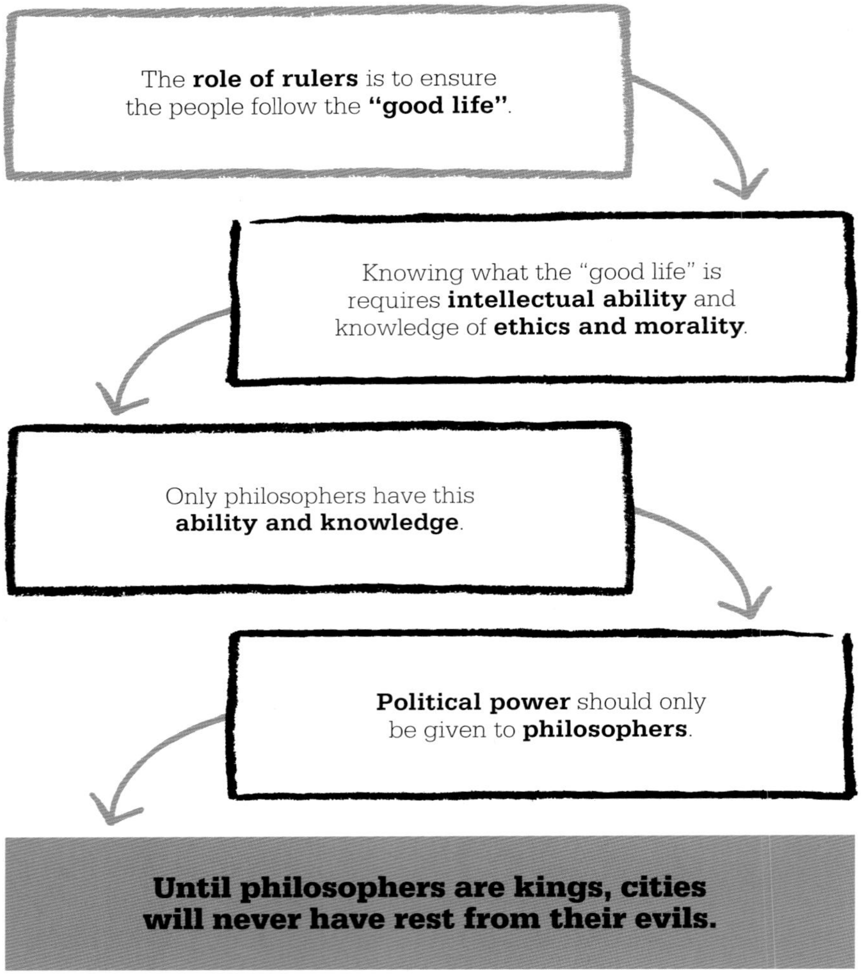

At the end of the 6th century BCE, a cultural "golden age" began in Greece which was to last for 200 years. Now referred to as the Classical period, it saw the flowering of literature, architecture, science, and above all, philosophy, all of which profoundly influenced the development of Western civilization.

At the very beginning of the Classical period, the people of the city-state of Athens overthrew their tyrannical leader and instituted a form of democracy. Under this system, government officials were chosen by a lottery from among the citizens, and decisions were taken by a democratic assembly. All the citizens could speak and vote at the assembly – they did not elect representatives to do this on their behalf. It should be noted, however, that the "citizens" were a minority of the population; they were free men aged over 30 whose parents were Athenians. Women, slaves, children, younger men, and foreigners or first-generation settlers, were excluded from the democratic process.

This political environment quickly made Athens a major cultural centre, attracting some of the foremost thinkers of the time. One of the greatest of these was an Athenian named Socrates, whose philosophical questioning of the generally accepted notions of justice and virtue gained him a following of young disciples. Unfortunately, it also attracted unwanted attention from the authorities, who persuaded the democratic assembly to issue Socrates with a death sentence, on charges of corrupting the young.

See also: Confucius 20–27 ▪ Mozi 32–33 ▪ Aristotle 40–43 ▪ Chanakya 44–47 ▪ Cicero 49 ▪ Augustine of Hippo 54–55 ▪ Al-Farabi 58–59

> Democracy passes into despotism.
> **Plato**

One of Socrates' young followers was Plato, who shared his teacher's inquisitive nature and sceptical attitude. Plato was to become disillusioned with the Athenian system after what he saw as its unfair treatment of his teacher.

Plato went on to become as influential a philosopher as Socrates, and towards the end of his career he turned his considerable intellect to the business of politics, most famously in the *Republic*. Unsurprisingly, given that he had seen Socrates condemned and was himself from a noble family, Plato had little sympathy for democracy. But neither did he find much to commend in any other existing form of government, all of which he believed led the state into "evils".

The good life

To understand what Plato meant by "evils" in this context, it is important to bear in mind the concept of *eudaimonia*, the "good life", which for ancient Greeks was a vital aim. "Living well" was not a question of achieving material wellbeing, honour, or mere pleasure, but rather living according to fundamental virtues such as wisdom, piety, and above all, justice. The purpose of the state, Plato believed, was to promote these virtues so that its citizens could lead this good life. Issues such as protection of property, liberty, and stability were only important in so far as they created conditions that allowed citizens to live well. In his opinion, however, no political system had yet existed that fulfilled this objective – and the defects within them encouraged what he saw as "evils", or the opposite of these virtues.

The reason for this, Plato maintained, is that rulers, whether in a monarchy, oligarchy (rule of the few), or democracy, tend to rule in their own interests rather than for the good of the state and its people. Plato explains that this is due to a general ignorance of the virtues that constitute the good life, which in turn leads people to desire the wrong things, especially the transitory pleasures of honour and wealth. These prizes come with political power, and the problem is intensified in the political arena. The desire to rule, for what Plato saw as the wrong reasons, leads to conflict among citizens. With everyone seeking increased power, this ultimately undermines the stability and unity of the state. Whoever emerges victorious from the power struggle deprives his opponents of the power to achieve their desires, which leads to injustice – an evil that is exactly contrary to the cornerstone of Plato's notion of the good life.

In contrast, Plato argued, there is a class of people who understand the meaning of the good life: philosophers. They alone recognize the worth of virtues above the pleasures of honour and money, and they have devoted their lives to the pursuit of the good life. Because of this, they do not lust after fame and fortune, and so have no desire for political power – paradoxically this is what qualifies them as ideal »

Socrates chose to drink poison rather than renounce his views. The trial and conviction of Socrates caused Plato to doubt the virtues of the democratic political system of Athens.

rulers. On face value, Plato's argument would seem to be simply that "philosophers know best", and (coming from a philosopher) might appear to contradict his assertion that they have no desire to rule, but behind it he gives a much richer and more subtle reasoning.

Ideal Forms

From Socrates, Plato had learned that virtue is not innate, but dependent on knowledge and wisdom, and in order to lead a virtuous life it is necessary first to understand the essential nature of virtue. Plato developed his mentor's ideas, showing that while we might recognize individual instances of qualities such as justice, goodness, or beauty, this does not allow us to understand what gives them their essential nature. We might imitate them – acting in a way that we think is just, for example – but this is mere mimicry rather than truly behaving according to those virtues.

In his Theory of Forms, Plato suggested the existence of ideal archetypes of these virtues (and of everything that exists) that consist of the essence of their true nature; this means that what we see as instances of these virtues are only examples of these Forms, and may show only a part of their nature. They are like inadequate reflections or shadows of the real Forms.

> The chief penalty is to be governed by someone worse if a man will not himself hold office and rule.
> **Plato**

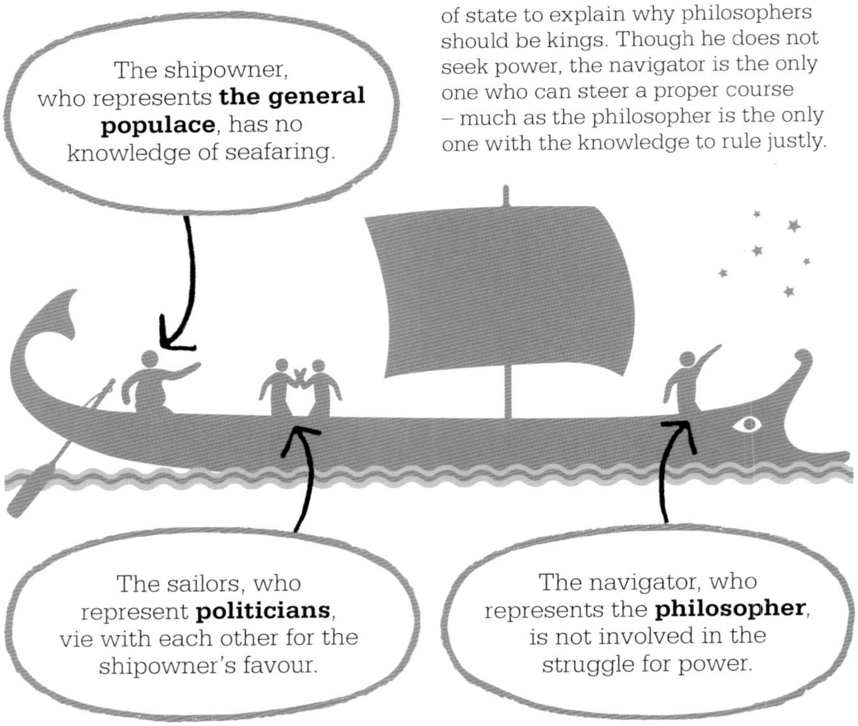

Plato used the metaphor of the ship of state to explain why philosophers should be kings. Though he does not seek power, the navigator is the only one who can steer a proper course – much as the philosopher is the only one with the knowledge to rule justly.

These ideal Forms, or Ideas, as Plato called them, exist in a realm outside the world we live in, accessible only via philosophical reasoning and enquiry. It is this that makes philosophers uniquely qualified to define what constitutes the good life, and of leading a truly virtuous life, rather than simply imitating individual examples of virtue. Plato had already demonstrated that to be good, the state has to be ruled by the virtuous, and while others value money or honour above all, only philosophers value knowledge and wisdom, and therefore virtue. It follows then that only the interests of philosophers benefit the state, and therefore "philosophers must become kings". Plato goes as far as to suggest that they should be compelled to take positions of power, in order to avoid the conflict and injustice inherent in other forms of government.

Educating kings

Plato recognizes that this is a utopian stance, and goes on to say, "...or those now called kings must genuinely and adequately philosophize", suggesting the education of a potential ruling class as a more practical proposition. In his later dialogues *Statesman* and *Laws*, he describes a model for a state in which this can be achieved, teaching the philosophical skills necessary to understanding the good life, in the same way as any other skills that can be of use to society. However, he points out that not every citizen has the aptitude

> Democracy… is full of variety and disorder, dispensing a sort of equality to equals and unequals alike.
> **Plato**

and intellectual ability to learn these skills. He suggests that where this education is appropriate – for a small, intellectual elite – it should be enforced rather than offered. Those chosen for power because of their "natural talents" should be separated from their families and reared in communes, so that their loyalties are to the state.

Plato's political writings were influential in the ancient world, in particular in the Roman empire, and echoed the notions of virtue and education in the political philosophy of Chinese scholars such as Confucius and Mozi. It is even possible that they influenced Chanakya in India when he wrote his treatise on training potential rulers. In medieval times, Plato's influence spread to the Islamic empire, and to Christian Europe, where Augustine incorporated them into the teachings of the Church. Later, Plato's ideas were overshadowed by those of Aristotle, whose advocacy of democracy chimed better with the political philosophers of the Renaissance.

Plato's political notions have been seen as unacceptably authoritarian and elitist by later thinkers, and they fell out of favour with many in the modern world while it struggled to establish democracy. He has been criticized as advocating a totalitarian, or at best paternalistic, system of government run by an elite that claims to know what is best for everyone else. Recently, however, his central notion of a political elite of "philosopher kings" has been reappraised by political thinkers. ■

Emperor Nero is said to have stood by and done nothing to help while a fire raged in the city of Rome. Plato's ideal of a philosopher king has been blamed by some for the rise of such tyrants.

Plato

Born around 427 BCE, Plato was originally called Aristocles, later acquiring the nickname Plato (meaning "broad") because of his muscular physique. From a noble Athenian family, he was probably expected to follow a career in politics, but instead became a disciple of the philosopher Socrates and was present when his mentor chose to die rather than renounce his views.

Plato travelled widely around the Mediterranean before returning to Athens, where he established a school of philosophy, the Academy, which numbered among its students the young Aristotle. While teaching, he wrote a number of books in the form of dialogues, generally featuring his teacher Socrates, exploring ideas of philosophy and politics. He is believed to have carried on teaching and writing well into his later years, and died at about the age of 80 in 348/347 BCE.

Key works

c.399–387 BCE *Crito*
c.380–360 BCE *Republic*
c.355–347 BCE *Statesman, Laws*

MAN IS BY NATURE A POLITICAL ANIMAL

ARISTOTLE (384–322 BCE)

IN CONTEXT

IDEOLOGY
Democracy

FOCUS
Political virtue

BEFORE
431 BCE Athenian statesman Pericles states that democracy provides equal justice for all.

c.380–360 BCE In the *Republic*, Plato advocates rule by "philosopher kings" who possess wisdom.

AFTER
13th century Thomas Aquinas incorporates Aristotle's ideas into Christian doctrine.

c.1300 Giles of Rome stresses the importance of the rule of law to living in a civil society.

1651 Thomas Hobbes proposes a social contract to prevent man from living in a "brutish" state of nature.

Ancient Greece was not a unified nation-state as we would recognize one today, but a collection of independent regional states with cities at their centre. Each city-state, or *polis*, had its own constitutional organization: some, such as Macedon, were ruled by a monarch, while others, most notably Athens, had a form of democracy in which at least some of the citizens could participate in their government.

Aristotle, who was brought up in Macedon and studied in Athens, was well acquainted with the concept of the *polis* and its various interpretations, and his analytical

See also: Plato 34–39 ▪ Cicero 49 ▪ Thomas Aquinas 62–69 ▪ Giles of Rome 70 ▪ Thomas Hobbes 96–103 ▪ Jean-Jacques Rousseau 118–25

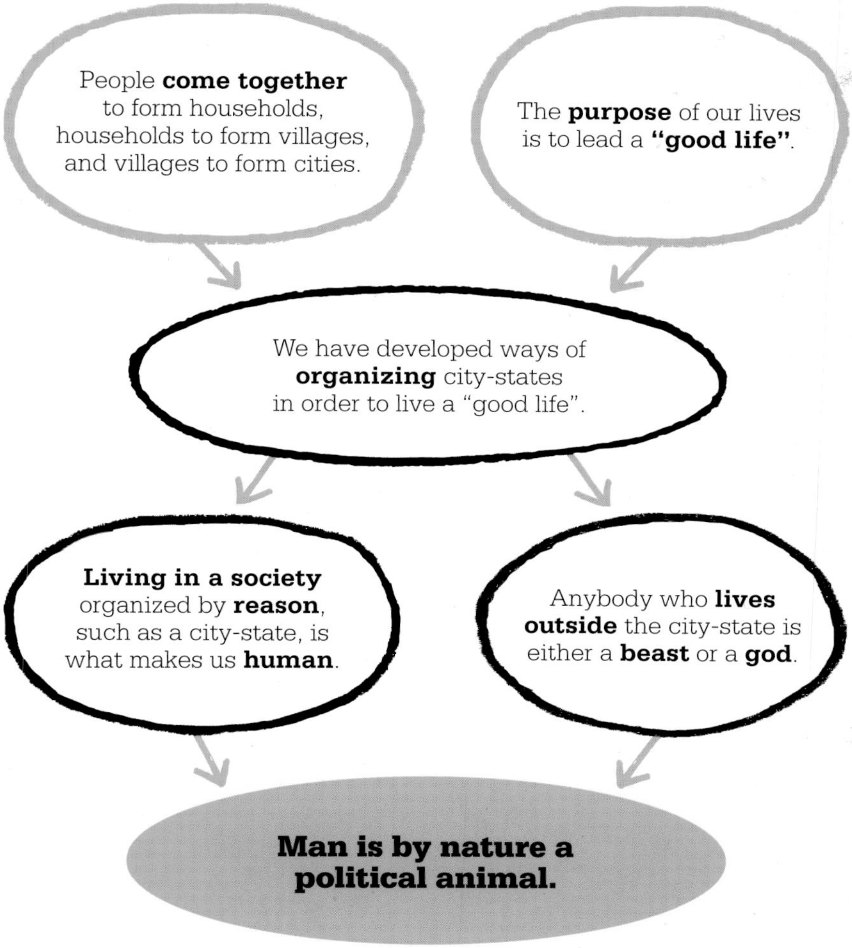

turn of mind made him well qualified to examine the merits of the city-state. He also spent some time in Ionia classifying animals and plants according to their characteristics. He was later to apply these skills of categorization to ethics and politics, which he saw as both natural and practical sciences. Unlike his mentor, Plato, Aristotle believed that knowledge was acquired through observation rather than intellectual reasoning, and that the science of politics should be based on empirical data, organized in the same way as the taxonomy of the natural world.

Naturally social

Aristotle observed that humans have a natural tendency to form social units: individuals come together to form households, households to form villages, and villages to form cities. Just as some animals – such as bees or cattle – are distinguished by their disposition to live in colonies »

Aristotle

The son of a physician to the royal family of Macedon, Aristotle was born in Stagira, Chalcidice, in the north-east of modern Greece. He was sent to Athens aged 17 to study with Plato at the Academy, and remained there until Plato's death 20 years later. Surprisingly, Aristotle was not appointed Plato's successor to lead the Academy. He moved to Ionia, where he made a study of the wildlife, until he was invited by Philip of Macedon to be tutor to the young Alexander the Great.

Aristotle returned to Athens in 335 BCE to establish a rival school to the Academy, at the Lyceum. While teaching there he formalized his ideas on the sciences, philosophy, and politics, compiling a large volume of writings, of which few have survived. After the death of Alexander in 323 BCE, anti-Macedonian feeling in Athens prompted him to leave the city for Euboea, where he died the following year.

Key works

c.350 BCE
Nicomachean Ethics
Politics
Rhetoric

or herds, humans are by nature social. Just as he might define a wolf by saying it is by nature a pack animal, Aristotle says that "Man is by nature a political animal". By this, Aristotle means simply that Man is an animal whose nature it is to live socially in a *polis*; he is not implying a natural tendency towards political activity in the modern sense of the word.

The idea that we have a tendency to live in large civil communities might seem relatively unenlightening today, but it is important to recognize that Aristotle is explicitly stating that the *polis* is just as much a creation of nature as an ants' nest. For him, it is inconceivable that humans can live in any other way. This contrasts markedly with ideas of civil society as an artificial construct that has taken us out of an uncivilized "state of nature" – something Aristotle would not have understood. Anyone living outside a *polis*, he believed, was not human – he must be either superior to men (that is, a god) or inferior to them (that is, a beast).

The good life

This idea of the *polis* as a natural phenomenon rather than a man-made one underpins Aristotle's ideas about ethics and the politics of the city-state. From his study of the natural world, he gained a notion that everything that exists has an aim or a purpose, and he decided that for humans, this is to lead a "good life". Aristotle takes this to mean the pursuit of virtues, such as justice, goodness, and beauty. The purpose of the *polis*, then, is to enable us to live according to these virtues. The ancient Greeks saw the structure of the state – which enables people to live together and protects the property and liberty of its citizens – as a means to the end of virtue.

Aristotle identified various "species" and "sub-species" within the *polis*. He found that what distinguishes Man from the other animals is his innate powers of reason and the faculty of speech, which give him a unique ability to form social groups and set up communities and partnerships. Within the community of a *polis*, the citizens develop an organization that ensures the security, economic stability, and justice of the state; not by imposing any form of social contract, but because it is in their nature to do so. For Aristotle, the different ways of organizing the life of the *polis* exist not so that people can live together (as they do this by their very nature), but so that they can live well. How well they succeed in achieving this goal, he observes, depends on the type of government they choose.

> Law is order, and good law is good order.
> **Aristotle**

Species of rule

An inveterate classifier of data, Aristotle devised a comprehensive taxonomy of the natural world, and in his later works, especially *Politics*, he set about applying the same methodical skills to systems of government. While Plato had reasoned theoretically about the ideal form of government, Aristotle chose to examine existing regimes to analyse their strengths and weaknesses. To do this, he asked two simple questions: who rules, and on whose behalf do they rule?

In answer to the first question, Aristotle observes that there are basically three types of rule: by a single person, by a select few, or by many. And in answer to the second question, the rule could be either on behalf of the population as a whole, which he considered true or good government, or in the self-

In ancient Athens, citizens debated political affairs at a stone dais called the Pnyx. To Aristotle, the active participation of citizens in government was essential for a healthy society.

interest of the ruler or ruling class, a defective form of government. In all, he identified six "species" of rule, which came in pairs. Monarchy is rule by an individual on behalf of all; rule by an individual in his own interests, or tyranny, is corrupted monarchy. Rule by aristocracy (which to the Greeks meant rule by the best, rather than rule by hereditary noble families) is rule by a few for the good of all; rule by a self-interested few, or oligarchy, is its corrupted form. Finally, polity is rule by the many for the benefit of all. Aristotle saw democracy as the corrupted form of this last form of rule, as in practice it entails ruling on behalf of the many, rather than every single individual.

Aristotle argues that the self-interest inherent in the defective forms of government leads to inequality and injustice. This translates into instability, which threatens the role of the state and its ability to encourage virtuous living. In practice, however, the city-states he studied did not all fall neatly into just one category, but exhibited characteristics from the various types.

Although Aristotle had a tendency to view the *polis* as a single "organism", of which the citizens are merely a part, he did also examine the role of the individual within the city-state. Again, he stresses Man's natural inclination to social interaction, and defines the citizen as one who shares in the structure of the civil community, not merely by electing representatives, but through active participation. When this participation is within a "good" form of government (monarchy, aristocracy, or polity), it fosters the ability of the citizen to lead a virtuous life. Under a "defective" regime (tyranny, oligarchy, or democracy), the citizen becomes involved with the self-interested pursuits of the ruler or ruling class – the tyrant's pursuit of power, the oligarchs' thirst for wealth, or the democrats' search for freedom. Of all the possible regimes, Aristotle concludes, polity provides the best opportunity to lead a good life.

Although Aristotle categorizes democracy as a "defective" form of regime, he argues that it is only second best to polity, and better than the "good" aristocracy or monarchy. While the individual citizen may not have the wisdom and virtue of a good ruler, collectively "the many" may prove to be better rulers than "the one".

The detailed description and analysis of the Classical Greek *polis* seems on the face of it to have little relevance to the nation-states that followed, but Aristotle's ideas had a growing influence on European political thought throughout the Middle Ages. Despite being criticised for his often authoritarian standpoint (and his defence of slavery and the inferior status of women), his arguments in favour of constitutional government anticipate ideas that emerged in the Enlightenment. ■

> The basis of a democratic state is liberty.
> **Aristotle**

Aristotle's Six Species of Government

	Rule By A Single Person	Rule By A Selected Few	Rule By The Many
True Government	 **Monarchy**	 **Aristocracy**	 **Polity**
Corrupt Government	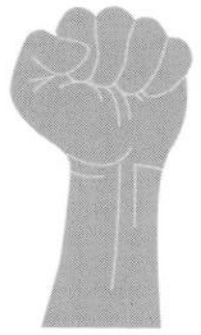 **Tyranny**	 **Oligarchy**	 **Democracy**

A SINGLE WHEEL DOES NOT MOVE

CHANAKYA c.350–c.275 BCE

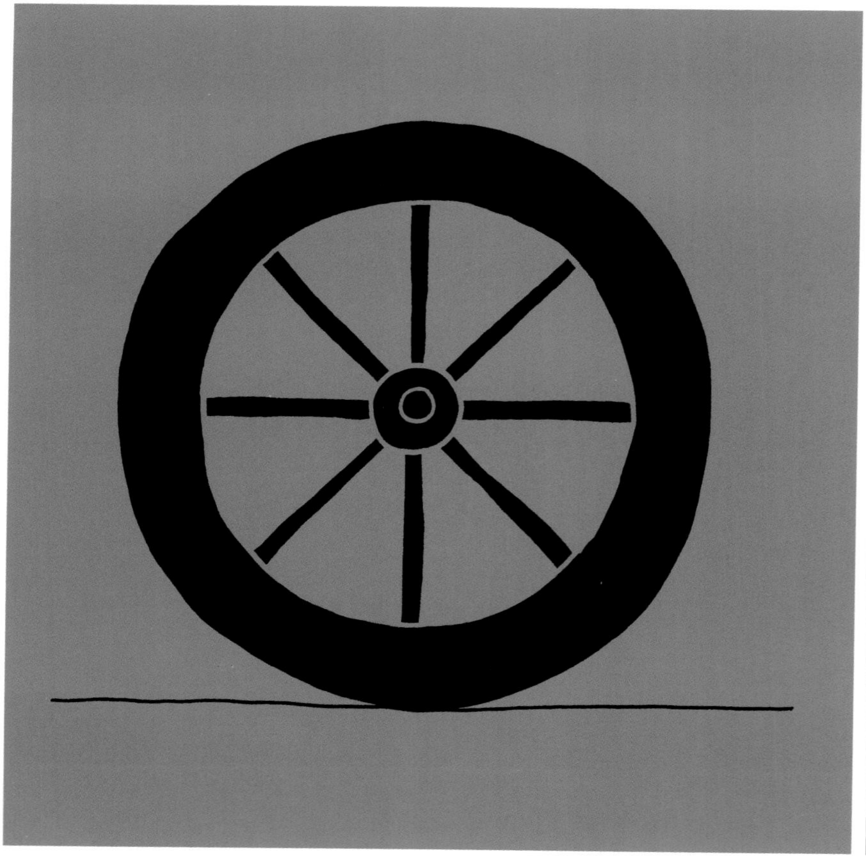

IN CONTEXT

IDEOLOGY
Realism

FOCUS
Utilitarian

BEFORE
6th century BCE The Chinese general Sun Tzu writes his treatise *The Art of War*, bringing an analytical approach to statecraft.

424 BCE Mahapadma Nanda establishes the Nanda dynasty, and relies on his generals for tactical advice.

AFTER
c.65 BCE The Mauryan empire, which Chanakya helped to found, reaches its height and rules over all but the southern tip of the Indian subcontinent.

1904 Texts of Chanakya's treatises are rediscovered and, in 1915, are translated into English.

During the 5th and 4th centuries BCE, the Nanda dynasty slowly gained control over the northern half of the Indian subcontinent, defeating its rivals one by one and holding off the threat of invasion by the Greeks and Persians from the West. The rulers of this expanding empire relied on generals for tactical advice in battle, but they also began to recognize the value of ministers to advise on matters of policy and government. Scholars, especially those from Takshashila, a university established *c.*600 BCE in Rawalpindi, now part of Pakistan, frequently became these ministers. Many important thinkers developed

See also: Confucius 20–27 ▪ Sun Tzu 28–31 ▪ Mozi 32–33 ▪ Plato 34–39 ▪ Aristotle 40–43 ▪ Niccolò Machiavelli 74–81

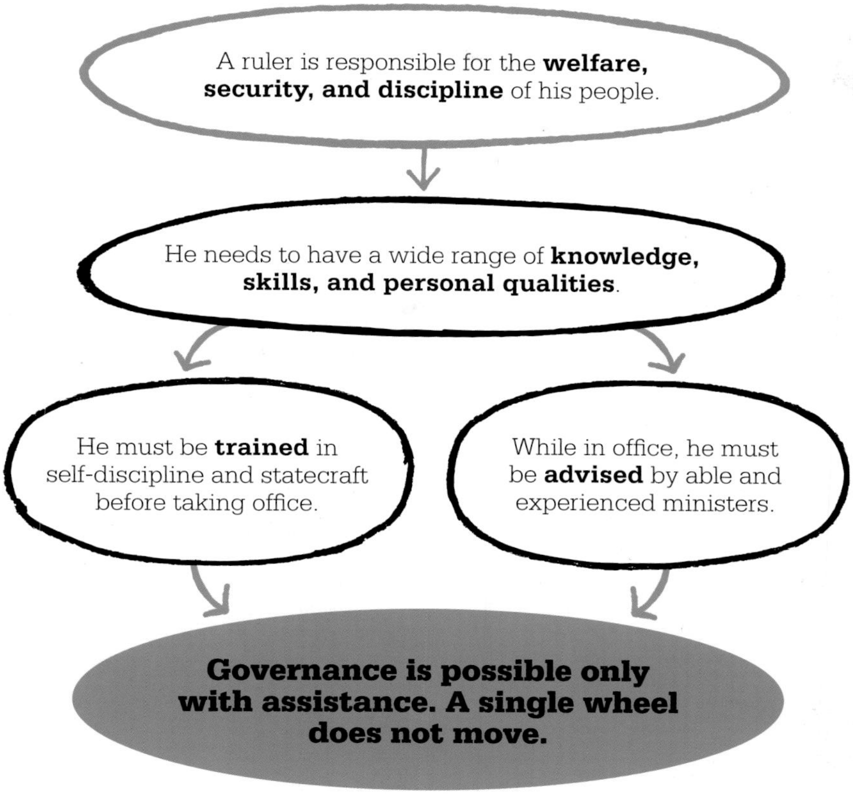

their ideas at Takshashila, but perhaps the most significant was Chanakya (also known as Kautilya and Vishnugupta). He wrote a treatise on statecraft titled *Arthashastra*, meaning "the science of material gain" or "the art of government". It combined the accumulated wisdom of the art of politics with Chanakya's own ideas, and was remarkable in its dispassionate, and at times ruthless, analysis of the business of politics.

Advising the sovereign

Although sections of the treatise dealt with the moral qualities desirable in the leader of a state, the emphasis was on the practical, describing in forthright terms how power could be gained and maintained, and for the first time in India, it explicitly described a civil structure in which ministers and advisors played a key role in the running of the state.

A commitment to the prosperity of the state lies at the heart of Chanakya's political thought, and he makes repeated references to the welfare of the people as the ultimate goal of government. This, he believed, was the responsibility of a sovereign who would ensure his people's wellbeing and security by administering order and justice, and leading his country to victory over rival states. The power to carry out his duties to his country and its people is dependent on several different factors, which Chanakya describes in *Arthashastra*: the personal qualities of the ruler, the abilities of his advisors, his territory and towns, his wealth, his army, and his allies.

The sovereign, as head of state, has the central role in this system of government. Chanakya emphasizes the importance of finding a ruler with the appropriate qualities, but then goes on to say that personal qualities of leadership are not sufficient on their own: the sovereign must also be trained for the job. He must learn the various skills of statecraft, such as military tactics and strategy, law, administration, and the arts of diplomacy and politics, but in addition he should be taught the skills of self-discipline and ethics in order to develop the moral authority necessary to command the»

The lion capital of Ashoka stood on top of a pillar in Sarnath at the centre of the Mauryan empire. Chanakya helped to found this powerful empire, which came to rule almost the whole of India.

> All things begin with counsel.
> **Chanakya**

loyalty and obedience of his people. Before taking office, the sovereign needs assistance from experienced and knowledgeable teachers.

Once instated, a wise sovereign does not rely solely on his own wisdom, but can turn to trusted ministers and advisors for counsel. In Chanakya's view, such individuals are as important as the sovereign in governing the state. In *Arthashastra*, Chanakya states: "Governance is possible only with assistance – a single wheel does not move." This is a warning to the sovereign not to be autocratic, but to arrive at decisions of state after consulting his ministers.

The appointment of ministers with the necessary qualifications is therefore just as important as the people's choice of leader. The ministers can provide a range of knowledge and skills. They must be utterly trustworthy, not only so that the sovereign can rely on their advice, but also to ensure that decisions are made in the interests of the state and its people – if necessary, preventing a corrupt ruler from acting in his own interests.

The end justifies the means

It was this recognition of the realities of human nature that distinguished Chanakya from other Indian political philosophers of the time. *Arthashastra* is not a work of moral philosophy, but a practical guide to governance, and in ensuring the welfare and security of the state it often advocates using whatever means are necessary. Although *Arthashastra* advocates a regime of learning and self-discipline for an ideal ruler, and mentions certain moral qualities, it doesn't flinch from describing how to use underhand methods to gain and maintain power. Chanakya was a shrewd observer of human weaknesses as well as strengths, and he was not above exploiting these to increase the sovereign's power and undermine that of the sovereign's enemies.

This is particularly noticeable in his advice on defending and acquiring territory. Here he recommends that the ruler and his ministers should carefully assess the strength of their enemies before deciding on a strategy to undermine them. They can then choose from a number of different tactics, ranging from conciliation, encouraging dissent in the enemy's ranks, and forming alliances of convenience with other rulers, to the simple use of military force. In deploying these tactics, the ruler should be ruthless, using trickery, bribery, and any other inducements deemed necessary. Although this seems contradictory to the moral authority Chanakya advocates in a leader, he stipulates that after victory has been achieved, the ruler should "substitute his virtues for the defeated enemy's vices, and where the enemy was good he shall be twice as good".

Intelligence and espionage

Arthashastra reminds rulers that military advisors are also needed, and the gathering of information is important for decision-making. A network of spies is vital in assessing the threat posed by neighbouring states or to judge the feasibility of acquiring territory; but

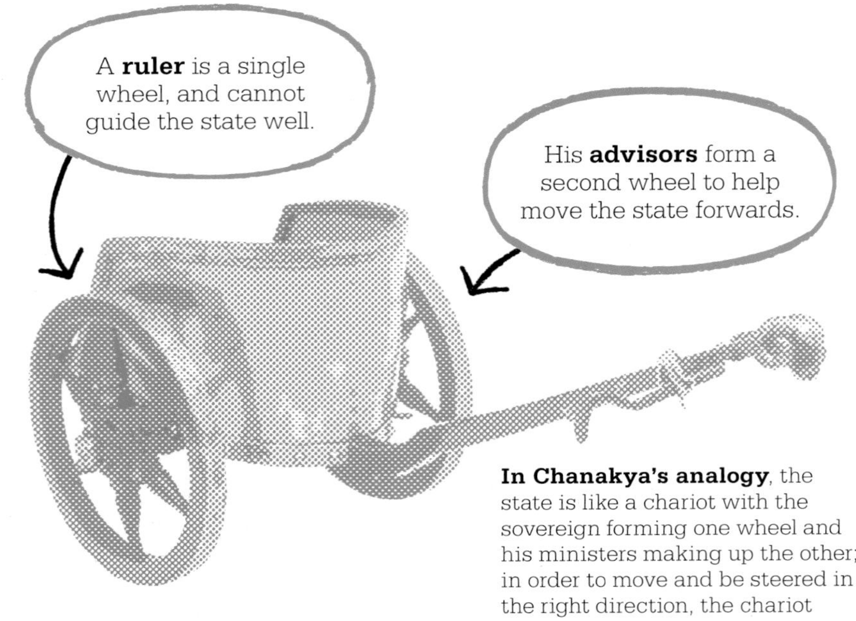

In Chanakya's analogy, the state is like a chariot with the sovereign forming one wheel and his ministers making up the other; in order to move and be steered in the right direction, the chariot needs both wheels.

> Through ministerial eyes others' weaknesses are seen.
> **Chanakya**

Chanakya goes further, suggesting that espionage within the state is also a necessary evil in order to ensure social stability. At home and in international relations, morality is of secondary importance to the protection of the state. The state's welfare is used as justification for clandestine operations, including political assassination should this be necessary, aimed at reducing the threat of opposition.

This amoral approach to taking and holding on to power, and the advocacy of a strict enforcement of law and order, can be seen either as shrewd political awareness or as ruthlessness, and has earned *Arthashastra* comparison with Machiavelli's *The Prince*, written around 2,000 years later. However, the central doctrine, of rule by a sovereign and ministers, has more in common with Confucius and Mozi, or Plato and Aristotle, whose ideas Chanakya may have come across as a student in Takshashila.

Elephants played a big role in Indian warfare, often terrifying enemies so much that they would withdraw rather than fight. Chanakya developed new strategies for warfare with elephants.

A proven philosophy

The advice contained in the pages of *Arthashastra* soon proved its usefulness when adopted by Chanakya's protegé Chandragupta Maurya, who successfully defeated King Nanda to establish the Maurya empire in around 321 BCE. This became the first empire to cover the majority of the Indian subcontinent, and Maurya also successfully held off the threat from Greek invaders led by Alexander the Great. Chanakya's ideas were to influence government and policy-making for several centuries, until India eventually succumbed to Islamic and Mughal rule in the Middle Ages.

The text of *Arthashastra* was rediscovered in the early 20th century, and regained some of its importance in Indian political thinking, gaining iconic status after India won independence from Britain in 1948. Despite its central place in Indian political history, it was little known in the West, and it is only recently that Chanakya has been recognized outside India as a significant political thinker. ■

Chanakya

The birthplace of Indian scholar Chanakya is not certain. It is known that he studied and taught in Takshashila (modern Taxila, Pakistan). Leaving Takshashila to become involved in government, he travelled to Pataliputra, where he became an advisor to King Dhana Nanda. There are many conflicting accounts, but all agree that he left the Nanda court after a dispute, and in revenge groomed the young Chandragupta Maurya to be Nanda's rival. Chandragupta overthrew Dhana Nanda and founded the Mauryan empire, which governed all modern-day India except the very south. Chanakya was Chandragupta's chief advisor, but is said to have starved himself to death after being falsely accused by Chandragupta's son, Bindusara, of poisoning his mother.

Key works

4th century BCE
Arthashastra
Neetishastra

IF EVIL MINISTERS ENJOY SAFETY AND PROFIT, THIS IS THE BEGINNING OF DOWNFALL

HAN FEI TZU (280–233 BCE)

IN CONTEXT

IDEOLOGY
Legalism

FOCUS
State laws

BEFORE
5th century BCE Confucius advocates a hierarchy based on traditional family relationships, with the sovereign and his ministers ruling by example.

4th century BCE Mozi proposes a purely meritocratic class of ministers and advisors chosen for their virtue and ability.

AFTER
2nd century BCE After the Warring States period ends, China's Han dynasty rejects Legalism and adopts Confucianism.

589–618 CE Legalist principles are revived during the Sui dynasty in an attempt to unify the Chinese empire.

During China's Warring States period, between the 5th and 3rd centuries BCE, rulers were vying for power over a unified Chinese empire, and a new political philosophy emerged to suit these turbulent times. Thinkers such as Shang Yang (390–338 BCE), Shen Dao (*c.* 350–275 BCE), and Shen Buhai (died 337 BCE) advocated a much more authoritarian approach to government, which became known as Legalism. Formalized and put into practice by Han Fei Tzu, Legalism rejected the Confucian idea of leading by example and Mozi's belief in the innate goodness of human nature, and instead took the more cynical view that people naturally acted to avoid punishment and achieve personal gain. The only way that this could be controlled, the Legalists argued, was by a system that emphasized the wellbeing of the state over the rights of the individual, with strict laws to punish undesirable behaviour.

> To govern the state by law is to praise the right and blame the wrong.
> **Han Fei Tzu**

Administration of these laws was handled by the ruler's ministers, who in turn were subject to laws that held them accountable, with punishments and favours given by the ruler. In this way, the hierarchy with the ruler at the top could be maintained, and corruption and intrigue among the bureaucracy could be controlled. It was vitally important to the safety of the state in times of war that the ruler could rely on his ministers and that they should be acting in the interests of the state rather than for their own personal advancement. ■

See also: Confucius 20–27 ▪ Sun Tzu 28–31 ▪ Mozi 32–33 ▪ Thomas Hobbes 96–103 ▪ Mao Zedong 260–65

THE GOVERNMENT IS BANDIED ABOUT LIKE A BALL

CICERO (106–43 BCE)

IN CONTEXT

IDEOLOGY
Republicanism

FOCUS
Mixed constitution

BEFORE
c.380 BCE Plato writes the *Republic*, outlining his ideas for an ideal city-state.

2nd century BCE Greek historian Polybius's *The Histories* describes the rise of the Roman Republic and its constitution with a separation of powers.

48 BCE Julius Caesar is given unprecedented powers, and his dictatorship marks the end of the Roman Republic.

AFTER
27 BCE Octavian is proclaimed Augustus, effectively the first emperor of Rome.

1734 Montesquieu writes *Considerations on the Causes of the Greatness of the Romans and Their Decline*.

The Roman Republic was founded in around 510 BCE along similar lines to the city-states of Greece. With only minor changes, it ruled for almost 500 years. This system of government combined elements of three different forms of regime – monarchy (replaced by the Consuls), aristocracy (the Senate), and democracy (the popular assembly) – each with distinct areas of power that balanced one another out. Known as a mixed constitution, it was considered by most Romans to be an ideal form of government that provided stability and prevented tyranny.

Checks and balances

Roman politician Cicero was a staunch defender of the system, particularly when it was threatened by the granting of dictatorial powers to Julius Caesar. He warned that a break-up of the Republic would prompt a return to a destructive cycle of governments. He said that from a monarchy, power can be passed to a tyrant; from the tyrant, it is taken by the aristocracy or the people; and from the people it will be seized by oligarchs or tyrants. Without the checks and balances of a mixed constitution, the government, he believed, would be "bandied about like a ball". True to Cicero's predictions, Rome came under the control of an emperor, Augustus, shortly after Caesar's death, and power was passed from him to a succession of despotic rulers. ■

The Roman standard carried the legend SPQR (the Senate and the People of Rome), celebrating the central institutions of the mixed constitution.

See also: Plato 34–39 ▪ Aristotle 40–43 ▪ Montesquieu 110–111 ▪ Benjamin Franklin 112–13 ▪ Thomas Jefferson 140–41 ▪ James Madison 150–53

MEDIEV
POLITIC
30 CE–1515 CE

AL
S

c.30 CE
According to Catholic tradition, St Peter is made the first **Bishop of Rome**, and his successors become known as popes.

306 CE
Constantine I becomes the first **Christian emperor** of the Roman empire.

380
Emperor Theodosius I establishes Christianity as the **official religion** of Rome.

c.413
Augustine of Hippo describes a **government without justice** as no better than a band of robbers.

622
Muhammad writes the **Constitution of Medina**, establishing the first Islamic government.

800
Charlemagne is crowned emperor of Rome, effectively founding the **Holy Roman empire**.

900
Al-Kindi brings **classical Greek texts**, including those of Plato and Aristotle, to the House of Wisdom in Baghdad.

c.940–950
In *The Virtuous City*, Al-Farabi applies the ideas of **Plato and Aristotle** to imagine an ideal Islamic state.

From its beginnings in the 1st century BCE, the Roman empire grew in strength, extending its reign over Europe, Mediterranean Africa, and the Middle East. By the 2nd century CE, it was at the height of its power, and Roman imperial culture, with its emphasis on prosperity and stability, threatened to replace the values of scholarship and philosophy associated with the republics of Athens and Rome. At the same time, a new religion was taking root within the empire: Christianity.

For the next millennium, political thinking was dominated by the Church in Europe, and political theory during the Middle Ages was shaped by Christian theology. In the 7th century, another powerful religion, Islam, emerged. It spread from Arabia into Asia and Africa, and also influenced political thinking in Christian Europe.

The impact of Christianity

Roman philosophers such as Plotinus returned to the ideas of Plato, and the "neo-Platonist" movement influenced early Christian thinkers. Augustine of Hippo interpreted Plato's ideas in the light of Christian faith to examine questions such as the difference between divine and human law, and whether there could be such a thing as a just war.

The pagan Roman empire had simply had little time for philosophy and theory, but in early Christian Europe, political thinking was subordinated to religious dogma, and the ideas of ancient Greece and Rome were largely neglected. A major factor in this subordination of ideas was the rise to political power of the Church and the papacy. Medieval Europe was effectively ruled by the Church, a situation that was formalized in 800 by the creation of the Holy Roman empire under Charlemagne.

Islamic influence

Meanwhile, in Arabia, Muhammad established Islam as a religion with an imperialist agenda, and it rapidly established itself as a major political as well as religious power. Unlike Christianity, Islam was open to secular political thinking and encouraged wide scholarship and the study of non-Muslim thinkers. Libraries were set up in cities throughout the Islamic empire to preserve classical texts, and

c.980–1037 Avicenna incorporates **rational philosophy** into Islamic theology, opening up space for new political ideas.

1086 King William I of England orders the compilation of the **Domesday Book** in one of the world's first government censuses.

1095 Christians launch the **First Crusade** to gain control of Jerusalem and the Holy Land from Islamic rule.

1100 Henry I of England issues the **Charter of Liberties**, making the monarch subject to laws preventing the abuse of power.

1300 Thomas Aquinas defines the **cardinal and theological virtues**, and makes a distinction between natural, human, and divine law.

1328 Marsilius of Padua sides with Holy Roman Emperor Louis IV and **secular rule** in the king's power struggle against Pope John XII.

1377 Ibn Khaldun states that the role of government is to **prevent injustice**.

1513 Niccolò Machiavelli writes *The Prince*, effectively starting **modern political science**.

scholars integrated the ideas of Plato and Aristotle into Islamic theology. Cities such as Baghdad became centres of learning, and scholars such as Al-Kindi, Al-Farabi, Ibn Sina (Avicenna), Ibn Rushd (Averroes), and Ibn Khaldun emerged as political theorists.

Meanwhile, in Europe, scholarship had become the preserve of the clergy, and the structure of society was prescribed by the Church, leaving little room for dissent. It would take Islamic influence to bring fresh ideas to medieval Europe, as scholars rediscovered the classical texts. In the 12th century, the texts that Islamic scholars had preserved and translated began to come to the notice of Christian scholars, particularly in Spain, where the two faiths co-existed. News of the rediscovery spread across the Christian world, and despite the suspicion of the Church authorities, there was a rush to find and translate not only the texts, but also their Islamic commentaries.

Difficult questions

A new generation of Christian philosophers became acquainted with classical thinking. Thomas Aquinas tried to integrate the ideas of Aristotle into Christian theology. This posed questions that had previously been avoided, on subjects such as the divine right of kings, and revived debate about secular versus divine law. The introduction of secular thinking into intellectual life had a profound effect within the Holy Roman empire. Separate nation-states were asserting their independence and rulers came into conflict with the papacy. The authority of the Church in civil affairs was brought into question, and philosophers such as Giles of Rome and Marsilius of Padua had to come down on one side or the other.

As the Middle Ages drew to an end, new nations challenged the authority of the Church, but people were also beginning to question the power of their monarchs. In England, King John was forced by his barons to concede some of his powers. In Italy, dynastic tyrants were replaced by republics such as Florence, where the Renaissance began. It was in Florence that Niccolò Machiavelli, a potent symbol of Renaissance thought, shocked the world by producing a political philosophy that was entirely pragmatic in its morality. ■

IF JUSTICE BE TAKEN AWAY, WHAT ARE GOVERNMENTS BUT GREAT BANDS OF ROBBERS?

AUGUSTINE OF HIPPO (354–430 CE)

IN CONTEXT

IDEOLOGY
Christianity

FOCUS
Just government

BEFORE
4th century BCE In the *Republic* and *Laws*, Plato stresses the importance of justice in an ideal state.

1st century BCE Cicero opposes the overthrow of the Roman Republic and its replacement with an emperor.

306 CE Constantine I becomes the first Christian emperor of the Roman empire.

AFTER
13th century Thomas Aquinas uses Augustine's arguments to define a just war.

14th century Ibn Khaldun says that government's role is to prevent injustice.

c. 1600 Francisco Suárez and the School of Salamanca create a philosophy of natural law.

In 380 CE, Christianity was effectively adopted as the official religion of the Roman empire, and as the Church's power and influence grew, its relationship with the state became a disputed issue. One of the first political philosophers to address this question was Augustine of Hippo, a scholar and teacher who became a convert to Christianity. In his attempt to integrate classical philosophy into the religion, he was greatly influenced by his study of Plato, which also formed the basis for his political thinking.

As a Roman citizen, Augustine believed in the tradition of a state bound by the rule of law, but as a scholar, he agreed with Aristotle

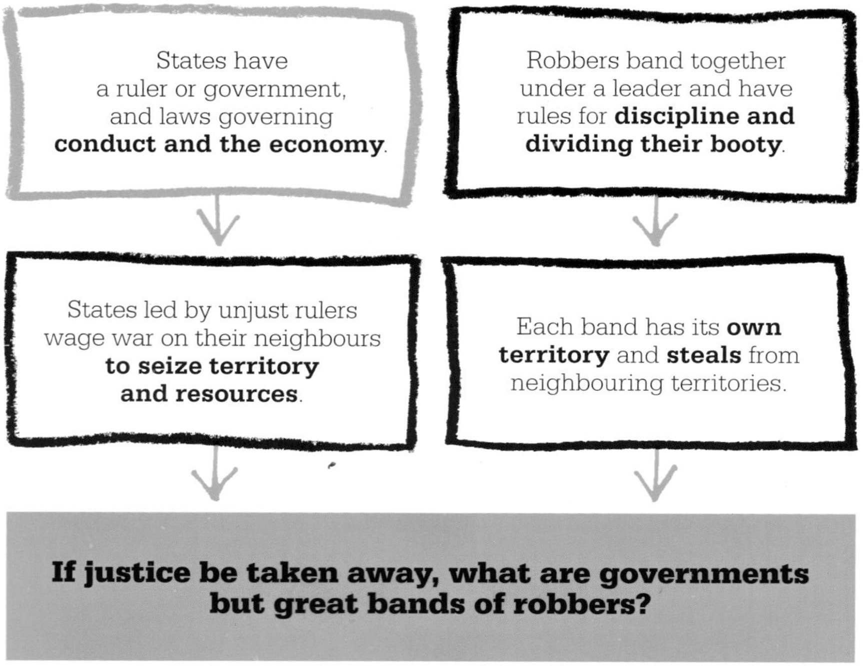

See also: Plato 34–39 ▪ Cicero 49 ▪ Thomas Aquinas 62–69 ▪ Francisco Suárez 90–91 ▪ Thomas Hobbes 96–103

> Without justice an association of men in the bond of law cannot possibly continue.
> **Augustine**

and Plato that the goal of the state was to enable its people to lead the good and virtuous life. For a Christian, this meant living by the divine laws prescribed by the Church. However, Augustine believed that, in practice, few men lived according to divine laws, and the vast majority lived in a state of sin. He distinguished between two kingdoms: the *civitas Dei* (city of God) and the *civitas terrea* (city of Earth). In the latter kingdom, sin predominates. Augustine sees the influence of the Church on the state as the only means to ensure that the laws of the land are made with reference to divine laws, allowing people to live in the *civitas Dei*. The presence of such just laws distinguishes a state from a band of robbers. Robbers and pirates join together under a leader to steal from their neighbours. The robbers may have rules, but they are not just rules. However, Augustine further points out that even in a sinful *civitas terrea*, the authority of the state can ensure order through the rule of law, and that order is something we all have a reason to want.

Just war

Augustine's emphasis on justice, with its roots in Christian doctrine, also applied to the business of war. While he believed all war to be evil, and that to attack and plunder other states was unjust, he conceded that a "just war" fought for a just cause, such as defending the state against aggression, or to restore peace, did exist, though it should be embarked upon with regret and only as a last resort.

This conflict between secular and divine law, and the attempt to reconcile the two, began the power struggle between Church and state that ran through the Middle Ages. ■

Augustine's vision of a state living according to Christian principles was outlined in his work *City of God*, in which he described the relationship between the Roman empire and God's law.

Augustine of Hippo

Aurelius Augustine was born in Thagaste (now Souk-Ahras, Algeria) in Roman North Africa, to a pagan father and a Christian mother. He studied Latin literature in Madaurus and rhetoric in Carthage, where he came across the Persian Manichean religion, and became interested in philosophy through the works of Cicero. He taught in Thagaste and Carthage until 373, when he moved to Rome and Milan, and there was inspired by theologian Bishop Ambrose to explore Plato's philosophy, and later to become a Christian. He was baptised in 387, and was ordained a priest in Thagaste in 391. He finally settled in Hippo (now Bone, Algeria), establishing a religious community and becoming its bishop in 396. As well as his autobiographical *Confessions*, he wrote a number of works on theology and philosophy. He died during a siege of Hippo by the Vandals in 430.

Key works

387–395 *On Free Will*
397–401 *Confessions*
413–425 *City of God*

FIGHTING HAS BEEN ENJOINED UPON YOU WHILE IT IS HATEFUL TO YOU

MUHAMMAD (570–632 CE)

IN CONTEXT

IDEOLOGY
Islam

FOCUS
Just war

BEFORE
6th century BCE In *The Art of War*, Sun Tzu argues that the military is essential to the state.

c.413 Augustine describes a government without justice as no better than a band of robbers.

AFTER
13th century Thomas Aquinas defines the conditions for a just war.

1095 Christians launch the First Crusade to wrest control of Jerusalem and the Holy Land from the Muslims.

1932 In *Towards Understanding Islam*, Abul Ala Maududi insists that Islam embraces all aspects of human life, including politics.

Islam is a **peaceful religion** and all Muslims wish to live in peace.

↓

But even believers in Islam need to **defend** themselves against invasion…

↓

…and **attack the unbelievers** who threaten their peace and religion.

↓

Fighting has been enjoined upon you while it is hateful to you.

Revered by Muslims as the prophet of the Islamic faith, Muhammad also laid the foundations for an Islamic empire; he was its political and military leader as much as its spiritual guide. Exiled from Mecca because of his faith, in 622 he travelled to Yathrib (on a journey that became known as the Hijra), where he gained huge numbers of followers, and ultimately organized the city into a unified Islamic city-state. The city was renamed Medina ("city of the Prophet"), and it became the world's first Islamic state. Muhammad created a constitution for the state – the Constitution of Medina – which formed the basis of an Islamic political tradition.

The constitution addressed the rights and duties of every group within the community, the rule of law, and the issue of war. It recognized the Jewish community of Medina as separate, and agreed reciprocal obligations with them. Among its edicts, it obliged the whole community – members of all the religions in Medina – to fight as one if the community came under threat. The key aims were peace within the Islamic state of Medina

See also: Augustine of Hippo 54–55 ▪ Al-Farabi 58–59 ▪ Thomas Aquinas 62–69 ▪ Ibn Khaldun 72–73 ▪ Abul Ala Maududi 278–79 ▪ Ali Shariati 323

Muslim pilgrims pray near the Prophet Muhammad Mosque in the holy city of Medina, Saudi Arabia, where Muhammad established the first Islamic state.

and the construction of a political structure that would help Muhammad gather followers and soldiers for his conquest of the Arabian peninsula.

The authority of the constitution was both spiritual and secular, stating, "Whenever you differ about a matter it must be referred to God and Muhammad." Since God spoke through Muhammad, his word carried unquestionable authority.

Peaceful but not pacifist

The constitution confirms much of the Islamic holy book known as the *Quran*, which it predates. However, the *Quran* is more detailed on religious duties than political practicalities. In the *Quran*, Islam is described as a peace-loving religion, but not a pacifist religion. Muhammad repeatedly stresses that Islam should be defended from unbelievers, and implies that this may in some cases mean taking pre-emptive action. Although violence should be abhorrent to a believer in Islam, it can be a necessary evil to protect and advance the religion, and Muhammad states that it is the moral obligation of all Muslims to defend the faith.

This duty is encapsulated in the Islamic idea of *jihad* (literally "struggle", or "striving"), which was originally directed against neighbouring cities that attacked Muhammad's Islamic state. As these were conquered one by one, fighting became a way of spreading the faith and, in political terms, expanding the Islamic empire.

While the *Quran* describes *jihad* as a religious duty, and fighting as hateful but necessary, it also states that there are strict rules governing the conduct of war. The conditions for a "just war" (just cause, right intention, proper authority, and last resort) are very similar to those that evolved in Christian Europe. ■

Muhammad

Muhammad was born in Mecca in 570, shortly after the death of his father. His mother died when he was six, and he was left in the care of his grandparents and an uncle, who employed him managing caravans trading with Syria. In his late 30s, he made regular visits to a cave on Mount Hira to pray, and in 610 he is said to have received his first revelation from the angel Gabriel. He began preaching, and slowly gained a following, but was eventually driven from Mecca with his disciples. Their escape to Medina in 622 is celebrated as the beginning of the Muslim calendar. By the time of his death in 632, nearly all of Arabia was under his rule.

Key works

c.622 *Constitution of Medina*
c.632 The *Quran*
8th and 9th centuries The *Hadith*

"Fight in the name of Allah and in the way of Allah. Fight against those who disbelieve in Allah."
Sunni Hadith

THE PEOPLE REFUSE THE RULE OF VIRTUOUS MEN

AL-FARABI (c.870–950)

IN CONTEXT

IDEOLOGY
Islam

FOCUS
Political virtue

BEFORE
c.380–360 BCE Plato proposes rule by "philosopher kings" in the *Republic*.

3rd century CE Philosophers such as Plotinus reinterpret Plato's works, introducing theological and mystical ideas.

9th century The Arab philosopher Al-Kindi brings Classical Greek texts to the House of Wisdom, Baghdad.

AFTER
c.980–1037 The Persian writer Avicenna incorporates rational philosophy into Islamic theology.

13th century Thomas Aquinas defines the cardinal and theological virtues, and differentiates between natural, human, and divine law.

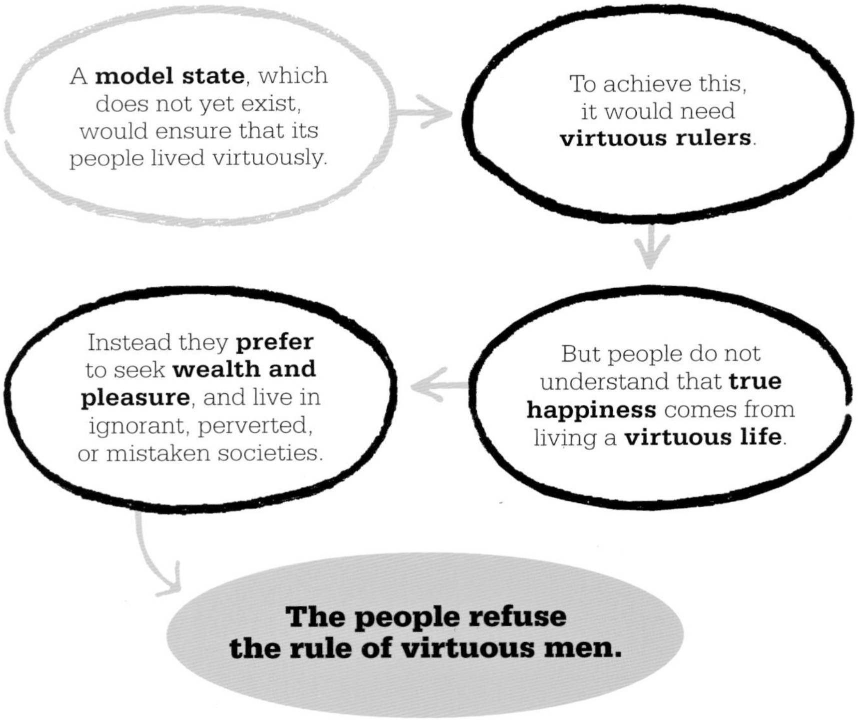

With the spread of the Islamic empire in the 7th and 8th centuries came a flourishing of culture and learning often referred to as the Islamic Golden Age. Libraries were established in many of the major cities of the empire, where texts of the great Greek and Roman thinkers were kept and translated. Baghdad, in particular, became a renowned centre of learning, and it was there that Al-Farabi built his reputation as a philosopher and commentator on the works of the Greek philosopher Aristotle.

See also: Plato 34–39 ▪ Aristotle 40–43 ▪ Augustine of Hippo 54–55 ▪ Thomas Aquinas 62–69

> The goal of the model state is not only to procure the material prosperity of its citizens, but also their future destiny.
> **Al-Farabi**

Like Aristotle, Al-Farabi believed that man by nature needs to live in a social structure such as a city-state in order to lead a good and happy life. He also believed that the city was only the minimum size in which this was possible, and felt the same principles could be applied to nation-states, empires, and even a world-state. However, it was Aristotle's teacher, Plato, who most influenced Al-Farabi's political thinking, in particular with his vision of the ideal state and how it would be ruled. Just as Plato advocated the rule of "philosopher kings" who alone understand the true nature of virtues such as justice, Al-Farabi, in *The Virtuous City*, describes a model city ruled by a virtuous leader who guides and instructs his people to live virtuous lives that will bring them true happiness.

Divine wisdom

Where Al-Farabi differs from Plato is in his conception of the nature and origin of the ideal ruler's virtue, which for Al-Farabi was divine wisdom. Rather than a philosopher king, Al-Farabi advocated rule by a "philosopher prophet" or, as he describes it, a just Imam.

However, Al-Farabi makes it clear that his Virtuous City is a political Utopia. He also describes the various forms of government that exist in the real world, pointing out their failings. He identifies three major reasons why they fall short of his ideal: they are ignorant, mistaken, or perverted. In an ignorant state, the people have no knowledge of how true happiness comes from leading a virtuous life; in a mistaken state, the people misunderstand the nature of virtue; in a perverted state, they know what constitutes a virtuous life, but choose not to pursue it. In all three types of imperfect state, the people pursue wealth and pleasure instead of the good life. Al-Farabi believed the souls of the ignorant and mistaken would simply disappear after death, while those of the perverted would suffer eternal sorrow. Only the souls of men from a Virtuous City could enjoy eternal happiness. However, as long as the ignorant, mistaken, and perverted citizens and their leaders pursue their earthly pleasures, they will reject the rule of a virtuous leader, as he will not give them what they believe they want, and so the model Virtuous City has yet to be achieved. ■

Al-Farabi developed his ideas in Baghdad, Iraq, which was a centre of learning in the Islamic Golden Age, and still boasts some of the oldest universities in the world.

Al-Farabi

Referred to as the "Second Teacher" (after Aristotle) among Islamic philosophers, little is known for certain of the life of Abu Nasr al-Farabi.

He was probably born in Farab (modern-day Otrar, Kazakhstan) in around 870, and went to school there and in Bukhara, now in Uzbekistan, before travelling to Baghdad to continue his studies in 901. In Baghdad, he studied alchemy and philosophy with both Christian and Islamic scholars. He also became a renowned musician and noted linguist. Although he spent most of his life in Baghdad as a *qadi* (judge) and teacher, Al-Farabi also travelled widely, visiting Egypt, Damascus, Harran, and Aleppo. It is believed that he wrote most of his works in his time in Aleppo, working for the court of Sayf al-Dawla, ruler of Syria.

Key works

c. 940–950
The Virtuous City
Epistle on the Intellect
Book of Letters

NO FREE MAN SHALL BE IMPRISONED, EXCEPT BY THE LAW OF THE LAND

BARONS OF KING JOHN (EARLY 13TH CENTURY)

IN CONTEXT

IDEOLOGY
Parliamentarism

FOCUS
Liberty

BEFORE
c.509 BCE The monarchy in Rome is overthrown and replaced by a republic.

1st century BCE Cicero argues for a return to the Roman Republic after Julius Caesar takes power from the Senate.

AFTER
1640s The English Civil War and subsequent overthrow of the monarchy establish that a monarch cannot govern without parliamentary consent.

1776 The US Declaration of Independence lists "Life, Liberty, and the pursuit of Happiness" as inherent rights.

1948 The United Nations General Assembly adopts the Universal Declaration of Human Rights in Paris.

King John of England became increasingly unpopular during his reign due to his mishandling of the wars with France and his high-handed attitude towards his feudal barons, who provided him with both knights and tax revenue. By 1215, he faced rebellion and was forced to negotiate with his barons when they arrived in London. They presented him with a document detailing their demands – modelled on the Charter of Liberties of 100 years earlier issued by King Henry I – which effectively reduced John's power and protected their own privileges. The "Articles of the Barons" included clauses relating to their property, rights, and duties, but also made the king subject to the law of the land.

> To no man will we sell, or deny, or delay, right or justice.
> **Magna Carta, Clause 40**

Freedom from tyranny

Clause 39, in particular, had profound implications: "No free man shall be seized or imprisoned, or stripped of his rights or possessions, or outlawed or exiled, or deprived of his standing in any other way, nor will we proceed with force against him, or send others to do so, except by the lawful judgment of his equals or by the law of the land." Implicit in the barons' demands was the concept of *habeas corpus*. This requires that a person under arrest be brought before a court, and protects individuals from arbitrary abuse of power. For the first time, the freedom of the individual from a tyrannical ruler was explicitly guaranteed. John had no choice but to accept the terms and attach his seal to what later became known as the *Magna Carta* (Latin for "Great Charter").

Unfortunately, John's assent was only a token, and much of the document was later ignored or repealed. Nevertheless, the

See also: Cicero 49 ▪ John Locke 104–09 ▪ Montesquieu 110–11 ▪ Jean-Jacques Rousseau 118–25 ▪ Oliver Cromwell 333

Free men have a **right to liberty**, protected by law.

A **despotic monarch** can **exploit** his subjects and **punish** them arbitrarily.

A monarch's **power should be limited** by the law of the land.

No free man shall be imprisoned, except by the law of the land.

key clauses remained, and the spirit of *Magna Carta* was highly influential in the political development of Britain. The restriction of the power of the monarch in favour of the rights of the "free man" – which at the time meant only the feudal landowners, and not the serfs – laid the foundations for an independent parliament. The rebellious De Montfort's Parliament in 1265 was the first such body, featuring elected representatives, knights, and burgesses (borough officials) as well as barons for the first time.

Towards a parliament

In the 17th century, the idea of making the English monarch bound by the law of the land came to a head in the English Civil War, and *Magna Carta* symbolized the cause of the Parliamentarians under Oliver Cromwell. Although at the time it applied only to a minority of already privileged citizens, *Magna Carta* pioneered the idea of laws to protect the liberty of the individual from despotic authority. It also inspired the bills of rights enshrined in many modern constitutions, particularly those of the former colonies of Britain, as well as many declarations of human rights. ■

The Houses of Parliament in London, England, has its origin in the insistence of the barons in 1215 that the monarch could not levy additional taxes without the consent of his royal council.

Feudal Barons of England

First created by William the Conqueror (1028–87), the barony was a form of feudal land tenure granted by the king, with certain duties and privileges allocated to the holder. The barons paid taxes to the king in return for their holding of the land, but also had an obligation, the *servitium debitum* ("service owed"), to provide a quota of knights to fight for the king when asked. In return, the barons were granted the privilege of participation in the king's council or parliament – but only when summoned to do so by the king. They did not meet regularly and, since the king's court often moved from place to place, they did not have a regular venue.

Although the barons at the time of King John (pictured above) forced *Magna Carta* on their king, the power of the feudal barony weakened during the 13th century, and was rendered all but obsolete during the English Civil War.

Key works

1100 *Charter of Liberties*
1215 *Magna Carta*

FOR WAR TO BE JUST THERE IS REQUIRED A JUST CAUSE

THOMAS AQUINAS (1225–1274)

IN CONTEXT

IDEOLOGY
Natural law

FOCUS
Just war

BEFORE
44 BCE In *De Officiis*, Cicero argues against war, except as a last resort in order to defend the state and restore peace.

5th century Augustine of Hippo argues that the state should promote virtue.

620s Muhammad calls on Muslims to fight in defence of Islam.

AFTER
1625 Hugo Grotius puts the theory of just war into the context of international law in *On the Law of War and Peace*.

1945 The United Nations (UN) Charter prohibits the use of force in international conflict unless authorized by the UN.

The Roman Catholic Church held a monopoly over learning for several centuries in medieval Europe. Ever since the adoption of Christianity as the official religion of the Roman empire by Constantine at the end of the 4th century CE, political thinking had been dominated by Christian teaching. The relationship between state and Church preoccupied philosophers and theologians, most notably Augustine of Hippo, who laid the foundations for the debate by integrating the political analysis of Plato's *Republic* with Christian doctrine. However, as translations of classical Greek texts became available in Europe in the 12th century through contact with Islamic scholars, some European thinkers began to take an interest in other philosophers – in particular, in Aristotle and his Islamic interpreter, the Andalusian polymath Averroes.

A reasoned method

By far the most significant of the Christian thinkers to emerge in the late Middle Ages was the Italian scholar Thomas Aquinas, a member of the newly formed Dominican religious order. An order that valued the tradition of scholasticism, the Dominicans used reasoning and inference as a method of education, rather than simply teaching Christian dogma. In this spirit, Aquinas set about reconciling Christian theology with the rational arguments put forward by philosophers such as Plato and Aristotle. As a priest, his concerns

> Peace is the work of justice indirectly, in so far as justice removes the obstacles to peace; but it is the work of charity, according to its very notion, that causes peace.
> **Thomas Aquinas**

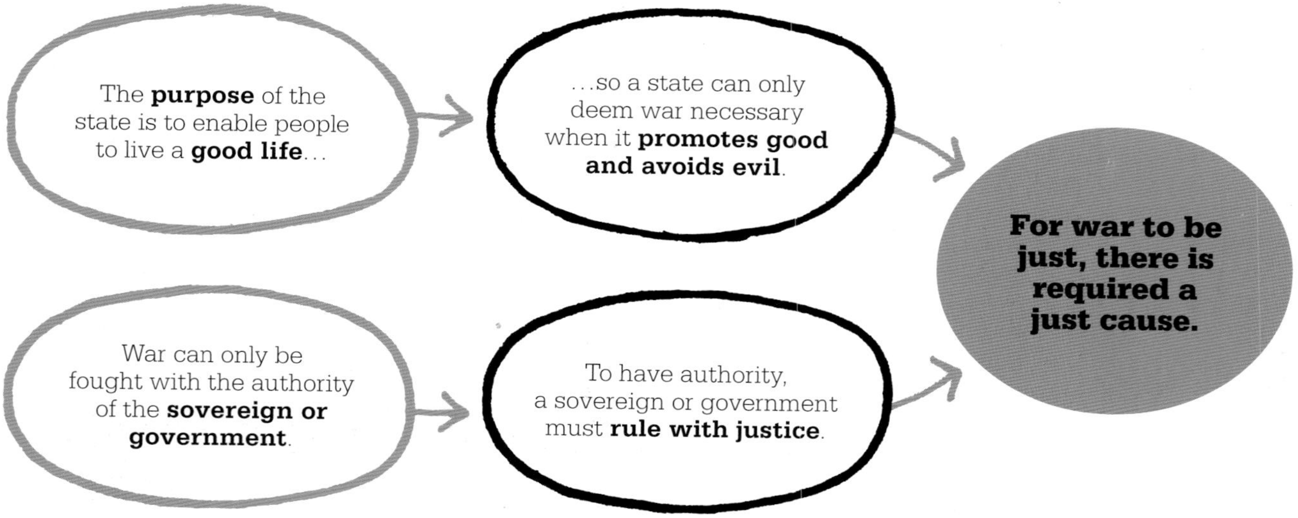

See also: Aristotle 40–43 ▪ Cicero 49 ▪ Augustine of Hippo 54–55 ▪ Muhammad 56–57 ▪ Marsilius of Padua 71 ▪ Francisco Suárez 90–91 ▪ Michael Walzer 324–25

were primarily theological, but since the Church was the dominant political power at the time, the distinction between theological and political was not as clear-cut as it is today. In arguing for an integration of the rational and the dogmatic, of philosophy and theology, Aquinas addressed the question of secular power versus divine authority, and the conflict between Church and state that was growing in many countries. He also used this method to examine ethical questions, such as when it might be justified to wage war.

Justice, the prime virtue

In his moral philosophy, Aquinas explicitly examines political issues, stressing that reasoning is as important in political thinking as it is in theological argument. As a starting point, he took the works of Augustine of Hippo, who had successfully integrated into his Christian beliefs the classical Greek notion that the purpose of the state is to promote a good and virtuous life. Augustine argued that this was in harmony with divine law – which, if adhered to, will prevent injustice. For Aquinas, steeped in the works of Plato and Aristotle, justice was the prime political virtue that underpinned »

Warfare for the protection of Christian values could be justified in Aquinas's thinking, including the First Crusade of 1096–99, in which Jerusalem was captured and thousands massacred.

Thomas Aquinas

The son of the Count of Aquino, Aquinas was born in Roccasecca, Italy, and was schooled in Monte Cassino and the University of Naples. Although expected to become a Benedictine monk, he joined the new Dominican order in 1244 and moved to Paris a year later. In about 1259, he taught in Naples, Orvieto, and the new school in Santa Sabina, and acted as a papal advisor in Rome.

He was sent back to Paris in 1269, probably due to a dispute over the compatibility of Averroes' and Aristotle's philosophies with Christian doctrine. In 1272, he set up a new Dominican university in Naples. While there, he had a mystical experience that prompted him to say that all he had written seemed "like straw" to him. Aquinas was summoned as an advisor to the Council of Lyons in 1274, but fell ill and died after an accident on the way.

Key works

1254–56 *Commentary on the Sentences*
c.1258–60 *Summa Contra Gentiles*
1267–73 *Summa Theologica*

> The only excuse, therefore, for going to war is that we may live in peace unharmed.
> **Cicero**

his entire political philosophy, and the notion of justice was the key element in governance. Just laws were the difference that distinguished good government from bad, bestowing upon it the legitimacy to rule. It was also justice that determined the morality of the actions of the state, a principle that can most clearly be seen in Aquinas's theory of a "just war".

Defining a just war

Using Augustine's arguments as his starting point, Aquinas agreed that although Christianity preached pacifism for its adherents, it was sometimes necessary to fight in order to preserve or restore peace in the face of aggression. However, such a war should be defensive, not pre-emptive, and waged only when certain conditions could be met. He called these conditions the *jus ad bellum* or "right to war" – which were distinct from the *jus in bello*, the rules of just conduct in a war – and believed that they would ensure the justice of the war.

Aquinas identified three distinct basic requirements for just war: rightful intention, authority of the sovereign, and a just cause. These principles have remained the basic criteria in just-war theory to the present day. The "rightful intention" for the Christian meant one thing only – the restoration of peace – but it is in the other two conditions that we can see a more secular approach. The "authority of the sovereign" implies that war can only be waged by an authority such as the state or its ruler, while the "just cause" limits its power to fighting a war only for the benefit of the people, rather than for personal gain or glory. For these criteria to be met, there must be a properly instituted government or ruler

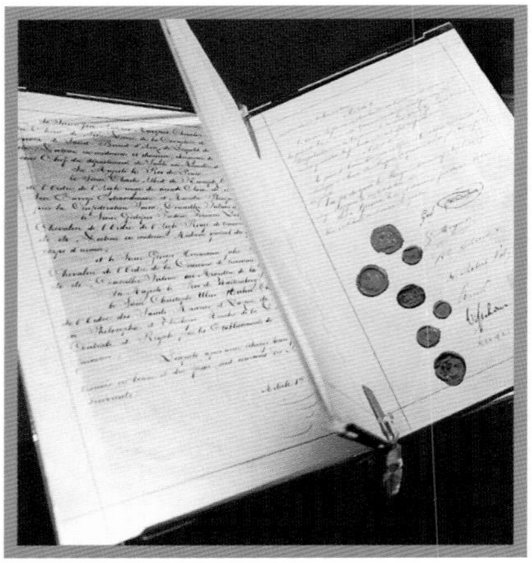

The Geneva Convention consists of four treaties signed between 1864 and 1949 – broadly based on the concepts of just war – defining fair treatment of soldiers and civilians in wartime.

bound by laws that ensure the justice of its actions, and this in turn needs to be based on a theory of legitimate governance, taking into account the demands of both the Church and the state.

Natural and human laws

This recognition of the role of the state and its authority distinguished Aquinas's political philosophy from other thinkers of the time. His emphasis on justice

The Right To War

For Aquinas, the only **rightful intention** of a just war is the restoration of peace.

A just war can only be waged under the **authority of the sovereign**.

For a war to be fought in a **just cause**, it must benefit the people.

The laws that we create for ourselves and our societies must be based on natural law, which in itself is a reflection of the eternal law that guides the entire universe.

Natural law is made clear to us through our God-given gift of reason. It guides our moral and ethical behaviour.

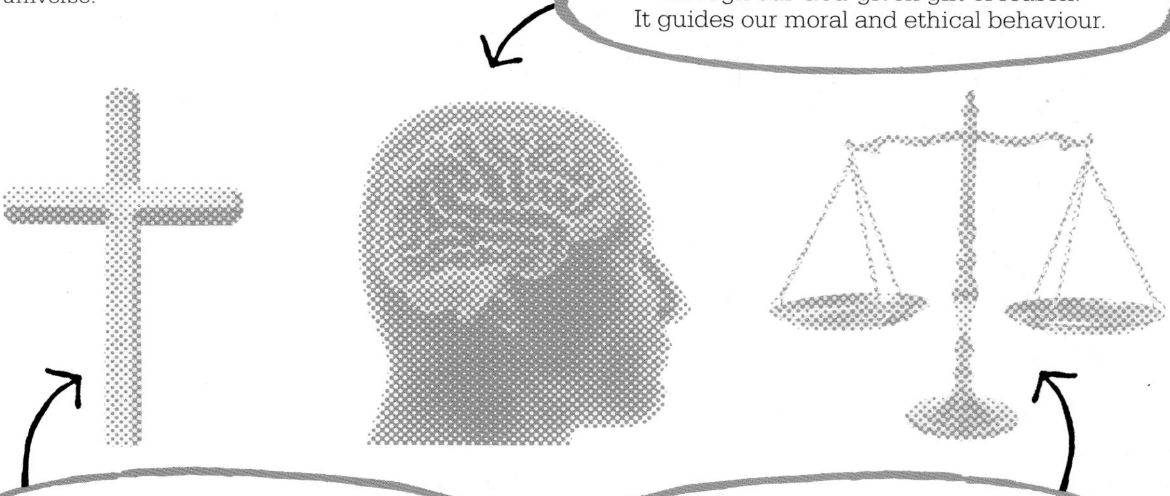

Eternal law is divine, and comes directly from God. The eternal law rules the entire universe.

Human laws on crime and punishment must be based on reason, so that they relate to the values we deduce from natural law.

as an essential virtue, influenced by his study of Plato and Aristotle, led him to consider the place of law in society, and this interest in law formed the basis for his political thinking. Unsurprisingly, given the increasing plurality of society at the time, this involved an examination of the differences between divine and human laws, and by implication the laws of the Church and those of the state.

As a Christian, Aquinas believed that the universe is ruled by an eternal divine law, and that humans – as the only rational creatures – have a unique relationship with it. Because of our ability to reason, we are subject to what he calls a "natural law", which we have arrived at by examining human nature and inferring a moral code of behaviour. Far from being a contradiction of God's law, however, Aquinas explained this as our participation in the eternal law.

Reason, he argues, is a God-given ability that enables us to devise for ourselves the natural law, which is – in effect – the way in which the eternal law applies to human beings in accordance with our nature as a social animal.

> Reason in man is rather like God in the world.
> **Thomas Aquinas**

However, natural law, which is concerned with morality and virtue, is not to be confused with the human laws that govern our day-to-day affairs, which we have created to enable the smooth running of our social communities. These man-made laws are, like their creators, by their very nature fallible, so they can lead to injustice and their authority can only be judged by comparison with natural law.

The urge for community

While Aquinas attributes natural law to our propensity for rational thought, the emergence of human laws is explained by another aspect of human nature – our need to form social communities. This idea is very much the same as proposed by Aristotle in *Politics* – which Aquinas had written a lengthy commentary on – that man is by »

The Kellogg-Briand Pact, signed in 1928 by 15 countries, forbade its signatories from starting wars. This accorded with Aquinas's principle that war should only be used to restore peace.

nature a "political animal". The urge to form social communities is something that defines us as humans distinct from other animals. Like Aristotle, Aquinas recognizes that humans naturally form family units, which in turn come together as villages, and ultimately form political societies, such as city-states or nation-states, providing an ordered social framework. Although he agreed in principle with Aristotle that such a state was the perfect community, his conception of it was not the same as the ancient Greek understanding, which was not compatible with the views of the Church in the 13th century.

According to the Greek philosophers, the aim of such a society was to enable its citizens to lead a "good life" in accordance with virtue and reason. Aquinas's interpretation was subtly different, bringing it in line with Christian theology and his own ideas of natural law. For him, the role of political society was to enable its citizens to develop their powers of reason, and through this, to acquire an understanding of moral sense – in other words, the natural law. They would then be able to live well, in accordance with natural law, and – as Christians – in accordance with divine law.

Ruling justly

The question that followed was this: what form of government is best suited to ensuring the aspirations of this political society? Again, Aquinas takes his lead from Aristotle, classifying various types of regime by the number of rulers and, crucially, whether their rule is just or unjust. Rule by a single individual is known as monarchy when it is just, but tyranny when unjust; similarly, just rule by a few is known as aristocracy, but when unjust, as an oligarchy; and just rule by the people is called a republic or polity, as opposed to the unjust rule of a democracy.

What determines whether these forms of government are just or unjust are the laws through which order is brought to the state. Aquinas defined law as "an ordinance of reason, for the common good, promulgated by one who has the care of the community". This definition sums up his criteria for just rule. The laws must be based on reason, rather than divine law imposed on the state by the Church in order that they satisfy our human need to deduce for ourselves the natural law.

> A just war is in the long run far better for a man's soul than the most prosperous peace.
> **Theodore Roosevelt**

Maintaining order

Aquinas goes on to explain that purely human laws are also necessary for the maintenance of order in society. Natural law guides our decisions of right and wrong, and the moral code that determines what constitutes a crime or injustice, but it is human law that decides what would be a fitting punishment and how this should be enforced. These human laws are essential to ordered, civilized society, and provide deterrents and incentives to potential wrongdoers to act with respect for the common good – and eventually to "do willingly what hitherto they did from fear, and become virtuous". The justice of human laws is judged by how well they measure up to natural law. If found to fall short, they should not be considered laws at all.

The second part of Aquinas's definition, however, is perhaps the deciding factor in judging the justice of a system of government. The laws imposed should be in the interests of the people as a whole, and not those of the ruler or rulers. Only with such laws can the state provide a framework in which its citizens can freely pursue their intellectual and moral development. However, the question still remains: who should rule? Aquinas, like Aristotle, believed that the majority did not have the reasoning power to fully appreciate the morality necessary for ruling, which implies that government should not be in the hands of the people, but a just individual, monarch, or aristocracy. But Aquinas also recognized the potential for these individuals to be corrupted, and argued instead for some form of mixed constitution.

The United Nations was established in 1945 after World War II with the intention of maintaining international peace and promoting principles that Aquinas would have called natural law.

Surprisingly, in view of his notion of the state existing to promote life according to Christian principles, Aquinas does not dismiss the possibility of a legitimate non-Christian ruler. Although his rule would not be perfect, a pagan could rule justly and in accordance with human laws, allowing his citizens to develop their powers of reason and eventually come to deduce a moral code. Living then according to natural law, they would in time become a Christian society.

A radical thinker

When viewed from our modern standpoint nearly 900 years later, it might appear that Aquinas was simply rediscovering and repeating Aristotle's political theories. However, when considered fully in context against a background of medieval Christianity, his views are revealed as a radical change in political thinking that challenged the conventional power of the Roman Catholic Church. Despite this, thanks to his scholarship and devoutness, his ideas were soon accepted by the established Church and have remained the basis for a large part of Catholic political philosophy to the present day.

In the criteria for a just war – rightful intention, authority of the sovereign, and just cause – we can see how these principles fit Aquinas's more general ideas of political justice based on natural law, and the principle of reason rather than divine authority. As well as influencing much subsequent just-war theory, Aquinas's notion of natural law was embraced by both theologians and experts on law. Over the centuries, the necessity of human law would become a key issue in the increasing conflict between Church and secular powers in Europe, as emerging nation-states asserted their independence from the papacy. ■

Aquinas's view of the requirements of a just war – rightful intention, authority, and just cause – still hold true today, and motivate many involved in anti-war movements.

TO LIVE POLITICALLY MEANS LIVING IN ACCORDANCE WITH GOOD LAWS

GILES OF ROME (c.1243–1316)

IN CONTEXT

IDEOLOGY
Constitutionalism

FOCUS
The rule of law

BEFORE
c.350 BCE In his *Politics*, Aristotle says that Man is a political animal by nature.

13th century Thomas Aquinas incorporates Aristotle's ideas into Christian philosophy and political thinking.

AFTER
1328 Marsilius of Padua sides with King Louis IV and secular rule in his power struggle against Pope John XXII.

c.1600 Francisco Suárez argues against the divine right of kings in *Tractatus de legibus ac deo legislatore*.

1651 Thomas Hobbes's *Leviathan* describes life in a state of nature as "solitary, poor, nasty, brutish, and short", and advocates a social contract to protect all citizens in society.

The teachings of the Greek philosopher Aristotle, long ignored in Europe, became accepted by the Church in the 13th century thanks largely to the work of the Dominican priest Thomas Aquinas and his protégé Giles of Rome. As well as writing important commentaries on Aristotle's works, Giles developed his ideas further, in particular the notion of man as a "political animal" – "political" in the Aristotelian sense of living in a *polis* or civil community, rather than referring to a political regime.

For Giles, being part of a civil society is "living politically", and is essential to living a good life according to virtue. This is because civil communities are regulated by laws that ensure and safeguard the morality of their citizens. Giles suggests that good laws should enforce virtues, such as justice. Being a member of society – living politically – requires adherence to these laws; not abiding by them means living outside society. It follows that it is the rule of law that distinguishes "political" life from tyranny, as a tyrant excludes himself from civil society by not adhering to the law.

King Philip IV of France arranged a public burning of the *Unam Sanctam*. This document attempted to force the king into submission to the papacy – a principle that Giles agreed with.

Although Giles believed that a hereditary monarchy was the form of government best suited to rule a political society, as an archbishop his loyalties were divided between the Church and secular power. Eventually, he sided with the pope by declaring that kings ought to be subordinate to the Church. ■

See also: Aristotle 40–43 ▪ Thomas Aquinas 62–69 ▪ Marsilius of Padua 71 ▪ Francisco Suárez 90–91 ▪ Thomas Hobbes 96–103

THE CHURCH SHOULD DEVOTE ITSELF TO IMITATING CHRIST AND GIVE UP ITS SECULAR POWER

MARSILIUS OF PADUA (1275–1343)

IN CONTEXT

IDEOLOGY
Secularism

FOCUS
Role of the Church

BEFORE
c.350 BCE Aristotle's *Politics* describes the role of the citizen in the administration and jurisdiction of the city-state.

c.30 CE According to Catholic belief, St Peter becomes the first Bishop of Rome. Subsequent bishops are known as "popes".

800 Charlemagne is crowned Emperor of Rome, initiating the Holy Roman Empire.

AFTER
1328 Ludwig of Bavaria, newly crowned Holy Roman Emperor, deposes Pope John XXII.

1517 German theologian Martin Luther criticizes the doctrines and rituals of the Catholic Church, prompting the beginning of the Protestant Reformation.

As an academic rather than a member of the clergy, Marsilius of Padua was in a better position than theologians to state openly what many of them believed: that the Church, and the papacy in particular, should not have any political power.

In his treatise *Defensor Pacis* (Defender of the Peace) – written in defence of the elected Holy Roman Emperor, Ludwig of Bavaria, in his power struggle with Pope John XXII – he argues convincingly that it is not the function of the Church to govern. He refutes the claim made by successive popes of a God-given "plenitude of power", believing that it was destructive to the state.

Using arguments from Aristotle's *Politics*, Marsilius describes effective government as originating with the people, who have rights that include choosing a ruler and participating in the legislative process. Management of human affairs is best conducted by legislation, administered by the people, not imposed by divine law, which even the Bible does not sanction. Christ himself, he points out, denied the clergy any coercive power over people in this world, stressing their role as teachers. The Church should therefore follow the example of Jesus and his disciples and return political power to the state. This secular state can then better manage the specialist areas of government, such as law and order, and economic and military matters, under a ruler chosen by a majority of the people. ■

> No elective official who derives his authority from election alone requires any further confirmation or approval.
> **Marsilius of Padua**

See also: Aristotle 40–43 ■ Augustine of Hippo 54–55 ■ Giles of Rome 70 ■ Niccolò Machiavelli 74–81

GOVERNMENT PREVENTS INJUSTICE, OTHER THAN SUCH AS IT COMMITS ITSELF

IBN KHALDUN (1332–1406)

IN CONTEXT

IDEOLOGY
Islam

FOCUS
Corruption of power

BEFORE
1027–256 BCE Historians in China during the Zhou dynasty describe the "Dynastic Cycle" of empires declining and being replaced.

c.950 Al-Farabi draws on Plato and Aristotle for *The Virtuous City*, his notion of an ideal Islamic state and the shortcomings of governments.

AFTER
1776 In *The Wealth of Nations*, British economist Adam Smith explains the principles behind the division of labour.

1974 US economist Arthur Laffer uses Ibn Khaldun's ideas on taxation to produce the Laffer curve, which demonstrated the relationship between rates of taxation and government revenue.

The unity of a political society comes from *asabiyyah*, or **community spirit**.

↓

This is the **basis for government**, and prevents injustice.

↓

As a society advances, social cohesion decreases and its **government becomes lax**...

↓

...**exploiting its citizens** for its own advantage, causing injustice.

↓

Eventually, **another government emerges** to take the place of the decadent regime.

↓

Government prevents injustice, other than such as it commits itself.

See also: Aristotle 40–43 ▪ Muhammad 56–57 ▪ Al-Farabi 58–59 ▪ Niccolò Machiavelli 74–81 ▪ Karl Marx 188–93

Described by British anthropologist Ernest Gellner as the best definition of government in the history of political theory, Ibn Khaldun's assertion that "government prevents injustice, other than such as it commits itself" could be taken for a cynical modern comment on political institutions, or for the realism of Machiavelli. In fact, this definition lies at the heart of an innovative 14th-century analysis of the causes of political instability.

Built on community

Unlike many other political thinkers of his time, Ibn Khaldun took a historical, sociological, and economic standpoint to examine the rise and fall of political institutions. Like Aristotle, he recognized that humans form social communities, which he ascribed to the Arabic concept of *asabiyyah* – which translates as "community spirit", "group solidarity", or simply "tribalism". This social cohesion gives rise to the institution of the state, whose purpose is to protect the interests of its citizens and defend them against attack.

Whatever form this government may take, it contains the seeds of its own destruction. As it gains more power, it becomes less concerned with the wellbeing of its citizens, and begins to act more in its own self-interest, exploiting people and creating injustice and disunity. What had started as an institution to prevent injustice is now committing injustices itself. The *asabiyyah* of the community declines, so conditions are ripe for another government to emerge and take the place of the decadent regime. Civilizations rise and fall in this way, Ibn Khaldun argues, in a cycle of political dynasties.

Corruption leads to decline

Ibn Khaldun also points out the economic consequences of the existence of a powerful elite. At the beginning of a political society, taxes are only used to provide for necessities to maintain the *asabiyyah*, but as it becomes more civilized, the rulers impose higher taxes to maintain their own, increasingly opulent, lifestyle. Not only is this an injustice that threatens the unity of the state, but it is also counterproductive – overtaxing discourages production, and leads in the long run to lower, not higher, revenues. This idea was rediscovered in the 20th century by US economist Arthur Laffer. Ibn Khaldun's theories on the division of labour and the labour theory of value also predate their "discovery" by mainstream economists.

Although he believed that the continuous cycle of political change was inevitable, Ibn Khaldun saw some forms of government as better than others. For him, *asabiyyah* is best maintained under a single ruler, such as a caliph in an Islamic state (which has the added benefit of religion to give social cohesion). It is maintained least satisfactorily under a tyrant. Government, he felt, is a necessary evil, but as it implies an inherent injustice of control of men by other men, its power should be kept to a minimum. ■

> "When a nation has become the victim of a psychological defeat, then that marks the end of a nation."
> **Ibn Khaldun**

Ibn Khaldun

Born in Tunis, Tunisia, in 1332, Ibn Khaldun was brought up in a politically active family and studied the Quran and Islamic law. He held official posts in the Maghreb region of North Africa, where he saw at first hand the political instability of many regimes. While working in Fez, he was imprisoned after a change of government, and after his release moved to Granada in southern Spain, where he led peace negotiations with the Castilian king Pedro the Cruel. He later returned to serve in several North African courts, but fled to the protection of a Berber tribe in the desert when his attempts at reform were rejected. In 1384, he settled in Cairo, where he completed his *History*. He made one final journey in 1401, to Damascus to negotiate peace between Egypt and the Mongol Khan Timur.

Key works

1377 *Introduction to History*
1377–1406 *History of the world*
1377–1406 *Autobiography*

A PRUDENT RULER CANNOT AND MUST NOT HONOUR HIS WORD

NICCOLÒ MACHIAVELLI (1469–1527)

IN CONTEXT

IDEOLOGY
Realism

FOCUS
Statecraft

BEFORE
4th century BCE Chanakya advises rulers to do whatever is necessary to achieve the wellbeing of the state.

3rd century BCE Han Fei Tzu assumes it is human nature to seek personal gain and avoid punishment, and his Legalist government makes strict laws.

51 BCE Roman politician Cicero advocates republican rule in *De Republica*.

AFTER
1651 Thomas Hobbes's *Leviathan* describes life in a state of nature as "nasty, brutish, and short".

1816–30 Carl von Clausewitz discusses the political aspects of warfare in *On War*.

Written by probably the best known (and most often misunderstood) of all political theorists, Niccolò Machiavelli's work gave rise to the term "Machiavellian", which epitomizes the manipulative, deceitful, and generally self-serving politician who believes that "the end justifies the means". However, this term fails to encapsulate the much broader, and innovative, political philosophy Machiavelli proposed in his treatise *The Prince*.

Machiavelli lived in turbulent political times at the beginning of the period that would come to be known as the Renaissance. This was a turning point in European history, when the medieval concept of a Christian world ruled with divine guidance was replaced by the idea that humans could control their own destiny. As the power of the Church was being eroded by Renaissance humanism, prosperous Italian city-states, such as Machiavelli's native Florence, had been established as republics, but were repeatedly threatened and taken over by rich and powerful families – such as the Medicis – seeking to extend their influence. Through his first-hand experience in public office for the Florentine Republic as a diplomat, and influenced by his study of classical Roman society and politics, Machiavelli developed an unconventional approach to the study of political theory.

A realistic approach

Rather than seeing society in terms of how it ought to be, Machiavelli tried to "go directly to the effectual truth of the thing rather than to the imagination of it", meaning that he sought to get to the heart of the matter and treat politics not as a branch of moral philosophy or ethics, but rather in purely practical and realistic terms.

Unlike previous political thinkers, he does not see the purpose of the state as nurturing the morality of its citizens, but rather as ensuring their wellbeing and security. Consequently, he replaces the concepts of right and wrong with notions such as usefulness, necessity, success, danger, and harm. By placing utility above morality, his ideas for the desirable qualities of a successful leader are based on

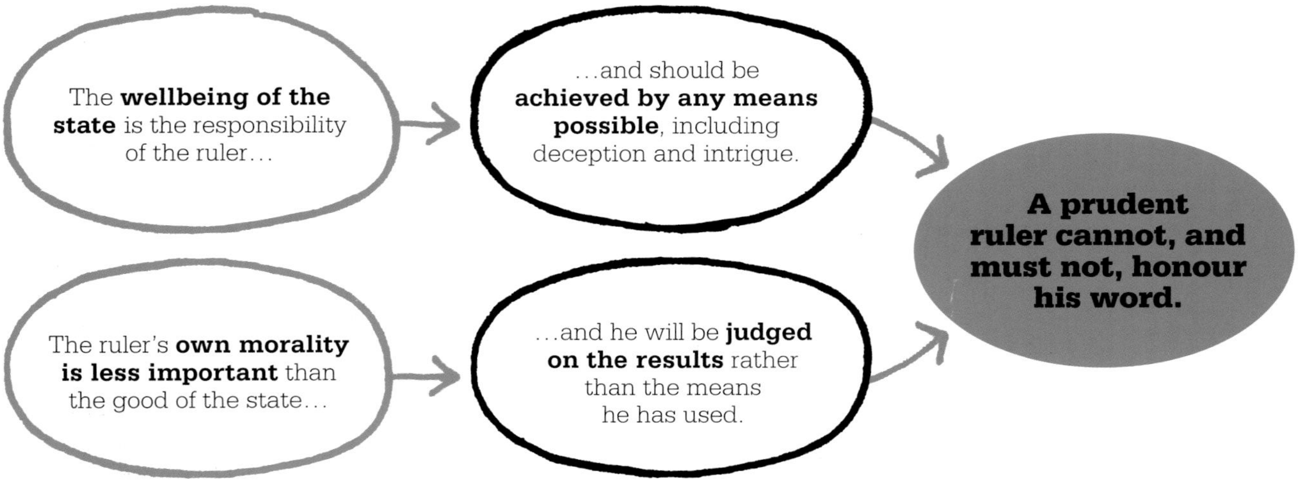

See also: Chanakya 44–47 ▪ Han Fei Tzu 48 ▪ Ibn Khaldun 72–73 ▪ Thomas Hobbes 96–103 ▪ Carl von Clausewitz 160 ▪ Antonio Gramsci 259

An effective leader can harness the weaker traits of humanity in his people to great effect, in the same way that a sheepdog can manipulate a herd of sheep.

effectiveness and prudence rather than any sort of ideology or moral rectitude.

At the centre of his political philosophy is the Renaissance idea of viewing human society in human terms, completely separated from the religious ideals imposed by the Christian Church. To achieve this, his starting point is an analysis of human nature based on his observations of human behaviour throughout history, which brings him to the conclusion that the majority of people are by nature selfish, short-sighted, fickle, and easily deceived. His view is realistic, if somewhat cynical, and very different from those of previous political thinkers. While they might appear to be an obstacle to creating an efficient, stable society, Machiavelli argues that some of these human failings can in fact be useful in establishing a successful society, though this requires the correct leadership.

Using human nature

Man's innate self-centredness, for example, is shown in his instinct for self-preservation. However, when threatened by aggression or a hostile environment, he reacts with acts of courage, hard work, and cooperation. Machiavelli draws a distinction between an original, fundamental human nature that has no virtues, and a socially acquired nature that acts in a virtuous manner and is beneficial to society. Other negative human traits can also be turned to the common good, such as the tendency to imitate rather than think as individuals. This, Machiavelli notes, leads people to follow a leader's example and act cooperatively. Further, traits such as fickleness and credulity allow humans to be easily manipulated by a skilful leader to behave in a benevolent way. Qualities such as selfishness, manifested in the human desire for personal gain and ambition, can be a powerful driving force if channelled correctly, and are especially useful personal qualities in a ruler.

The two key elements to transforming the undesirable, original human nature into a benevolent social nature are social organization and what Machiavelli describes as "prudent" leadership, by which he means leadership that is useful to the success of the state.

Advice for new rulers

Machiavelli's famous (and now infamous) treatise *The Prince* was written in the style of the »

Sandro Botticelli's *Adoration of the Magi*, painted in 1475, includes representations of the powerful Medici family, who ruled Florence at the time Machiavelli wrote *The Prince*.

practical guides for leaders known as "Mirrors of Princes", which were common in the Middle Ages and the Renaissance. It is addressed to a new ruler – and is dedicated to a member of the powerful Medici family – with advice on how basic human nature can be engineered and manipulated for the good of the state. Later interpretations, however, hint that Machiavelli was using the genre somewhat cleverly, by exposing to a wider audience the secrets already known to the ruling classes. Having explained man's essentially self-centred but malleable nature, he then turns his attention to the qualities that are necessary for a ruler to govern prudently.

> A prince never lacks legitimate reasons to break his promise.
> **Niccolò Machiavelli**

Leadership qualities

Confusingly, Machiavelli uses the word *virtù* to describe these leadership qualities, but this is very different from our modern idea of moral virtue, as well as the concept of virtue as understood by the Church. Machiavelli was a Christian, and as such he advocates Christian virtues in day-to-day life, but when dealing with the actions of a ruler, he believes that morality must take second place to utility and the security of the state. In this respect, his ideas hark back to the Roman quality of "virtue" embodied by the military leader who is motivated by ambition and the pursuit of glory, properties that are almost the exact opposite of the Christian virtue of modesty. Machiavelli notes, however, that these motivations are also a manifestation of human nature's inherent self-interest, and similarly can be harnessed for the common good.

Machiavelli takes the analogy between military and political leaders further, pointing out other aspects of *virtù*, such as boldness, discipline, and organization. He also stresses the importance of analysing a situation rationally before taking action, and basing that action not on how people should ideally behave but how they will behave (meaning in their own self-interest). In Machiavelli's opinion, social conflict is an inevitable result of the selfishness of human nature (this is in contrast to the medieval Christian view that selfishness was not a natural condition). In order to deal with this selfishness, a leader needs to employ the tactics of war.

Although Machiavelli believes that to a large extent man is master of his own fate, he recognizes that there is also an element of chance at play, which he refers to as *fortuna*. The ruler must battle against this possibility, as well as against the fickleness of human nature, which also corresponds to *fortuna*. He sees that political life, in particular, can be seen as a continuous contest between the elements of *virtù* and *fortuna*, and in this regard is analogous to a state of war.

Conspiracy is useful

By analysing politics using military theory, Machiavelli concludes that the essence of most political life

> In judging policies we should consider the results that have been achieved through them rather than the means by which they have been executed.
> **Niccolò Machiavelli**

is conspiracy. Just as success in war is dependent on espionage, intelligence, counter-intelligence, and deception, political success requires secrecy, intrigue, and deceit. The idea of conspiracy had long been known to military theorists, and was practised by many political leaders, but Machiavelli was the first in the West to explicitly propose a theory of political conspiracy. Deceit was considered contrary to the idea that a state should safeguard the morality of its citizens, and Machiavelli's suggestions were a shocking departure from conventional thinking.

According to Machiavelli, while intrigue and deceit are not morally justifiable in private life, they are prudent for successful leadership, and excusable when used for the common good. More than that, Machiavelli asserts that in order to mould the undesirable aspects of human nature, it is essential that a ruler is deceitful and – out of prudence – does not honour his word, as to do so would jeopardize his rule, threatening the stability of the state. For the leader, then, compelled to deal with the inevitable conflicts that face him, the ends do justify the means.

The end is what counts

A prince's success as a ruler is judged by the consequences of his actions and their benefit to the state, not by his morality or ideology. As Machiavelli puts it in *The Prince*: "In the actions of all men, especially princes, where there is no recourse to justice, the end is all that counts. A prince should only be concerned with conquering or maintaining a state, for the means will always be judged to be honourable and praiseworthy by each and every person, because the masses always follow appearances and the outcomes of affairs, and the world is nothing other than the masses." He does, however, stress that this is a matter of expediency, and not a model for social behaviour. It is only excusable when done for the public good. It is also important that the methods of intrigue and deception should be a means to an end and not become an end in themselves, so these methods need to be restricted to political and military leaders, and strictly controlled.

Another tactic Machiavelli borrows from the military is the use of force and violence, which again is morally indefensible in private life, but excusable when employed for the common good. Such a policy creates fear, which is a means of ensuring the security of the ruler. Machiavelli tackles the question of whether it is better for a leader to be feared or loved with characteristic pragmatism. In an ideal world, he should be both loved and feared, but in reality the two seldom go together. Fear will keep the leader in a much stronger position, and is therefore better for the wellbeing of the state. Rulers »

Though Machiavelli did not sanction the use of questionable methods to get things done in private life, he argued that the ruler should use all means necessary to secure the future of the state.

> Since love and fear can hardly exist together, if we must choose between them, it is far safer to be feared than loved.
> **Niccolò Machiavelli**

Italian dictator Benito Mussolini was a forceful and ruthless leader, more feared than loved. He claimed inspiration from *The Prince*.

who have gained power through exercising their *virtù* are in the most secure position, having defeated any opposition and earned respect from the people, but to maintain this support and hold on to power, they must continually assert their authority.

An ideal republic

While *The Prince* is addressed to the would-be successful ruler, Machiavelli was a statesman in the Republic of Florence, and in his less well-known work *Discourses on Livy*, he strongly advocated republicanism rather than any form of monarchy or oligarchy. Despite remaining a lifelong Catholic, he was also opposed to any interference in political life by the Church. The form of government he favoured was modelled on the Roman Republic, with a mixed constitution and participation by its citizens, protected by a properly constituted citizens' army as opposed to a militia of hired mercenaries. This, he argued, would protect the liberty of the citizens, and minimize any social conflict between the common people and a ruling elite. However, to found such a republic, or reform an existing state, requires the leadership of an individual who possesses the appropriate *virtù* and prudence. Though it may require a strong leader and some scurrilous means to begin with, once a political society is established, the ruler can then introduce the necessary laws and social organization to enable it to continue as an ideal republic – this would be a pragmatic means to achieve a desirable end.

Machiavelli's philosophy, based on personal experience and an objective study of history, challenged the dominance of the Church and conventional ideas of political morality, and led to his works being banned by the Catholic authorities. By treating politics as a practical and not a philosophical or ethical subject of study, he replaced morality with utility as the purpose of the state, and shifted the emphasis from the moral intention of a political action to focus primarily on its consequences.

Enduring legacy

The Prince was very influential in the centuries following Machiavelli's death, particularly among leaders such as Henry VIII of England, Holy Roman Emperor Charles V, Oliver Cromwell, and Napoleon, and the book was acknowledged as an inspiration by such diverse figures as Marxist theorist Antonio Gramsci and Fascist dictator Benito Mussolini.

Machiavelli's critics, too, came from all sides of the political spectrum, with Catholics accusing him of supporting the Protestant cause, and vice versa. His importance to mainstream political thinking was immense – he was clearly very much a product of the Renaissance, with its emphasis on humanism rather than religion, and empiricism rather than faith and dogma, and he was the first to take an objective, scientific approach to political history.

This objectivity also underlies his perhaps cynical analysis of human nature, which was a precursor to Thomas Hobbes's brutal description of life in a state of nature. His concept of utility became a mainstay of 19th-century liberalism. In a more general sense, by divorcing morality and ideology from politics, his work was the basis for a movement that later became known as political realism, with particular relevance in international relations.

"Machiavellian" behaviour

The term "Machiavellian" is in common usage today, and is usually applied pejoratively to

> Everyone sees what you appear to be, but few really know what you are.
> **Niccolò Machiavelli**

politicians who are perceived (or discovered) to be acting manipulatively and deceitfully. US president Richard Nixon, who attempted to cover up a break-in and wiretapping of his opponent's headquarters and was forced to resign over the scandal, is a modern-day example of such underhand behaviour. It is also possible that Machiavelli may have been making a less obvious point in *The Prince*: perhaps he was saying that those who have been successful rulers may have behaved in just as "Machiavellian" a way, but their actions have not been so closely examined. How they achieved their success has been overlooked because the focus has shifted to what they achieved. It seems that we tend to judge leaders on their results rather than the means used to achieved them.

Expanding this argument further, we might consider how often the losers of a war are found to be morally questionable, while the victors are seen as above reproach – the notion that history is written by the victors. Criticizing Machiavelli leads us to examine ourselves and the extent to which we are prepared to overlook the dubious machinations of our governments if the outcome works in our favour. ■

Richard Nixon resigned as US president in 1974. He authorized a break-in and wiretap at the Democratic National Committee headquarters: actions described as "Machiavellian".

Niccolò Machiavelli

Born in Florence, Niccolò Machiavelli was the son of a lawyer, and is believed to have studied at the University of Florence, but little is known of his life until he became a government official in 1498 in the government of the Republic of Florence. He spent the next 14 years travelling around Italy, France, and Spain on diplomatic business.

In 1512, Florence was attacked and returned to the rule of the Medici family. Machiavelli was imprisoned and tortured unjustly for conspiring against the Medici, and when released retired to a farm outside Florence. There, he devoted himself to writing, including *The Prince* and other political and philosophical books. He tried to regain favour with the Medici, with little success. After they were overthrown in 1527, he was denied a post with the new republican government because of his links with the Medici. He died later that year.

Key works

c.1513 (pub. 1532) *The Prince*
c.1517 (pub. 1531) *Discourses on Livy*
1519–21 *The Art of War*

RATIONA
ENLIGHT
1515–1770

LITY AND
ENMENT

1517
Martin Luther nails his **95 Theses** to a church door in Wittenberg, questioning the authority of the Catholic Church.

1532
Spanish explorer Francisco Pizarro **conquers the Incas** in South America.

1576
Jean Bodin describes the **best form of government** in *Six Books of the Republic.*

1590
Following the seige of Odawara, **Japan is unified** under Toyotomi Hideyoshi, who imposes a strict class system.

1597
In *Metaphysical Disputations*, Francisco Suárez revisits the **political ideas of Thomas Aquinas**.

1602
The Dutch East India Company is founded, becoming the **first multinational corporation**.

1620
The Pilgrim Fathers establish the **colony of Plymouth** in Massachusetts, USA.

1625
Hugo Grotius lays the **foundations for international law** in *De jure belli ac pacis.*

The roots of most modern Western political thought can be traced back to scholarship in the "Age of Reason", which followed the Middle Ages in Europe. The invention of the printing press, the rise of nation-states, and the discovery of the Americas were some of the factors that influenced the transition from the Middle Ages to the Age of Reason. The questioning of religious orthodoxy – prompted in 1517 by Martin Luther's *95 Theses* – led to the Protestant Reformation, and later the Catholic counter-reformation.

Overlapping spheres of authority and governance in Europe led to fierce battles between and within civil and religious groups. In the absence of religious doctrine, people needed a new way to organize and legitimize political order. Two concepts became fundamental: the "divine right of kings" to rule, granted by God; and "natural law", which analysed human behaviour to arrive at valid moral principles. Both concepts were used to argue for an absolutist state.

Absolute sovereignty

In France, Jean Bodin argued in favour of a strong central power with absolute sovereignty, to avoid the factional strife that followed the decline of papal authority in Europe. Thomas Hobbes wrote during a time of bloody civil war in England. He agreed with Bodin on the need for a strong sovereign, but not on the divine right of kings, which Bodin's work was often used to legitimize. For Hobbes, the power to rule was granted not by God but via a social contract with the ruled. The idea that the power to govern is granted by the people via an implicit or explicit contract – and that rulers can legitimately be removed from power if they break the contract – is still central to modern understandings of political systems.

Further key insights were offered by Johannes Althusius, who saw politics as the art of uniting people in associations to ensure peace and prosperity, and Montesquieu, who emphasized that government should be based on a principle of the separation of legislative and executive powers. All such thinkers spoke against a strong, centralized state.

Towards Enlightenment

Theologians such as Francisco de Vitoria and Francisco Suárez, both part of the School of

1643

Five-year-old Louis XIV, later known as **the Sun King** for his absolutist rule, begins his 72-year reign in France.

1649

Charles I of England is **executed** at the end of the English Civil War.

1651

Thomas Hobbes argues for **absolutism** in *Leviathan*.

1689

A **Bill of Rights** is passed by the English Parliament.

1689

In *Two Treatises on Government*, John Locke argues that government can only rule with the **consent of the people**.

1733

French author Voltaire praises **Britain's political freedom** in "Letters concerning the English nation".

1748

Montesquieu argues for the **separation of powers** in *The Spirit of Laws*.

1758

Benjamin Franklin paves the way for **capitalism in the US** in his essay "The Way to Wealth".

Salamanca, began to interpret the Bible using arguments based on rationality. This led de Vitoria to criticize the colonial conquests being made at the time in the name of the Church. Suárez distinguished between man-made laws, natural laws, and divine guidance. He argued against the divine right of kings as a misguided merging of those three sources of laws.

Later scholars of the period would base their analysis not on theology, but on pure reason. These are closer to so-called "Enlightenment ideals". Immanuel Kant coined the term Enlightenment in 1784 to describe the capacity and freedom to use one's own intelligence without the guidance of others.

While scholars such as Bodin and Hobbes had focused on political stability and used the concept of natural law to argue for absolutism, Enlightenment writers used natural law as a cornerstone in liberal theories and international law, asserting that humans had rights that trumped man-made laws.

Individual rights

Hugo Grotius, considered the father of international law, placed liberty and rights firmly in the possession of individuals, as opposed to thinking of them as qualities bestowed by God. This idea was key to the development of liberalism, and to the conceptual separation of rights and duties in legal matters. John Locke further championed individual rights and freedom. He argued that the purpose of government and law was to preserve and enlarge human freedom. Like Hobbes, he believed in the social contract, but his more optimistic view of human nature led him to the conclusion that government should be limited and protective, not absolute.

The American Enlightenment not only shaped the Declaration of Independence, but was also closely linked to the ideals of the French Revolution of 1789, which is often seen as the culmination of the European Enlightenment. Benjamin Franklin was a central figure in this period, and his views on entrepreneurialism as a civic virtue were highly influential for the development of capitalism.

Human rights, freedom, checks and balances, international law, representative democracy, and reason are all modern concepts that were first truly explored by the thinkers of this age. ■

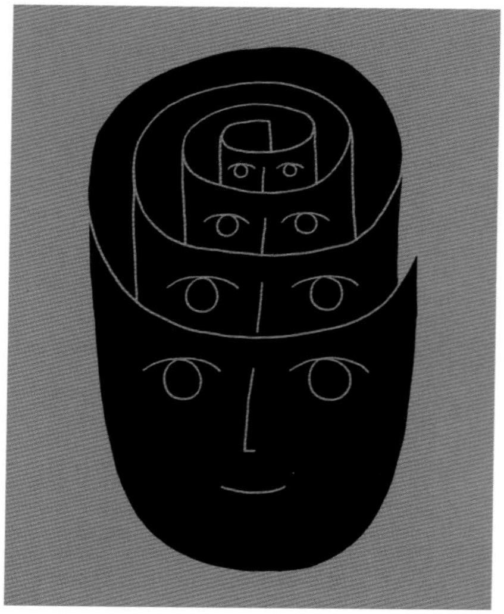

IN THE BEGINNING, EVERYTHING WAS COMMON TO ALL

FRANCISCO DE VITORIA (c.1483–1546)

IN CONTEXT

IDEOLOGY
Just war

FOCUS
Colonialism

BEFORE

1267–72 Thomas Aquinas writes *Summa Theologica*, the most influential work of Christian theology in the West.

1492 Genoese explorer Christopher Columbus lands in the New World, leading to a race for conquest in the Old World.

AFTER

1625 Drawing on de Vitoria's teachings, Hugo Grotius publishes *On the Law of War and Peace*, a seminal work for the formulation of international law.

1899 The first Hague Conference takes place, resulting in the first formal convention on the laws of war and war crimes.

Francisco de Vitoria was central among the group of theologians at the University of Salamanca, Spain, who founded the School of Salamanca in the early 16th century. They revolutionized the concept of natural law by emphasizing individual liberty, rights, and equality.

With the discovery of the New World and the decline of papal authority, European states were competing to colonize as much of the newly conquered land as possible. The School of Salamanca was the first and the most potent intellectual force to criticize these actions. De Vitoria believed that the origin of law emanated from nature itself. Given that all humans are born from and share the same nature, he argued that all had equal rights to life and liberty.

Illegitimate conquests

De Vitoria's principle of natural law and the universality of rights ran counter to the dominant view of the Church and the European colonial powers. Flowing from Christian dogma, the dominant morality held that it was legitimate to conquer and rule the indigenous Americans.

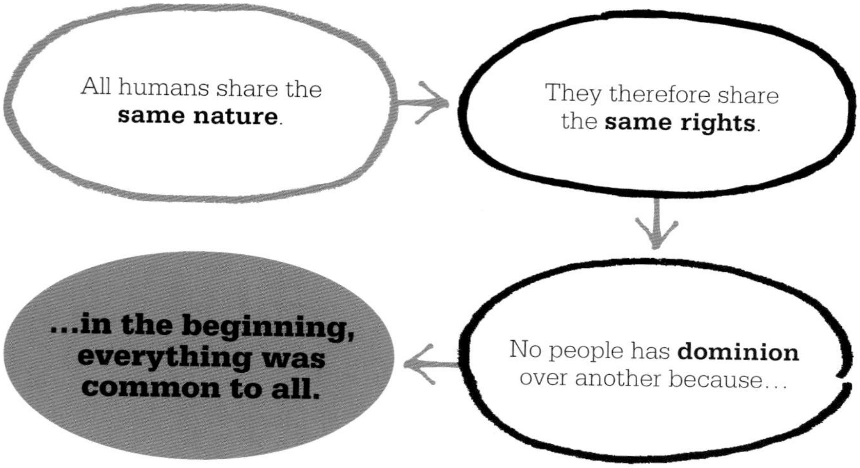

See also: Thomas Aquinas 62–69 ▪ Francisco Suárez 90–91 ▪ Hugo Grotius 94–95 ▪

De Vitoria regarded the conquest as illegitimate, based on the logic that "in the beginning, everything was common to all". If unbelievers were not necessarily evil, and Christians could conduct evil acts, it was not logical to consider Christians to have rights over unbelievers.

This view also undermined the divine right of kings to rule. It led to many disagreements between de Vitoria and Charles V, King of Spain and Holy Roman Emperor, but the king nevertheless still went to de Vitoria for counsel.

> Ownership and dominion are based either on natural law or human law; therefore they are not destroyed by want of faith.
> **Francisco de Vitoria**

Can war be just?

De Vitoria's principle of natural law and the rights of people also related to his scholarship on the theory of just war. The moral and religious justifications for war were fiercely debated at the time of the conquest of the New World. The central issue was how the teachings of Christ could be reconciled with political realities. Drawing from the works of Thomas Aquinas, who distinguished between just cause and just conduct of war, the School of Salamanca further developed this body of thought. De Vitoria did not accept religious arguments as justifications for war. War was not justified simply because people were unbelievers, or because they refused conversion. Belief could not be forced – it was an act of free will bestowed by God.

De Vitoria not only separated issues of justice and morality from religion, but also laid the foundation for future scholarship on international law and human rights. The doctrine that warring states have responsibilities, and that non-combatants have rights – enshrined in the Hague and Geneva conventions – can be traced back to his teachings. Today, de Vitoria's doctrine is still quoted when discussing the rights of indigenous people in international law. ■

De Vitoria deplored the conquest of the Americas, rejecting the assumed superiority of the Christian conquistadors over the non-believing indigenous population.

Francisco de Vitoria

Francisco was born in the small Basque town of Vitoria. Prior to taking up his post at the university in Salamanca, de Vitoria spent 18 formative years in Paris, where he studied at the Sorbonne University and lectured in a Dominican college.

De Vitoria became a Dominican friar, a professor of theology at the University of Salamanca, and was elected *prima* chair of theology – the most senior position in the department – in 1526. He was the founding member of the School of Salamanca – an influential group of scholars that included Domingo de Soto, Martin de Azpilcueta, Tomas de Mercado, and Francisco Suárez – who strove to redefine man's relationship with God within the Catholic tradition. De Vitoria studied the teachings of fellow Dominican and theologian Thomas Aquinas, whose work was a cornerstone of the School of Salamanca.

Key works

1532 *Of Indians*
1532 *Of the Spanish War Against the Barbarians*
1557 *Theological Reflections*

SOVEREIGNTY IS THE ABSOLUTE AND PERPETUAL POWER OF A COMMONWEALTH

JEAN BODIN (1529–1596)

IN CONTEXT

IDEOLOGY
Absolutism

FOCUS
Power of the sovereign

BEFORE
380 BCE In the *Republic*, Plato argues that the ideal state would be ruled by a philosopher king.

1532 CE Niccolò Machiavelli's *The Prince* is published, providing practical advice to sovereigns.

AFTER
1648 The Peace of Westphalia creates the modern system of European nation-states.

1651 In *Leviathan*, Thomas Hobbes argues that rule by an absolute sovereign nonetheless involves a social contract with the people.

1922 Carl Schmitt insists that a sovereign ruler has the right to suspend law in exceptional circumstances, such as war.

Competing power structures lead to **civil war and chaos**...

...so there must be a **single sovereign with absolute power**, answerable only to God.

For a sovereign's power to be absolute, it must be **perpetual** and not granted by others or limited in time.

Sovereignty is the absolute and perpetual power of a commonwealth.

The idea that states should be sovereign within their own territory owes much to the writing of French jurist Jean Bodin. After living through the French Wars of Religion (1562–98), a period of civil war fought primarily between Catholics and Huguenot Protestants, Bodin saw the dangers of the complex, overlapping power structures of his time. The Church, the nobility, and the monarch all competed for the allegiance of their subjects, and this struggle often resulted in civil war and disorder. The German theologian Martin Luther – and later thinkers such as English philosopher John Locke and American Founding Father Thomas Jefferson – argued for a separation of Church and state to avoid such conflict. To Bodin, however, a strong central sovereignty was the key to ensuring peace and prosperity.

In his treatise *Six Books of the Republic*, Bodin argued that sovereignty had to be absolute and perpetual to be effective. Absolute sovereignty would create a stronger central authority over its territory. To avoid conflict, the sovereign should not be bound by laws, obligations, or conditions, either

See also: Plato 34–39 ▪ Thomas Aquinas 62–63 ▪ Niccolò Machiavelli 74–81 ▪ Thomas Hobbes 96–103 ▪ John Locke 104–09 ▪ Carl Schmitt 254–57

> The sovereign Prince is accountable only to God.
> **Jean Bodin**

from outside factions or from his own subjects. Bodin's insistence on the need for absolute sovereignty formed an intellectual pillar supporting the rise of absolute monarchy in Europe. He also argued that sovereignty needed to be perpetual. Power could neither be granted to the sovereign by others nor be limited in time, as this would contradict the principle of absolutism. Bodin used the Latin term *res publica* ("*république*" in French, or "commonwealth" in English) for matters of public law, and believed that any political society must have a sovereign who is free to make and break the law for the commonwealth to prosper.

The divine right of kings

For Bodin, the source of legitimacy for the sovereign was rooted in natural law and the divine right of kings – society's moral code and a monarch's right to rule both came directly from God. In this, Bodin was opposed to the concept that a sovereign's legitimacy arises from a social contract between ruler and subjects, an idea later developed by Enlightenment thinkers such as French philosopher Jean-Jacques Rousseau. Although Bodin disliked democracy as a form of popular government, he did not agree with the Machiavellian position that a sovereign could act and rule unconditionally. Rulers needed to have absolute power, but they in turn were accountable to God and natural law.

The Peace of Westphalia, a series of treaties agreed between European powers in 1648, was based on Bodin's views on the primacy of sovereignty in each territory, and moved Europe from its medieval political system of a local hierarchy to the modern state system. The Westphalian system has been the organizing framework for international relations ever since, based on the principles of sovereign territories' political self-determination, mutual recognition, and non-interference in the domestic affairs of other states. ■

In the French Wars of Religion, Catholic forces saw the pope as the ultimate power, while Protestants backed the authority of the king.

Jean Bodin

The son of a wealthy tailor, Jean Bodin was born near Angers in northwest France in 1529. He joined the Carmelite religious order when still very young, and travelled to Paris in 1545 to study under the philosopher Guillaume Prévost. He then studied law in Toulouse, returning to Paris in 1560, where he was made a counsel to the king, and later became the king's prosecutor.

Bodin wrote on a wide range of subjects, including history, economics, natural history, law, witchcraft, and religion. His works were influential in his lifetime and long after his death, but his religious views were far from orthodox and much debated. Although Bodin was a Catholic, he questioned the authority of the pope and, in later years, attempted to start a constructive dialogue with other faiths.

Key work

1576 *Six Books of the Republic*

THE NATURAL LAW IS THE FOUNDATION OF HUMAN LAW

FRANCISCO SUÁREZ (1548–1617)

IN CONTEXT

IDEOLOGY
Philosophy of law

FOCUS
Natural and human law

BEFORE
1274 Thomas Aquinas distinguishes between natural law and human law in his *Summa Theologia*.

1517 The Protestant Reformation questions the doctrines of the Catholic Church, and is used to justify the divine right of kings.

AFTER
1613 King James I of England bans Suárez's treatise against Anglicanism, since it criticizes the divine right of kings.

1625 Hugo Grotius writes the first systematic treatise on international law.

1787 The Constitution of the United States refers to natural law as the basis for positive law.

In 16th-century Europe, events such as the Protestant Reformation, the discovery of the Americas, and the rise of humanism made the question of whether laws were derived from nature, God, or fellow human beings particularly topical. Thomas Aquinas had linked natural law with divine law, saying that human laws should be judged by their conformity to natural law, which in turn should be understood in the context of divine law. Natural law refers to universal rules of morality that can be derived by analysing nature – including humans, as part of nature – whereas human law (also called positive law) refers to the man-made laws of a particular society.

Breaking human laws

Spanish philosopher Francisco Suárez continued in Aquinas's tradition, arguing that natural law is the foundation of human law. He described how human laws could be unjust, and placed a greater emphasis on individual liberty and freedom. Man-made laws could, in the view of Suárez,

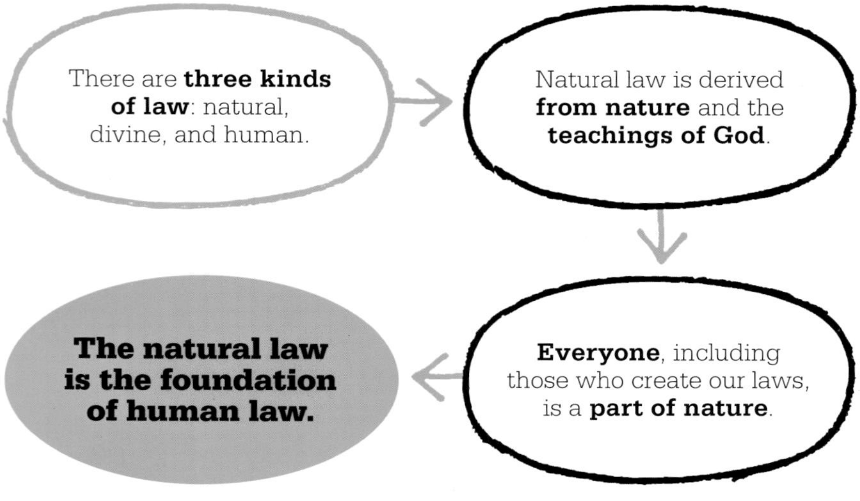

See also: Thomas Aquinas 62–69 ■ Francisco de Vitoria 86–87 ■ Hugo Grotius 94–95 ■ John Locke 104–09

The University of Salamanca was home to the School of Salamanca, a group of theologians that included Suárez, who sought to square the ideas of Aquinas with a changing world.

be broken in certain cases. For example, power and authority can be conferred on a ruler by the people, but can also be taken away from the ruler if their laws are unjust. No man-made laws should override people's natural rights to life and liberty. And since the origin of the state's authority and power is human, it should be secondary to sacred authority.

A divine right?

Suárez's ideas were controversial, as monarchs across northern Europe claimed divine and absolute authority – the so-called "divine right" of kings. Suárez's conclusions challenged the notion that the ruler was accountable only to God, and not to the Church or to his or her subjects. By distinguishing between different sources of laws – natural, divine, and human – Suárez rejected the mixing of the secular and the sacred, and separated the realms of power. He also introduced the notion of the social contract, proposing that the ruler governs by the consent of the people, who can also legitimately withdraw their consent if the ruler does not respect the demands of natural law.

International law

Suárez made a distinction between international law and natural law, seeing the former as primarily based on custom and positive law rather than universal rules. Today, the distinction between natural law and positive law remains, both in national jurisdictions and international law. English common law has been greatly influenced by natural law theories, while the US Declaration of Independence and its Constitution refer to natural law. ■

> There is no doubt that God is the sufficient cause and, as it were, the teacher of the natural law. But it does not follow from this that He is the lawgiver.
> **Francisco Suárez**

Francisco Suárez

Suárez was born in the south of Spain and became a Jesuit student in Salamanca at the age of 16. As a theologian and philosopher, he wrote in the same scholastic tradition as Thomas Aquinas, and had considerable influence on the development of international law and the theory of just war. His most influential work was his 1597 *Metaphysical Disputations*, but he was a productive scholar who wrote many other significant treatises on the relationship between natural law, the state and Church, and theology. Suárez was a dedicated Jesuit – hardworking, disciplined, humble, and pious. He was regarded by contemporaries as one of the greatest living philosophers. Pope Paul V called him *Doctor Eximius et Pius*, an honorary title, and Pope Gregory XIII is said to have attended his first lecture in Rome.

Key works

1597 *Metaphysical Disputations*
1612 *On Laws*
1613 *Defence of the Catholic and Apostolic Faith against the Errors of Anglicanism*

POLITICS IS THE ART OF ASSOCIATING MEN

JOHANNES ALTHUSIUS (1557–1638)

IN CONTEXT

IDEOLOGY
Federalism

FOCUS
Consociation

BEFORE
c.350 BCE Aristotle argues that humans are naturally sociable beings.

1576 Jean Bodin advocates state sovereignty across Europe, centralizing power and authority in the monarch.

AFTER
1762 Jean-Jacques Rousseau claims that the central idea of the social contract must be that sovereignty belongs to the people.

1787 The last four articles of the Constitution of the United States of America express the principles of its federalist system of government.

1789 The French Revolution overthrows the king and claims sovereignty for the people.

Humans **associate in groups** at different levels: families, guilds, cities, provinces, and states.

The purpose of the **state** is to **protect members** of its associations and their communications.

Elected state representatives must **reflect the many views** of these differing associations.

Politics is the art of associating men.

Political thinkers have long pondered the balance of power between government, communities, and individuals. In the 16th and 17th centuries the prevailing idea was of a centralized state with power vested in a sovereign. However, the radical views of Calvinist political philosopher Johannes Althusius on the role of the state, sovereignty, and politics paved the way for the modern concept of federalism.

Althusius redefined politics from an activity relating only to the state, to one that permeates many aspects of social life and unfolds in political associations well below the level of the state. In the first chapter of his major work, *Politica*, he introduces the idea of "consociation", which has formed the basis of federalist thinking ever since.

Althusius claimed that human communities – from private ones, such as families and guilds, to

See also: Aristotle 40–43 ▪ Jean Bodin 88–89 ▪ Thomas Hobbes 96–103 ▪ Jean-Jacques Rousseau 118–25 ▪ Thomas Jefferson 140–41 ▪ Michel Foucault 310–11

The communal aspects of village life, such as dances, are an example of Althusius's idea of a consociation: individuals forming a group based on shared needs, services, or values.

public ones, such as cities – are autonomous entities that came into being through a form of social contract. Like Aristotle, Althusius believed that people are sociable, and in order to live peaceably together, they are happy to share goods and services and respect one another's rights. Each consociation of individuals begins when someone recognizes a shared need, service, or set of values, and is willing to contribute to the welfare of a group.

Bottom-up, not top-down

Absolute sovereignty, as advocated by Bodin and Hobbes, was seen by Althusius as illogical and repressive. He believed power and authority should move upwards via consociations, not down from a sovereign. While consociations are independently subordinate to the state, collectively, they are superior to the state. The government sits at the top of a hierarchy of consociations, and its task is to administer the commonwealth made up of the various interacting groups. It, too, is a part of the social contract, recognizing and sharing the aims, values, goods, and services of its people and coordinating their communications.

In Althusius's theory, sovereignty belongs to the people, not the monarch. The elected representatives of the government do not represent individuals or a single common will, but a plurality of wills – of all the communities that exist within the one larger community of the nation.

Althusius's focus on symbiotic associations distinguishes his idea of federalism from the federal governments that we know today, such as that recognized in the US Constitution. Modern federalism is based on individualism, not social groups. However, both concepts see the state as a political association, not a single entity independent of its constituent units. ■

> This mutual communication, or common enterprise, involves things, services, and common rights.
> **Johannes Althusius**

Johannes Althusius

Althusius was born in 1557 in Diedenshausen in Westphalia, a Calvinist area of Germany. Under the patronage of a local count he studied law, philosophy, and theology in Cologne from 1581. After a series of academic appointments, in 1602 he became president of the College of Herborn. In 1604, a year after the publication of *Politica*, his most important work, he was elected a municipal trustee of the city of Emden.

Althusius later became a council member and city elder, acting as a diplomat and lawyer for the city until his death in 1638. Although *Politica* was widely popular in Althusius's time, his work was overlooked for the next two centuries since it contradicted the prevailing principle of absolute sovereignty. In the 19th century, Otto von Gierke revived interest in Althusius's ideas, and today he is considered the forefather of federalism.

Key works

1603 *Politics: A Digest of its Methods* (also known as *Politica*)
1617 *Dicaelogicae*

LIBERTY IS THE POWER THAT WE HAVE OVER OURSELVES

HUGO GROTIUS (1583–1645)

IN CONTEXT

IDEOLOGY
Natural law

FOCUS
Individual rights

BEFORE
1517 The protection of liberty is seen as the fundamental political task of a republic by Niccolò Machiavelli in his *Discourses*.

1532 Francisco de Vitoria lectures on the rights of peoples at the University of Salamanca.

AFTER
1789 The French Revolution – with its demands for liberty, equality, and fraternity – transforms France and the rest of Europe.

1958 Political theorist Isaiah Berlin lectures on the Two Concepts of Liberty: negative liberty (non-interference and the opportunity to be free) and positive liberty (the ability to be one's own master).

Life and property are **natural rights** of all individuals.

↓

People have the **powers to claim** these rights.

↓

The state has **no legitimate powers** to take these liberties away.

↓

Liberty is the power we have over ourselves.

The notions of individual liberty and individual rights came to the fore relatively late in human history. During the medieval era, rights were collective and judged in relation to natural or divine law. Individuals did not possess rights: rights flowed from nature or God. Liberty was rarely discussed in relation to individuals; rather, individuals had a duty to carry out God's plan. In the 16th century, at the University of Salamanca, first Francisco de Vitoria and later Francisco Suárez had begun to theorize on the natural rights of individuals. However, it was Hugo Grotius who decisively changed medieval thinking, by clearly asserting that liberty and rights were in the possession of individuals.

See also: Francisco de Vitoria 86–87 ▪ Francisco Suárez 90–91 ▪ John Locke 104–09 ▪ John Stuart Mill 174–81

Grotius redefined natural law, and laid out a new conception of rights and liberty. The idea of divine influence on natural law was discarded. Instead, the study of human nature was seen as sufficient to inform law- and policy-makers. Put simply, human behaviour produces the natural law. People have certain natural rights that are intrinsic to them, and which are not bestowed by God or the sovereign. Rather, liberty is a natural right.

Power over ourselves

By viewing liberty as the power that people have over themselves, Grotius distinguished between a person's ability to do something and their freedom from constraints. Since man has a right to life and property, Grotius argued, he is also granted the powers to take the necessary action to fulfill those rights. The state does not have legitimate superior authority in such circumstances. Thus, by connecting rights with the individual, the concept of individual freedom, or liberty, becomes more than just a question of free will. It also includes the freedom to act without constraints. This focus on human agency marked a clear break from the thinking of earlier times.

Grotius regarded rights as abilities or powers possessed by individuals, and his philosophy also allowed for the commodification of rights. Rights could be "traded" with, for example, a sovereign. In this case, the power of the state would come from the voluntary transfer of rights by individuals. Grotius distinguished between two classes of relations. Relations of unequals could be between "Parents and Children, Masters and Servants, King and Subject", while relations between "Brothers, Citizens, Friends, and Allies" were relations of equals.

Grotius's idea that people are natural bearers of rights has become a cornerstone for the theory of liberalism. However, his belief that some people have a right to superiority is certainly not in line with modern liberal thinking. ■

Freedom of the seas was considered by Grotius to be a natural right, and he used this belief to justify the Dutch East India fleet breaking the monopolies set up by other nations.

Hugo Grotius

Hugo Grotius was born in 1583 in the city of Delft in the south of Holland during the Dutch Revolt against Spain. Considered by many to be a child prodigy, Grotius entered the University of Leiden at the age of 11, and received his doctorate when he was 16. By the age of 24, he was advocate general for Holland. During a tumultuous period in Dutch history, Grotius was sentenced to life imprisonment in Loevestein Castle for his views on restraining the powers of the Church in civil matters.

Grotius escaped to Paris, reportedly in a trunk, and there he wrote his most famous work *De Jure Belli ac Pacis*. Grotius is widely held to be the father of international and maritime law. His themes of natural law and individual liberty were later taken up by liberal philosophers such as John Locke.

Key works

1605 *De Jure Praedae Commentarius*
1609 *Mare Liberum* (originally part of *De Jure Praedae Commentarius*)
1625 *De Jure Belli ac Pacis*

THE CONDITION OF MAN IS A CONDITION OF WAR

THOMAS HOBBES (1588–1679)

IN CONTEXT

IDEOLOGY
Realism

FOCUS
Social contract

BEFORE
1578 The concepts of sovereignty and the divine right of kings emerge, influenced by *The Six Books of the Republic* by Jean Bodin.

1642–51 The English Civil War temporarily establishes the precedent that the monarch cannot rule without the consent of Parliament.

AFTER
1688 The Glorious Revolution in England leads to the 1689 Bill of Rights, which limits the powers of the monarch in law.

1689 John Locke opposes absolutist rule, arguing that government should represent the people and protect their rights to life, health, liberty, and possessions.

The Enlightenment period that followed the Middle Ages in Europe introduced new views on human nature that were not based on religious doctrine, but were instead founded on rational thought. Disagreement between some Enlightenment thinkers often derived from differences in opinion concerning the true nature of the human condition and human behaviour. To settle such abstract, fundamental differences, scholars began to state their views on the so-called "state of nature" – the theoretical condition of mankind before the introduction of social structures and norms.

Many thinkers believed that by analysing the human "instincts" and behaviours of this state of nature, one could design a system of government that met the needs of its citizens and would promote good behaviours and counteract bad ones. For example, if humans were able to see beyond narrow self-interests and work for the public good, then they could enjoy the benefits of democratic rights. However, if they mainly cared about their own interests and maximizing their own power, then a strong, controlling authority was required in order to prevent chaos. English writer Thomas Hobbes was one of the first Enlightenment philosophers to base his argument explicitly on an articulated view of the state of nature. Hobbes's view was that human beings needed to be ruled by government, as the state of nature was a terrible, "dog-eat-dog" world.

The cruel state of nature

In his most famous work, *Leviathan*, Hobbes portrays humans as rational agents who seek to maximize power and act

> Without a common power to keep them all in awe, they [men] are in that condition called war.
> **Thomas Hobbes**

Thomas Hobbes

Born in 1588, Thomas Hobbes was educated at Oxford University in England and would later work as a tutor for William Cavendish, Earl of Devonshire. Due to the English Civil War, he spent a decade in exile in Paris where he wrote *Leviathan*, which has had a profound influence on the way we perceive the role of government and the social contract as a basis for legitimacy to govern. Hobbes's political philosophy was influenced by his interest in science, and his correspondence with philosophers including René Descartes (1596–1650). Drawing from scientific writings, Hobbes believed that everything could be reduced to its primary components, even human nature. He was inspired by the simplicity and elegance of geometry and physics, and revolutionized political theory by applying such scientific method to its reasoning. He returned to England in 1651, dying in 1679.

Key works

1628 *History of the Peloponnesian War*
1650 *Treatise on Human Nature*
1651 *Leviathan*

See also: Plato 34–39 ▪ Jean Bodin 88–89 ▪ John Locke 104–09 ▪ Jean-Jacques Rousseau 118–25 ▪ John Rawls 298–303

The frontispiece of *Leviathan* depicts a ruler, composed of tiny faces, rising up over the land and holding a sword and sceptre, symbolizing earthly and ecclesiastical powers respectively.

according to self-interest, because acting otherwise would threaten their self-preservation. The title is suggestive of Hobbes's views on the state and human nature. Leviathan is the name of a monster in the biblical book of Job, and for Hobbes the state is the "great Leviathan… which is but an Artificial Man; though of greater stature and strength than the Natural, for whose protection and defence it was intended; and in which, the Sovereignty is an Artificial Soul, as giving life and motion to the whole body." The state is thus a cruel, artificial construct, but is necessary nonetheless for the sake of the protection of its citizens.

Left ungoverned, men will terrorize each other in a **state of nature**…

…in which individuals will stop at nothing to ensure their own **self-preservation or self-promotion**.

In the state of nature, the condition of man is a condition of war of everyone against everyone.

To avert a descent into the state of nature, men must **enter into a social contract**, submitting to the authority and protection of a sovereign.

The sovereign must be an absolute ruler with **indivisible and unlimited power**, to prevent factional strife and chaos.

If a sovereign fails in their duty, **the social contract is broken** and individuals may take action, leading back to a state of nature.

The book was written during the English Civil War (1642–51), and argues against challenges to royal authority. The state of nature – the warring of all against one another – was for Hobbes comparable to civil war, and could only be avoided if men handed over their arms to a third party – the sovereign – via a social contract that ensured that all others would do the same. The reason rational agents would surrender their freedom to an absolute ruler was » that life in the state of nature was so "solitary, poor, nasty, brutish, and short" that freedom would always be a secondary concern, an ill-afforded luxury. Hobbes stated that while people would have natural rights in such a state of nature, the overriding concern would be to do whatever was necessary to secure survival. All actions could be justified – rights would not protect the individual.

Rule by social contract

With no common authority to solve disputes or protect the weak, it would be up to each individual to decide what he or she needs – and needs to do – to survive. In the state of nature, men are naturally free and independent, with no duties to others. Hobbes assumes that there will always be a scarcity of goods, and that people are equally vulnerable. Some people will go into conflict to secure food and shelter, while others will be willing to do so in order to obtain power and glory. A state of constant fear will ensue, leading to pre-emptive attacks.

Hobbes sees this state of war and chaos as the natural end point of uncontrolled human freedom. In order to prevent it, the state needs to have indivisible power and authority to control its subjects. This is similar to a description of sovereignty by French jurist Jean Bodin, which was also born out of a period of civil war. However, Hobbes did not base authority on the divine right of kings, but on the idea of a social contract that all rational people would agree upon.

While the concept of man's state of nature was deeply influential among Hobbes's contemporaries and future political theorists, it was often interpreted differently. Hobbes used the state of nature to refer to a hypothetical situation, a sort of rational reconstruction of how life without order and government would be. This differed from the way later thinkers, including John Locke and Jean-Jacques Rousseau, would use the concept in their own works on the social contract and ideal forms of government. Locke and Rousseau did not consider the state of nature to be a rational construct, but an actual state of affairs.

A necessary evil

Enlightenment thinkers referred to the concept of a social contract between the ruled and the ruler to answer questions of the political legitimacy of various modes of governance. To rule legitimately, there must be either an explicit or tacit agreement that the sovereign will protect his citizens and their natural rights if they agree to surrender their individual freedom and submit to subordination.

Hobbes argued that humans had two principal choices in life – they could either live without government (the state of nature) or with government. For Hobbes, a social contract bestowing indivisible authority to a sovereign was a necessary evil to avoid the cruel fate that awaited man if a strong power could not keep the destructive impulses of individuals in check. Hobbes believed that, "During the time men live without a common power to keep them all in awe, they are in that condition called war; and such a war, as is of every man, against every man." However, unlike earlier scholars who had argued for the divine right of kings to rule, Hobbes truly saw the relationship between the ruled and the ruler as contractual. The contract was primarily made

Hobbes wrote *Leviathan* as the English Civil War was waged. His view of the "state of nature" that a sovereign protected against seemed to be borne out by the savagery of the war.

Hobbes saw the state of nature as undesirable, stating that the people must willingly subject themselves to a ruler or sovereign in order to protect society.

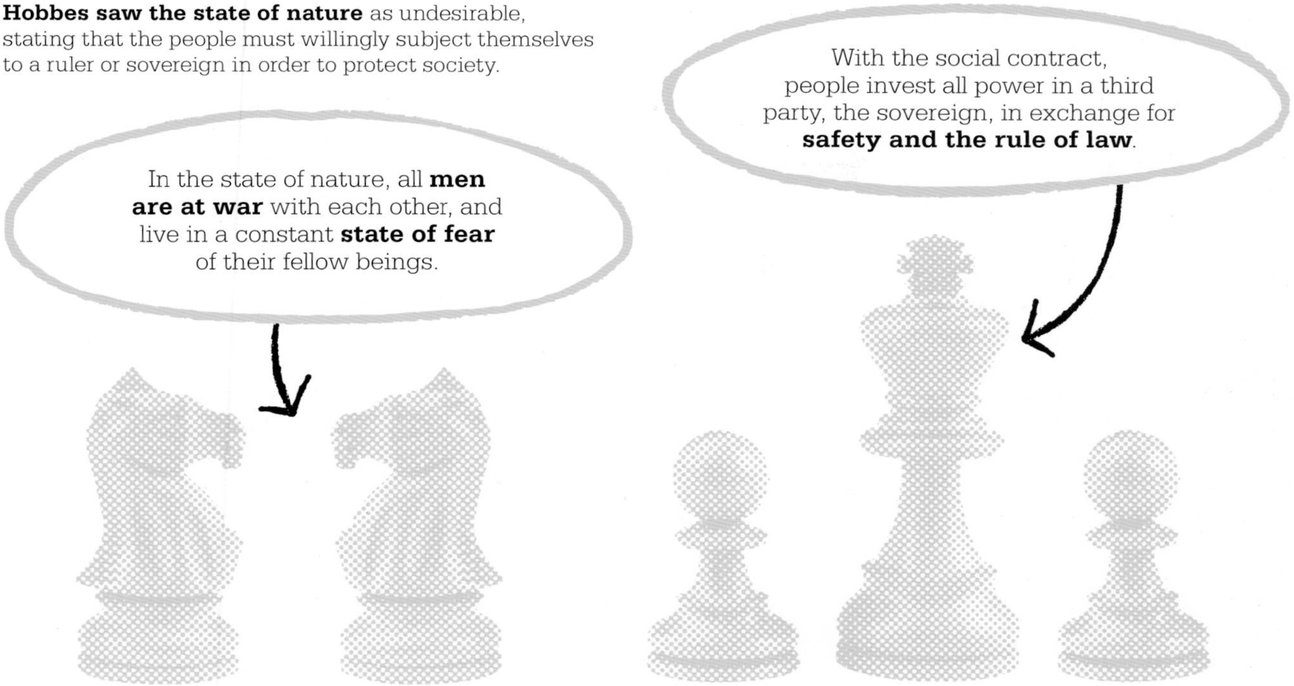

between the individuals in a society, while the sovereign was an outside, third party.

Collective action

Because people are rational, they can see that the state of nature is undesirable, and that peace is good. However, because each individual has to protect their own interests in the state of nature, a "collective action problem" arises. Although Hobbes did not coin this term, his dilemma of individuals in the state of nature not trusting each other to lay down arms is very similar to this modern concept, where a problem exists that can only be overcome if individuals – all of whom stand to gain from the successful outcome – act collectively. Hobbes's solution was radical: invest all power in a third party – the sovereign. Contemporary scholars have identified many ways in which individuals overcome collective action problems without the need for a strong government. British philosopher Margaret Gilbert has suggested that collective action involves joint commitment to a course of action in which, in effect, people act as parts of one person with one aim. Nevertheless, governments are still the main regulators of conflict and providers of public goods.

> The obligation of subjects to the sovereign is understood to last as long, and no longer, than the power lasteth by which he is able to protect them.
> **Thomas Hobbes**

Hobbes's contractual view of government authority also affected the duties of the sovereign. Only so long as the sovereign could protect his subjects were they bound by the social contract. However, Hobbes did not encourage popular revolutions, nor religious influence on state matters, and he did not favour democratic rule. The main aim of government was stability and peace, not individual freedom.

Pragmatic politics

Hobbes's views on the social contract did legitimize changes in government. When the English king, Charles I, was dethroned in 1649 by Oliver Cromwell, according to Hobbes's thinking the social contract was held intact, since one ruler was merely replaced with another. In other words, Hobbes »

Oliver Cromwell led the anti-Royalist forces that deposed King Charles I in 1649. Hobbes believed the social contract was still intact, since rule had passed unbroken to Parliament.

was an anti-democrat and an absolutist, but also a pragmatist. Although he did not take a decisive stance on which mode of government was best, he clearly preferred Charles I's monarchy as a good, stable form of government. However, he also regarded parliamentary sovereignty as a suitable form of government, as long as the legislative assembly contained an odd number of members to prevent a situation of political stalemate.

The logic behind Hobbes's version of the social contract was questioned by many scholars. John Locke provided a sarcastic critique by questioning why one would believe that "Men are so foolish that they take care to avoid what Mischiefs may be done to them by Pole-cats, or Foxes, but are content, nay think it Safety, to be devoured by Lions." For Locke, authoritarian rule is just as dangerous as civil disorder – he preferred the state of nature to subordination. Hobbes believed, however, that only governments with indivisible and unlimited power would prevent the otherwise inevitable disintegration of society into civil war. For Hobbes, anyone arguing for individual freedoms and rights had not grasped that the basic security that civilized life took for granted would only endure as long as strong, centralized rule existed. Political obedience was needed to keep the peace. Citizens had a right to defend themselves if their lives were threatened, but in all other questions the government was to be obeyed to prevent factional strife or political paralysis.

Against a state of nature

Hobbes delivered a strong argument for absolutism based on his deliberations on the nature of man. His opponents – arguing against absolutism – responded by challenging his portrayal of human beings as hungry for power and strife. Jean-Jacques Rousseau saw the life of man in the state of nature in a romantic light, as a life of innocence and simplicity, in contrast to life in modern society, which was dishonest. Therefore, one should not try to escape from the state of nature, rather it should be re-created as best as possible in the mode of government. Rousseau therefore advocated direct democracy in small communities. While Hobbes lived his life with the English Civil War as a reference point, Rousseau lived in the tranquil city of Geneva, Switzerland. It is telling how their different backgrounds shaped their political theories. Unlike Hobbes, Rousseau regarded the state of nature as a historical description of

> Nothing is so gentle as man in his primitive state, when placed by nature at an equal distance from the stupidity of brutes and the fatal enlightenment of civil man.
> **Jean-Jacques Rousseau**

man in a pre-social state of nature. Political theorists have since vacillated between the extremes of Hobbes and Rousseau, viewing the condition of man either as a condition of war or as people living in accordance with nature.

Two other influential philosophers – Locke and Scottish philosopher David Hume – also criticized Hobbes. Locke writes on the state of nature in his two treatises of government (1690), and refers to the laws of nature that govern this condition. In contrast to Hobbes, he states that even in the state of nature no man has the right to harm another. Hume adds to the debate by stating that human beings are naturally social, and that the savage condition described by Hobbes is therefore improbable.

The Hobbes method

Today, scholars continue to use Hobbes's method and the concept of a state of nature to argue for and against different political systems. John Rawls used Hobbes's notion of what made a stable society when formulating what rational people would be able to agree upon. In *A Theory of Justice* (1971), Rawls argues that people would choose a condition where everyone had some basic rights and economic safeguards if forced to choose under a "veil of ignorance", not knowing whether they would have a privileged position in this imagined society. Hobbes did not, however, theorize on the ideal society, but on the necessity of strong government.

> To this war of every man against every man… nothing can be unjust… where there is no common power, there is no law, where no law, no injustice.
> **Thomas Hobbes**

While most scholars today would consider Hobbes's view of the human condition to be pessimistic, he maintains a significant influence on political thought. The realist tradition in international relations, which stresses the study of power, departs from Hobbes's premise that the condition of man is a condition of war. Nevertheless, the anarchical condition that Hobbes described in the state of nature is also taken to be true for the international system, where states are the main actors. Realist views of the international system still dominate today, despite the end of the Cold War. The main difference from Hobbes's theory is that, at the international level, it is not possible to rely on the Leviathan of the state to subdue destructive pursuits of power and self-interest. States cannot trust each other, and are therefore doomed to arms races and wars. ■

The Triumph of Death (1562) by Pieter Bruegel the Elder depicts anarchy breaking out as Death comes to rich and poor alike. Hobbes saw the state of nature as similarly anarchic and brutal.

THE END OF LAW IS TO PRESERVE AND ENLARGE FREEDOM

JOHN LOCKE (1632–1704)

IN CONTEXT

IDEOLOGY
Liberalism

FOCUS
The rule of law

BEFORE
1642 A series of conflicts known as the English Civil War breaks out, due to concerns that Charles I would attempt to introduce absolutism in England.

1661 Louis XIV begins his personal rule of France, and embodies absolutism in the phrase *"L'état, c'est moi"*, saying that he is the state.

AFTER
1689 The English Bill of Rights secures the rights of Parliament and elections free of royal interference.

18th century Popular revolutions in France and America lead to the establishment of republics based on liberalist principles.

An important question in political theory concerns the role of government and the functions it should perform. Equally important is the question of what gives the government a right to govern, and where the boundaries of government authority should be. Some medieval scholars argued that kings had a right to rule that had been bestowed upon them by God, while others proclaimed that the nobility had a birthright to rule. Enlightenment thinkers started to challenge these doctrines. But if the power to rule was not to be granted by divine will or by birth, other sources of legitimacy had to be found.

English philosopher John Locke was the first to articulate the liberal principles of government: namely that the purpose of government was to preserve its citizens' rights to freedom, life, and property, to pursue the public good; and to punish people who violated the rights of others. Law-making was therefore the supreme function of government. For Locke, one of the main reasons people would be willing to enter into a social contract and submit to being ruled by a government, is that they expect the government to regulate disagreements and conflicts in a neutral manner. Following this logic, Locke was also able to describe the characteristics of an illegitimate government. It followed that a government that did not respect and protect people's natural rights – or unnecessarily constrained their liberty – was not legitimate. Locke was therefore opposed to absolutist rule. Unlike his contemporary Thomas Hobbes, who believed that an absolute sovereign was required to save people from a brutal "state of nature", Locke maintained that the powers and functions of government had to be limited.

The centrality of laws

Much of Locke's writing on political philosophy centred on rights and laws. He defined political power as "a Right of making Laws with Penalties of Death". He contended that one of the primary reasons why people would voluntarily leave the lawless state of nature was that no independent judges existed in such a situation. It was preferable to grant government a monopoly on

John Locke

John Locke lived in – and shaped – one of the most transformative centuries in English history. A series of civil wars pitted Protestants, Anglicans, and Catholics against each other, and power vacillated between the king and the Parliament. Locke was born in 1632 close to Bristol, England. He lived in exile in France and Holland for large periods of time due to suspicions that he was involved in an assassination plot against King Charles II. His book *Two Treatises of Government* provided the intellectual foundation for the Glorious Revolution of 1688, which transferred the balance of power permanently from the king to Parliament. He promoted the idea that people are not born with innate ideas, but with a mind like a blank slate – a very modern way of viewing the self.

Key works

1689 *Two Treatises of Government*
1689 *A Letter Concerning Toleration*
1690 *An Essay Concerning Human Understanding*

See also: Thomas Hobbes 96–103 ▪ Montesquieu 110–11 ▪ Jean-Jacques Rousseau 118–25 ▪ Thomas Jefferson 140–41 ▪ Robert Nozick 326–27

Humans are **rational, independent agents** with natural rights. → They join political society **to be protected** by the rule of law. → **The end of law should be to preserve and enlarge freedom.**

violence and sentencing to ensure fair rule of law. Moreover, for Locke, a legitimate government upholds the principle of separation of the legislative and executive powers. The legislative power is superior to the executive – the former has supreme power to establish general rules in the affairs of government, whereas the latter is only responsible for enforcing the law in specific cases.

One reason for the centrality of laws in Locke's writings is that laws protect liberty. The purpose of law is not to abolish or restrain, but to preserve and enlarge freedom. In political society, Locke believes that "where there is no law there is no freedom". Laws, therefore, both constrain and enable freedom. To live in freedom is not to live without laws in the state of nature. Locke points out that "freedom is not, as we are told, liberty for every man to do what he lists (for who could be free when every other man's humour might domineer over him?), but a liberty to dispose, and order as he lists, his person, actions, possessions, and his whole property, within the allowance of those laws." In other words, laws can not only preserve, but also enable liberty to be exercised. Without laws, our freedom would be limited by an anarchical, uncertain state of nature, and in practice there may be no freedom at all.

> In all the states of created beings capable of law, where there is no law, there is no freedom.
> **John Locke**

Man's initial condition

Locke says that laws should be designed – and enforced – with man's initial condition and nature in mind. Like most social contract theorists, he considers men to be equal, free, and independent. According to Locke, the state of nature is a situation in which people coexist, often in relative harmony, but there is no legitimate political power or judge to settle disputes in a neutral way. Locke writes that "men living according to reason, without a common superior on Earth to judge between them, is properly the state of nature."

Unlike Hobbes, Locke does not equate the state of nature with war. A state of war is a situation in which people do not uphold natural law, or the law of reason as Locke calls it. Where Hobbes would see human beings acting as "power maximizers", mainly concerned with self-preservation, Locke finds that people can act according to reason and with tolerance in the state of nature. Conflicts are therefore not necessarily common in a state of nature. However, when »

Opposed to absolutist rule, Locke as a child had witnessed the execution of King Charles I in 1649 for being "a tyrant, traitor, murderer and public enemy to the good of this nation".

The Role Of Government

Governments must **craft good laws**...

...that **protect the rights** of the people...

...and **enforce them** with the public good in mind.

population density increases, resources become scarce, and the introduction of money leads to economic inequality, conflicts increase, and human society begins to need laws, regulators, and judges to settle disputes in an objective manner.

The purpose of government

The question of legitimacy was at the heart of Locke's political thinking. Following the example of Hobbes, he sought to deduce the legitimate role of government, based on an understanding of the human state of nature.

Locke agrees with Hobbes that a legitimate government is based on a social contract between individuals in a society. The problem with the state of nature is that there are no judges or police to enforce the law. People are willing to enter civil society in order for government to take up this role. This is, therefore, a legitimate role for government. Another important aspect of legitimate government is rule by consent of the people. For Locke, this did not have to mean democracy – a majority of people could reasonably decide that a monarch, aristocracy, or a democratic assembly should rule. The important point was that the people granted the right to rule, and were entitled to take back this privilege.

Locke argued against a strong, absolutist sovereign – as advocated by Thomas Hobbes – as such a powerful figure would limit individual freedom unnecessarily. For Locke, total subordination was dangerous. He wrote: "I have reason to conclude that he who would get me into his power without my consent would use me as he pleased when he got me there, and destroy me too when he had a fancy to it; for nobody can desire to have me in his absolute power unless it be to compel me by force to that which is against the right of my freedom, i.e. make me a slave."

The English Bill of Rights, ratified by King William III in 1689, established limits on the king's power, conforming with Locke's contention that a monarch only rules by the consent of the people.

Rather, Locke favours a limited role for government. Government should protect people's private property, keep the peace, secure public commodities for the whole people, and as far as possible, protect citizens against foreign invasions. For Locke, "This is the original, this is the use, and these are the bounds of the legislative (which is the supreme) power in every commonwealth." The purpose of government is to do what is missing in the state of nature to ensure people's freedom and prosperity. There is no need to enslave people under absolute rule. The primary function of government is to craft good laws to protect people's rights, and to enforce those laws with the public good in mind.

The right to revolt

Locke's distinction between legitimate and illegitimate governments also carries with it the idea that opposition to illegitimate rule is acceptable. Locke describes a range of scenarios in which people would have a right to revolt in order to take back the power they had given the government. For example, people can legitimately rebel if: elected representatives of the people are prevented from assembly; foreign powers are bestowed with authority over people; the election system or procedures are changed without public consent; the rule of law is not upheld; or the government seeks to deprive people of their rights. Locke regarded illegitimate rule as tantamount to slavery. He even went as far as to condone regicide – the execution of a monarch – in circumstances where the monarch has broken the social contract with his people. As the son of Puritans who had supported the Parliamentarian cause in the English Civil War, this was no mere theoretical concern – Locke's writing gives a clear justification for the execution of Charles I.

Locke's legacy

The political philosophy of John Locke has, since his time, become known as "liberalism" – the belief in the principles of liberty and equality. The revolutions in France and North America near the end of the 18th century were founded on liberal ideas. In fact, Thomas Jefferson, one of the architects of the American Constitution and the Declaration of Independence, revered Locke, and used many of his phrases in the founding documents. The emphasis on protection of "life, liberty, or property" found in the Bill of Rights in the Constitution, and the inalienable rights to "Life, Liberty, and the pursuit of Happiness" in the Declaration can all be traced directly back to John Locke's philosophy a century earlier. ■

> "A Bill of Rights is what the people are entitled to against every government, and what no just government should refuse, or rest on inference."
> **Thomas Jefferson**

For a government to be legitimate, according to Locke, assemblies of elected representatives of the people, such as the House of Commons, must be allowed to meet and debate.

WHEN LEGISLATIVE AND EXECUTIVE POWERS ARE UNITED IN THE SAME BODY, THERE CAN BE NO LIBERTY

MONTESQUIEU (1689–1755)

IN CONTEXT

IDEOLOGY
Constitutional politics

FOCUS
Separation of powers

BEFORE
509 BCE After the overthrow of King Lucius Tarquinius Superbus, the Roman Republic is founded, in which a tripartite system of government evolves.

1689 After the "Glorious Revolution" in England, a constitutional monarchy is established.

AFTER
1787 The Constitution of the United States is adopted in Philadelphia.

1789–99 During the French Revolution, a secular democratic republic replaces rule by the monarchy and the Church.

1856 Alexis de Tocqueville publishes *The Old Regime and the Revolution*, an analysis of the fall of the French monarchy.

During the 18th-century Age of Enlightenment, the traditional authority of the Church was undermined by scientific discoveries, and the idea of monarchs ruling by divine right was called into question. In Europe, particularly France, many political philosophers began to investigate the power of the monarchy, clergy, and aristocracy. Foremost among these were Voltaire, Jean-Jacques Rousseau, and Montesquieu.

Rousseau argued for power to be shifted from the monarchy to the people, and Voltaire for a separation

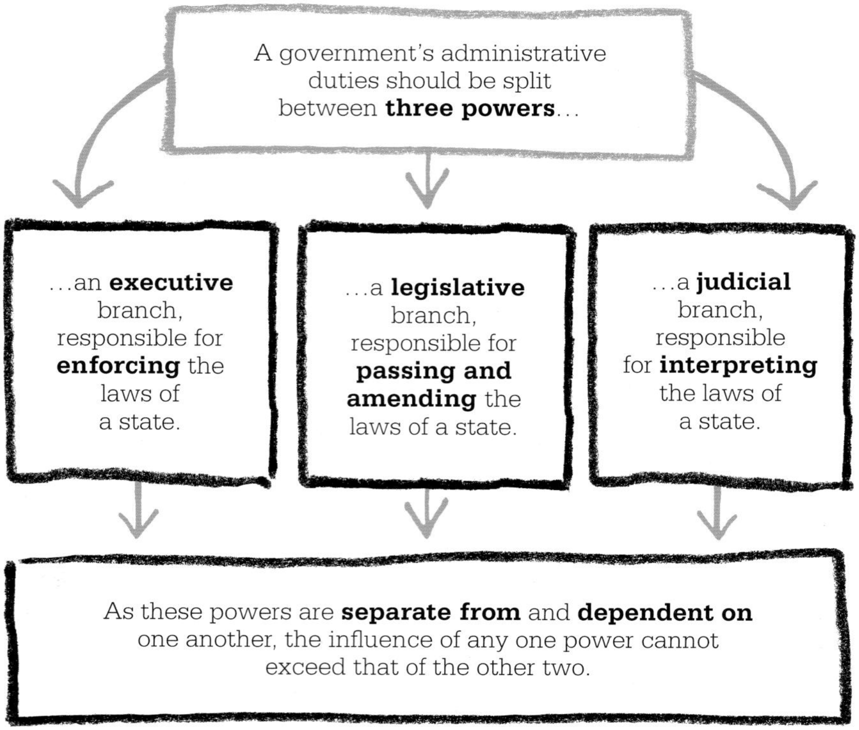

See also: Cicero 49 ▪ Jean-Jacques Rousseau 118–25 ▪ Thomas Jefferson 140–41 ▪ James Madison 150–53 ▪ Alexis de Tocqueville 170–71 ▪ Henry David Thoreau 186–87 ▪ Noam Chomsky 314–15

> The deterioration of a government begins almost always by the decay of its principles.
> **Montesquieu**

of Church and State. Montesquieu was less concerned with who took the reins of government; of more importance to him was the existence of a constitution that would protect against despotism. This could be achieved, he argued, by a separation of the powers of government.

Montesquieu argued that despotism was the single greatest threat to the liberty of the citizen, and both monarchies and republics risked degeneration into despotism unless regulated by a constitution that prevented it. At the heart of his argument was the division of the administrative power of a state into three distinct categories: the executive (responsible for the administration and enforcement of laws), the legislative (responsible for the passing, repealing, and amending of laws), and the judicial (responsible for interpreting and applying the laws).

Separation of powers

This distinction between the different branches of governmental power, sometimes known as the *trias politica*, was not new – the ancient Greeks and Romans had recognized a similar division. Where Montesquieu was innovative was in his advocacy of separate bodies to exercise these powers. This would create a balance, ensuring stable government with minimal risk of decline into despotism. The separation of powers ensured that no one administrative body could become all-powerful, as each would be able to restrict any abuse of power by the others. Although Montesquieu's ideas were inevitably met with hostility by the authorities in France, his principle of the separation of powers was hugely influential, especially in America, where it became a cornerstone of the Constitution of the United States. Following the French Revolution, it also formed a model for the new republic, and as democracies were established worldwide over the next century, some form of the tripartite system was generally enshrined in their constitutions. ■

The United States Congress is the legislative branch of the federal US government; its powers are separate and distinct from those of the President (executive branch) and the Judiciary.

Montesquieu

Montesquieu was born Charles-Louis de Secondat near Bordeaux in France, and inherited the title of Baron de Montesquieu on the death of his uncle in 1716. He studied law at Bordeaux, but his marriage in 1715 brought him a substantial dowry, which, along with his inheritance, allowed him to concentrate on his literary career, starting with the satirical *Persian Letters*.

Montesquieu was elected to the Paris Academy in 1728, and began a series of travels to Italy, Hungary, Turkey, and England. After his return to Bordeaux in 1731, he worked on his history of the Roman empire as well as his masterwork, *The Spirit of the Laws*, which was published anonymously in 1748. Praised elsewhere in Europe, it had a hostile reception in France. Montesquieu died of a fever in Paris in 1755.

Key works

1721 *Persian Letters*
1734 *Considerations on the Causes of the Greatness of the Romans and Their Decline*
1748 *The Spirit of the Laws*

INDEPENDENT ENTREPRENEURS MAKE GOOD CITIZENS

BENJAMIN FRANKLIN (1706–1790)

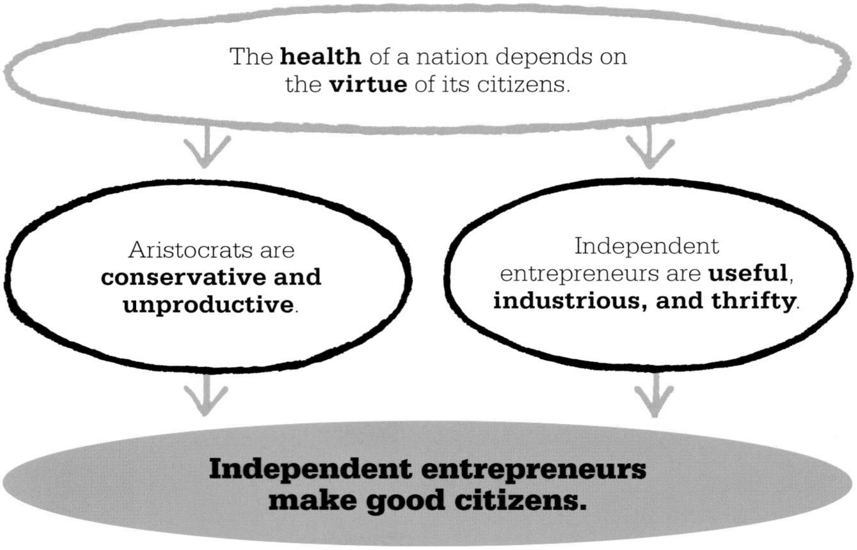

IN CONTEXT

IDEOLOGY
Liberalism

FOCUS
Entrepreneurial citizens

BEFORE
1760 Britain seizes France's North American colonies, raising the stakes in its land acquisition in the New World.

1776 Thirteen colonies declare their independence from Britain to become the United States of America.

AFTER
1879 Thomas Paine's *Declaration of the Rights of Man and of the Citizen* is published in France.

1868 Black people are granted citizenship in the United States following the ratification of the 14th amendment to the US Constitution.

1919 Women are granted the vote in the United States through the 19th amendment.

The period before and after the independence of the United States from British rule was revolutionary intellectually as much as politically. Labelled the American Enlightenment, its leading thinkers were inspired by European Enlightenment writers such as John Locke, Edmund Burke, Jean-Jacques Rousseau, Voltaire, and Montesquieu. When designing their new system of government, the Founding Fathers of the new state favoured liberal and republican principles. They opposed centralized, absolute authority and aristocratic privileges. Instead, pluralist ideals, protection of individual rights, and universal citizenship were the cornerstones. The view of human nature that underpinned this new system of government stemmed from classical republicanism, which saw civic virtue as the foundation for a good society. In the view of one of the Founding Fathers, Benjamin Franklin, individual entrepreneurs

See also: John Locke 104–09 ▪ Montesquieu 110–11 ▪ Edmund Burke 130–33 ▪ Thomas Paine 134–39 ▪ Thomas Jefferson 140–41

made good, virtuous citizens. In this, Franklin articulated the future capitalist spirit of the United States.

Entrepreneurial virtue

While liberals tend to focus on individuals' rights – for example, to life and property – classical republicans place greater emphasis on the individual's duties to the commonwealth as a citizen, and the virtues that citizens need to fulfil this role. The concept of virtue was important to earlier classical republicans, such as Italian diplomat Niccolò Machiavelli, in describing the characteristics of rulers. But the virtues of individual citizens were rarely discussed.

Franklin discusses virtue at an individual level. In his view, a prosperous nation is built on the virtues of individual, hard-working, and productive citizens, not on the characteristics of the ruler or a social class such as the aristocracy. In common with many of Europe's Enlightenment thinkers, Franklin believed that merchants and scientists were the real driving forces of society, but he also placed more emphasis on the importance of personal traits and individual responsibilities. He regarded entrepreneurship to be a personal trait that had important virtue.

The entrepreneurial spirit and philanthropy shown by Bill Gates, founder of Microsoft – the pioneering manufacturer of PCs – are central to Franklin's notion of good citizenship.

> Lose no time; be always employ'd in something useful; cut off all unnecessary actions.
> **Benjamin Franklin**

Promoting the public good

Entrepreneurship is today widely associated with the capitalist system. For example, to the Austrian economist Joseph Schumpeter, entrepreneurship was central to the process of "creative destruction" that shapes the capitalist system. However, Franklin's view of entrepreneurs differed markedly from the modern image of a capitalist businessman. Firstly, he saw entrepreneurship as a virtue only when it promoted the public good, via philanthropy for example. Secondly, he saw an important role for voluntary organizations in order to temper individualism. ■

Benjamin Franklin

Benjamin Franklin was the son of a soap- and candle-maker who rose to become a statesman, scientist, and inventor. Born in 1706 in Boston, he played a leading role in the long process that brought the United States into being. As a statesman, Franklin opposed the British Stamp Act, was the US ambassador in London and Paris, and is considered one of the most important Founding Fathers of the United States.

As a scientist, Franklin is best known for his experiments with electricity. Among his many inventions are the lightning rod, the open stove, bifocal glasses, and the flexible urinary catheter. As an entrepreneur, he was a successful newspaper editor, printer, and author of popular literature. Although he never occupied the highest office in the United States, few other Americans have had a more lasting influence on the country's political landscape.

Key works

1733 *Poor Richard's Almanack*
1787 *United States Constitution*
1790 *Autobiography*

REVOLUT THOUGHT 1770–1848

ONARY
S

1776

In *Common Sense*, Thomas Paine demands **freedom from British rule** for the American colonies.

1783

The American colonies are victorious in the **War of Independence** against the British empire.

1788

Immanuel Kant's *Critique of Practical Reason* argues for moral and political judgments to be **framed by reason**.

1789

The Bastille, a prison in Paris, is **stormed by a crowd**, sparking the French Revolution.

1790

Edmund Burke denounces the **violence of the revolution** in *Reflections on the Revolution in France*.

1792

France is **proclaimed a republic** by the newly established National Convention.

1798

The Irish Rebellion, inspired by the French and American revolutions, **fails to overthrow** British rule.

1804

Haiti gains independence from France, becoming the **first black republic** in the Americas.

The 17th century had seen immense progress in the understanding of the natural world. New approaches to the problems presented by discoveries in science in turn helped inform different ways to approach social problems. English philosopher Thomas Hobbes had introduced the notion of the "social contract", based on his ideas of how rational (but selfish) individuals would function in the state of nature, while another Englishman, John Locke, had provided a rational argument for private property. These early, enlightened efforts to rationalize social structure would, however, be subverted by writers also claiming to work in the tradition known as the Enlightenment. This was a great intellectual movement that aimed to clear away the centuries of scholasticism from human knowledge and reform society using reason, rather than faith.

Sovereignty of the people

A Swiss-born French philosopher named Jean-Jacques Rousseau used the social contract to offer a radical new view of how politics could function in the modern age. Whereas many Enlightenment thinkers – French philosopher Voltaire among them – encouraged enlightened despots to rule wisely, and were against the rule of the mob, Rousseau argued that true sovereignty resided only with the people. He was not the first to offer a critique of existing authority, but he was the first to do so within a framework of thought drawn from Enlightenment sources. Far from being a movement of the elite, the Enlightenment's emphasis on rationality and progress made it, Rousseau believed, a movement for the masses.

The decades after Rousseau's death in 1778 were marked by conflicts over these new views of society. Enlightenment ideals began to shape events in the latter part of the 18th century, most spectacularly in the American and French revolutions of the 1770s and 1780s. For example, Thomas Paine's simple argument for independence, a republic, and democracy in *Common Sense* popularized the demands of the American revolutionaries, and the pamphlet became an instant bestseller. In France, the most radical faction of the revolution, the Jacobins, idolized Rousseau, and arranged

1806
After nearly 1,000 years of existence, the **Holy Roman empire is dissolved** by the Treaty of Pressburg.

1810
Wars of independence begin in **Latin America**, led by Venezuelan army officer Simón Bolívar.

1815
French emperor **Napoleon Bonaparte is defeated** by a British-led coalition at the Battle of Waterloo.

1820
Georg Hegel's *Elements of the Philosophy of Right* argues that freedom derives from **complex social arrangements**.

1821
The Greek War for Independence against Ottoman rule begins, sparking further **nationalist revolts** in the Balkans.

1831
The Merthyr Uprising of mine workers in South Wales is suppressed; the **red flag** as a symbol of revolution is flown for the first time.

1837
The Upper Canada rebellion, led by republicans, fails to overthrow **British rule in Canada**.

1839
A People's Charter for democratic reform is launched in Britain, including **secret ballots** and **universal adult male suffrage**.

for his reburial in the Panthéon in Paris as a national hero, opposite the equally iconic Voltaire.

Belief that society could be reconstructed in a rational fashion, even through a radical break with the past, was gaining ground at the beginning of the 19th century. By the 1850s, revolutions had shaken Europe and national liberation movements had been successful across Latin America. British writer Mary Wollstonecraft helped to expand the argument that the ideals of Enlightened freedom should not exclude half of humanity, and that women's rights were an integral part of a just society.

New conservatism

In reaction to these and other radical thinkers, a new and more sophisticated style of conservative thought developed, exemplified by the Irish philosopher and politician Edmund Burke.

Burke used the language of freedom and rights to justify the rule of the wisest, and believed that it was more important to maintain social stability than to attempt radical reform. Healthy societies, Burke believed, could only develop over many generations. The bloody Reign of Terror that followed the revolution in France demonstrated for Burke the failings of radicalism.

Meanwhile, a distinctive style of liberal argument in defence of rights also began to develop. Proceeding on the basis of simple claims about humanity's desire for happiness, English philosopher Jeremy Bentham constructed a justification for limited democratic freedoms that respected property and identified the limits of government. Certain rights had been won in the past, but the need for government to balance competing claims would, Bentham held, limit any great extension of those rights in the future.

A more ambiguous variant of the same conclusions was provided by German philosopher Georg Hegel who, starting from an admiration for the French Revolution, argued for the need to understand freedom as possible only in a fully developed civil society, and ended his life a supporter of the autocratic Prussian state. His complex arguments provided a framework with which the next generation of thinkers would attempt to understand the failings of the post-revolutionary world. ■

TO RENOUNCE LIBERTY IS TO RENOUNCE BEING A MAN

JEAN-JACQUES ROUSSEAU (1712–1778)

IN CONTEXT

IDEOLOGY
Republicanism

FOCUS
The general will

BEFORE
1513 Niccolò Machiavelli's *The Prince* offers a modern form of politics in which a ruler's morality and the concerns of state are strictly separate.

1651 Thomas Hobbes's *Leviathan* argues for the foundation of the state on the basis of the social contract.

AFTER
1789 The Jacobin Club begins meeting in Paris. Its extremist members attempt to apply Rousseau's principles to revolutionary politics.

1791 In Britain, Edmund Burke blames Rousseau for the "excesses" of the French Revolution.

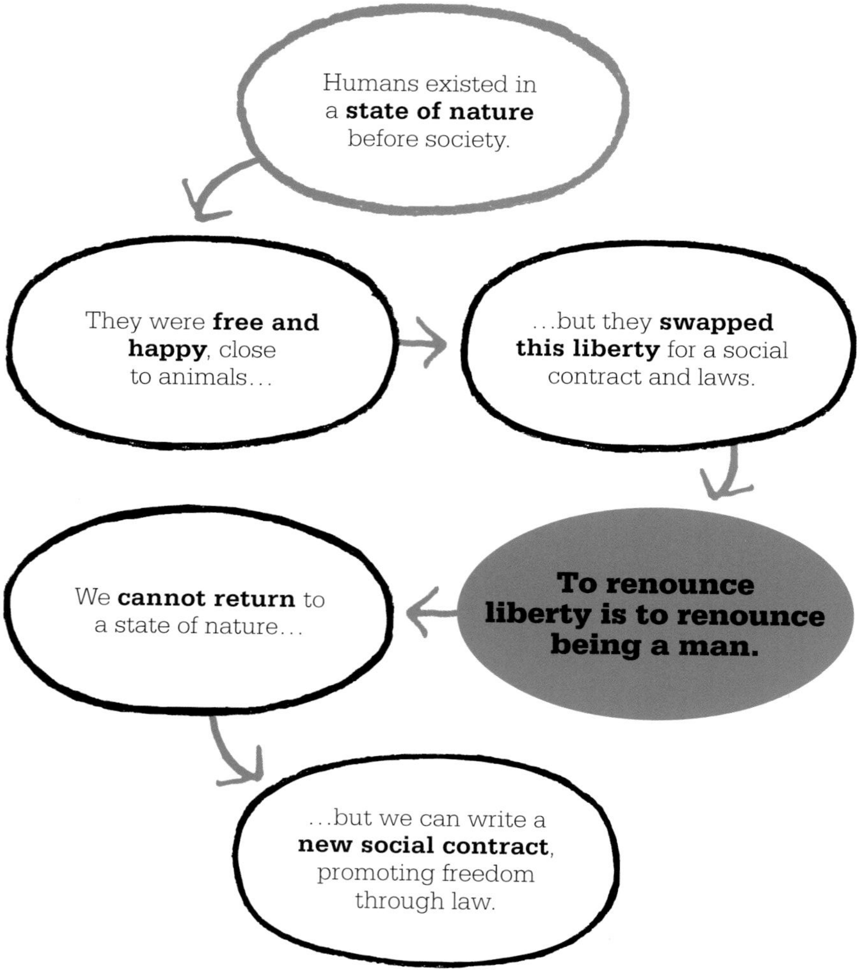

For centuries in Western Europe, a certain style of thinking about human affairs prevailed. Under the sway of the Catholic Church, the writings of ancient Greece and Rome had been steadily studied and rehabilitated, with outstanding intellectuals such as Augustine of Hippo and Thomas Aquinas rediscovering ancient thinkers. A scholastic approach, treating history and society as essentially unchanging and the higher purpose of morality as fixed by God, had come to dominate the ways in which society was considered. It took the upheavals associated with the development of capitalism and urban life to begin to tear this approach apart.

Rethinking the status quo

In the 16th century, Niccolò Machiavelli, in a radical departure with the past, had turned the scholastic tradition on its head in *The Prince*, drawing on ancient examples not to act as a guide to a moral life, but to demonstrate how an effective statecraft or politics could be cynically performed. Thomas Hobbes, writing his *Leviathan* during the English Civil War of the mid-17th century, used the scientific method of deduction, rather than the reading of ancient texts, to argue for the necessity of a strong state to preserve security among the people.

However, it was Jean-Jacques Rousseau, an idiosyncratic Swiss exile from Geneva whose personal life scandalized polite society, who proposed the most radical break with the past. Rousseau's autobiographical *Confessions*, published after his death, reveal

See also: Ibn Khaldun 72–73 ▪ Niccolò Machiavelli 74–81 ▪ Hugo Grotius 94–95 ▪ Thomas Hobbes 96–103 ▪ Edmund Burke 130–33 ▪ Hannah Arendt 282–83

> You are undone if you once forget that the fruits of the Earth belong to us all, and the Earth itself to nobody.
> **Jean-Jacques Rousseau**

that it was during his time in the Italian island-port of Venice – while working as an underpaid ambassadorial secretary – that he decided "everything depends entirely on politics". People were not inherently evil, but could become so under evil governments. The virtues he saw in Geneva, and the vices in Venice – in particular, the sad decline of the city-state from its glorious past – could be traced not to human character, but to human institutions.

Society shaped by politics

In his *Discourse on Inequality* of 1754, Rousseau broke with previous political philosophy. The ancient Greeks and others writing on society – including Ibn Khaldun in the 14th century – viewed political processes as subject to their own laws, working with an unchanging human nature. The Greeks, in particular, had a cyclical view of political change in which good or virtuous modes of government – whether monarchy, democracy, or aristocracy – would degenerate into various forms of tyranny before the cycle was renewed again. Society, as such, did not change, merely its form of government.

Rousseau disagreed. If, as he argued, society could be shaped by its political institutions, there was – in theory – no limit to the ability of political action to reshape society for the better.

This assertion marked Rousseau out as a distinctively modern thinker. Nobody before him had systematically thought of society as something distinct from its political institutions, as an entity that was itself capable of being studied and acted upon. Rousseau was the first, even among the philosophers of the Enlightenment, to reason in terms of social relations among people.

This new theory begged an obvious question: if human society was open to political change, why, then was it so obviously imperfect?

On property and inequality

Rousseau provided, again, an exceptional answer, and one that scandalized his fellow philosophers. As his starting point, he asked that we consider humans without society. Thomas Hobbes had argued such people would be savages, living lives that were "poor, nasty, brutish, and short", but Rousseau asserted quite the opposite. Human beings free from society were well-disposed, happy creatures, content in their state of nature. Only two principles guided them: the first, a natural self-love and desire for self-preservation; the second, a compassion for their fellow human beings. The combination of the two ensured that humanity reproduced itself, generation after generation, in a state close to that of other animals. »

The corruption Rousseau found in Venice exemplified for him the way in which bad government causes people to be bad. He contrasted this with the propriety of his home town, Geneva.

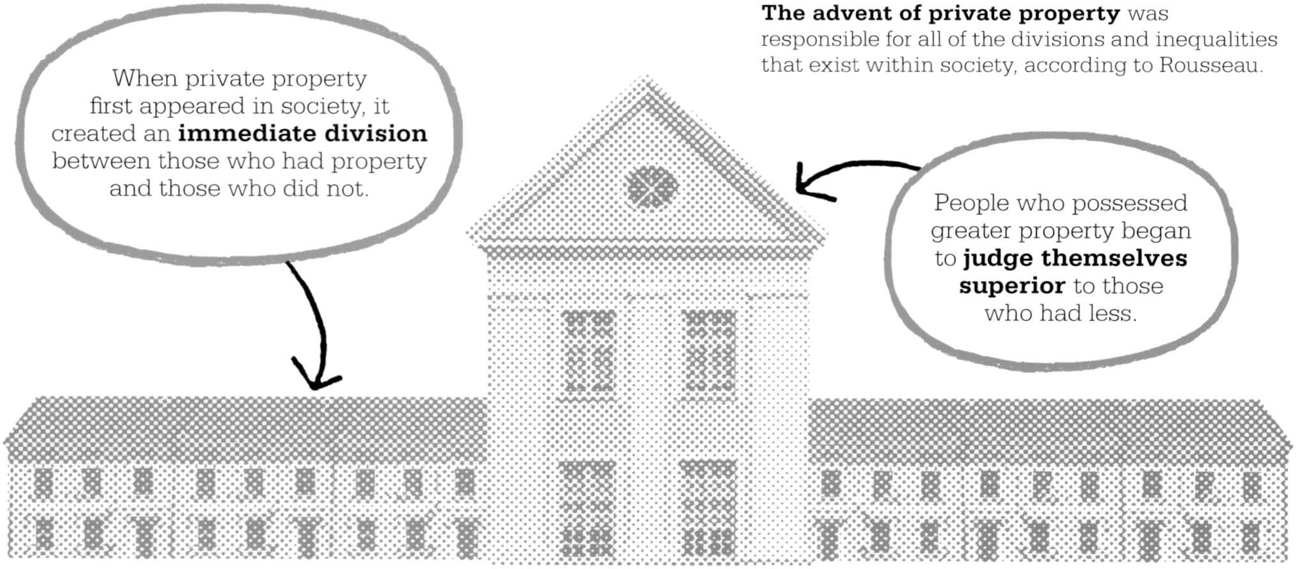

The advent of private property was responsible for all of the divisions and inequalities that exist within society, according to Rousseau.

This happy condition was, however, brutally brought to a close by the creation of civil society and, in particular, the development of private property. The arrival of private property imposed an immediate inequality on humanity that did not previously exist – between those who possessed property, and those who did not. By instituting this inequality, private property provided the foundations of further divisions in society – between those of master and slave, and then in the separation of families. On the foundation of these new divisions, private property then provided the mechanism by which a natural self-love turned into destructive love of self, now driven by jealousy and pride, and capable of turning against other human beings. It became possible to possess, and acquire, and to judge oneself against others on the basis of this material wealth. Civil society was the result of division and conflict working against a natural harmony.

> The mere impulse of appetite is slavery, while obedience to the law we prescribe to ourselves is liberty.
> **Jean-Jacques Rousseau**

The loss of liberty

Rousseau built on this argument in *The Social Contract*, published in 1762. "Man was born free, and he is everywhere in chains," he wrote. Whereas his earlier writings had been resolutely bleak in their opposition to conventional society, *The Social Contract* sought to provide the positive foundations for politics. Like Hobbes and Hugo Grotius before him, Rousseau saw the emergence of a sovereign power in society as the result of a social contract. People could choose to forfeit their own rights to a government, handing over their full liberty to a sovereign in return for the king – in Hobbes's account – providing security and protection. Hobbes argued that life without a sovereign pushed humanity back to a vile state of nature. By handing over a degree of liberty – in particular, liberty to use force – and swearing obedience, a people could guarantee peace, since the sovereign could end disputes and enforce punishments.

Rousseau rejected this. It was impossible, he thought, for any person or persons to hand over their liberty without also handing over their humanity and therefore destroying morality. A sovereign could not hold absolute authority, since it was impossible for a free man to enslave himself. Establishing a ruler superior to the rest of society transformed humanity's natural equality into a permanent, political inequality. For Rousseau, the social contract envisaged by Hobbes was a form of hoax by the rich against the poor – there was no other way that the poor would agree to a state of affairs in which the social contract preserved inequality.

The societies that existed, then, were not formed in the state of nature, deriving their legitimacy from improvement over that time. Rather, Rousseau argued, they were formed after we had left the state of nature, and property rights – with the resultant inequalities – had been established. Once property rights were in place, conflicts would ensue over the distribution of those rights. It was civil society and property that led to war, with the state as the agency through which war could be pursued.

Revising the social contract

What Rousseau offered in *The Social Contract* was the possibility of this dire situation transforming into its opposite. The state and civil society were burdens on individuals, depriving them of a natural freedom. But they could be changed into positive extensions of our freedom, if political institutions and society were organized effectively. The social contract, instead of being a pact written in fear of our evil natures, could be a contract written in the hope of improving ourselves. The state of nature might have been free, but it meant people had no greater ideals than that of their animal appetites. More sophisticated desires could only appear outside the state of nature, in civil society. To achieve this, a new kind of social contract would be written.

Where Hobbes saw law only as a restraint, and freedom existing only in the absence of law, Rousseau argued that laws could become an extension of our freedom, provided that those subject to the law also prescribed the law. Freedom could be won within the state, rather than against it. To achieve this, the whole people must become sovereign. A legitimate state is one that offers greater freedom than is obtainable in the raw state of nature. To secure that positive freedom, a people must also be equal. In Rousseau's new world, liberty and equality march together, rather than in opposition.

Popular sovereignty

In *The Social Contract*, Rousseau laid down, in outline, many of the claims that would underlie the development of the left in politics over subsequent centuries: a belief that freedom and equality were partners, not enemies; a belief in the ability of law and the state to improve society; and a belief in the people as a sovereign entity, from which the state gained its legitimacy. Despite the »

Hobbes and Rousseau compared

	In the state of nature...	The social contract...	Freedom...
Hobbes	 ...life is nasty, brutish, and short.	 ...is necessary to guarantee peace and avoid the state of nature.	 ...can exist only in the absence of law.
Rousseau	 ...people are contented, happy creatures.	 ...preserves inequalities and destroys a person's humanity.	 ...can be won within the bounds of law.

Rousseau was not against property, so long as it was distributed fairly. He considered a small, agrarian republic in which all citizens were smallholders to be an ideal form of state.

vehemence of his attack on private property, Rousseau was not a socialist. He believed that the total abolition of private property would pitch liberty and equality into conflict, whereas a moderately fair distribution of property could enhance freedom. Indeed, he later went on to argue for an agrarian republic of smallholding farmers. Nonetheless, Rousseau's ideas were, for the time, dramatically radical. By investing the whole people with sovereignty, and by identifying sovereignty with equality, he offered a challenge to an entire existing tradition of Western political thought.

A new contract

Rousseau did not equate this idea of popular sovereignty with democracy as such, fearing that a directly democratic government, requiring all citizens to participate, was uniquely prone to corruption and civil war. Instead, he envisaged sovereignty being invested in popular assemblies capable of delegating the tasks of government – via a new social contract, or a constitution – to an executive. The sovereign people would embody the "general will", an expression of popular assent. Day-to-day government, however, would depend on specific decisions, requiring a "particular will".

It was in this very distinction, Rousseau thought, that conflict between the "general will" and the "particular will" opened up, paving the way for the corruption of the sovereign people. It was this corruption that so marked the world of Rousseau's time, in his view. Instead of acting as a collective, sovereign body, the people were consumed by the pursuit of private interests. In place of the freedom of popular sovereignty, society had pushed people into separate, private spheres of endeavour, whether in the arts, science, or literature, or in the division of labour. This numbed people into habitual deference, and instilled a spirit of passivity.

To ensure the government was an authentic expression of the popular, general will, Rousseau believed that participation in its assemblies and procedures should be compulsory, removing – as far as possible – the temptations of the private will. But this belief in the necessity of combating private desires is exactly where Rousseau's later, liberal critics have found the deepest fault.

Private versus general will

The "general will", however desirable in theory, could easily be vested in deeply oppressive

Jean-Jacques Rousseau

Jean-Jacques Rousseau was born in Geneva, Switzerland. The son of a freeman entitled to vote in city elections, he never wavered in his appreciation of Geneva's liberal institutions. Inheriting a large library and a voracious appetite for reading, Rousseau received no formal education. At the age of 15, an introduction to the noblewoman Françoise-Louise de Warens led to his conversion to Catholicism, exile from Geneva, and disownment by his father.

Rousseau began studying in earnest in his 20s and was appointed secretary to the ambassador to Venice in 1743. He left soon after for Paris, where he built a reputation as a controversial essayist. When his books were banned in France and Geneva, he fled briefly to London, but soon returned to France where he spent the rest of his life.

Key works

1754 *Discourse on the Origin and Basis of Inequality Among Men*
1762 *Emile*
1762 *The Social Contract*
1770 *Confessions*

The French Revolution began when an angry mob stormed the Bastille in Paris on 14 July 1789. The medieval fortress and prison was a symbol of royal power.

> We are approaching a state of crisis and the age of revolutions.
> **Jean-Jacques Rousseau**

arrangements. Not least was the difficulty in actually ascertaining the "general will". The road for an individual or a group claiming to express the general will, when merely exercising their own particular wills, was clearly wide open. Rousseau, in desiring to make the people sovereign, could be presented as the forefather of totalitarianism. What repressive regime since his time has not attempted to claim the support of "the people"?

Indeed, Rousseau's provisions against factions and divisions among the people – which he, like Machiavelli, saw as undermining the state – could certainly turn into a tyranny of the majority, in which unpopular minorities suffer at the hands of those exercising the "general will". Rousseau's recommendation for dealing with this dilemma was to recognize the inevitability of factions, and to multiply them indefinitely – making so many particular wills that no one of them would stand a chance of representing the general will, nor would any one faction be dominant enough to oppose the general will.

States formed under illegitimate social contracts based on the fraud of the powerful were not capable of expressing this will, precisely because their subjects were bound to them only by deference to authority, not by mutual assent. However, if the apparent contracts between rulers and ruled were illegitimate, based on a denial of people's sovereignty rather than its expression, it would follow that the people had every right to depose their rulers. That, at least, is how the more radical of Rousseau's later followers came to interpret him. Rousseau himself was at best ambiguous on the issue of outright revolt, frequently denouncing violence and civil unrest and urging respect for existing laws.

A revolutionary icon

Rousseau's belief in the sovereignty of the people, and the perfectibility of both people and society, has had an immense impact. In the French Revolution, the Jacobins adopted him as a figurehead for their own belief in the necessity of a ruthlessly complete, egalitarian transformation of French society. In 1794, he was reinterred in the Panthéon, Paris, as a national hero. Over the next two centuries, Rousseau's work also acted as a touchstone for all those who wished to see society radically overhauled for the common good, from Karl Marx onwards.

Similarly, the arguments against Rousseau, during his life and after, have helped to shape both conservative and liberal thought. In 1791, Edmund Burke, one of the founders of modern conservatism, held Rousseau to be almost personally responsible for the French Revolution and what he saw as its excesses. Writing almost 200 years later, the radical-liberal philosopher Hannah Arendt believed the errors in Rousseau's thinking helped to drive the Revolution away from its liberal roots. ■

NO GENERALLY VALID PRINCIPLE OF LEGISLATION CAN BE BASED ON HAPPINESS

IMMANUEL KANT (1724–1804)

IN CONTEXT

IDEOLOGY
Freedom

FOCUS
Personal responsibility

BEFORE
380 BCE Plato argues in the *Republic* that the state's main aim is to ensure the happiness of all people.

1689 In his *Second Treatise on Government*, John Locke states that by a "social contract" people delegate their right of self-protection to government.

AFTER
1851 Pierre-Joseph Proudhon argues that the social contract should be between individuals, not between individuals and government.

1971 In his book *A Theory of Justice*, John Rawls combines Kant's idea of autonomy with Social Choice theory.

In 1793, the great German philosopher Immanuel Kant wrote an essay entitled "On the Common Saying: 'That may be right in theory, but it does not work in practice'", which is often now referred to simply as *Theory and Practice*. The essay was written in a year of momentous political change: George Washington became the first president of the US, the German city of Mainz declared itself an independent republic, and the French Revolution reached its height with the execution of King Louis XVI and Marie Antoinette. Kant's essay examined not only political theory and practice, but also the

See also: Plato 34–39 ▪ Thomas Hobbes 96–103 ▪ John Locke 104–09 ▪ Jean-Jacques Rousseau 118–25 ▪ Jeremy Bentham 144–49 ▪ John Rawls 298–303

Happiness is gained and felt in **different ways** by different people.

→ This means that it **cannot** be used to **generate fixed principles** that are equally applicable to everyone.

→ Since **laws** must be agreed as **applicable to all**, and reflective of the **common will**…

→ **…no generally valid principle of legislation can be based on happiness.**

legitimacy of government itself. This was a topic that had become literally a matter of life or death.

In stating that "no generally valid principle of legislation can be based on happiness", Kant argues with a position taken by the Greek philosopher Plato some 2,000 years earlier. Kant's essay states that happiness does not work as a basis for law. No one can – nor should – try to define what happiness is for someone else, so a rule based on happiness cannot be applied consistently. "For… the highly conflicting and variable illusions as to what happiness is," Kant wrote, "… make all fixed principles impossible, so that happiness alone can never be a suitable principle of legislation." What is crucial instead, he believed, is that the state ensures people's freedom within the law "so that each remains free to seek his happiness in whatever way he thinks best, so long as he does not violate the lawful freedom and rights of his fellow subjects at large."

Kant considers what would happen in a society where people live "in a state of nature", free to pursue their own desires. He sees the main problem as a conflict of interests. What do you do, for instance, if your neighbour moves into your house and throws you out, and there are no laws to stop him or give you any redress? Kant claims that a state of nature is a recipe for anarchy, in which disputes cannot be settled peacefully. For this reason, people willingly "abandon the state of nature… in order to submit to external public and lawful coercion." Kant's position follows on from the English philosopher John Locke's earlier idea of the social contract, which says that people make a contract with the state in which they each freely consent to give up some of their freedom in exchange for the state's protection.

The consent of all

Kant asserts that governments must remember that they govern only by the people's consent – not »

King Louis XVI of France was executed in 1793. For Kant, the French Revolution was a warning to all governments that they must rule for the good of all the people.

the consent of a few people, nor even a majority, but of the entire population. What counts is that no one among the population might potentially object to a proposed law. "For if the law is such that a whole people could not possibly agree to it, it is unjust; but if it is at least possible that a people could agree to it, it is our duty to consider the law just."

Kant's idea acts as an important guide for the citizen as well as the government, because he is also saying that if a government passes a law that you consider wrong, it is still your moral duty to obey it. You might think it is wrong to pay taxes to your government to fund a war, but you should not withhold your taxes because you feel the war is unjust or unnecessary, because "it is at least possible that the war is inevitable and the tax indispensable".

However, for Kant, although subjects have a duty to obey the law, they also have to take individual responsibility for their moral choices. He says that morals have a "categorical imperative". By this, he means that an individual should only follow rules or maxims that they believe should apply to everyone. Each person, he says, must act as though they were law-makers through each of the moral choices they make.

> No one can compel me to be happy in accordance with his conception of the welfare of others.
> **Immanuel Kant**

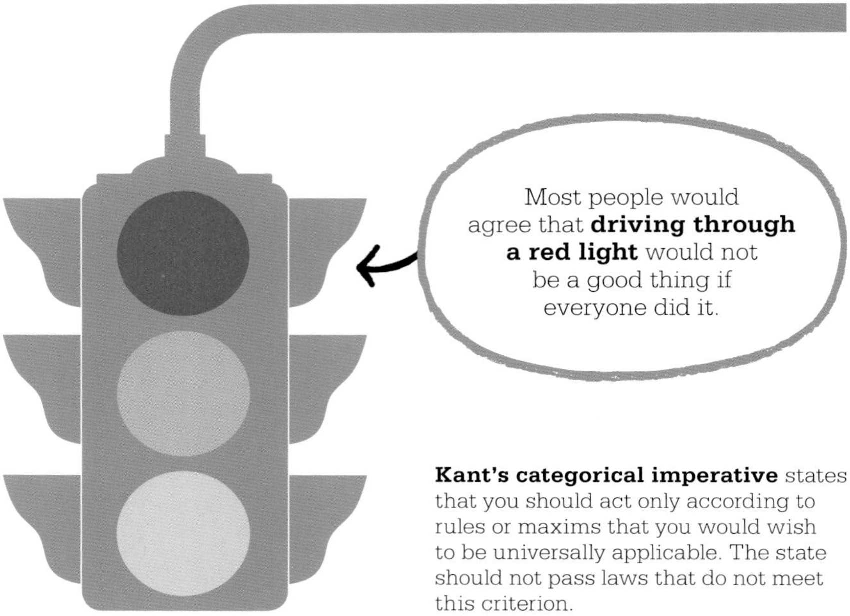

Kant's categorical imperative states that you should act only according to rules or maxims that you would wish to be universally applicable. The state should not pass laws that do not meet this criterion.

The will of the people

At the heart of Kant's philosophy – and applicable to both morality and politics – is the notion of autonomy. This is the idea that the human will is and must be wholly independent. Freedom is not being unbound by any law, but being bound by laws of one's own making. The link between morals and state laws is direct: the legitimacy of both morality and laws is that they are based on the rational desires of the people; the social contract is "based on a coalition of the wills of all private individuals in a nation". State laws must be literally "the will of the people". So, if we agree to be governed, we must rationally agree to obey every law the government passes. By the same token, though, the laws of an external government, such as an occupying force or colonial power, have no legitimacy.

Kant asks whether a government has a role in promoting the happiness of its people. He is clear that since only an individual can decide what makes him happy, any legislation designed to improve people's lot must be based on their actual wishes, not what the government believes will be good for them. Nor should a government compel individuals to make other people happy. It cannot, for example, force you to go and see your grandmother regularly, even though it might be good for the country's general happiness if grandmothers were properly appreciated.

A state without happiness?

Some commentators have argued that Kant does not see happiness as playing any part in government thinking. If this were the case, however, the state would do no more than protect its citizens physically. It would have no business providing education, building things such as hospitals, art galleries and museums, roads,

> All right consists solely in the restriction of the freedom of others.
> **Immanuel Kant**

and railways, or in looking after people's welfare in any way. This position may be logically consistent, but it is not a recipe for a state that very many of us would want to live under.

All the same, in the last 50 years, some thinkers have used this interpretation of Kant as a basis for the privatization of state industries, and for the dismantling of the welfare system on the grounds that it is an infringement of individual freedom to expect people to pay taxes for other people's happiness. However, other commentators believe this is a misunderstanding of Kant's position. They claim that Kant is not necessarily saying the promotion of happiness should not play a part in the thinking of the state – just that happiness cannot be the sole criterion. In addition, Kant points out that happiness can only be found after a solid constitution, outlining the role of the state, is already in place. In *Theory and Practice*, he says "the doctrine that 'the public welfare is the supreme law of the state' retains its value and authority undiminished; but the public welfare which demands first consideration lies precisely in that legal constitution which guarantees everyone his freedom within the law."

Rights and happiness

Two years before *Theory and Practice,* in an essay entitled *Perpetual Peace*, Kant wrote that governments have two sets of duties: to protect the rights and liberties of the people as a matter of justice; and to promote the happiness of the people, as long as they can do this without diminishing the rights and freedom of the people.

In recent years, commentators have wondered whether governments, perhaps still powerfully influenced by the narrower interpretation of Kant's advice, have concentrated too much on economics and justice and left happiness out of the picture. Responding to these criticisms, in 2008 France's then president Nicolas Sarkozy commissioned a report from a team led by US economist Joseph Stiglitz to measure his country's "wellbeing". ■

Intervention in Afghanistan may be unpopular with the public in the US and Europe but, according to Kant, this discontent does not give individuals the right to withhold their taxes.

Immanuel Kant

The German philosopher Immanuel Kant was born in Königsberg, Prussia (now Kaliningrad in Russia), and lived there his whole life. The fourth of nine children of Lutheran parents, he was educated at a Lutheran school, where he gained a love of Latin but took a strong dislike to religious introspection. At the age of 16, he enrolled as a theology student, but soon became fascinated by philosophy, mathematics, and physics.

Kant worked at the University of Königsberg as an unpaid lecturer and sub-librarian for 15 years before becoming a professor of logic and metaphysics at the age of 46. He gained international fame with the publication of his *Critiques*, and continued to teach for the rest of his life. He is considered by many to be the greatest thinker of the 18th century.

Key works

1781 *Critique of Pure Reason* (revised 1787)
1788 *Critique of Practical Reason*
1793 *Theory and Practice*

THE PASSIONS OF INDIVIDUALS SHOULD BE SUBJECTED

EDMUND BURKE (1729–1797)

IN CONTEXT

IDEOLOGY
Conservativism

FOCUS
Political tradition

BEFORE
1688 English landowners force the abdication of James II in the Glorious Revolution.

1748 Montesquieu asserts that liberty is maintained in England by a balance of power in different parts of society.

AFTER
1790–91 Paine's *Rights of Man* and Wollstonecraft's *A Vindication of the Rights of Woman* counter Burke's work.

1867–94 Marx's *Capital* states that the overthrow of the status quo is inevitable.

1962 Michael Oakeshott upholds the importance of tradition in public institutions.

In 1790, British statesman and political theorist Edmund Burke wrote one of the first and most cogent criticisms of the revolution in France, which had begun the previous year. His pamphlet, entitled "Reflections on the French Revolution", suggested that the passions of individuals should not be allowed to dictate political judgments.

When the revolution began, Burke had been surprised by it, but not overtly critical. He was shocked by the ferocity of the insurgents, but admired their revolutionary spirit – much as he had admired the American revolutionaries in their quarrel with the English crown.

See also: Jean-Jacques Rousseau 118–25 ▪ Thomas Paine 134–39 ▪ Thomas Jefferson 140–41 ▪ Georg Hegel 156–59 ▪ Karl Marx 188–93 ▪ Vladimir Lenin 226–33 ▪ Michael Oakeshott 276–77 ▪ Michel Foucault 310–11

By the time Burke was writing his pamphlet, the revolution had gathered momentum. Food was scarce, and rumours abounded that the king and aristocrats were set to overthrow the Third Estate (the rebellious people). Peasants rose up against their ruling lords, who – in fear for their lives – granted them their freedom through the Declaration of the Rights of Man and of the Citizen. This affirmed that all people had "natural rights" to liberty, property, and security, and to resist oppression.

However, the king refused to sanction the Declaration, and on 5 October 1789 crowds of Parisians marched to Versailles to join the peasants in forcing the king and his family back to Paris. For Burke, this was a step too far, and it provoked him to write his critical pamphlet – which has been seen ever since as the classic rebuttal to would-be revolutionaries.

Government as organism

Burke was a Whig, a member of a British political party that favoured the gradual progress of society – as opposed to the Tory party, which strove to maintain the status quo. Burke championed emancipation for Catholics in Ireland and for India from the corrupt East India Company. But, unlike other Whigs, he believed the continuity of government was sacrosanct. In *Reflections*, he argues that government is like a living thing, with a past and a future. We cannot kill it and start anew, as the French revolutionaries aimed to do.

Burke sees government as a complex organism that grows over time into the subtle, living form that it is today. The nuances of its political being – from the behaviour of monarchs to the inherited aristocratic codes of behaviour – have developed over generations in such an elaborate way that nobody can understand how it all works. The habit of government is so deep-rooted among the ruling class, he says, that they barely have to think about it. Anyone believing they can use their powers of reason to destroy society and build a better one from scratch – such as Enlightenment thinker Jean-Jacques Rousseau – is foolish and arrogant.

Abstract rights

Burke is particularly damning of the Enlightenment concept of natural rights. They may be all »

John Bull is tempted by the devil, who hangs from the Tree of Liberty, symbolizing the fear of French revolutionary zeal spreading to England at the time of Burke's writings.

Government is a **human invention** to oversee human needs in society.

↓

But some human needs and desires **conflict** with those of other people.

↓

Government must **judge** between conflicting wants to produce the **fairest outcome**.

↓

The individual's passions must be subjected to the government's laws.

very well in theory, he says, but that's where the problem lies: "their abstract perfection is their practical defect". Also, for Burke, a theoretical right to a good or service is of no use whatever if there is no means to procure it. There is no end to what people may reasonably claim as rights. In reality, rights are simply what people want, and it is the government's task to mediate between the wants of people. Some wants can even include restraint on the wants of others.

It is a fundamental rule of any civil society, Burke says, "that no man should be judge in his own cause". To live in a free and just society, a man must give up his right to determine many things he deems essential. In claiming that "the passions of individuals should be subjected", Burke means that society must control the unruly will of the individual for the good of the rest. If everyone is allowed to behave as he wishes, expressing every passion and whim, the result is chaos. Indeed, not just individuals but the masses as a whole must be so constrained, "by a power out of themselves".

This refereeing role requires "a deep knowledge of human nature and human necessities", and is so complex that theoretical rights are a distraction.

Habit and prejudice

Burke was sceptical of individual rights, arguing instead for tradition and habit. He viewed government as an inheritance to be carried forward safely into the future, and made a distinction between England's Glorious Revolution of 1688 and France's ongoing turmoil. The English revolution, which replaced the Catholic-leaning King James II with the Protestant William and Mary, was about preserving the status quo against a wayward monarch, not fabricating a new government, which would fill Burke with "disgust and horror".

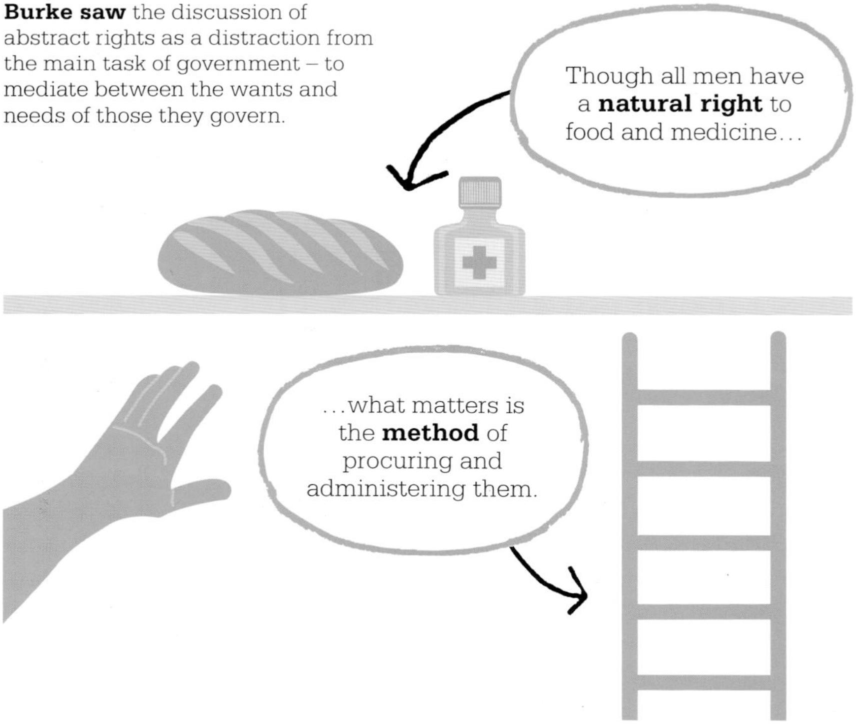

Burke saw the discussion of abstract rights as a distraction from the main task of government – to mediate between the wants and needs of those they govern.

> The social contract… is between those who are living, those who are dead, and those who are to be born.
> **Edmund Burke**

Burke defended an unthinking emotional response to respect the king and parliament as "the general bank and capital of nations". He saw this as far superior to the vagaries of individual reason, but regarded prejudice as an age-old wisdom that could produce a fast, automatic response in emergencies that left the rational man hesitating.

The consequences of ignoring these traditions may be dire, Burke warned. New men entering the political fray would not be able to run an existing government, let alone a new one. Struggles between factions trying to step into the power vacuum would inevitably lead to bloodshed and terror – and a chaos so consuming that the military would have to take over.

The Burke revolution

Burke's prediction of both the Terror in the French Revolution, which occurred in 1793 and 1794, and the rise of Napoleon Bonaparte in 1799, earned him a reputation as something of a seer. His arguments

Napoleon Bonaparte swept to power in 1799, fulfilling Edmund Burke's 1790 prediction that a military dictatorship would follow the revolutionary overthrow of the monarchy in France.

appealed to those on the right, but were also a surprise to those on the left. Thomas Jefferson, then living in France as a US diplomat, wrote, "The Revolution in France does not astonish me as much as the revolution in Mr Burke". In England, Thomas Paine immediately wrote *The Rights of Man* – published in 1791 – to challenge Burke's argument against natural rights.

The power of property

Burke believed that society's stability was underpinned by inherited property – the massive inherited properties of the landowning aristocracy. Only such rich landowners had the power, self-interest, and inherited political skill, Burke asserted, to prevent the monarchy over-reaching itself. The great size of their landholdings also acted as a natural protection for the lesser properties around them. In any case, he argued, the redistribution from the few to the many could only ever result in "inconceivably small" gains.

Although Napoleon was eventually defeated, the revolutions that rolled on through Europe long after Burke's death gave his ideas a special place in the hearts of those frightened by the uprisings. Burke's plea for the continuity of government and society seemed to some to be a beacon of sanity in a mad world. However, for Karl Marx – who was particularly critical of Burke's ideas on property – and many others, Burke's defence of inequality was unacceptable. Burke argued persuasively against the trashing of tradition, but according to his critics, this leads ultimately to the defence of societies in which the majority are kept in a life of servitude, with no prospect of betterment and no say in their future. Burke's defence of prejudice, intended as a call for sympathy for people's natural inclinations, can end up as an argument for blind bigotry. His assertion that the passions of individuals should be subjected is potentially a justification for censorship, the persecution of dissenters, and a police state. ■

> "The great feudal lords created an incomparably larger proletariat by the forcible driving of the peasantry from the land."
> **Karl Marx**

Edmund Burke

Born in Dublin, Ireland, in 1729, Burke was raised as a Protestant, while his sister, Juliana, was raised a Catholic. He initially trained as a lawyer, but soon gave up law to become a writer. In 1756, he published *A Vindication of Natural Society*, a satire of Tory leader Lord Bolingbroke's views on religion. Soon after, he became private secretary to Lord Rockingham, the Whig prime minister.

In 1774, Burke became a Member of Parliament, later losing his seat due to the unpopularity of his views on the emancipation of Catholics. His fight for the abolition of capital punishment earned him a reputation as a progressive. However, his criticism of the French Revolution caused a spilt with the radical wing of his Whig party, and today he is remembered more for his conservative philosophy than his liberal views.

Key works

1756 *A Vindication of Natural Society*
1770 *Thoughts on the Cause of the Present Discontents*
1790 *Reflections on the Revolution in France*

RIGHTS DEPENDENT ON PROPERTY ARE THE MOST PRECARIOUS

THOMAS PAINE (1737–1809)

IN CONTEXT

IDEOLOGY
Republicanism

FOCUS
Universal male suffrage

BEFORE
508 BCE Democracy in Athens gives all male citizens a vote.

1647 A radical part of Oliver Cromwell's New Model Army calls for universal male suffrage and an end to monarchy.

1762 Jean-Jacques Rousseau publishes *The Social Contract*, arguing that sovereignty lies with the whole people.

AFTER
1839–48 Chartism, a mass movement in Britain, calls for universal male suffrage.

1871 A newly united German empire grants universal male suffrage.

1917–19 As World War I ends, democratic republics replace monarchies across Europe.

Current rights to vote depend on **ownership of property**.

Property owners **abuse their position of privilege** to run society for their **own benefit**.

This breeds resentment among the poor, who will **rise up against the rich** if their needs are neglected.

Rights dependent on property are the most precarious.

Rights should be granted without property qualification.

The English Revolution, which reached the peak of its radicalism with the trial and execution of King Charles I in 1649, had fizzled out by the end of the 17th century. The "Glorious Revolution" of 1688 had seen the restoration of the monarchy, now subordinate to Parliament, and the stabilization of the British state. No formal constitution was written, and the brief experiment with a republic under Oliver Cromwell was over. The new government was a hybrid made of a corrupt and unrepresentative Lower House in the Commons, a corrupt and unelected Upper House in the Lords, and a monarch who was still nominally head of state.

The 1689 Bill of Rights that set out the parameters for the new government was a compromise that satisfied few, least of all those most obviously excluded from it: the Irish, Catholics, and non-conformists; the poor and the artisans; even the more prosperous middle classes and employees of the state. It was from this milieu that Thomas Paine emerged, after emigrating to America in 1774. In a series of incendiary and wildly popular pamphlets, he sought to reclaim arguments for democracy and republicanism that had been made during Cromwell's time.

The case for democracy

In *Common Sense*, published anonymously in Philadelphia in 1776, Paine made the case for a radical break by Britain's North American colonists from both the British empire and constitutional monarchy. Like Hobbes and Rousseau before him, he argued that people come to form natural attachments to each other, creating

See also: Thomas Hobbes 96–103 ▪ John Locke 104–09 ▪ Jean-Jacques Rousseau 118–25 ▪ Edmund Burke 130–33 ▪ Thomas Jefferson 140–41 ▪ Oliver Cromwell 333 ▪ John Lilburne 333 ▪ George Washington 334

> When we are planning for posterity, we ought to remember that virtue is not hereditary.
> **Thomas Paine**

a society from individuals. As these attachments of family, friendship, or trade become more complex, they in turn create a need for regulation. These regulations are systematized into laws, and a government is erected to create and enforce those laws. These laws are intended to act for the people, but there are too many people to make collective decisions. Democracy is required, to elect representatives.

Democracy, Paine held, was the most natural way to balance the needs of society with those of government. Voting would act as the regulating instrument between society and government, allowing society to shape government so that it more closely corresponded to social needs. Institutions such as monarchy were unnatural, since the hereditary principle stood apart from society as a whole, and monarchs could act in their own interests.

Even a mixed state with a constitutional monarchy, as advocated by John Locke, would be dangerous, since a monarch could easily obtain more power and circumvent laws. Paine believed it was better to do away with the monarch entirely.

It followed that America's best course of action in its war with the British empire was to refuse any compromise on the issue of the monarchy. Only with full independence could a democratic society be built. Paine's clear and unequivocal call for a democratic republic was an immediate success in the midst of the Revolutionary War against the British empire. Returning to England in 1787, he visited France two years later, and became a firm supporter of the French Revolution.

Reflections on revolution

On returning from France, Paine had a rude awakening. Edmund Burke, MP for Bristol and one of the founders of modern conservative thought, had strongly supported the rights of American colonies to independence. Burke and Paine had been on friendly terms since Paine's arrival back in England, but Burke had ferociously denounced the French Revolution, claiming in his 1790 *Reflections on the Revolution in France* that by its radicalism it threatened the very order of society. Burke viewed society as an organic whole, not amenable to sudden change. The American Revolution and Britain's "Glorious Revolution" did not directly threaten long-established rights, but merely corrected some clear deformities in the system. In particular, they did not threaten the rights of property. But the situation in France, with its violent overthrow of the *ancien regime*, was clearly different.

Burke's opposition caused Paine to defend his position. He replied with *The Rights of Man*, printed in early 1791. Despite official »

The inattentive judges in William Hogarth's satirical *The Bench* (1758) are portrayed as members of an idle, incompetent, and venal judiciary that has little regard for society's rights.

The French National Assembly has its roots in the French Revolution's National Convention, which was the country's first governing assembly to be elected by universal male suffrage.

censorship, it became the best-known and widest-circulated of all English defences of the revolution in France. Paine argued for the rights of every generation to remake its political and social institutions as it saw fit, not bound by existing authority. A hereditary monarch had no claim to superiority over this right. Rights, not property, were the only hereditary principle, transmitted across the generations. A second part to the pamphlet, published in 1792, argued for a major programme of social welfare. By the end of the year, the two volumes had sold 200,000 copies.

An end to monarchy

Under threat of prosecution, and with "Church and King" mobs burning his figure in effigy, Paine offered a still more radical step. His *Letter Addressed to the Addresses on the Late Proclamation* was written against "the numerous rotten boroughs and corporation addresses" that had published the royal proclamation against "seditious libel" – the writing and printing of texts that attacked the state. Paine, denouncing this and other abuses as a new tyranny, called for an elected National Convention to draft a new, republican constitution for England. This was a direct call for revolution in all but name, taking France's republican National Convention as its model. Paine had returned to France shortly before the *Address* was published, and in his absence was found guilty of seditious libel.

The argument in the *Address* is brief, but tackles Burke head on. Although England's Bill of Rights of 1689 gave guarantees about the rights all subjects would enjoy in a constitutional monarchy, it was open to abuse. Paine detailed some of the most obnoxious instances of corruption, but he wanted to go further and tackle the system itself. By defending hereditary property as the supreme law, this system drove the corruption and abuse. The tyranny of William Pitt's government was a direct result of its defence of property. At the top of the regime was a hereditary monarch, and Parliament acted merely as a defence of Crown and property. Reform of the corrupt Parliament was not enough: the whole system had to be transformed, from the top down.

Universal male suffrage

Paine asserted that sovereignty should not lie with the monarch, but with the people, who have an

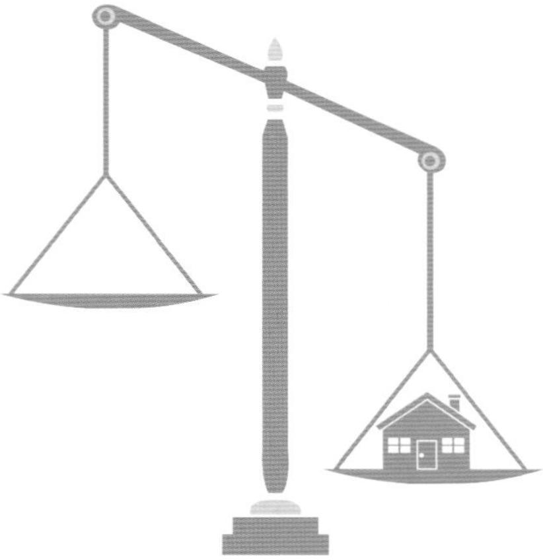

Property qualifications for voting create inequalities between the rich and the poor, leading to corruption and a monopoly of power.

Universal male suffrage redresses the balance – the rights of the rich and the poor must then be considered in the creation of policies.

> It will always be found, that when the rich protect the rights of the poor, the poor will protect the property of the rich.
> **Thomas Paine**

absolute right to make or unmake laws and governments as they see fit. The existing system contained no mechanism to allow the people to change the government. It was therefore necessary, Paine argued, to sidestep the system by electing a new assembly – a National Convention, as in France.

Paine attempted to popularize an argument made by Rousseau: that the "general will" of the people should be sovereign in a nation, and that with transparent and fair elections to the Convention, private interests and corrupt practices would be squeezed out. Universal male suffrage would determine the delegates to the Convention, and these delegates would be charged with drafting a new constitution for Britain. It was England's property qualification for voting that Paine held most responsible for the corruption and venality of the electoral system. Only in a system where the rights of both rich and poor were equally considered would each respect the other, and neither seek to rob the other.

A legacy for reform

Paine's short pamphlet never quite achieved the success of either *Common Sense* or *The Rights of Man*, but the radical argument presented in the *Address* – for a republic, a new constitution, and a National Convention elected by universal male suffrage – formed the core of reformers' demands in Britain for the next 50 years. The London Corresponding Society, from the 1790s onwards, called for a National Convention; the Chartists of the 1840s actually held a National Convention, which thoroughly alarmed the authorities; and the hated property qualification for voting was eventually removed in the 1867 Second Reform Act.

A Chartist Convention held a mass meeting at Kennington Common in London on 10 April 1848, demanding electoral reforms of the kind advocated by Thomas Paine.

It was in Paine's adopted countries of America and France that his ideas had the most impact – perhaps especially in the United States, where he is credited as one of the Founding Fathers of independence and the Constitution, and where his writings swayed thousands towards the cause of democracy and republicanism. ■

Thomas Paine

Thomas Paine was born in Thetford, England. He emigrated to America in 1774, having lost his job as a tax collector after agitating for better pay and conditions. With a recommendation from Benjamin Franklin, he became editor of a local magazine in Pennsylvania.

Common Sense was published in 1776, selling 100,000 copies in three months, among a colonial population of two million. In 1781, Paine helped to negotiate large sums from the French king for the American Revolution. Returning to London in 1790, and inspired by the French Revolution, he wrote *The Rights of Man*, which led to a charge of seditious libel. After fleeing to France, he was elected to the National Convention there, and avoided execution during the Terror. He returned to America in 1802 at President Jefferson's invitation, and died seven years later in New York.

Key works

1776 *Common Sense*
1791 *The Rights of Man*
1792 *Letter Addressed to the Addresses on the Late Proclamation*

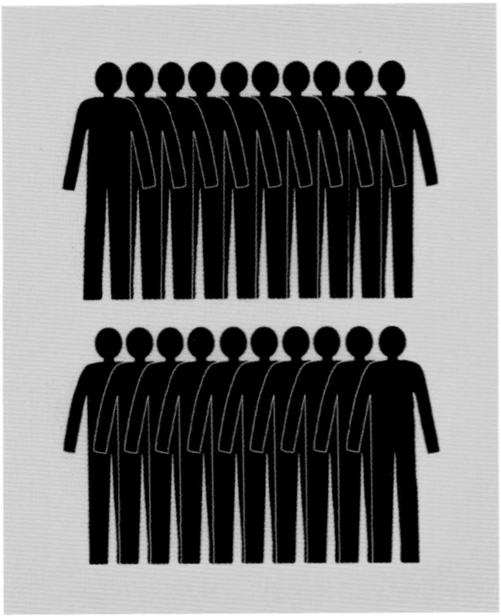

ALL MEN ARE CREATED EQUAL

THOMAS JEFFERSON (1742–1826)

IN CONTEXT

IDEOLOGY
Nationalism

FOCUS
Universal rights

BEFORE
1649 England's King Charles I is tried and executed for acting "against the public interest, common right, liberty, justice, and peace of the people".

1689 John Locke refutes the divine right of kings and insists sovereignty lies in the people.

AFTER
1789 The French Revolution's *Declaration of the Rights of Man and Citizen* asserts that all men "are born and remain free with equal rights".

1948 The UN adopts the *Universal Declaration of Human Rights*.

1998 DNA evidence suggests that Jefferson may have fathered the children of his slave Sarah Hemings.

The American Declaration of Independence is one of the most famous texts in the English language. Its assertion that all people hold the right to "Life, Liberty, and the Pursuit of Happiness" still helps to define how we think about a good life, and the conditions that make it possible.

The Declaration was drafted during the American Revolution, a revolt of Britain's 13 American colonies against rule by the Crown. By 1763, Britain had won a series of wars against France for possession of these colonies, and was now taxing them to offset the huge cost of the wars. Britain's Parliament did not have a single MP from the American colonies, yet it was making decisions on their behalf. Protests in Boston against taxation without representation led to British military intervention, which spiralled into war. At the First Continental Congress of 1774, the colonists demanded their own parliament. A year later, at the Second Congress, with King George III spurning their demands, they pushed for total independence.

> The God who gave us life gave us liberty at the same time; the hand of force may destroy but cannot disjoin them.
> **Thomas Jefferson**

From Old World to New

Thomas Jefferson, a delegate to the Second Continental Congress, was appointed to draft a declaration of independence. He was a key figure in the American Enlightenment, the intellectual movement that was a prelude to the revolution.

Colonists from Europe could look back to the Old World and see absolute monarchies and corrupt oligarchies presiding over squalid, unequal societies, which were often at war, with religious tolerance and minimal freedoms thrown aside. Jefferson and other intellectuals in the New World looked to thinkers such as English liberal philosopher John Locke, who stressed the

See also: Hugo Grotius 94–95 ▪ John Locke 104–09 ▪ Jean-Jacques Rousseau 118–25 ▪ Thomas Paine 134–39 ▪ George Washington 334

All men are created equal. They are endowed with inherent and inalienable rights.

Hereditary rule transgresses the inalienable rights of men.

Only a **republic is compatible** with the inalienable rights of men.

The **colonies must break** with European hereditary rule and **become independent republics**.

"natural rights" of humanity, and the need for government to hold to a "social contract" with the governed.

While Locke had defended Britain's constitutional monarchy, Jefferson and others took a far more radical message from his writings. To Locke's support for private property and freedom of thought, Jefferson added republicanism. In this, he was highly influenced by Thomas Paine, whose pamphlet *Common Sense* early in 1776 popularized the arguments for a republic. The Declaration of Independence marked a break not only with colonialism, but with all hereditary rule, which was held to be incompatible with the notion that "all men are created equal" and to transgress their "inalienable rights".

Signed on 4 July 1776 by representatives of 13 states, the full text still retains its original force in its denunciation of the arbitrary rule of monarchs. It helped shape the French Revolution and, from Gandhi to Ho Chi Minh, inspired leaders of future independence movements. ■

Jefferson presented the first draft of the Declaration of Independence to the Congress. The final version was read aloud in the streets in the hope that it would inspire men to sign up to fight.

Thomas Jefferson

Thomas Jefferson was born in Shadwell, Virginia. He was a plantation owner, and later a lawyer, who became the third president of the United States in 1801. A key figure in the Enlightenment, he was appointed as the principal author of the Declaration of Independence in June 1776, while serving as a delegate from Virginia to the Second Continental Congress.

As a planter, Jefferson owned well over 100 slaves, and he struggled to reconcile this position with his beliefs in equality. His text denouncing slavery in the original draft of the Declaration was excised by the Congress. Following victory over Britain in 1783, Jefferson's subsequent move to ban slavery in the new republic was defeated by a single vote in Congress.

After losing the presidency in 1808, Jefferson remained active in public life, founding the University of Virginia in 1819. He died on 4 July 1826.

Key works

1776 *Declaration of Independence*
1785 *Notes on the State of Virginia*

EACH NATIONALITY CONTAINS ITS CENTRE OF HAPPINESS WITHIN ITSELF

JOHANN GOTTFRIED HERDER (1744–1803)

IN CONTEXT

IDEOLOGY
Nationalism

FOCUS
Cultural identity

BEFORE
98 CE The Roman senator and historian Tacitus hails German virtues in *Germania*.

1748 Montesquieu argues that national character and the nature of a government are reflections of climate.

AFTER
1808 German philosopher Johann Fichte develops the concept of the *Volk* or "people" in the movement for Romantic Nationalism.

1867 Karl Marx criticizes nationalism as a "false consciousness" that prevents people from realizing they deserve better.

1925 Adolf Hitler champions the racial supremacy of the German nation in *Mein Kampf*.

People are **shaped by** the places they grow up...

↓

...because shared languages and landscapes help to create a **national spirit**, or *Volksgeist*.

↓

This national spirit forges a community with a **particular national character**.

↓

People depend on this **national community** for happiness.

↓

Each nationality contains its centre of happiness within itself.

In 18th-century Europe, Enlightenment philosophers tried to show how the light of reason could lead the human race out of superstition. Johann Herder, however, believed that a search for universal truths based solely on reason was flawed, since it neglected the fact that human nature varies according to cultural and physical environments. People need a sense of belonging, and their outlook is shaped by the places they grow up in.

National spirit

Herder argued that language is crucial in forming a sense of self, and so the natural grouping for humanity is the nation – not necessarily the state, but the cultural nation with its shared language, customs, and folk-memory. He believed that a community is forged by a national spirit – the *Volksgeist* – which emerges from language and reflects the physical character of the homeland. He saw nature and the landscape as nurturing and supporting the people, binding them with their national character.

People depend on this national community for happiness. "Each nation has its centre of happiness

See also: Montesquieu 110–11 ▪ Guissepe Mazzini 172–73 ▪ Karl Marx 188–93 ▪ Friedrich Nietzsche 196–99 ▪ Theodor Herzl 208–09 ▪ Marcus Garvey 252 ▪ Adolf Hitler 337

> It is nature which educates people: the most natural state is therefore one nation, an extended family with one national character.
> **Johann Gottfried Herder**

within itself," Herder asserts, "just as every sphere has its own centre of gravity." If people are taken out of their national environment, they lose contact with this centre of gravity and are deprived of this natural happiness. Herder was not only concerned about emigration, but also immigration, which he believed upset the organic unity of national culture – the only true basis of government. "Nothing is more manifestly contrary to the purpose of political government than the unnatural enlargement of states, the mixing of various races and nationalities under one sceptre." Herder was referring to the perils of colonialism and empire building, but his ideas can be related to modern multiculturalism.

Rising nationalism

Herder's ideas were an inspiration for the rising tide of Romantic nationalism that swept through Europe in the 19th century as a range of peoples – from the Greeks to the Belgians – asserted their nationhood and self-determination. But national or racial superiority was often assumed, culminating in the German persecution of the Jews, and in "ethnic cleansing". Although the Holocaust cannot be laid directly at Herder's door, he did state that Jews are "alien to this part of the world [Germany]". Herder's idea of a national centre of gravity also ignores the diversity of views and cultures within each nation, and leads to national stereotyping. His emphasis on national culture neglects other influences – such as economics, politics, and social contacts with different people – making his views less credible in the modern, globalized world. Arguably, he overestimated the prominence of nationality in people's priorities, which can be swayed by anything from family ties to religious views. ■

Nationalism as championed by Herder became an important part of the Nazi party's ideology. This travel brochure from 1938 depicts an Aryan couple enjoying traditional folk dancing.

Johann Gottfried Herder

Herder was born in Mohrungen in Prussia (now Morag in Poland) in 1744. At 17, he studied under Kant and was mentored by Johan Hamann at the University of Königsberg. After graduation, he taught in Riga before travelling to Paris and then Strasbourg, where he met the writer Goethe, on whom he had a profound influence. The German Romantic literary movement led by Goethe was inspired partly by Herder's claim that poets are the creators of nations. Goethe's influence gained Herder a post at the court of Weimar, where he developed his ideas of language, nationality, and people's response to the world. He began to collect folk songs capturing the *Volksgeist* – the "spirit" – of the German people. Herder was made a noble by the elector-prince of Bavaria and so was able to call himself "von" Herder. He died in Weimar in 1803.

Key works

1772 *Treatise on the Origin of Language*
1773 *Voices of the People in their Songs*

GOVERNMENT HAS BUT A CHOICE OF EVILS

JEREMY BENTHAM (1748–1832)

IN CONTEXT

IDEOLOGY
Utilitarianism

FOCUS
Public policy

BEFORE
1748 Montesquieu asserts in *The Spirit of the Laws* that liberty in England is maintained by the balance between the power of different parts of society.

1748 David Hume suggests that good and bad can be seen in terms of usefulness.

1762 Jean-Jacques Rousseau argues in *The Social Contract* that every law the people have not ratified in person is not a law.

AFTER
1861 John Stuart Mill warns of the "tyranny of the majority", and states that government should only interfere with individual liberties if they cause harm to others.

The idea that government has but a choice of evils runs right through the work of English philosopher Jeremy Bentham, from as early as 1769, when he was a young trainee lawyer, to the end of his life 50 years later, when he had become a hugely influential figure in British and European political thought.

The year 1769, Bentham wrote half a century later, was "a most interesting year". At the time, he was reading the works of philosophers such as Montesquieu, Beccaria, and Voltaire – all forward-thinking leaders of the continental Enlightenment. But it was the work of two British writers – David Hume and Joseph Priestley – that set off great sparks of revelation in young Bentham's mind.

Morality and happiness

In *An Enquiry Concerning Human Understanding* (1748), Hume says that one way to distinguish good and bad is by usefulness. A good quality is only really good if it is put to good use. But for the sharp, no-nonsense lawyer Bentham this was still too vague. What if you consider usefulness, or "utility", to be the only moral quality? What if you decide whether an action is good or not entirely by its usefulness, by whether it produces a good effect – crucially, whether it makes people happier or not?

Looked at in this way, all morality is at root about creating happiness and avoiding misery. Any other description is an unnecessary elaboration or, worse, a deliberate veiling of the truth. Religions are often guilty of this obfuscation, Bentham says, but so too are those high-flown political idealists who assert people's rights and so miss the point that it is all really about making people happy.

This is true, Bentham argues, not just on a personal and moral level, but on a public and political level, too. And if both private morality and public policy are reduced to this simple aim, everyone can agree – and men and women of good will can work together to achieve the same end.

So what, then, is a happy, useful outcome? Bentham is a realist and accepts that even the best action produces some bad along with the good. If one child has two sweets, another has one, and a third has

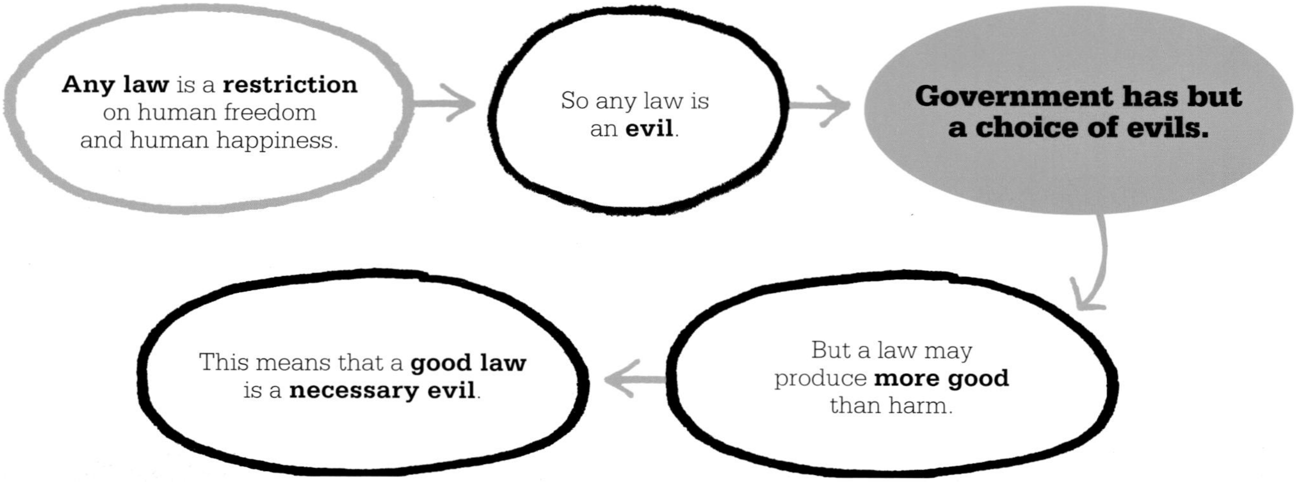

See also: Jean-Jacques Rousseau 118–25 ▪ Immanuel Kant 126–29 ▪ John Stuart Mill 174–81 ▪ Friedrich Hayek 270–75 ▪ John Rawls 298–303

none, the fairest action for the children's parents would be to take a sweet from the child with two and give it to the one with none. This still leads to one of the children losing a sweet. Similarly, any government action will work to the advantage of some but the disadvantage of others. For Bentham, such actions should be judged according to the following criterion: an action is good if it produces more pleasure than pain.

The greatest good

Reading Priestley's *An Essay on the First Principles of Government* (1768) sparked off the second great revelation of 1769 for Bentham. He draws from Priestley the idea that a good act is one that produces the greatest happiness for the greatest number. In other words, it's all about arithmetic. Politics can be simplified to one question – does it make more people happy than it makes sad? Bentham developed a mathematical method, which he called "felicific calculus", to work out whether a given government act produced more happiness or less.

This is where the idea that "government has but a choice of evils" comes in. Any law is a restriction on human liberty, argues Bentham – an interference with the individual's freedom to act completely as he or she wants. Therefore, every law is necessarily an evil. But doing nothing may also be an evil. The decision rests on the arithmetic. A new law can be justified if, and only if, it does more good than harm. He likens government to a doctor who should only intervene if he is sure the treatment will do more good than harm – an apt analogy for Bentham's time, when doctors frequently made patients more ill by bleeding them, draining some of their blood in an attempt to clear out disease. When deciding the punishment for a criminal, for instance, the law-maker must take into account not just the direct effects of the mischief, but the secondary effects, too – a robbery does not just harm the victim, but creates alarm in the community. The punishment must also make the robber worse off, so that it outweighs any profit he gained by committing the crime.

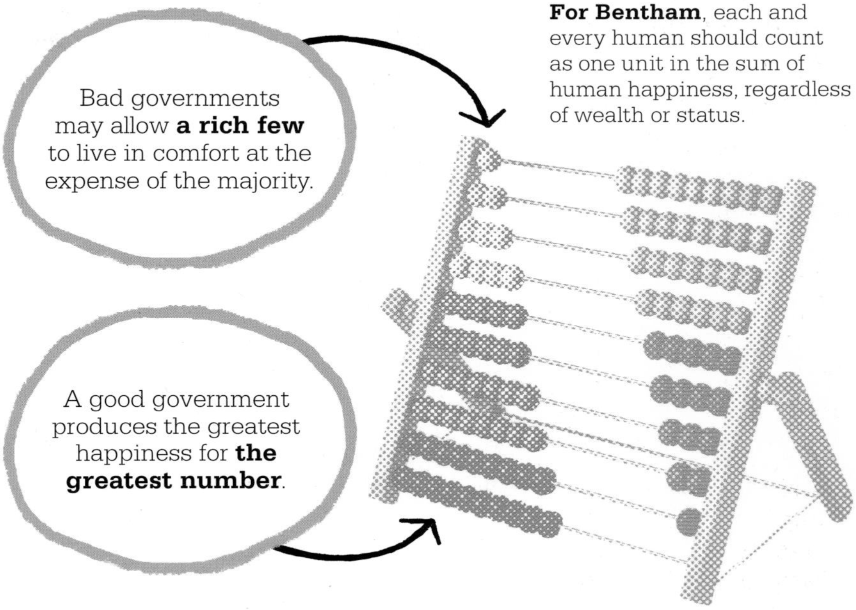

For Bentham, each and every human should count as one unit in the sum of human happiness, regardless of wealth or status.

Hands-off government

Bentham extended his idea into the field of economics, endorsing the view of Scottish economist Adam Smith, who argued that markets work best without government restrictions. Since Bentham's time, many people have used his warning to law-makers as a justification for "hands-off" government – for scaling back bureaucracy and for deregulation. His views have even been used as an argument in favour of a conservative government that avoids introducing new laws, especially new laws that try to change people's behaviour. »

> It is the greatest good to the greatest number of people which is the measure of right and wrong.
> **Jeremy Bentham**

> Good is pleasure or exemption from pain… Evil is pain or loss of pleasure.
> **Jeremy Bentham**

However, Bentham's arguments also have far more radical implications. Governments cannot stand still until everyone is infinitely happy, which will never happen. This means there is always work to do. Just as most people continue to search for happiness throughout their lives, governments must constantly strive to make ever more people happy.

Bentham's moral arithmetic highlights not just the benefits of happiness, but its cost. It makes it clear that for someone to be happy, someone else may have to pay a price. For a very rich few to live in comfort, for instance, many others must live in discomfort. Each person only counts as one unit in Bentham's sum of human happiness. This means that this imbalance is immoral, and it is every government's duty to continually work to redress the situation.

Inequalities in society mean that a rich minority exists alongside the poor. For Bentham this is morally unacceptable, and a government's role is to ensure that a balance is reached.

Pragmatic democracy

So how can rulers be persuaded to spread the wealth, when that would seem to make them less happy? The answer, Bentham argues, is more democracy, meaning the extension of the franchise. If rulers fail to increase human happiness for the greatest number, they get voted out at the next election. In a democracy, politicians have a vested interest in increasing happiness for the majority to ensure they are re-elected. While other thinkers, from Rousseau to Paine, were pushing for democracy as a natural right – without which a man is denied his humanity – Bentham argued for it entirely pragmatically: as a means to an end. The idea of natural laws and rights is, to Bentham, nothing more than "nonsense on stilts".

With their costs and benefits, profit and loss, Bentham's arguments for extending voting rights appealed to hard-nosed British industrialists and businessmen – the rising new power base in the Industrial Revolution – in a way that no amount of idealism and talk of man's natural rights could. Bentham's down-to-earth, "utilitarian" arguments helped to shift Britain towards parliamentary reform and liberalism in the 1830s. Today, a Benthamite approach is a useful everyday benchmark for public policy decisions, encouraging governments to consider whether each policy is, on balance, good for the majority of people.

Bentham's ideas were satirized by Charles Dickens, whose character Mr Gradgrind, in the novel *Hard Times*, runs a school based on cold, hard facts, leaving little room for fun.

Hard facts

However, there are some real problems with Bentham's ideal-free recipe of utilitarianism. The English author Charles Dickens hated the new breed of utilitarians that followed Bentham, and satirized them mercilessly in his novel *Hard Times* (1854), depicting them as killjoys stamping on the imagination and sapping the human spirit with their insistence on reducing life to hard facts. It is not a picture that Bentham, a deeply empathetic man, would necessarily recognize, but it was a clear reference to his reduction of every issue to arithmetic.

One recurring criticism of Bentham's idea is that it encourages "scapegoating". The greatest happiness principle can permit huge injustices if the overall effect is general happiness. After a terrible terrorist bombing, for instance, the police are under great pressure to find the perpetrators. The general population will be much happier and the alarm will subside if the police arrest anyone who appears to fit the bill, even if they are not actually the guilty party (provided there are no further attacks).

Following Bentham's argument, some critics claim, it is morally acceptable to punish the innocent if their suffering is outweighed by an increase in the happiness of the general population. Supporters of Bentham can get round this problem by saying that the general population would be unhappy to live in a society in which innocent people are made scapegoats. But that issue only arises if the population finds out the truth; if the targeting of scapegoats is kept secret, it would appear justified according to Bentham's logic. ■

Utilitarian arguments have been used to justify the prosecution of innocent people – such as Gerry Conlon, accused of IRA bombings – on the basis that the majority is made happier.

Jeremy Bentham

Jeremy Bentham was born in Houndsditch, London, in 1748, to a family who were financially comfortable. He was expected to become a lawyer, and he went to Oxford University aged just 12, graduating to train as a barrister in London at 15. But the chicanery of the legal profession depressed him, and he became more interested in legal science and philosophy.

Bentham retired to London's Westminster to write, and for the next 40 years, he turned out works of commentary and ideas on legal and moral matters. He began by criticizing the leading legal authority William Blackstone for his assumption that there was nothing essentially wrong with Britain's laws, then he went on to develop a complete theory of morals and policy. This was the basis of the utilitarian ethic that had already come to dominate British political life by the time of his death in 1832.

Key works

1776 *Fragment on Government*
1780 *Introduction to Principles of Morals and Legislation*
1787 *Panopticon*

THE PEOPLE HAVE A RIGHT TO KEEP AND BEAR ARMS

JAMES MADISON (1751–1836)

IN CONTEXT

IDEOLOGY
Federalism

FOCUS
Armed citizenry

BEFORE
44–43 BCE Cicero argues in his *Philippics* that people must be able to defend themselves, just as wild beasts do in nature.

1651 Thomas Hobbes argues in *Leviathan* that by nature, men have a right to defend themselves forcefully.

AFTER
1968 After the assassinations of Robert Kennedy and Martin Luther King in the US, federal restrictions on gun ownership are introduced.

2008 The US Supreme Court decides that the Second Amendment protects an individual's right to keep a gun at home for self-defence.

Even as the Founding Fathers were putting the finishing touches to the US Constitution in 1788, demands came for the addition of a Bill of Rights. The idea that the people have a right to keep and bear arms appears as the Second Amendment in this Bill with the words "the right of the people to keep and bear Arms, shall not be infringed". The exact wording is crucial, since it has become the focus of modern debate over gun control, and how much freedom US citizens have by law to own and carry guns.

The architect of the Bill of Rights was Virginia-born James Madison, who was also one of the

See also: Cicero 49 ▪ Thomas Hobbes 96–103 ▪ John Locke 104–09 ▪ Montesquieu 110–11 ▪ Pierre-Joseph Proudhon 183 ▪ Jane Addams 211 ▪ Mahatma Gandhi 220–25 ▪ Robert Nozick 326–27

The central, federal government may be swayed by the **power of the majority**.

Driven by the majority, the federal government may use a standing army to **enforce its will** on states.

People in each state must be able to form militias to **defend themselves** against an oppressive federal army.

The right of the people to keep and bear arms shall not be infringed.

main creators of the Constitution itself. This makes him possibly unique among political thinkers in that he was able to put his ideas directly into practice – ideas that are still, two centuries on, the basis of the political way of life of the world's most powerful nation. Indeed, in later becoming US president, Madison climbed to the very peak of the political edifice that he had himself created.

The Bill of Rights is considered by some as the very embodiment of the Enlightenment thinking on natural rights, which began with John Locke and culminated in Thomas Paine's inspirational call for the Rights of Man. Though the latter stressed the importance of democracy (the universal right to vote) as a principle in his treatise, Madison's intentions were more pragmatic. They were rooted in the tradition of English politics – where parliament sought to prevent the sovereign overreaching his power, rather than striving to protect basic universal freedoms.

Defence from the majority

As he admitted in a letter to Thomas Jefferson, the only reason Madison put forward the Bill of Rights was to satisfy the demands of others. He personally believed that the establishment of the Constitution by itself, and so the creation of proper government, should have been enough to guarantee that fundamental rights are protected. Indeed, he admitted that the addition of a Bill of Rights implied that the Constitution was flawed, and could not protect these rights in itself. There was also a risk that defining specific rights would impair protection of rights that were not specified. Moreover, Madison acknowledged that bills of rights had not had a happy history in the United States.

But there were also strong reasons why a bill of rights might be a good idea. Like most of the US's Founding Fathers, Madison was nervous of the power of the majority. "A democracy," wrote Thomas Jefferson, "is nothing more than mob rule, where fifty-one percent of the people may take away the rights of the other forty-nine." A Bill of Rights might help protect the minority against the mass of the people.

"In our Governments," Madison wrote, "the real power lies in the majority of the Community, and the invasion of private rights is chiefly to be apprehended, not from acts of Government contrary to the sense of its constituents, but from acts in which the Government is the »

Shay's Rebellion in 1786–87 saw a rebel militia seize Massachusetts' court house. Quashed by government forces, it encouraged the principle of strong government in the US Constitution.

Though Madison believed that the existence of the Constitution would ensure that basic rights were protected under a federal government, he formulated the Bill of Rights as an extra measure to counteract the power of the majority in a democracy.

mere instrument of the major number of the constituents." In other words, the Bill of Rights was actually intended to protect property owners against the democratic instincts of the majority.

Militias legitimized

Madison also had a simple political reason for creating the Bill of Rights. He knew he would not gain support for the Constitution from the delegates of some individual states if he did not. After all, the War of Independence had been fought to challenge the tyranny of centralized power, so these delegates were wary of a new central government. They would only ratify the Constitution if they had some guarantee of protection against it. So rights were not natural laws, but the states' (and property owners') protection against the federal government.

This is where the Second Amendment came in. Madison ensured that states or citizens would not be deprived of the ability to protect themselves by forming a militia against an overbearing national government, just as they had done against the British crown. Such a situation envisaged a community banding together to resist an army of oppression. The Second Amendment actually says in its final version: "A well regulated Militia, being necessary to the security of a free State, the right of the people to keep and bear Arms, shall not be infringed."

> The ultimate authority... resides in the people alone.
> **James Madison**

The amendment, then, was about a militia and "the people" (in other words, the community) protecting the state, not people as individuals.

Individual self-defence

Madison was not talking about individuals carrying arms to defend themselves against individual criminal acts. Yet that is how his words in the Second Amendment have come to be used, and many Americans now claim that the right to carry guns is enshrined in the Constitution – challenging any move to institute gun controls as unconstitutional.

Attempts to overturn this interpretation in the courts have repeatedly met with failure, with the insistence that the US Constitution upholds citizens' rights to bear arms in defence of themselves as well as the state. Many argue even further that, regardless of Madison's intentions, owning and carrying a gun should be considered a basic freedom.

A century before Madison's bill, English philosopher John Locke, in identifying the right to self-defence as a natural right, took his cue from an imagined "natural" time before civilization. Just as a wild animal will defend itself with violence if cornered, so, Locke argues, may humans. The implication is that government is in some way an unnatural imposition from which people need protection. In retrospect, some commentators have put a Lockean gloss on the Bill of Rights, and assume that it is confirming self-defence by violent means as a natural, inalienable right.

However, it seems possible that Madison and his fellow Founding Fathers were more in tune with Scottish philosopher David Hume's view of government than with Locke's. Hume is too pragmatic to pay much attention to the idea of a natural time of freedom before rights were curtailed by civilization. For Hume, people want government because it makes sense, and rights are something negotiated and agreed upon, like every other aspect of law. So there is nothing fundamental about the right to bear arms – it is simply a matter that people generally agree about, or not. According to Hume, freedoms and rights are just examples of tenets on which people concur – and perhaps decide mutually to enshrine in law to ensure that they are adhered to. Taking this view, there is no fundamental principle at stake in the right to bear arms – rather, it is a consensus. And consensus does not necessarily require a democratic majority.

Lasting controversy

Gun control remains a hot issue in the US, with powerful lobbies – such as the National Rifle Association (NRA) – campaigning against any restrictions on gun ownership at all. Those against gun control appear to have the upper hand, with most states allowing people to own firearms. Still, there are very few states where gun ownership is entirely unregulated, and there are arguments over whether, for instance, people should be allowed to carry concealed guns. The high level of gun crime in the US, and the increasing frequency of mass murders – such as the cinema killings in Aurora, Colorado in July 2012 – have led many to question whether unrestricted ownership of firearms is appropriate in a nation that is no longer a frontier state.

Natural self-defence as used by wild animals against attack is cited by exponents of natural law to justify the right of an individual to defend themselves by any means.

It is remarkable that Madison's Bill of Rights is still, with only a few changes, at the heart of the US political system. Some, maybe even Madison himself, would argue that a good government would have protected these rights without need of a bill. Yet the US Bill of Rights remains perhaps the most powerful meld of political theory and practice ever devised. ■

James Madison

James Madison Jr was born in Port Conway, Virginia. His father owned Montpelier, the largest tobacco plantation in Orange County, worked by 100 or so slaves. In 1769, Madison enrolled at the College of New Jersey, now Princeton University. During the American War of Independence, he served in the Virginia legislature and was the protégé of Thomas Jefferson. At 29, he became the youngest delegate to the Continental Congress in 1780, and gained respect for his ability to draft laws and build coalitions. Madison's draft – the Virginia Plan – formed the basis of the US Constitution. He co-wrote the 85 *Federalist Papers* to explain the theory of the Constitution and ensure its ratification. Madison was one of the leaders of the emerging Democratic-Republican party. He followed Jefferson to become the fourth US president in 1809, and held the office for two terms.

Key works

1787 *United States Constitution*
1788 *Federalist Papers*
1789 *The Bill of Rights*

THE MOST RESPECTABLE WOMEN ARE THE MOST OPPRESSED

MARY WOLLSTONECRAFT (1759–1797)

IN CONTEXT

IDEOLOGY
Feminism

FOCUS
Women's emancipation

BEFORE
1589 *Her Protection for Women* by English novelist Jane Anger castigates men for seeing women merely as objects of sexual desire.

1791 In *Declaration of the Rights of Woman*, French playwright Olympe de Gouges writes: "Woman is born free and remains equal to man".

AFTER
1840s In the US and UK, women's property is legally protected from their husbands.

1869 In *The Subjection of Women*, John Stuart Mill argues that women should be given the right to vote.

1893 In New Zealand, women are given the vote – one of the first countries to do so.

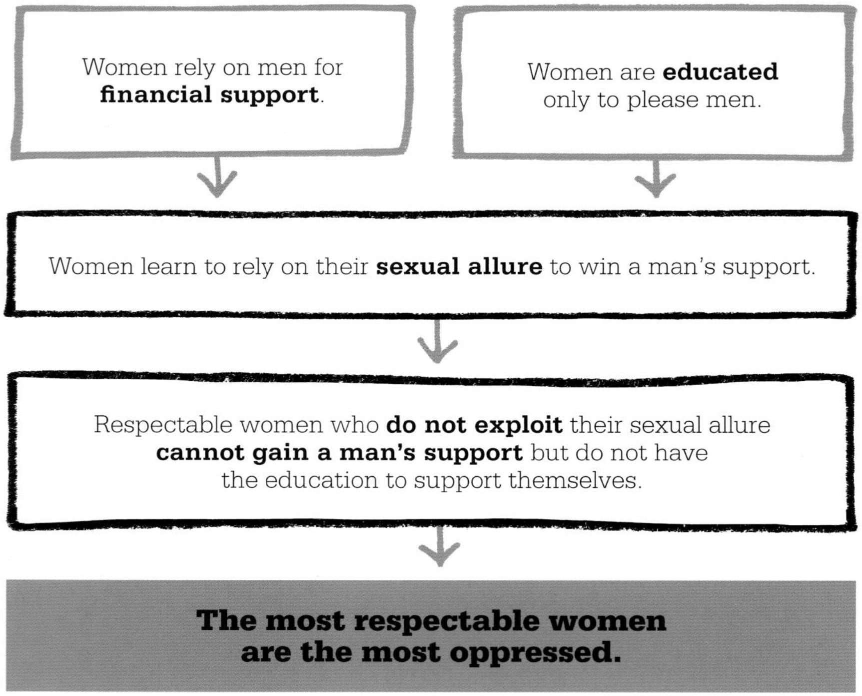

Published in 1792, British writer Mary Wollstonecraft's *A Vindication of the Rights of Woman* is seen as one of the first great feminist tracts. It was written at a time of intellectual and political ferment. The Enlightenment had established the rights of men at the centre of political debate, which culminated in France in the Revolution against the monarchy in the very year that Wollstonecraft wrote *A Vindication*. Yet few talked about the position of women in society. Indeed, French philosopher Jean-Jacques Rousseau, an ardent advocate of political freedom, argued in his work *Émile* that

See also: John Stuart Mill 174–81 ▪ Emmeline Pankhurst 207 ▪ Simone de Beauvoir 284–89

> How much more respectable is the woman who earns her own bread by fulfilling any duty, than the most accomplished beauty.
> **Mary Wollstonecraft**

women should only be educated to make them good wives able to give pleasure to men.

Freedom to work

Wollstonecraft wrote *A Vindication* to show how wrong Rousseau was about women. The rejuvenation of the world could only happen, she argued, if women were happy, as well as men. Yet women were trapped by a web of expectations due to their dependence on men. They were forced to trade on their looks and to connive to win the affections of a man. Respectable women – women who did not indulge in this game of seduction – were put at a huge disadvantage.

Wollstonecraft argued that women needed the freedom to earn a living, granting them autonomy from men. To achieve this freedom required education. To those who argued that women were inferior to men intellectually, she insisted that this misapprehension was simply due to a woman's lack of education. She argued that there were many occupations women could pursue with the right education and opportunities: "How many women thus waste life away the prey of discontent, who might have practised as physicians, regulated a farm, managed a shop, and stood erect, supported by their own industry?" Independence and education for women would also be good for men, because marriages might be based on mutual affection and respect. Wollstonecraft proposed reforms to education, such as combining private and public education, and a more democratic, participatory approach to schooling.

Wollstonecraft's proposals for the education and emancipation of women were largely overlooked in her lifetime, and for a time after her death she was better known for her unconventional lifestyle than her ideas. However, later campaigners – such as Emily Davies, who set up Girton College for women at the University of Cambridge in 1869 – were strongly influenced by her ideas. Change was nonetheless slow to come – it was more than 150 years after the publication of *A Vindication* that the University of Cambridge finally offered full degrees to women. ■

Feminine charms were essential for a woman to advance in 18th-century European society. Wollstonecraft abhorred the fact that a woman had to attract a man to provide for her.

Mary Wollstonecraft

Wollstonecraft was born in 1759 to a family whose fortunes were in decline. In her early 20s she set up a progressive school in London, and then became a governess in Ireland to the children of Lady Kingsborough, whose vanity and disdain did much to foster Mary's views on women.

In 1787, she returned to London to write for the radical magazine *Analytical Review*. In 1792, she went to France to celebrate the Revolution and fell in love with American author Gilbert Imlay. They had a child, but did not marry, and the relationship failed. After a move to Sweden, and a failed suicide attempt, she returned to London and married William Godwin. She died in 1797 giving birth to their only child, Mary, who wrote the novel *Frankenstein* under her married name of Shelley.

Key works

1787 *Thoughts on the Education of Daughters*
1790 *A Vindication of the Rights of Men*
1792 *A Vindication of the Rights of Woman*
1796 *The Wrongs of Woman, or Maria*

THE SLAVE FEELS SELF-EXISTENCE TO BE SOMETHING EXTERNAL

GEORG HEGEL (1770–1831)

IN CONTEXT

IDEOLOGY
Idealism

FOCUS
Human consciousness

BEFORE
350 BCE Aristotle claims that slavery is natural because some people are natural leaders, while some are subservient.

1649 René Descartes argues that consciousness is self-evident because you cannot deny your mind's existence at the same time as using your mind to do the denying.

AFTER
1840s Karl Marx uses Hegel's dialectic method in his analysis of the class struggle.

1883 Friedrich Nietzsche creates his image of the *Übermensch* (overman) who trusts his own intuitive sense of what is good and evil.

The German philosopher Georg Hegel's great work *The Phenomenology of Mind* (or "*Spirit*") appears at first to have little to do with politics, as it deals with difficult and abstract arguments about the nature of human consciousness. However, his conclusions regarding the way we reach a state of self-awareness have profound implications for the way society is organized, and pose difficult questions concerning the nature of human relations.

Hegel's philosophy is focused on how the thinking mind views the world. He wants to understand how

See also: Aristotle 40–43 ▪ Hugo Grotius 94–95 ▪ Jean-Jacques Rousseau 118–25 ▪ Karl Marx 188–93 ▪ Friedrich Nietzsche 196–99

When two spirits or consciousnesses meet, they **battle for recognition**.

↓

The spirit that **prefers liberty to life** becomes the **Master**; the spirit that **prefers life to liberty** becomes the **Slave**.

↓

The existence of the **Master's consciousness is affirmed** through the Slave.

↓

The Slave **discovers his consciousness** through his work for the Master in the tangible, external world.

↓

The Slave feels self-existence to be something external.

each human consciousness creates its own worldview. Crucial to his argument is his emphasis on self-consciousness. For Hegel, the human mind, or spirit, desires recognition, and indeed needs that recognition in order to achieve self-awareness. This is why human consciousness, for Hegel, is a social, interactive process. It is possible to live in isolation without being fully aware, Hegel believes. But for the mind to fully exist – to be free – it must be self-conscious, and it can only become self-conscious by seeing another consciousness react to it.

Master–Slave

According to Hegel, when two minds meet, what matters to both is being recognized: receiving from the other the confirmation of their own existence. However, there is only room for one worldview in the mind of each individual, so a struggle ensues about who is going to acknowledge whom – whose worldview is to triumph. Hegel describes how each mind must try to kill the other. The problem is, though, that if one destroys the other, the loser will no longer be able to give the affirmation the winner needs. The way out of »

Georg Hegel

Georg Hegel was born in Stuttgart in the German Duchy of Württemberg. Much of his life was lived in the calm of Protestant southern Germany, but against the backdrop of the French Revolution. He was a student at Tübingen University at the height of the Revolution and he encountered Napoleon at Jena, where he completed *The Phenomenology of Mind*.

After eight years as rector at the Gymnasium in Nuremberg, he married Marie von Tucher and worked on his great book on logic. In 1816, after the early death of his wife, he moved to Heidelberg, and many of his ideas are contained in notes from the lectures he gave to philosophy students there. He died in 1831 after returning to Berlin during a cholera epidemic. Perhaps appropriately for such a complex thinker, it is said that his last words were "And he didn't understand me".

Key works

1807 *The Phenomenology of Mind*
1812–16 *The Science of Logic*
1821 *The Philosophy of Right*

this dilemma is a Master–Slave relationship, in which one person "gives in" to the other. The one who values liberty more than life becomes Master; the one who values life more than liberty becomes Slave. This relationship evolves not only in literal master and slave situations, but in any situation where two minds meet.

Hegel appears to be implying that slaves are only slaves because they prefer to submit rather than die, and they collude with their masters. He wrote, "it is solely by risking life that freedom is obtained". He asserts that terror of death is the cause of oppression throughout history, and at the root of slavery and class distinction. He admired Napoleon for this reason, and praised Napoleon's willingness to risk his own life in order to achieve his aims. Hegel is suggesting that slavery is primarily a state of mind, which finds echoes in the later case of escaped American slave Frederick Douglass (1818–1890). Dragged back to his master, Douglass decided to stand up and fight, even if it might mean death, and afterwards wrote, "however long I might remain a slave in form, the day had passed forever when I could be a slave in fact".

Napoleon Bonaparte's vision for a new order and courage in battle made him a man "whom it is impossible not to admire", according to Hegel, to whom his was a "Master" mentality.

Dialectical relationship

Today, the choice between death and slavery seems an unacceptable one to have to make. But it may be that Hegel's arguments about the Master–Slave relationship are much less literal, and far more subtle and complex. He suggests ways in which the Slave might in fact benefit more from the relationship than the Master. He describes the development of their relationship as a dialectic. By this he means a particular kind of argument that begins with a thesis (the minds) and its antithesis (the result of the encounter between minds), which together produce a synthesis (the resolution into Master and Slave). This dialectic is not necessarily a description of a real struggle between a slaveowner and slave. Hegel is talking about a struggle for domination between minds – and there is no room in his conception for cooperation: there must be a resolution into Master and Slave.

Hegel asserted that a Slave, while engaged in tangible work, would come to experience a realization of his own existence (and therefore become "free") in a way that his Master would not.

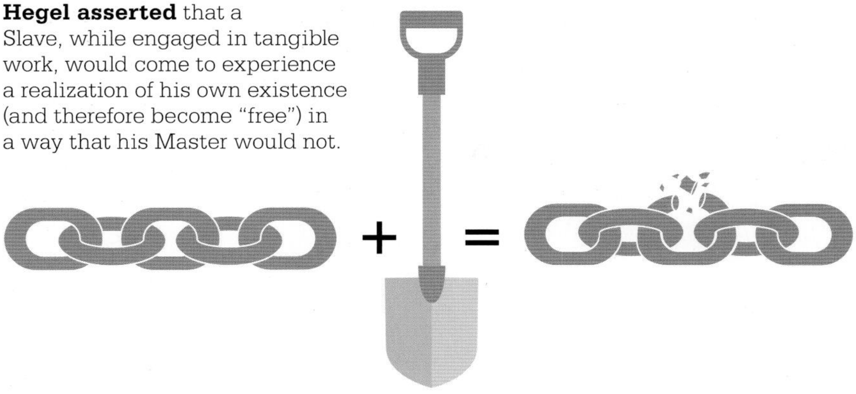

He goes on to show how the relationship develops further. The synthesis seems to confirm the existence of the Master's mind. At first, everything appears to revolve around him, and his ability to get the Slave to serve his needs confirms his own freedom and self-consciousness. The Slave's independent self-consciousness, meanwhile, is totally dissolved. However, at this point another dialectic relationship develops.

Since the Master does nothing, he relies on the Slave to affirm his existence and freedom. He is, in fact, in a dependent relationship with the Slave, which means that he is anything but free. The Slave, however, is working with real things – with nature – even if only for his Master. This reaffirms his existence in a tangible, external way that the idle Master cannot hope to emulate: "In [his work for] the Master, the Slave feels self-existence to be something external, an objective fact." In making things, and making things happen, "self-existence comes to be felt explicitly, as his own proper being, and [the Slave] attains the consciousness that he himself exists in his own right." So now their situations become inverted – the Master disappears as an independent mind, while the Slave emerges as one. Ultimately, for Hegel, the Master–Slave dialectic may be more harmful to the Master than it is to the Slave.

Slave ideologies

So what happens when the Slave reaches this new kind of self-realization – yet is not ready for a fight to the death? At this point, Hegel argues, the Slave finds "slave ideologies" that justify his position, including stoicism (in which he rejects external freedom for mental freedom), scepticism (in which he doubts the value of external freedom), and unhappy consciousness (in which he finds religion and escape but only in another world).

> If a man is a slave, his own will is responsible for his slavery... the wrong of slavery lies at the door not of enslavers or conquerors but of the slaves and conquered themselves.
> **Georg Hegel**

Hegel finds these Master–Slave relationships in many places – in the wars between stronger states and weaker states, and conflicts between social classes and other groupings. For Hegel, human existence is an endless fight to the death for recognition, and this fight can never properly be resolved.

Hegel's influence

Karl Marx was strongly influenced by Hegel's ideas and adopted his idea of the dialectic, but found Hegel too abstract and mystical in his concentration on consciousness. Instead, Marx chose a materialist approach. Some find Hegel's argument that only fear keeps people enslaved inspirational; others consider that his insistence that submission is a choice is a case of blaming the victim and does not relate well to the real world, in which power relations are complex. Hegel remains one of the hardest political philosophers to understand, and one of the most controversial. ■

A slave, about to be whipped by his master, could be to blame for his position, following Hegel's logic. Critics of Hegel argue that this position is clearly unjust.

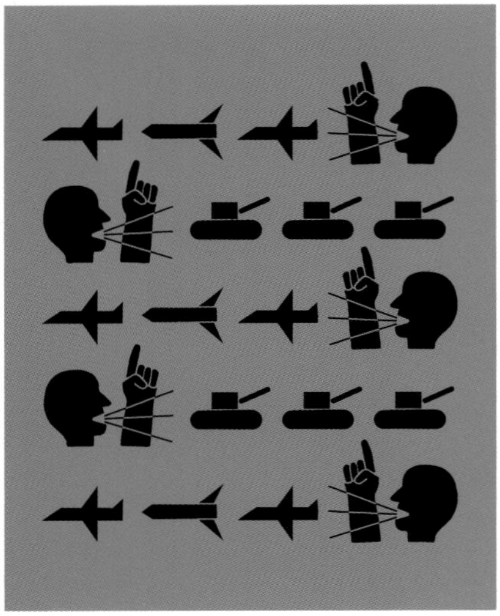

WAR IS THE CONTINUATION OF POLITIK BY OTHER MEANS

CARL VON CLAUSEWITZ (1780–1831)

IN CONTEXT

IDEOLOGY
Realism

FOCUS
Diplomacy and war

BEFORE
5th century BCE Sun Tzu states that the art of war is vital to the state.

1513 Niccolò Machiavelli argues that even in peacetime, a prince must be ready and armed in preparation for war.

1807 Georg Hegel states that history is a struggle for recognition that leads to a master and slave relationship.

AFTER
1935 German general Erich Friedrich Wilhelm Ludendorff develops his notion of a "Total War" that mobilizes the entire physical and moral forces of a nation.

1945 Adolf Hitler cites "the great Clausewitz" in his last testament in the bunker.

Few phrases from military theory have been as influential as Prussian soldier Carl von Clausewitz's statement that "war is the continuation of *Politik* by other means", taken from his book *On War*, published after his death in 1832. The phrase is one of a series of truisms Clausewitz coins as he attempts to put war in context by examining its philosophical basis, much as philosophers would explore the role of the state. The German word *Politik* translates as both politics and policy, covering both the principles of governance and its practicalities.

War leads to politics

For Clausewitz, war is a clash of opposing wills. "War is nothing but a duel on an extensive scale," he writes, "an act of violence intended to compel our opponent to fulfil our will." The aim is to disarm your enemy, so that you become the master. But there is no single, decisive blow in war – a defeated state seeks to repair the damage of defeat by using politics. Clausewitz is keen to emphasize that the business of war is serious in intent, and no mere adventure. It is always, he says, a political act, because one state wishes to impose its will on another – or risk submission.

War is simply the means to a political end that might well be achieved through other means. His point is not to highlight the cynicism of politicians who go to war, but to ensure that those who wage war are always aware of its overriding political goal. ■

Otto von Bismarck declared Wilhelm I of Prussia Emperor of Germany in 1871. Bismarck had provoked war with France to achieve this political end.

See also: Sun Tzu 28–31 ▪ Niccolò Machiavelli 74–81 ▪ Thomas Hobbes 96–103 ▪ Georg Hegel 156–59 ▪ Smedley D. Butler 247

ABOLITION AND THE UNION CANNOT CO-EXIST

JOHN C. CALHOUN (1794–1850)

IN CONTEXT

IDEOLOGY
State's rights

FOCUS
Slavery

BEFORE
5th century BCE Aristotle says that some people are naturally slaves and slavery helps build skills and virtues.

426 CE Augustine states that the primary cause of slavery is sin, which brings some under the domination of others as a punishment from God.

1690 John Locke argues against the idea of natural slaves and that prisoners of war can be enslaved.

AFTER
1854 In his speech in Peoria, Illinois, Abraham Lincoln outlines his moral, economic, political, and legal arguments against slavery.

1865 Slaves are emancipated in the United States.

The United States Senator John C. Calhoun made an impassioned speech on the issue of slavery in 1837. Throughout the 1830s, pressure for the abolition of slavery had been building in the US, and Southern slaveholders were feeling beleaguered. In retaliation, they argued that there were natural inequalities ordained by God, which meant that some are suited to command and others to labour. Moreover, they claimed, black slavery could avert conflicts between workers and employers, and the tyranny of wage slavery that threatened the wellbeing of the nation every bit as much as the abolitionist cause.

Good for both races

It was the sending of the issue to the Senate committee that prompted Calhoun to stress that Congress had no place interfering with the basic right to own slaves guaranteed by the Constitution. To go down the route of abolition would mean that the slaveholding and non-slaveholding states would live under different political systems. "The conflicting elements would burst the Union asunder, powerful as are the links which hold it together. Abolition and the Union cannot co-exist." Instead of defending slavery as a necessary evil, he asserts that black slavery is, in fact, a positive good for both races. "Never before has the black race of Central Africa," he claims, "...attained a condition so civilized and so improved, not only physically, but morally and intellectually." ■

> "The relation now existing in the slaveholding states... is a positive good."
> **John C. Calhoun**

See also: Aristotle 40–43 ■ Thomas Jefferson 140–41 ■ Abraham Lincoln 182 ■ Henry David Thoreau 186–87 ■ Marcus Garvey 252 ■ Nelson Mandela 294–95

A STATE TOO EXTENSIVE IN ITSELF ULTIMATELY FALLS INTO DECAY

SIMÓN BOLÍVAR (1783–1830)

IN CONTEXT

IDEOLOGY
Liberal republicanism

FOCUS
Revolutionary warfare

BEFORE

1494 In the Treaty of Tordesillas, the territories of the Americas are divided between Spain and Portugal.

1762 Jean-Jacques Rousseau argues against the divine right of kings to rule.

AFTER

1918 Following World War I, US president Woodrow Wilson lays out a reconstruction plan for Europe based on liberal nationalist principles.

1964 Che Guevara addresses the United Nations, arguing that Latin America has yet to gain true independence.

1999 Hugo Chavéz becomes president of Venezuela with a political ideology he describes as Bolivarian.

A **small republic**...

...has no reason to expand its boundaries...

...and so **avoids injustice and instability**.

An **empire**...

...must make conquered lands into **colonies**.

This leads to a **degeneration of justice** and a fall into **despotism**.

A state too extensive in itself, or by virtue of its dependencies, ultimately falls into decay.

Christopher Columbus claimed America for Spain in 1492, opening the way for an empire that would extend over five continents. The Spanish would rely on the collaboration of local elites to manage their lands. Venezuelan revolutionary Simón Bolívar saw this aspect of their empire as a source of dynamism but also as a potential weakness.

Small but strong republics

Spain's power began to crumble in 1808 when Napoleon invaded and placed his brother on the

See also: Niccolò Machiavelli 74–81 ▪ Jean-Jacques Rousseau 118–25 ▪ Jeremy Bentham 144–49 ▪ Che Guevara 312–13

> The distinctive feature of small republics is permanence.
> **Simón Bolívar**

throne. Bolívar recognized this as an opportunity for the Spanish American countries to throw off the yoke of colonialism. During an 18-year fight for freedom, Bolívar was exiled for a year in Jamaica. As he planned for the future, he pondered how he could ensure a state large enough to govern, but small enough to foster the greatest happiness for its people.

Bolívar considered the question in "The Jamaica Letter". In this letter, he explained his reason for rejecting monarchies: kingdoms were inherently expansionist, driven by a king's "constant desire to increase his possessions". A republic, on the other hand, was "limited to the matter of its preservation, prosperity, and glory".

Bolívar believed that Spanish America should become 17 independent republics, and the ambition of these must be to educate; to help people in their fair ambitions; and to protect the rights of all citizens. Each would have no reason to expand its boundaries, because this used up valuable resources while bringing no advantages. In addition, "a state too extensive in itself, or by virtue of its dependencies, ultimately falls into decay". Worse still, "its free government becomes a tyranny", its founding principles are disregarded and it "degenerates into despotism". Small republics, he said, enjoyed permanence; large ones veered towards empire and instability.

American republics

The independent republics that emerged in Spanish America after the wars of liberation reflected Bolívar's vision in their size if not in their freedoms, as political power came to be monopolized by small elites. In this, they perhaps reflected Bolívar's own elitist instincts and ambivalence towards full democracy.

The revolutionary vision of "El Libertador" is still revered in Latin America, though Bolívar's name has been misappropriated by politicians to sanction actions he would have deplored. ■

Bolivar's portrait is held aloft during a pro-Hugo Chávez rally in Venezuela. Chávez describes his political movement as a Bolivarian revolution, stressing its anti-imperialist stance.

Simón Bolívar

Born to aristocratic parents in Venezuela, Simón Bolívar was tutored by renowned scholar Simón Rodríguez, who introduced him to the ideals of the European Enlightenment. At age 16, after completing his military training, Bolívar travelled through Mexico and France, then on to Spain, where he married, though his wife died eight months later.

In 1804, Bolívar witnessed Napoleon Bonaparte become emperor of France. He was inspired by the nationalist ideas he encountered in Europe and vowed not to rest until South America gained independence from Spain. Bolívar led the liberation of modern-day Ecuador, Colombia, Venezuela, Panama, northern Peru, and northwest Brazil from Spain. Retreating from his earlier idealism, Bolívar felt forced to declare himself dictator of the new state of Gran Colombia in 1828. He died two years later, disillusioned with the results of the revolutions he had inspired.

Key works

1812 *The Cartagena Manifesto*
1815 *The Jamaica Letter*

AN EDUCATED AND WISE GOVERNMENT RECOGNIZES THE DEVELOPMENTAL NEEDS OF ITS SOCIETY

JOSÉ MARÍA LUIS MORA (1780–1850)

IN CONTEXT

IDEOLOGY
Liberalism

FOCUS
Modernization

BEFORE
1776 The leaders of the American Revolution declare that they are reorganizing the political system to the benefit of the human condition.

1788 Immanuel Kant argues that progress is not automatic, but must be fostered through education.

AFTER
1848 Auguste Comte suggests that society progresses through three stages to an enlightened rational age of science.

1971 Peruvian priest Gustavo Gutiérrez writes *A Theology of Liberation*, arguing that Christians must lead a liberation from unjust economic, political, or social conditions.

Mexico in the 1830s was a turbulent place. The protracted War of Independence had left the country bitter and divided. Despite finally becoming independent from Spain in 1821, Mexico was to have 75 presidents in the next 55 years, and the power of the rich landowners, the army, and the Church remained as solid as ever. Strongly influenced by the Enlightenment philosophers of the 18th century, and also by political developments in France and the United States, Latin American liberals believed that this entrenched power was blocking the progress of society. Young Mexican liberal José María Luis Mora challenged the obstinate conservatism he found in his country. He argued that a society has to move forward or it will die. Just as a child needs nurturing by its parents as it grows, so "a wise government recognizes the developmental needs of its society".

Mora's call for modernization fell on deaf ears. He was jailed for opposing the elevation of Maximilian to emperor, and exiled to Paris after upsetting President Santa Anna. Fifty years after independence, Mexico was poorer, per capita, than ever. ■

Emperor Maximilian was installed as monarch of Mexico in 1864, to strong opposition from liberals such as Mora. Three years later, Maximilian was overthrown and executed.

See also: Plato 34–39 ▪ Immanuel Kant 126–29 ▪ Auguste Comte 165 ▪ Karl Marx 188–93 ▪ Antonio Gramsci 259

THE TENDENCY TO ATTACK "THE FAMILY" IS A SYMPTOM OF SOCIAL CHAOS

AUGUSTE COMTE (1798–1857)

IN CONTEXT

IDEOLOGY
Positivism

FOCUS
The family

BEFORE
14th century Ibn Khaldun's *Muqaddimah* uses scientific reasoning to examine social cohesion and conflict.

1821 In France, early socialist Henri de Saint-Simon argues that the new industrial society will bring forth a new Utopia, with a new kind of politics led by men of science.

1835 Belgian philosopher Adolphe Quetelet puts forward the idea of a social science to study the average man.

AFTER
1848 Karl Marx argues for the abolition of the family in the *Communist Manifesto*.

1962 Michael Oakeshott argues that society cannot be understood rationally.

French philosopher Auguste Comte's defence of the family in his *Course in Positive Philosophy* (1830–48) is based on more than mere sentimental attachment. Comte's "positivist" philosophy takes the view that in any true understanding of society, the only valid data comes from the senses, and from the logical analysis of this data. Society, he argues, operates according to laws, just like the physical world of natural science. It is the task of the scientist of society to study it and tease out these laws.

Family is the social unit

It is crucial, believes Comte, to look at general laws and not become obsessed by idiosyncratic individual views. "The scientific spirit forbids us to regard society as composed of individuals. The true social unit is the family." It is on the basis of families that society is constructed – a social science that starts with the demands of individuals is doomed to failure. It is also within the family that individual whims are harnessed for the good of society. Humans are driven by both personal instinct and social instincts. "In a family, the social and the personal instincts are blended and reconciled; in a family, too, the principle of subordination and mutual cooperation is exemplified." Comte's position stresses social bonds, but is in conflict with socialism – Marxists who argue for the abolition of the family are, in Comte's view, arguing for the very destruction of human society. ■

> "Families become tribes and tribes become nations."
> **Auguste Comte**

See also: Ibn Khaldun 72–73 ▪ Karl Marx 188–93 ▪ Max Weber 214–15 ▪ Michael Oakeshott 276–77 ▪ Ayn Rand 280–81

THE RISE
THE MAS
1848–1910

OF
SES

1848

Karl Marx and Friedrich Engels publish the *Communist Manifesto* as **unrest sweeps across Europe**.

1864

The **Taiping Rebellion** in China collapses after taking 20 million lives.

1865

Victory for the North in the US Civil War sees the nationwide **abolition of slavery**.

1868

The Meiji Restoration in Japan **ends feudal rule** of the shogunate.

1871

The **Paris Commune** is established, and proclaimed as the first government of the workers.

1871

Germany is unified as a single nation-state under Kaiser Wilhelm.

1872

Friedrich Nietzsche's first major work, *The Birth of Tragedy*, is published.

1873

A financial crisis triggers the severe **Long Depression** in Europe and the US.

The revolutions and wars of the late 18th and early 19th centuries left an uncertain legacy in Europe. The Treaty of Paris in 1815 ended the Napoleonic Wars, and for almost a century there were few conflicts between the European powers. The world economy continued to grow, driven by industrialization and the rapid growth of railways and telecommunications. It was just about possible to believe that the political settlements enacted in the first part of the 19th century would provide a stable institutional framework for humanity. German philosopher Georg Hegel thought the most perfect form of the state had been achieved in Prussia in the 1830s, while European colonialism was presented by many as a civilizing mission for the rest of the world. Once political and civil rights had been secured, a just society would emerge.

Communist thoughts

Two young scholars of Hegel, Friedrich Engels and Karl Marx, violently disagreed with his conclusions. They pointed to the creation – through industrialization – of a new class of propertyless workers, who enjoyed increased political freedom, but suffered a form of economic slavery. Using the tools of analysis developed by Hegel, they believed they could show how this class had the potential to push civil and political rights into the realm of economics.

Marx and Engels wrote their *Communist Manifesto* as revolutionary movements were gathering momentum across Europe. They attempted to provide a radical template through which a new kind of mass politics would come into existence. New workers' parties, such as Germany's SPD, adopted the manifesto as their guiding light and looked with confidence to a future in which the great mass of the people would exercise political and economic power. Politics was shifted from the concern of the elites to a mass activity, with millions joining political organizations and – as the right to vote spread – millions more participating in elections.

The old order in retreat

In the US, differences over the place of slavery in the new territories led to civil war. Victory for the Union saw an end to slavery across the country and provided new vigour to

1876
Britain's queen Victoria is declared **Empress of India**.

1889
The **"Second International"** organization of socialist and labour parties is founded in Paris.

1890
The **Wounded Knee Massacre** ends the Indian Wars in the US, marking the end of the "Old West".

1895
Theodor Herzl writes *The Jewish State*, starting the modern **Zionist movement**.

1905
Max Weber's *The Protestant Ethic and the Spirit of Capitalism* is published.

1905
A revolution in Russia is put down, but wins **concessions from the tsar**.

1908
In *Reflections on Violence*, Georges Sorel argues in favour of **violent revolution**.

1909
The Minority Report in Britain recommends the creation of a **welfare state**.

the nation, marking the start of its rise in economic and political power. To the south, the new republics of Latin America struggled to achieve the political stability that their constitutions had promised, and power passed back and forth between sections of a narrow elite. Much of the region stagnated, but demands for reform would lead to the outbreak of revolution in Mexico in 1910.

In Asia, the first anti-colonial organizations were set up to fight for political rights, and a section of Japan's traditional rulers instituted a thoroughgoing modernization that swept away the old feudal order. Across the world, the old regimes appeared to be in retreat.

However, whatever some Marxists may have believed, progress towards political power for the masses was not guaranteed. Friedrich Nietzsche was prominent among those who expressed a profound cynicism about the ability of society to be reformed by the masses. His ideas were adapted later by Max Weber, who attempted to reimagine society not as a place of class struggle, as in Marxist thinking, but as a battle for power between competing belief systems.

Reform movements

Liberals and conservatives adapted themselves to a changed world by forming mass membership parties of their own, and sought to manage the growing demands for welfare and economic justice from the left. Liberal philosophy had been given a firm theoretical base by thinkers such as Britain's John Stuart Mill, who held that the rights of the individual should be the basis for a just society, rather than the class struggle of the Marxists.

Increasingly, socialists seeking social ownership of production also began to see the possibilities for reform from within the capitalist system. Eduard Bernstein argued for reform through the ballot box, taking advantage of the universal male suffrage now established in the newly unified Germany. In Britain, reformist socialists such as Sidney and Beatrice Webb advocated a comprehensive system of welfare to protect the poor.

Meanwhile, in Russia, Vladimir Lenin and others agitated tirelessly for a socialist revolution. Tensions between Europe's old elites were also starting to grow. The stage was set for the tumultuous changes that were about to sweep the world. ■

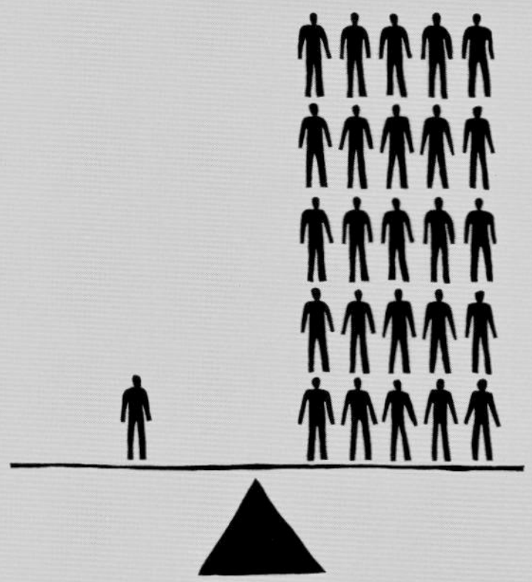

SOCIALISM IS A NEW SYSTEM OF SERFDOM

ALEXIS DE TOCQUEVILLE (1805–1859)

IN CONTEXT

IDEOLOGY
Liberalism

FOCUS
Classless society

BEFORE
380 BCE Plato argues that democracy is inferior to other forms of government.

1798 The French Revolution begins, leading to the establishment of a republic.

1817 Socialist theorist Henri de Saint-Simon argues for a new type of society based entirely on socialist principles.

AFTER
1922 The Soviet Union is established, bringing communist rule to much of Eastern Europe.

1989 The Berlin Wall falls, heralding the end of socialism throughout Eastern Europe and the increased expansion of capitalist, democratic systems of government.

Socialism **ignores** the highest human virtues.

Socialism **undermines** private property.

Socialism **stifles** the individual.

Socialism is a new system of serfdom.

In September 1848, Alexis de Tocqueville made an impassioned speech in France's Constituent Assembly, which had been elected after the overthrow of King Louis-Philippe that February. He argued that the ideals of the French Revolution of 1789 implied a democratic future for France and a rejection of socialism.

De Tocqueville attacked socialism on three counts. First, he argued that socialism plays on "men's material passions" – its aim is the generation of wealth. It ignores the loftiest human ideals of generosity and virtue, which were the seeds of the revolution. Second, socialism undermines the principle of private property, which he saw as vital to liberty. Even if socialist states do not seize property, they weaken it. Finally, his strongest criticism was that socialism is contemptuous of the individual.

Under socialism, de Tocqueville believed, individual initiative is snuffed out by an overbearing state. The state directs society as a whole, but increasingly becomes the "master of each man". While democracy enhances personal autonomy, socialism reduces it. Socialism and democracy can never go together – they are opposites.

A classless society

De Tocqueville believed that the ideals of the French Revolution had been betrayed. The revolution of 1789 was about liberty for all, which meant the abolition of class

See also: Plato 34–39 ▪ Aristotle 40–43 ▪ Montesquieu 110–11 ▪ Jean-Jacques Rousseau 118–25 ▪ John Stuart Mill 174–81 ▪ Max Weber 214–15

> Democracy aims at equality in liberty. Socialism desires equality in constraint and in servitude.
> **Alexis de Tocqueville**

divisions. But since then, the upper classes had become more privileged and corrupt. The lower classes burned with anger and disaffection, and were therefore more easily seduced by socialist ideas.

The solution, de Tocqueville claimed, was not to be found in socialism, but in a reassertion of the original revolutionary ideal of a free, classless society. Socialism, by pitting property owners against the proletariat, would reinstate social divisions, betraying this vision. The establishment of a socialist system would be like reverting to the pre-revolutionary monarchy. The domineering socialist state was, for de Tocqueville, incompatible with freedom and competition.

De Tocqueville espoused a democratic society in which individual enterprise could flourish, but the poor and vulnerable would be protected through the Christian ideal of charity. As a model for this he pointed to the US, which he believed had achieved the most advanced version of democracy.

De Tocqueville's contrast between democracy-as-freedom and socialism-as-confinement became a recurring motif in 19th- and 20th-century debates. His speech was made in a year in which revolutions and uprisings spread across Europe, fomented in part by socialist ideas. However, after 1848, the uprisings fizzled out, and for a time, socialism failed to take root in the way he had feared. ■

Under socialism, de Tocqueville argued, workers would be mere cogs in the overbearing machinery of the state.

Alexis de Tocqueville

De Tocqueville was born in Paris to aristocratic parents. When Louis-Philippe d'Orléans came to the throne in 1830, de Tocqueville took up a post in the new government, but political changes made his position precarious so he left France for the US. The result was his most famous work, *Democracy in America*, in which he argued that democracy and equality had progressed furthest in the US. He also warned of the dangers of democracy – materialism and excessive individualism.

After the 1848 revolution de Tocqueville became a member of the Constituent Assembly in France, which was responsible for devising the constitution of the Second Republic. He withdrew from politics after his opposition to Louis-Napoléon Bonaparte's coup of 1851 led to a night in prison. Dogged by ill health for much of his life, he died of tuberculosis eight years later aged 53.

Key works

1835, 1840 *Democracy in America*
1856 *The Old Regime and the Revolution*

SAY NOT I, BUT WE

GIUSEPPE MAZZINI (1805–1872)

IN CONTEXT

IDEOLOGY
Nationalism

FOCUS
Rights and duties

BEFORE
1789 *The Declaration of the Rights of Man and of the Citizen*, issued during the French Revolution, defines the universal rights of citizens.

1793 German philosopher Johann Gottfried Herder argues for the importance of the nation.

AFTER
1859 In *On Liberty*, John Stuart Mill argues for the rights of the individual.

1861 Italy is unified.

1950s Nationalist movements rise around the world as colonies gain independence.

1957 The Treaty of Rome, signed by six European nations, founds the European Economic Community.

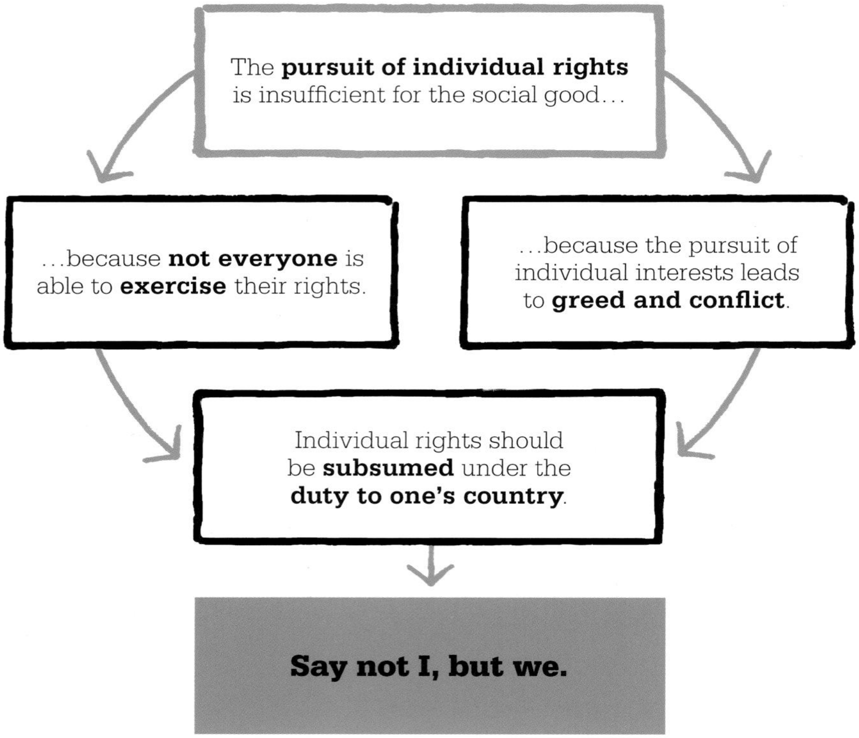

The Italian political thinker and activist Giuseppe Mazzini called on people to unite around the idea of the nation state. In his *Essay on the Duties of Man: Addressed to Workingmen*, he asked for people to place duty to their country above individual interests. Mazzini's nationalism arose from a critique of the political changes that had taken place in Europe over the previous century. The animating idea behind these upheavals had been liberty, which

See also: Johann Gottfried Herder 142–43 ▪ Simón Bolívar 162–63 ▪ John Stuart Mill 174–81 ▪ Theodor Herzl 208–09 ▪ Gianfranco Miglio 296

> In labouring for our own country on the right principle, we labour for Humanity.
> **Giuseppe Mazzini**

was to be obtained through the pursuit of individual rights. The working masses hoped that rights would deliver material wellbeing.

Mazzini believed that the advancement of liberty had not been matched by progress in the condition of the workers, despite the overall expansion of wealth and commerce. Economic development had benefited the privileged few, but not the many. For Mazzini, the narrow pursuit of individual rights raised two problems. First, liberty was an "illusion and a bitter irony" for most people, who were in no position to exercise it: the right to education, for example, meant nothing to those who didn't have the resources or time to pursue it. Second, striving for individual material interests led people to trample on each other, weakening mankind's common bonds.

Duty before rights

Mazzini argued that the pursuit of rights came second to a higher call of duty towards humanity. This duty required individuals to cooperate towards common aims. However, it would be hard for an individual acting alone to directly serve humanity in all its vastness. Instead, according to Mazzini, God had created separate countries, dividing humanity into branches. A country was the "workshop" through which the individual could serve mankind. Duty to country – thinking in terms of "we", not "I" – would connect individuals to the broader collective of humanity.

A procession through the streets of Turin marked the unification of Italy in 1861. Mazzini is seen as a founding father of the modern Italian state.

For Mazzini, a country was múch more than a group of individuals in a geographical area: it was an association of people united by brotherhood. Mazzini's ideas inspired revolutionaries in Europe's 1848 uprisings at a time when Italy was emerging as a unified state. In the 20th century, they roused nationalists during the struggles against colonial rule. Mazzini's dream of cooperation between European nations was realized with the creation of the European Economic Community in 1957. ■

Giuseppe Mazzini

The son of a doctor, Giuseppe Mazzini was born in Genoa, Italy. In his 20s he became involved with underground politics, and by 1831 had been imprisoned and then exiled for his activities. He founded a political organization, Young Italy, which fought for a unified Italy through agitation and uprising. Following his example, activists across Europe set up similar organizations.

In the wake of the 1848 European uprisings, Mazzini returned to Italy to lead a republic in Rome. After the republic fell, he found himself once more in exile. By the early 1860s, he was back in Italy, at a time when a northern Italian kingdom was being established. This didn't conform to Mazzini's republican vision, and he refused to take up his seat in the new parliament. He died in Pisa in 1872, two years after the unification of Italy had been completed with the Capture of Rome.

Key works

1852 *On Nationality*
1860 *The Duties of Man and Other Essays*

THAT SO FEW DARE TO BE ECCENTRIC MARKS THE CHIEF DANGER OF THE TIME

JOHN STUART MILL (1806–1873)

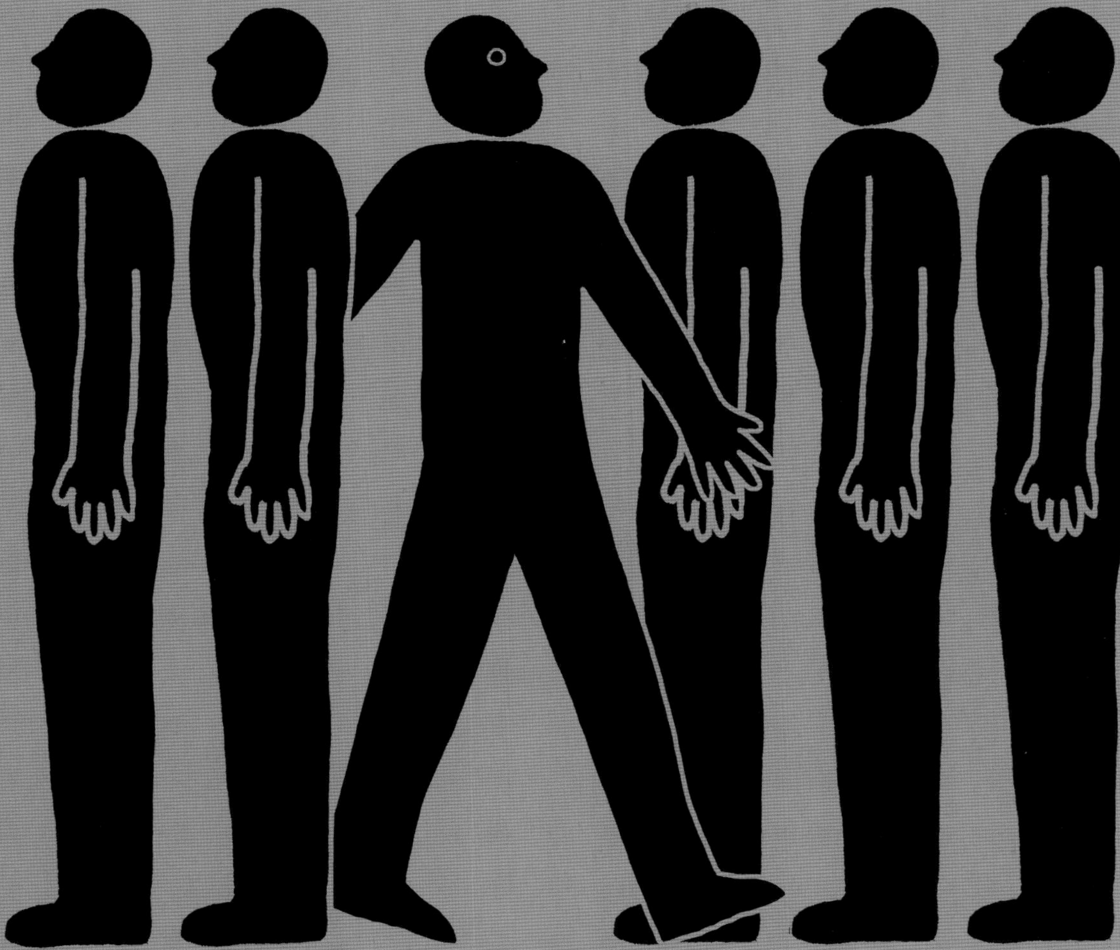

IN CONTEXT

IDEOLOGY
Liberalism

FOCUS
Individual liberty

BEFORE
1690 John Locke, an opposer of authoritarian governments, pioneers liberal thought.

1776 The American Declaration of Independence states that all men are created equal, with rights to liberty, life, and happiness.

AFTER
1940s Liberals lose faith in free markets after the Great Depression, and argue for a welfare state.

1958 British scholar Isaiah Berlin distinguishes "negative" from "positive" liberty.

1974 US philosopher Robert Nozick argues that personal liberties are sacrosanct.

In *On Liberty*, John Stuart Mill made a famous defence of an important tenet of liberalism: that individuality is the foundation of a healthy society. His investigations were motivated by a basic question of political theory – that of the appropriate balance between individual freedom and social control.

Mill argued that the transformations of the political conditions of the mid-19th century necessitated a fresh look at this matter. In earlier times, when absolutist monarchies wielded power, rulers' rapacity could not be kept in check by the ballot box. Because of this, the interests of the state were considered to be opposed to those of the individual, and government interference was viewed with suspicion.

The expansion of democratic systems of government in the 19th century was assumed to have resolved this tension. Regular elections made the masses the ultimate rulers, bringing into alignment the interests of the state with those of the people. In this setting, it was thought that interference by the government could not be to the detriment of the individuals who had elected it.

Tyranny of the majority

Mill warned about the complacency of this view. He said that the elected government distils the views of the majority, and this majority might end up wanting to oppress the minority. This "tyranny of the majority" meant that there was a risk that interference by even elected governments would have harmful effects. At least as serious as political tyranny was the risk of the social tyranny of public opinion, which tends to lead to conformity of belief and action. These forms of tyranny were all the more serious, argued Mill, because people's opinions were often unthinking, rooted in little more than self-interest and personal preference. Ultimately, the received wisdom is then nothing more than the interests of a society's most dominant groups.

Britain at the time was still going through the transition towards a modern democracy, and Mill said that people did not yet

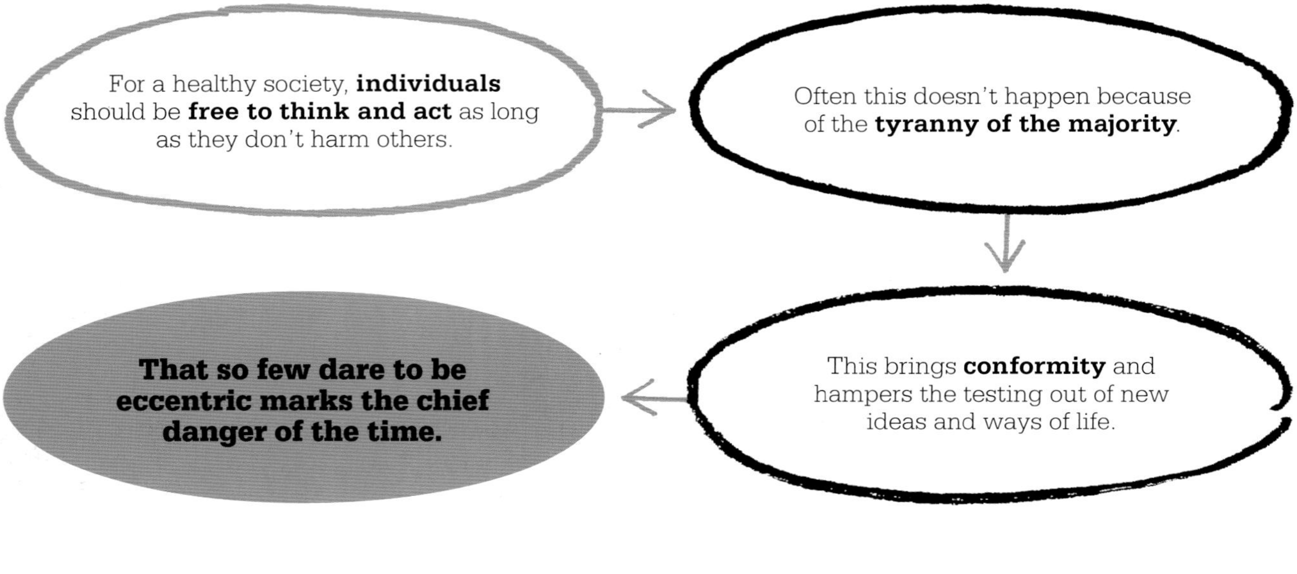

See also: Thomas Hobbes 96–103 ▪ John Locke 104–09 ▪ Jeremy Bentham 144–49 ▪ Alexis De Tocqueville 170–71 ▪ Robert Nozick 236–37 ▪ John Rawls 298–303

Freedom of action – such as the right of assembly at this gay pride parade in Paris – was central to Mill's idea of individual liberty, alongside freedom of thought and freedom of opinion.

appreciate the dangers. The prevailing mistrust of government was a relic from the era in which the state was viewed as a threat to individuals, and the potential for tyranny by a democratic majority was not yet widely understood. This confusion meant that the government's actions were both unnecessarily called for and unjustifiably condemned. Also, the tyranny of public opinion was on the rise and Mill feared a general tendency for society to increase its control over the individual.

Justifiable interference

A moral dam was needed to stop this trend, so Mill attempted to set out a clear principle to define the right balance between individual autonomy and government interference. He argued that society could only justifiably interfere with individuals' liberties in order to prevent harm to others. Concern for the individual's own good might justify an attempt to persuade him to take a different course of action, but not to compel him to do so: "Over himself, over his own body and mind, the individual is sovereign," Mill said. This principle of individual liberty applied to thought, to the expression of opinions, and to actions.

> The struggle between Liberty and Authority is the most conspicuous feature in the portions of history with which we are earliest familiar.
> **John Stuart Mill**

Mill argued that if this principle is undermined, the whole of society suffers. Without freedom of thought, for example, human knowledge and innovation would be restricted. To demonstrate this, Mill put forward an account of how humans arrive at truth. Because human minds are fallible, the truth or falsity of an idea only becomes known by testing it in the bubbling cauldron of opposing ideas. By stifling ideas, society might lose a true idea. It might also suppress a false idea that would have been useful to test and potentially reveal the truth of another idea. Mill rejected the argument that some ideas are more socially useful than others irrespective of their truth. He believed that this argument assumes infallibility in deciding which beliefs are useful. Although heretics were no longer burned at the stake, Mill believed that the social intolerance of unorthodox opinions threatened to dull minds and cramp the development of society.

A profusion of ideas

Even when society's received wisdoms were true, Mill argued that it was important to maintain a profusion of ideas – for a true idea to keep its vitality and power, it needs to be constantly challenged and probed. This was particularly the case with ideas about society and politics, which can never attain the certainty of mathematical truths. Testing ideas is best done by hearing the views of those who hold conflicting opinions. Where there are no dissenters, their »

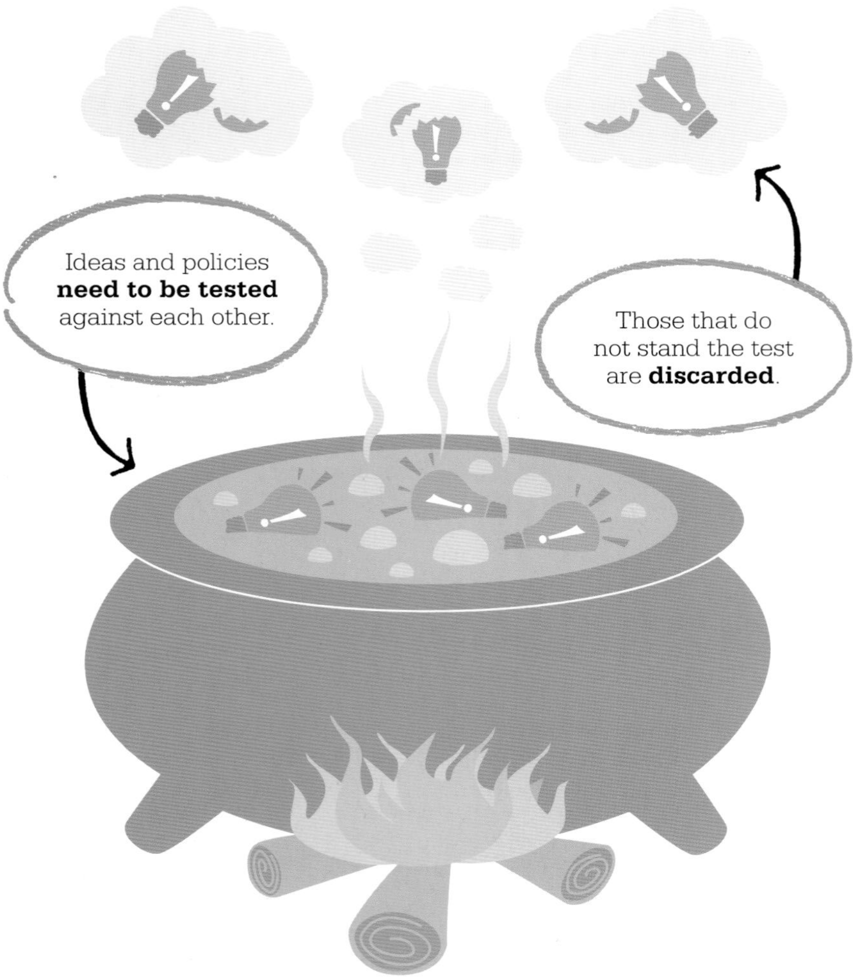

In Mill's bubbling cauldron of ideas, each idea must constantly be tested against other ideas. The cauldron acts like a still. False, or broken, ideas evaporate away as they are rejected, while true ideas are left in the mix, and grow stronger.

> "The tyranny of the majority" is now generally included among the evils against which society requires to be on its guard.
> **John Stuart Mill**

views must be imagined. Without this discussion and argument, people will not appreciate the basis of even true ideas, which then become dead dogmas, parroted without any real understanding. Correct principles of behaviour and morality, when they have been converted into barren slogans, can no longer motivate authentic action.

Mill used his principle of liberty to defend the individual's freedom to act. However, he acknowledged that freedom of action would necessarily be more limited than freedom of thought, because an action is more capable of hurting others than a thought. Like freedom of ideas, individuality – the freedom to live an unorthodox life – promotes social innovation: "the worth of different modes of life should be proved practically," he said. Although people might usefully draw on traditions as a guide to their own lives, they should do so creatively in ways that are especially relevant to their particular circumstances and preferences. Mill believed that when people automatically follow customs – in a similar way to the impact of unthinkingly held opinions – ways of living become sterile, and the individual's moral faculties are weakened.

Experimenting for all

As with the free expression of ideas, those who act in new ways provide a benefit to society as a whole, even to conventional people. Non-conformists discover new ways of doing things, some of which can then be adopted by others. But social innovators need to be free to experiment for these benefits to be realized.

Given the power of the majority view, free spirits and eccentrics help to inspire people towards new ways of doing things. When Mill wrote *On Liberty*, the Industrial Revolution had made Britain the most economically advanced country in the world. Mill believed that this success had come from the relative plurality of thought and freedom of action that existed in Europe. He contrasted the dynamism of Europe with the stagnation of China, which he believed had declined because customs and traditions had hardened and suppressed individuality. In Britain, economic development had brought mass education, faster communications, and greater opportunities for previously excluded social classes. But this progress also brought a greater homogeneity of tastes and, with it, a decline in individuality. He believed that if this trend continued, England would suffer the same fate as China. Mill thought that English society had already become too conformist and unappreciative of the value of individuality and originality. People acted in accordance with social rank, not their consciences. This is why he believed that a lack of eccentricity was such a danger.

The harm principle

Mill's criterion of harm was a useful and easily stated principle to define the appropriate boundary between state and individual, expressed at a time when the relationship between the government and the people was going through rapid change.

Policies on smoking during the 20th century illustrate how the principle can be used as a way of thinking about government restrictions on individual behaviour. Although it had long been understood that tobacco did people harm, society had never prevented individuals from smoking. Instead, health information was supplied to persuade people to stop smoking and, by the late 20th century, smoking was declining in the US and many European countries.

This was in line with Mill's principle of liberty: people could freely smoke even though it harmed them, because it did not harm others. Then new medical information came to light showing that passive smoking was harmful. This meant that smoking in public places now violated the harm principle. The principle was reapplied, and smoking bans in public places were initiated to reflect this new knowledge. With its rapid decline in popularity, smoking has in a sense become a habit of eccentrics, but despite the increasing evidence about the health dangers, few would advocate an outright ban.

> Wherever there is an ascendant class, a large portion of the morality of the country emanates from its class interests, and its feelings of class superiority.
> **John Stuart Mill**

Harm versus happiness

The harm principle may not always deliver the results imagined by liberals, however. For example, if people found homosexuality immoral and repugnant, they might argue that the mere knowledge that homosexuality was being practised would harm them. They might argue that the state should intervene to uphold sexual morals. This raises the issue of the underlying ethical basis for Mill's defence of the individual. *On Liberty* was written in the context of the philosophical system of utilitarianism, which Mill espoused. Mill was a follower of the English philosopher Jeremy Bentham, who argued that the »

Demonstrators protest at a neo-Nazi rally. Mill held that individual liberty – such as the neo-Nazis' right to gather – could be opposed if it led to more unhappiness than happiness.

morality of actions should be judged according to the extent to which they contribute to the sum total of human happiness. For instance, instead of judging lying as wrong in itself, one would need to condemn it because its various consequences – when reckoned together – cause more unhappiness than happiness. Mill refined and developed Bentham's theory, for example by making a distinction between "higher" and "lower" pleasures, meaning that it would be better to be born an unhappy Socrates than a happy pig, because only a Socrates has the possibility of experiencing higher pleasures.

One might perceive a conflict between utilitarianism and the approach taken in *On Liberty*, because the defence of individual liberty sounds like a separate principle, which might conflict with the happiness principle that takes precedence in a utilitarian approach. If homosexuality made the majority unhappy, for instance, utilitarianism would recommend that it should be banned, which would be a clear infringement of individual liberty. Despite this apparent conflict, Mill maintains that utility is still the ultimate, overarching principle in his system.

A religious preacher addresses onlookers at Speaker's Corner in Hyde Park, London. Mill argued against censorship and for freedom of speech, whatever the opinion being expressed.

Mill is not making an absolutist argument for individual autonomy. One way of viewing his argument is as concrete application of the happiness principle in the area of state versus individual action: Mill argues that liberty leads to social innovation and the growth of knowledge, which then contribute to happiness. This leaves open the possibility that Mill may have been too optimistic in thinking that the happiness principle always points towards liberty. He may even have been too optimistic with respect to the expression of opinions, not just to behavioural norms. For example, some might argue that the banning of the expression of certain opinions – the declaration of support for Adolf Hitler in today's Germany, for example – reduces unhappiness and is therefore justifiable on utilitarian grounds.

Negative liberty

Another criticism that could be levelled at Mill's arguments concerns the way in which he believes that truth bubbles up from the cauldron of opposing ideas. He believes that this cauldron bubbles most vigorously when society completely avoids any interference with individual thought or action. This is a notion of liberty that the British political theorist and philosopher Isaiah Berlin later called "negative liberty", which he defines as the absence of constraints on actions.

Leftist critics consider negative liberty alone to be insufficient. They point out that oppressed groups – such as the poorest in society, or women without rights – might have no way of expressing their unorthodox views: they are marginalized, which means that they have little access to the media and institutions in which opinions are expressed and publicized. For this reason, those on the left often argue that negative liberties are meaningless without "positive liberties", which actively help to give marginalized people the power to express their opinions and influence policy. If he had witnessed the achievements of feminism over the 20th century, Mill might well have argued that women did manage to obtain political equality through the vigorous expression of their views. However, leftists would counter once more that formal political rights mean little without positive liberties, such as the provision of equal pay and guaranteed employment rights.

> The liberty of the individual must be thus far limited; he must not make himself a nuisance to other people.
> **John Stuart Mill**

Pragmatic liberalism

Mill's political philosophies – utilitarianism and his defence of liberty – have had a profound influence on the development of liberal democracies throughout the world. His is perhaps the most famous and frequently cited argument for a pragmatic form of liberalism, which is tied to a principle of collective wellbeing rather than arguing for abstract, inalienable rights.

In modern liberal democracies, particularly in the UK and the US, many debates – such as those on sexual morality, smoking, and even the role of free markets in the economy – have been structured around the considerations that Mill put forward nearly two centuries ago. But even in these countries, many social constraints on individual actions are justified by more than just the minimal criterion of negative liberty. Bans on recreational drugs, for example, depend on a paternalistic principle, and even in free market countries, the government regulates commerce and attempts to make economic outcomes more equal. These are all actions that may be considered to go beyond Mill's condition for intervention, but as the debates about the appropriate scope of social control continue unabated, those arguing for more liberal stances often invoke the arguments made by Mill. ■

Mill's Three Basic Liberties

The liberty of **thought and ideas** – absolute freedom of opinion of sentiment, and the freedom to express them in speech or writing.

The liberty to pursue one's own **tastes and pursuits** – to live our lives exactly how we see fit, so long as this does no harm to others in society.

The liberty of **combination among individuals** – the right to unite with others for any non-harmful purpose, so long as members are not coerced.

John Stuart Mill

Born in London in 1806, John Stuart Mill became one of the most influential philosophers of the 19th century. His father, James Mill, was part of the circle of thinkers of the leader of utilitarian philosophy, Jeremy Bentham. The elder Mill set out to ensure that his precocious son became a great thinker – as a young boy Mill studied Latin, Greek, history, mathematics, and economics. But at the age of 20, Mill realized that these intellectual exertions had stunted his emotional life, and he suffered from a bout of deep depression.

From 1830, Mill developed a close friendship with Harriet Taylor, marrying her in 1851 after the death of her husband. Harriet was influential to Mill's development, helping him to broaden his conception of human life from the ascetic ethic of his father, to one that valued emotion and individuality. This is said to have influenced his thinking on utilitarianism and liberty.

Key works

1859 *On Liberty*
1865 *Utilitarianism*
1869 *The Subjection of Women*

NO MAN IS GOOD ENOUGH TO GOVERN ANOTHER MAN, WITHOUT THAT OTHER'S CONSENT

ABRAHAM LINCOLN (1809–1865)

IN CONTEXT

IDEOLOGY
Abolitionism

FOCUS
Equal rights

BEFORE
1776 The Constitution of the United States establishes the new republic.

1789 In the French Revolution the Declaration of Rights states that "men are born and remain free and equal in rights".

AFTER
1860 Lincoln's election as the 16th US president provokes the secession of Southern states in defence of their right to maintain slavery.

1865 With the surrender of General Robert E. Lee of the Confederacy, the US Civil War ends in victory for the Union.

1964 The US Civil Rights Act bans job discrimination on the basis of "race, color, religion, or national origin".

The foundation of the United States of America after the Revolutionary War against Britain left the nature of the new republic unresolved. Although the country was formally committed to the equality of "all men" through the Declaration of Independence of 1776, slavery saw millions of Africans transported across the Atlantic to plantations throughout the Southern states. The 1820 Missouri Compromise outlawed slavery in the northern states, but not in the South.

Abraham Lincoln's statement that "no man is good enough to govern another man, without that other's consent" comes from a speech of 1854. He argued against the right of states to maintain their own laws, by contesting that the foundation of the United States on the right to individual liberty overrode the right to "self-government". The republic was built on liberty and equality, not on political convenience or as a compromise among states that retained their own authority. Considered a moderate opponent of slavery, Lincoln had previously argued against extending slavery, but not for abolishing it. Yet this speech heralds the defence of republican virtues that became the rallying call for northern states when the Civil War erupted in 1861. Lincoln's message became more radical, and led to the Emancipation Proclamation of 1863 and the outlawing of slavery across the United States in 1865. ■

> One section of our country believes slavery is right and ought to be extended, while the other believes it is wrong and ought not to be extended.
> **Abraham Lincoln**

See also: Hugo Grotius 94–95 ■ Jean-Jacques Rousseau 118–25 ■ Thomas Jefferson 140–41 ■ John C. Calhoun 161

PROPERTY IS THEFT

PIERRE-JOSEPH PROUDHON (1809–1865)

IN CONTEXT

IDEOLOGY
Socialism, mutualism

FOCUS
Private property

BEFORE
462 BCE Plato advocates collective ownership, arguing that it promotes the pursuit of common goals.

1689 John Locke argues that human beings have a natural right to property.

AFTER
1848 In the *Communist Manifesto*, Karl Marx and Friedrich Engels outline their vision of a society with no property.

1974 US philosopher Robert Nozick argues for the moral primacy of private property.

2000 Peruvian economist Hernando de Soto claims that secure property rights are essential for lifting developing countries out of poverty.

Pierre-Joseph Proudhon, the French politician and thinker, made his famous assertion that property is theft at a time when many in France felt frustrated by the outcomes of the revolutions of the previous few decades. When Proudhon published *What is Property?*, 10 years had passed since the 1830 revolution that had ended the Bourbon monarchy. It was hoped that the new July monarchy would finally bring about the vision of freedom and equality embodied by the 1789 French Revolution. But by 1840, class conflict was rife, and the elite had grown rich while the masses remained in poverty. Many saw the result of the political struggles not as liberty and equality, but as corruption and rising inequality.

Proudhon said that the rights to liberty, equality, and security were natural, absolute, and inviolable, and were the very basis of society. However, he claimed that the apparent right to property was not the same as these. In fact, he maintained that property undermined these fundamental rights: while the liberty of the rich and the poor can co-exist, the property of the wealthy sits alongside the poverty of the many. Thus, property was inherently antisocial. Property was a primary issue of the working-class and socialist movements that were emerging in Europe in the 19th century, and Proudhon's fiery declaration encapsulates the revolutionary ferment of the time. ■

> The downfall and death of societies are due to the power of accumulation possessed by property.
> **Pierre-Joseph Proudhon**

See also: Hugo Grotius 94–95 ■ Thomas Paine 134–39 ■ Mikhail Bakunin 184–85 ■ Karl Marx 188–93 ■ Leon Trotsky 242–45

THE PRIVILEGED MAN IS A MAN DEPRAVED IN INTELLECT AND HEART

MIKHAIL BAKUNIN (1814–1876)

IN CONTEXT

IDEOLOGY
Anarchism

FOCUS
Corruption of power

BEFORE
1793 English political philosopher William Godwin outlines an anarchist philosophy, arguing that government corrupts society.

1840 Pierre-Joseph Proudhon imagines a just form of society devoid of political authority.

AFTER
1892 Peter Kropotkin proposes "anarchist communism", arguing for a form of cooperative distribution as well as production.

1936 Spain's anarchist union, the CNT, boasts more than 1 million members.

1999 Anarchist ideas re-emerge around anti-capitalist demonstrations in Seattle, USA.

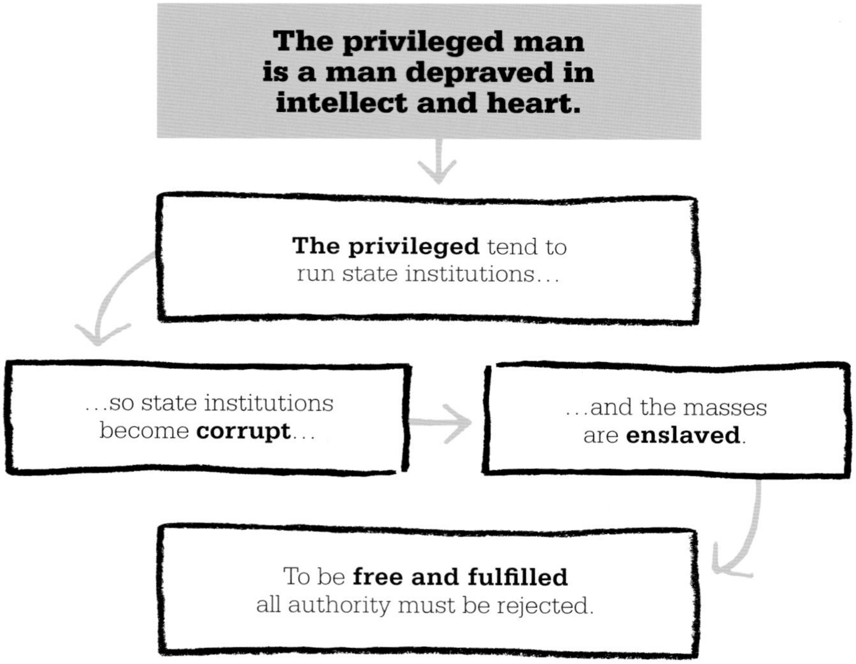

In Europe in the 19th century, modern nation states emerged, democracy spread, and the relationship between individuals and authority was recast. In *God and the State*, Russian revolutionary Mikhail Bakunin investigated the requirements for the moral and political fulfilment of human society.

At the time, society was seen as an association of individuals under the authority of a government or the Church. Bakunin argued that humans become truly fulfilled by exercising their capacity to think and by rebelling against authority, whether of gods or of man. He made a searing attack on "religious hallucination", arguing that it is a

See also: Georg Hegel 156–59 ▪ Pierre-Joseph Proudhon 183 ▪ Karl Marx 188–93 ▪ Peter Kropotkin 206

tool of oppression to keep people servile, and that it helps the powerful to maintain their position. Life for the masses is wretched, and solace can come from belief in God. But living in accordance with religion dulls the intellect, so it cannot allow human liberation. Bakunin argued that the oppressors of the people – priests, monarchs, bankers, police, and politicians – would agree with Voltaire's dictum that if there was no God, it would be necessary to invent him. Bakunin insisted instead that freedom required the abolition of God.

Acquiescence to the man-made institution of the state would also enslave people. The laws of nature unavoidably constrain what men can do, but Bakunin claimed that once these laws were discovered and known to all, no political organizations would be required to regulate society. Everyone could consciously obey natural laws because every individual would know them to be true. But as soon as an external authority, such as the state, imposes laws – even true ones – individuals are no longer free.

Power corrupts

Bakunin argued that, when acting as society's guardians, even learned, well-informed people inevitably become corrupt. They abandon the pursuit of truth, seeking instead the protection of their own power. The masses, kept in ignorance, need their protection. Bakunin believed that accordingly, privilege kills the heart and mind.

The implication was, for Bakunin, that all authority must be rejected, even that based on universal suffrage. This was the basis of his philosophy of anarchism, which he said would light the path to human freedom. Bakunin's writings and activism helped to inspire the emergence of anarchist movements in the 19th century. His ideas propelled the rise of a distinct strand of revolutionary thought, which sat alongside Marxist beliefs. ■

St Basil's Cathedral in Moscow represents the authorities that Bakunin called on people to rebel against, and instead exercise their own freedoms.

> The idea of God implies the abdication of human reason and justice.
> **Mikhail Bakunin**

Mikhail Bakunin

Bakunin's rebelliousness was first in evidence when he deserted the Russian army as a young man. He spent time in Moscow and Berlin, immersing himself in German philosophy and Hegelian thought. He began writing revolutionary material, which drew attention from the Russian authorities, and was arrested in 1849 when, inspired by the 1848 uprising in Paris, he tried to foment insurrection.

After eight years in prison in Russia, Bakunin travelled to London and then Italy, where he recommenced his revolutionary activities. In 1868, he joined the First International, an association of left-wing revolutionary groups, but a disagreement with Karl Marx led to his expulsion. Although both men believed in revolution, Bakunin rejected what he saw as the authoritarianism of the socialist state. Bakunin died in Switzerland, agitating for revolution until the end.

Key works

1865–66 *The Revolutionary Catechism*
1871 *God and the State*
1873 *Statism and Anarchy*

THAT GOVERNMENT IS BEST WHICH GOVERNS NOT AT ALL

HENRY DAVID THOREAU (1817–1862)

IN CONTEXT

IDEOLOGY
Individualism

FOCUS
Direct action

BEFORE

380 BCE In Plato's dialogue the *Crito*, Socrates refuses the chance to escape execution, arguing that as a citizen of Athens he has a duty to obey its laws.

1819 English poet Percy Bysshe Shelley writes *Masque of Anarchy*, which imagines the potential of non-violent resistance to injustice.

AFTER

Early 20th century Suffragettes break the law in the UK to protest at the lack of voting rights for women.

1920s Mahatma Gandhi applies his version of civil disobedience, *Satyagraha*, to the cause of Indian independence.

Progress comes from the **ingenuity of the people**, not from government.

↓

Governments can be useful, but they often bring about **harm and injustice**.

↓

The best thing governments can do is to **let people flourish**.

↓

That government is best which governs not at all.

In his essay *Civil Disobedience*, published in 1849, American writer Henry David Thoreau argued that an individual should do what his moral conscience, not the law, tells him is right. If he does not do this, governments will quickly become the agents of injustice. Thoreau saw evidence for his view in the government of the United States before the Civil War, and in particular in the existence of slavery. The essay was written shortly after the end of the Mexican–American War (1846–1848), in which the US had taken territory from Mexico. Thoreau had vehemently opposed the war, which he saw as an attempt to extend slavery into new territories.

For Thoreau, the existence of slavery rendered the US government illegitimate. He said that he could not recognize any government that was also the government of slaves. Thoreau held that the state easily becomes the vehicle for this kind of injustice when its citizens passively collude with it. He likened men with dulled moral senses to pieces of wood or stones from which the machinery of oppression can be fashioned. For him, it was not just the slave

See also: Peter Kropotkin 206 ▪ Emmeline Pankhurst 207 ▪ Mahatma Gandhi 220–25 ▪ Martin Luther King 316–21 ▪ Robert Nozick 326–27

The bondage of slaves such as these in South Carolina was not only a crime by the slave owners, according to Thoreau. All citizens who allowed the practice were morally implicated.

owners who were morally culpable for slavery. Citizens of the state of Massachusetts might seem to have had little to do with the slavery of the South, but by acquiescing to a government that legitimized it, they allowed it to endure.

The logical conclusion of Thoreau's thinking is summed up by his statement that the best government is that which governs not at all. According to Thoreau, progress in America came not from government but from the ingenuity of the people, so the best thing government could do was to get out of people's way and let them flourish.

Thoreau said that a disaffected individual must do more than just register disapproval at election time: the ballot box is part of the state, but the individual's moral conscience stands above and outside such institutions. "Cast your whole vote, not a strip of paper merely, but your whole influence," he urged. An individual's sense of natural justice may call for direct actions independent of the machinery of government or the views of the majority. For Thoreau, these actions were: the withdrawal of recognition of the state; non-cooperation with its officials; or the withholding of taxes. Thoreau himself was briefly jailed in 1846 for refusing to pay the Massachusetts poll tax because of his opposition to slavery.

Thoreau influenced later thinkers and activists, such as Martin Luther King, who cited him as an inspiration. In the 1960s, as the civil rights struggle gathered momentum in the US, Thoreau's ideas gained a renewed relevance for activists engaged in acts of civil disobedience. ■

Henry David Thoreau

Born in 1817 in the town of Concord, Massachusetts, Henry David Thoreau was the son of a pencil maker. He attended Harvard University, where he studied rhetoric, classics, philosophy, and science. He ran a school with his brother John until John's death in 1842.

At the age of 28, Thoreau built a cabin at Walden Pond on land owned by the writer Ralph Waldo Emerson, and lived there for two years. His book *Walden*, an investigation of simple living and self-sufficiency, extolled the benefits of solitude and man's direct experience of nature. Thoreau joined Emerson and the "transcendentalists" – who believed in the basic goodness of the individual. In 1862 he died of tuberculosis. His last words – said to have been "Moose, Indian" – perhaps exemplified his love for the natural life.

Key works

1849 *Resistance to Civil Government, or Civil Disobedience*
1854 *Walden*
1863 *Life without Principle*

COMMUNISM IS THE RIDDLE OF HISTORY SOLVED

KARL MARX (1818–1883)

IN CONTEXT

IDEOLOGY
Communism

FOCUS
Alienation of labour

BEFORE

380 BCE Plato argues that the ideal society has strong limitations on private property.

1807 Georg Hegel puts forward a philosophy of history that inspires Marx's theories.

1819 French writer Henri de Saint-Simon advocates a form of socialism.

AFTER

1917 Vladimir Lenin leads the Bolshevik Revolution in Russia, inspired by Marx's ideas.

1940s Communism spreads across the world and the Cold War begins.

1991 The Soviet Union breaks up, and nations in Eastern Europe adopt capitalist economic systems.

Over the middle decades of the 19th century, Karl Marx – philosopher, historian, and iconic revolutionary – made one of the most ambitious analyses of capitalism ever attempted. He sought to uncover laws governing the transition of societies between different economic systems, as part of his investigations into the changing nature of work and its implications for human fulfilment. Marx's work addressed central concerns of the time: how the rise of industrial capitalism affected living conditions and society's moral health, and whether better economic and political arrangements might be worked out and put into practice.

Marx was active in a period that saw new revolutionary ideas emerging in Europe that led to the uprisings of 1848. In the *Economic and Philosophic Manuscripts* of 1844, he sketched out important elements of his economic thought, considering how capitalist organization blights the lives of workers. He argued that communism solves a problem that bedevils capitalism – the organization of work. In the *Manuscripts*, Marx developed the notion of "alienated labour", the separation of human beings from their true nature and potential for fulfilment. Marx saw various kinds of alienation as inevitable in capitalist labour markets.

> Private property is thus the product… of alienated labour.
> **Karl Marx**

The fulfilment of work

Marx believed that work has the potential to be one of the most fulfilling of all human activities. The worker puts his effort and ingenuity into the transformation of the objects of nature into products. The goods that he creates then

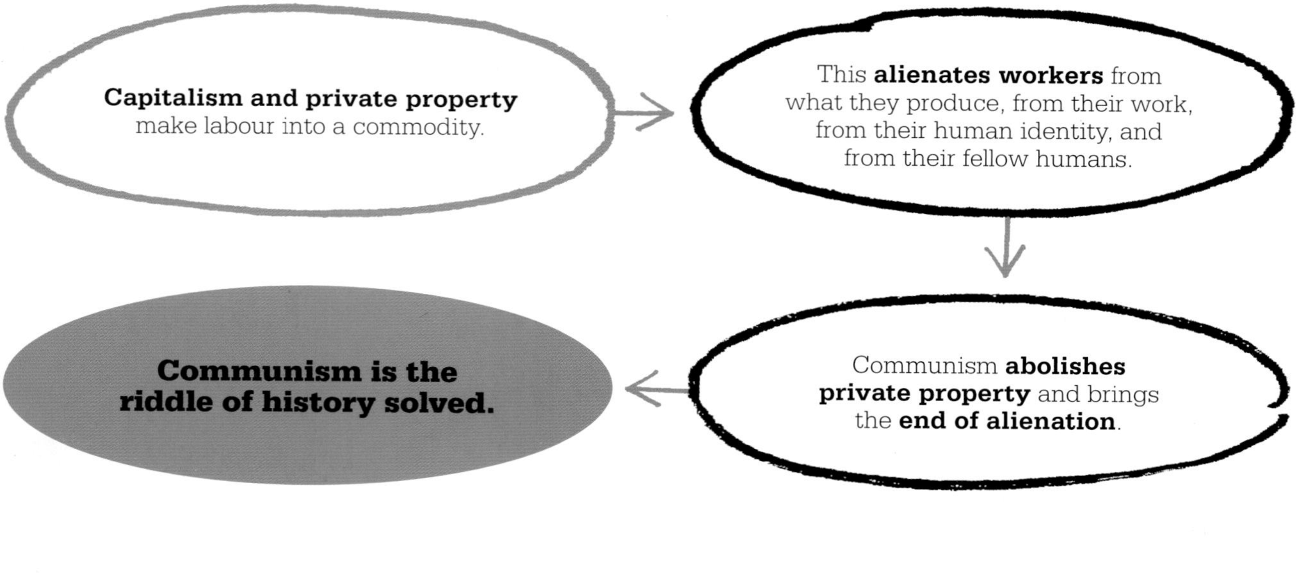

See also: Francisco de Vitoria 86–87 ■ Georg Hegel 156–59 ■ Pierre-Joseph Proudhon 183 ■ Vladimir Lenin 226–33 ■ Rosa Luxemburg 234–35 ■ Joseph Stalin 240–41 ■ Jomo Kenyatta 258

Under a capitalist system, according to Marx, the worker becomes disconnected from the products that he creates the moment they are handed over to his employer. This causes the worker to lose his self-identity.

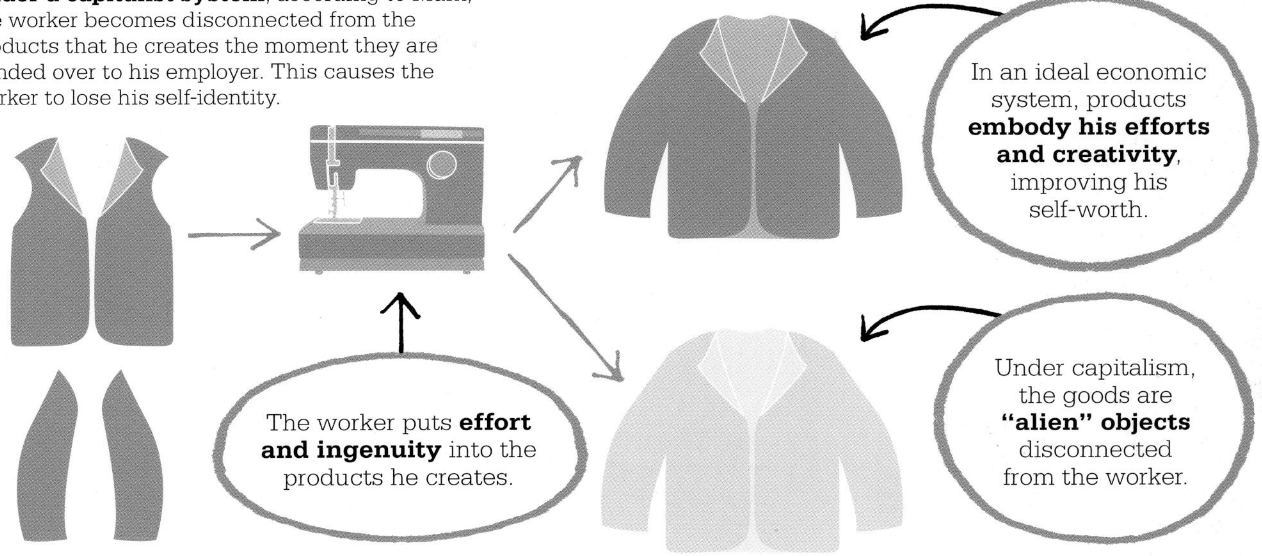

embody his effort and creativity. Under capitalism, the existence of private property separates society into capitalists – who own productive resources, such as factories and machines – and workers – who possess nothing except for their labour. Labour becomes a commodity to be bought and sold, and workers are hired by capitalists to produce goods that are then sold for profit. Marx argued that this removes the fulfilling quality of work, leading to alienation and dissatisfaction.

One form of this alienation arises from the fact that goods made by a worker who is employed by a capitalist do not belong to the worker, and cannot be kept by him. A suit cut by a tailor in a clothes factory is the property of the capitalist who owns the factory – the worker makes the suit and then hands it over to his employer. To the worker, the goods that he makes become "alien" objects with which he has little real connection. As he creates more goods that contribute to a world that he stands outside of, his inner life shrinks and his fulfilment is stunted. The worker may produce beautiful objects for other people to use and enjoy, but he creates only dullness and limitation for himself.

Workers disconnected

Marx said that workers also suffer from alienation through the very act of working. Under capitalism, workers' activity does not arise out of their inherent creativity, but from the practical necessity of working for someone else. The worker does not like work, since it crushes his body and mind and makes him unhappy – it becomes a kind of forced activity that, given the choice, he would not do. Like the goods that he eventually produces, the activity of work becomes something that is external to the worker and with which he has little real connection: "The worker therefore only feels himself outside his work, and in his work he feels outside himself." The worker becomes someone else's subject. His labour is no longer his own and his activity is no longer spontaneous and creative, but directed by another who treats him as a mere tool of production. »

> Communism is the positive transcendence of private property as human self-estrangement.
> **Karl Marx**

Marx predicted a global revolution as workers took control of the means of production. Revolution in Russia was followed by China, where propaganda stressed the values of communism.

The worker's alienation from the fruits of his labour and from the activity of working estranges him from his human identity – what Marx calls his "species-being". This is because human identity is rooted in people's ability to transform the raw material of nature into objects. Workers in capitalist systems lose the connection with this basic identity – economic necessity makes productive activity a means to an end, rather than the way in which an individual's fundamental identity is embodied and played out. Activity is what makes up life, and once this becomes alien to the worker, the worker loses the sense of his human self.

Private property to blame

These forms of alienation – from the goods produced, from the activity of work, and from human identity – cause people to become increasingly alienated from each other. Since the labour market estranges people from their own essential identity, they become estranged from each other's identity too. The worker is placed into a relationship of confrontation with the capitalist, who owns the fruits of the work and who controls the worker's labour activity for his own enrichment.

> There is no other definition of communism valid for us than that of the abolition of the exploitation of man by man.
> **Che Guevara**

Marx believed that private property lay at the root of the alienation of the worker. The division of society into property-owning capitalists and property-less workers is what leads to the alienation of workers. In turn, alienation itself reinforces this division and perpetuates private property. An aspect of the system of private property is exchange and the "division of labour". Labour becomes specialized: one worker makes the head of the pin, one worker the point, and another assembles the pin. Capitalists specialize in different kinds of goods and trade them with each other. In all of this, the worker becomes a mere cog, a small part of the larger economic machine.

Marx saw the process of the alienation of the worker and the strengthening of private property as a basic law of capitalism, which sets up a tension in human society as people become estranged from their essential nature. A solution is not to be found in higher wages, because workers would remain enslaved even if they were paid more. Alienated labour goes with private property, so "the downfall of one must therefore involve the downfall of the other".

Communism the solution

For Marx, communism resolves the tension caused by the alienation of the worker by abolishing private property, and finally solves the riddle thrown up by capitalism. It resolves the conflict between man and nature, and between human beings, and in so doing reconnects man to his fundamental humanity. Alienation made work and interactions between people into means of economic gain rather than ends in themselves. Under communism, these activities are restored to their rightful place as ends, the manifestation of true human values. For example, association between workers now arises out of a feeling of brotherhood rather than as something that has to be done. Communism brings the return of "man to himself as a social being".

Underlying the statement that communism solves history's riddle is a view of history that Marx went on to develop more fully in his later work. He believed that historical developments are determined by "material" – or economic – factors. Human beings have material needs and possess the ability to produce goods to satisfy them. Production of these goods can be organized in different ways, each of which gives rise to different kinds of social and political arrangements, which in turn lead to particular beliefs and ideologies. Marx believed that material economic factors were the fundamental determinant, and therefore the motor, of history.

Overturning capitalism

Capitalism – a particular way of organizing production – is a response to the material needs of human beings. Capitalism arose as older feudal forms of production died out. As the forces of production develop under capitalism, the suffering of workers becomes obvious, and history moves inevitably towards revolution and the ushering in of communism to replace it.

Friedrich Engels was the son of a German industrialist. He met Marx in 1842 and initially disliked him, but the pair went on to formulate one of the most far-reaching manifestos ever seen.

The legacy of Marx

It is hard to overstate Marx's influence. His work led to new schools of thought in the fields of economics, political theory, history, cultural studies, anthropology, and philosophy, to name just a few. The appeal of Marx's ideas comes from their broad interpretation of the world and their message of transformation and liberation. The prediction that he and Friedrich Engels made in their *Communist Manifesto* of 1848 – that the end of capitalism would be brought about through communist revolution – profoundly influenced 20th-century politics. Communist systems emerged in Europe and in Asia, and communist ideas influenced many governments and revolutionary movements throughout the century.

One challenge in assessing Marx's legacy is separating what he really meant from what was done in his name, particularly since communist ideology was used to justify totalitarianism and oppression in many places and at different times. By the end of the 20th century, communism in Eastern Europe had all but collapsed, and the wealthiest nations were firmly capitalist. So, even if aspects of Marx's analysis of capitalist society still had a ring of truth, many critics see history as having refuted him, particularly in his prediction of the collapse of capitalism. More recently, Marx's ideas echo once more in claims that the global economic crisis of the early 21st century is a sign of deep contradictions that are inherent in the capitalist system. ■

Karl Marx

Marx was born in Prussia to liberal Jewish parents who converted to Protestantism in response to anti-Jewish laws. As a journalist he increasingly turned to radical politics and economics. In 1843 he moved to Paris, where he met Friedrich Engels, with whom he co-wrote the *Communist Manifesto* in 1848.

After the revolutions of that year, Marx was expelled from Prussia, Belgium, and Paris before ending up in London, where he studied economics and history intensively. This eventually led to his major work, *Capital*. Marx found it hard to support himself and lived in poverty in the slum district of Soho, sustained by the financial support of Engels. He and his wife suffered from poor health, and several of their children died. Marx himself died before the final two volumes of *Capital* could be published.

Key works

1844 *Economic and Philosophic Manuscripts*
1848 *Communist Manifesto*
1867 *Capital Volume I*
(*Volumes II* and *III* published 1885 and 1894, posthumously)

THE MEN WHO PROCLAIMED THE REPUBLIC BECAME THE ASSASSINS OF FREEDOM

ALEXANDER HERZEN (1812–1870)

IN CONTEXT

IDEOLOGY
Socialism

FOCUS
Revolutionary criticism

BEFORE
1748 Montesquieu analyses different forms of government, distinguishing republics from monarchies and despotisms.

1789 The French Revolution begins, stimulating a period of revolutionary activity in France and beyond.

AFTER
1861 Serfdom is abolished in Russia by Tsar Alexander II, after growing pressure from liberals and radicals.

1890 The German Social Democratic Party is legalized, and starts on the road towards a reformist socialist party.

1917 The Russian Revolution sweeps away the tsarist regime, bringing the Bolsheviks to power.

The Russian revolutionary Alexander Herzen began his collection of essays *From the Other Shore* in 1848, the year of the failed revolutions in Europe. In it he conjured the image of a ship sailing for new lands that runs into gales and storms, representing the hopes and uncertainties of the time. But by 1850, in the collection's later essays, Herzen believed that real revolutionary fervour had been dampened, and betrayed by a more conservative vision of reform.

In one essay, Herzen lampooned the republican celebrations held in France in September 1848. He argued that beneath the pomp and slogans, the "old Catholic-feudal order" remained intact. He claimed that this had prevented realization of the authentic ideal of revolution – true liberty for all. Many of the liberals who professed to support revolution were in fact scared of its logical conclusion – the sweeping away of the old order entirely. Instead, Herzen claimed, they sought to secure freedom for their own circle, not for the worker with his "axe and blackened hands". The architects of the republic had, in a sense, broken the chains but left the prison walls standing, making them "assassins of freedom". Herzen believed that society was suffering contradictions that were dulling its vitality and creativity. Many shared his disappointment with the 1848 revolutions, and his writings influenced the populist movements that followed. ■

The penal colonies of French Guiana were extended in the 19th century. Despite the French Revolution of 1789, feudal-era punishments continued.

See also: Jean-Jacques Rousseau 118–25 ▪ Georg Hegel 156–59 ▪ Vladimir Lenin 226–33 ▪ Mao Zedong 260–65 ▪ Che Guevara 312–13

WE MUST LOOK FOR A CENTRAL AXIS FOR OUR NATION

ITO HIROBUMI (1841–1909)

IN CONTEXT

IDEOLOGY
Consititutional monarchy

FOCUS
Modernization

BEFORE

1600 Establishment of the Tokugawa Shogunate by Ieyasu brings to an end two centuries of internal conflict.

1688 The Glorious Revolution brings about a constitutional monarchy in Britain.

1791 The French constitutional monarchy, in which King Louis XVI shares power with the Legislative Assembly, fails.

1871–1919 Germany becomes a federation of states, each with its own monarch.

AFTER

1901 The new Commonwealth of Australia adopts a federal constitutional monarchy.

2008 Bhutan becomes a constitutional monarchy.

From the 17th to the 19th centuries, strict isolation and rigorously controlled trade kept Japan closed to the outside world. That changed when Commodore Matthew Perry forced the Japanese to sign a trade deal with the US in 1853. A national crisis ensued, and a section of Japan's feudal rulers – the shoguns – including Prince Ito Hirobumi, began to argue for radical reforms to preserve Japan's independence, using Western models of society. But a society as distinctive as Japan's could not easily switch to Western modes of rule. Instead, under the guise of returning the emperor to power, an alliance of powerful reformers, including Hirobumi, overthrew the shogunate in 1867, proclaiming a new imperial rule. Samurai were disarmed, feudal lands turned over to the state, and caste divisions abolished.

> “Since government is concerned with the administration of the country, it does not follow that its acts are always favourable to all individuals.”
> **Ito Hirobumi**

Meiji Constitution

The leaders of this revolt wanted to unite Western advances with traditional Japanese virtues. Hirobumi drafted the 1890 Meiji Constitution, in which the emperor remained as head of state and focal point for the nation, but government was exercised by a cabinet of ministers. As with constitutional monarchies elsewhere, it was hoped this would provide a "central axis" for Japanese society on which it could advance as a whole. In fact, the constitution provided the framework for Japan's economic and military development over the next 60 years. ■

See also: Barons of King John 60–61 ▪ John Locke 104–09 ▪ Tokugawa Ieyasu 333

THE WILL TO POWER

FRIEDRICH NIETZSCHE (1844–1900)

IN CONTEXT

IDEOLOGY
Nihilism

FOCUS
Morality

BEFORE
1781 Kant's *Critique of Pure Reason* describes the gap between our thought and the world it attempts to apprehend.

1818 Schopenhauer publishes *The World as Will and Representation*, taking Kant's insight and suggesting that the gap can never be closed.

AFTER
1937 Bataille dismisses any political interpretation of Nietzsche as inadequate.

1990 *The End of History and the Last Man* by Francis Fukuyama adopts Nietzsche's metaphor of the Last Man to describe the apparent triumph of free-market capitalism.

The name of Friedrich Nietzsche still invites hostility. His elusive, wide-ranging writings and visceral critique of morality would spark controversy even without his largely unwarranted tainting with fascism. Like Marx and Freud, he was – in French philosopher Paul Ricoeur's words – a leading light in the "school of suspicion", intent on stripping away the veil from received notions and comforting beliefs. His philosophy was nihilist, which means that he thought it impossible to find meaning in existence.

Opposed to the systematic thought of traditional philosophy, he nonetheless left numerous hints

See also: Immanuel Kant 126–29 ▪ Jeremy Bentham 144–49 ▪ Georg Hegel 156–59 ▪ Karl Marx 188–93

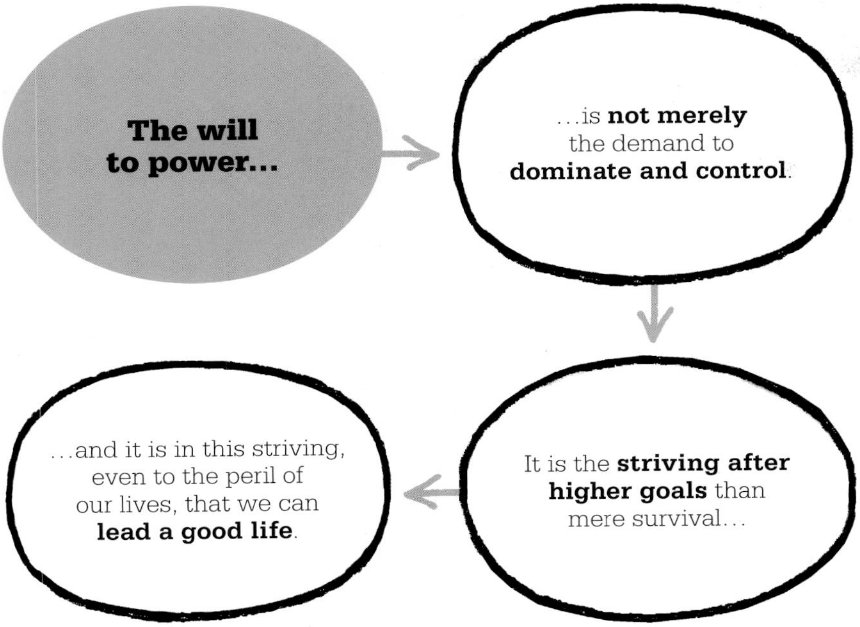

towards a political philosophy. This has little to do with the popular perception of him as a prototypical Nazi. Nietzsche was not an anti-Semite, considering it – and its accompanying nationalism – a means by which failed individuals blamed others for their own failings. He broke with his friend Richard Wagner partly due to the latter's increasingly strident racism and nationalism. This did not prevent Nietzsche's works being mauled by his sister, who assumed editing duties as illness incapacitated him towards the end of his life. She attempted to present his many writings in a more favourable light to the German nationalist and anti-Semitic circles in which she moved.

Will to power

Nietzsche's famous phrase "will to power" first appears in a short book that he considered to be his masterpiece, *Thus Spake Zarathustra*. In this dense, literary text, the protagonist, Zarathustra – a Germanized name for Zoroaster, founder of the ancient Persian religion – surveys a fallen world, and seeks to teach a new way of thinking and living to the people. It is not a standard work of philosophy, or of politics; stylistically, it is something closer to an epic poem, and its central arguments are rarely presented directly, favouring instead a figurative address. But the main themes are clear.

For Nietzsche, will to power is not merely a demand to dominate and control. He did not necessarily intend to describe a will to power over others. Rather, he intended it to denote the endless striving after goals and the highest achievements in life that he thought motivated human behaviour – whatever »

Friedrich Nietzsche

Nietzsche was born in Prussia to strongly religious parents. After completing his studies in theology and philology, he rejected religion. At the tender age of 24, he was appointed Professor of Classical Philology at Basel, where he met and befriended Richard Wagner, who was a marked influence on his early writings. His academic concerns drifted away from philology and into questions of philosophy. Nietzsche took a nihilistic position that stressed the meaninglessness of existence, but argued that Greek tragedy overcame this nihilism by affirming its meaninglessness – a theme that would recur throughout his later writings.

Beset by illness, Nietzsche resigned his teaching post in 1879 after a bout of diptheria and moved frequently around Europe, continually writing, but with limited reception. He suffered a severe mental breakdown in 1889, and died shortly after at the age of 56.

Key works

1872 *The Birth of Tragedy*
1883–85 *Thus Spake Zarathustra*
1886 *Beyond Good and Evil*

these goals may be in practice. In developing the concept, he was heavily influenced by his reading of the German philosopher Arthur Schopenhauer. The latter's bleak depiction of a reality in which no values could become meaningful was brightened, if at all, only by the "will to live" – a desperate striving of all life in the universe to avoid the finality of death. Nietzsche's development of the same concept is, by contrast, positive: not a struggle against, but a struggle for.

Nietzsche suggests that the will to power is stronger than the will to life itself. Even the most privileged humans strive after goals that mean risking their lives. There are higher values than crude survival, and what should mark out a good life is the willingness to reach after them.

Criticizing contentment

The will to power was a response to the utilitarian thinking that was coming to dominate social philosophy, in which people simply strive after their own happiness and the greatest goal in life is to be content. Nietzsche thought that utilitarianism, and the social philosophy it engendered, was the debased expression of the thinking of the English bourgeoisie – happy, and entirely philistine.

> The priests are the most evil enemies… in them hatred grows to monstrous and uncanny proportions, to the most spiritual and poisonous kind of hatred.
> **Friedrich Nietzsche**

Thus Spake Zarathustra contains an argument against this style of social thought. It describes the Last Man, a pitiable creature who is content, looks passively out on the world, "and blinks". The Last Man is a harbinger of the end of history itself, when all meaningful struggles have ceased.

But if we are not meant simply to be content with the world, and instead must strive after higher goals, the question remains as to what those goals should be. Nietzsche was clear on what they should not be. Zarathustra, the first to found a system of morality, must now be the man to destroy it. The morality we have is debased and the god we worship little more than the expression of our own inadequacies. "God is dead", wrote Nietzsche. Likewise we, as people who remain trapped by this morality, must overcome it. "Man is something to be surpassed. How have you overcome him?" demands Zarathustra of the crowd.

Rejecting the old morality

Nietzsche's later *Beyond Good and Evil* and the *Genealogy of Morals* clarify his argument that we should break with conventional morality. Both provide a history, and a criticism, of Western morality, in which "good" is necessarily paired with its opposite, "evil". Nietzsche believed that this form of moral thinking was at the root of all our current systems of morality, and was itself based on little more than the preferences of ancient, aristocratic orders. Starting with ancient Greece, "master" morality arose as the primary system of moral thinking, dividing the world up into the "good" and the "bad", the "life-affirming" and the "life-denying". The aristocratic virtues of health, strength, and wealth all fell into the good; the contrasting "slave" virtues of illness, weakness, and poverty were the bad.

Nietzsche decried the social philosophy of the utilitarians as equivalent to pigs in a sty – passive, philistine, and ultimately concerned solely with their own contentment.

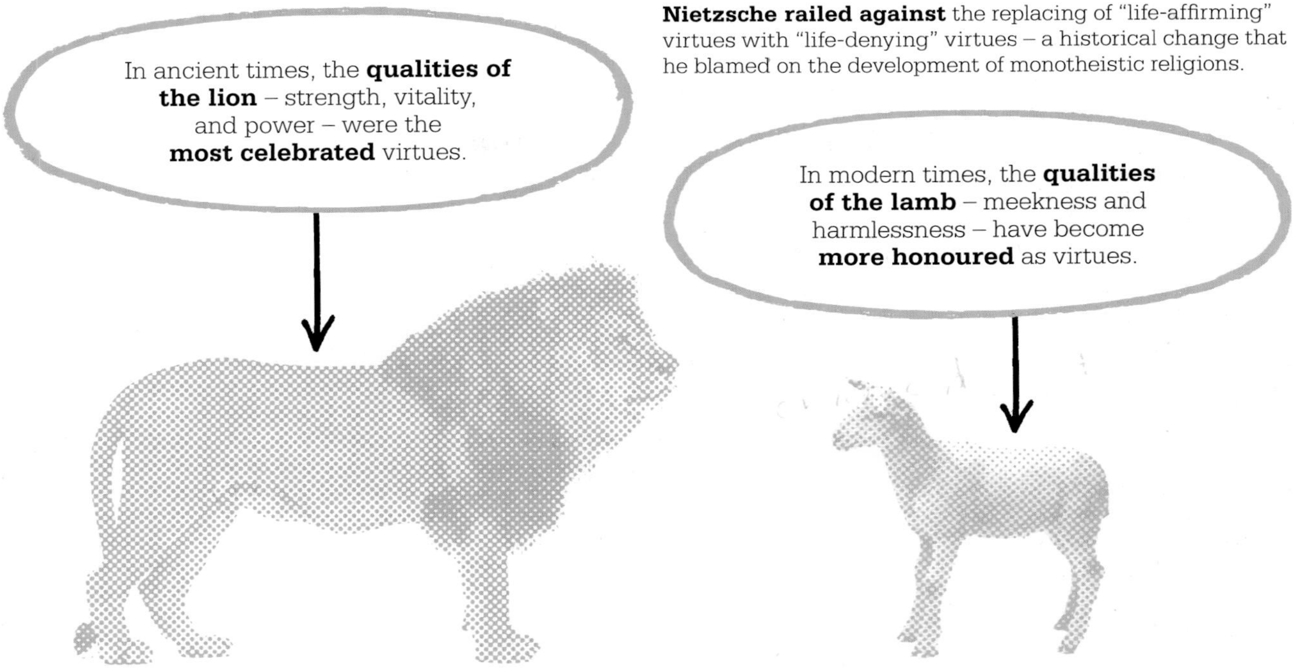

Nietzsche railed against the replacing of "life-affirming" virtues with "life-denying" virtues – a historical change that he blamed on the development of monotheistic religions.

But in response to the morality of the masters, the slaves themselves developed their own moral system. This new slave morality took the antitheses of the master morality, and presented them as good in themselves. The values of the master morality became inverted: where the master morality praised strength, the slave morality praised weakness, and so on. This allowed slaves to live with their true position in life without being overwhelmed by self-hatred and resentment. By denying, for example, the natural inequality of people in favour of a spurious, ideal equality between slaves and masters, slave morality offered a means for slaves to think as if they were equal to their masters – when, in simple reality, they were not. Nietzsche associated this slave morality particularly with Christianity and Judaism, which he portrayed as offering illusory solutions to the problems of life.

Thus Spake Zarathustra offers, in place of the toppled deities of organized religion, the figure of the "overman" (*Übermensch* in German). Humanity is merely a bridge between animals and the overman to come. But the overman is not a finished being, and still less the literal, biological evolution from humanity. An overman is a man who has mastered himself and can seek his own truths, remaining "faithful to the earth" and rejecting those who offer "otherworldly truths", of whatever kind.

Anti-political thinking

Such intense individualism has led some to suggest that Nietzsche was an anti-politician. Although political in tone, Nietzsche's rejection of morality suggests a nihilism that had little to do with understanding how a public sphere operates. He wrote only of individuals, never of movements or organizations. He was, in this sense, "beyond Right or Left", as French philosopher Georges Bataille argued. Yet he has come to have a deep influence on political thinkers of the Right and the Left. French philosopher Gilles Deleuze, in *Nietzsche and Philosophy*, emphasized Nietzsche's concern with the will to power. Deleuze placed the will to power as the drive to differentiate, to make all things different, and the centre of an "empirical" rejection of all transcendental or otherworldly claims about the existing world. Nietzsche became a philosopher of difference, in Deleuze's hands, and also of resistance to constraints. Conventional morality led only to "sad passions" that "disparage life". Nietzsche has subsequently come to occupy a critical place among post-structuralist thinkers concerned to overhaul systems of domination – including those purporting to liberate, such as Marxism. ■

IT IS THE MYTH THAT IS ALONE IMPORTANT

GEORGES SOREL (1847–1922)

IN CONTEXT

IDEOLOGY
Syndicalism

FOCUS
The heroic myth

BEFORE
1848 Karl Marx and Friedrich Engels publish the *Communist Manifesto*, as revolutions sweep across Europe.

1864 The International Workingmen's Association, the "First International", is founded in London, uniting socialists and anarchists.

1872 A split between anarchists and socialists leads to the collapse of the First International.

AFTER
1911 Admirers of Sorel form the Cercle Proudhon group to promote anti-democratic ideas.

1919 Novelist Enrico Corradini claims Italy is a "proletarian nation", seeking to unite Italian nationalism with syndicalism.

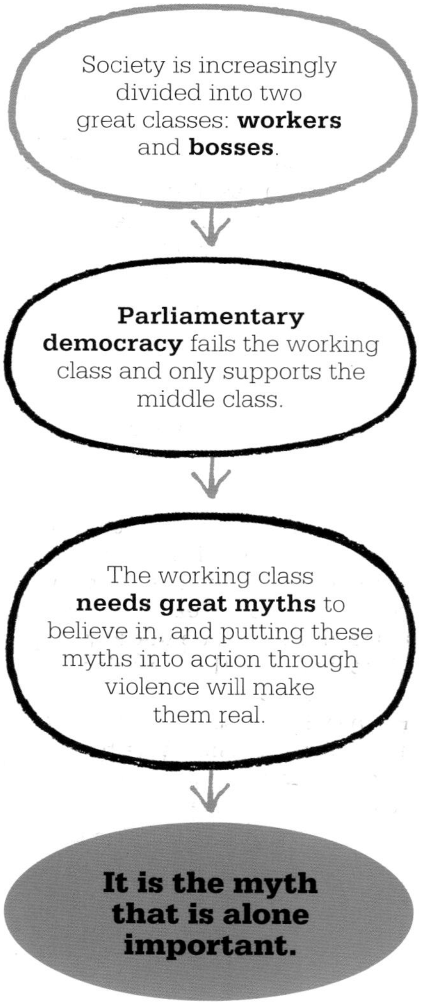

At the turn of the 20th century, Europe had well-developed capitalist societies. Alongside the incredible concentrations of industry and wealth that capitalism had created, a great new social force had emerged – the industrial working class. Political parties laying claim to the votes of the workers had formed, and these became stable organizations with increasing electoral significance. However, as the parties became entangled in parliamentary politics, seeking to eke out minor concessions from the system, they appeared to many radicals to be merely another prop for existing society.

Georges Sorel sought to challenge this bureaucratization in what became a unique body of work, synthesizing influences from Karl Marx, Friedrich Nietzsche, and French philosopher Henri Bergson. In his major collection of essays, *Reflections on Violence*, he rejects objective science as simply a system of "fictions", constructed to impose order on a reality that was inherently chaotic and irrational. He believed that to treat human society, the most chaotic of all parts of that reality, as if it were something

See also: Karl Marx 188–93 ▪ Friedrich Nietzsche 196–99 ▪ Eduard Bernstein 202–03 ▪ Vladimir Lenin 226–33 ▪ Rosa Luxemberg 234–35

> It is to violence that Socialism owes those high ethical values by means of which it brings salvation to the modern world.
> **Georges Sorel**

to be rationally understood, was an insult to the power of human imagination and creativity.

The power of myth

In place of objective science and theories about society, Sorel proposes that great myths could be used to change reality. Indeed, by believing in heroic myths about themselves and about the new world to come, the masses could overthrow existing society. Parliamentary democracy had failed, since it merely provided the means for the "mediocre" new middle classes to rule over the rest of society – including those socialists now committed to parliamentary politics. Rationality and order had been substituted for freedom and action. Orthodox Marxism, too, contained the seeds of middle-class rule, in that it attempted to offer a "scientific" understanding of society in which economics determines history.

To break the hold of bourgeois rationality, a myth has to be both believed and put into action. Sorel sees violence as the means through which myths can become real. He details examples of such myths and movements – from the Christian militants of the early Church, through the French Revolution, to the revolutionary syndicalists, or trade unionists, of his own day. Syndicalism was the most militant wing of the trade union movement, rejecting political manoeuvring as a corruption of workers' interests. The general strike – a mass stoppage of all work – was the pinnacle of syndicalist strategy, and Sorel sees it as the modern myth that will found a new society. "Heroic violence" is to be welcomed as the ethical and necessary route to establishing the new world.

Sorel's work is ambiguous. He rejects political classifications, and his thought does not sit easily on either the political left or right, though it has been used by both. ■

The miners' strikes in the UK during the 1980s were an example of mass protests that came to be imbued with a heroic power, much in the vein of Sorel's radical thinking.

Georges Sorel

Born in Cherbourg, France, and trained as an engineer, Georges Sorel retired in his 50s to study social problems. Self-taught as a social theorist, he initially identified with the "revisionist" wing of Marxism associated with Eduard Bernstein, before seeking a more radical challenge to parliamentary politics. His essays won a growing readership across the French radical left. At first, he supported revolutionary syndicalism and the foundation of the French union federation (CGT), opposed to parliamentary politics. But he became disillusioned, and turned to the far-right movement Action Francaise, believing an alliance of aristocrats and workers could overturn middle-class French society. He later denounced World War I, and supported the Bolsheviks in Russia. By the end of his life, he was ambivalent about both Bolshevism and fascism.

Key works

1908 *Reflections on Violence*
1908 *The Illusions of Progress*
1919 *Matériaux d'une Thérie du Prolétariat*

WE HAVE TO TAKE WORKING MEN AS THEY ARE

EDUARD BERNSTEIN (1850–1932)

IN CONTEXT

IDEOLOGY
Socialism

FOCUS
Revisionism

BEFORE
1848 Karl Marx and Friedrich Engels publish the *Communist Manifesto*.

1871 The German Social Democratic Party (SPD) adopts Marxism, voting to accept the Gotha Programme – a radical socialist manifesto.

AFTER
1917 The October Revolution overthrows the capitalist system in Russia.

1919 A communist revolution in Germany is put down.

1945 A Labour government is elected in the UK on a platform of welfare reform to create a mixed economy.

1959 The SPD formally repudiates Marxism at the Bad Godesberg Conference.

By the early 1890s, the left-wing German Social Democratic Party (SPD) had reasons for optimism. A decade of illegality from 1878 had merely strengthened its support. As the leading party of European socialism, its progress was followed by leftists across the continent, and debates within its ranks set the intellectual framework in which the movement operated. When it was legalized in 1890, the SPD looked to be set for power.

Yet there was a problem, as leading SPD member Eduard Bernstein pointed out. The party was dedicated to a socialist future and its policy was guided by Marxism. But as the party became more established, and without the pressure-cooker conditions of

---

Socialists expected **capitalism** to produce **poverty**.

Yet capitalism has **increased the wealth** of workers.

Capitalism has proved to be a **stable**, **secure** system.

This means that **workers accept** capitalism.

We have to take working men as they are.

Socialists should argue for **piecemeal reforms** under capitalism.

See also: Karl Marx 188–93 ▪ Vladimir Lenin 226–233 ▪ Rosa Luxemburg 234–35

illegality, its day-to-day activities lacked direction. While SPD members still pronounced on the need for the transformation of society, in practice it followed a gradualist path, eking out changes through parliamentary legislation.

Bernstein challenged this contradiction head on. From the 1890s, he argued that many of Marx's predictions – such as the inevitable impoverishment of working people and their march towards revolution – had failed to come true. Rather, capitalism was proving to be a stable system under which minor reforms could be won, leading step by step to socialism.

Gradual change

The publication of Bernstein's *Evolutionary Socialism* in 1899 fuelled a row within the SPD that would define the key argument for socialist thinkers over the next century. Was capitalism to be accepted, and minor improvements won – or was it to be overthrown? At the heart of this debate was an argument over what happened in workers' heads. For Marx, the working class would lead society into socialism once it realized its potential to do so. But in reality, "class consciousness" – awareness of class – had led not to revolutionary conclusions, but to workers voting, in increasing numbers, for a party that offered piecemeal reforms within the capitalist system.

Workers in Germany have won the right to strike for better pay and conditions. Bernstein saw that the working class could win significant concessions within capitalism.

> In all advanced countries we see the privileges of the capitalist bourgeoisie yielding step by step to democratic organizations.
> **Eduard Bernstein**

Bernstein proposed abandoning the idea that workers would come to revolutionary conclusions. Instead, socialists should examine workers' existing beliefs about the world, and work outwards from that point. This was the first theoretically robust case for a "reformist", or gradualist, socialism.

Orthodox Marxists responded ferociously, and Bernstein's views were never formally adopted by the SPD in his lifetime. It was not until the Bad Godesburg conference of 1959 that the party formally renounced Marxism. Nonetheless, its actual political activity had long been following the lines Bernstein had advocated, whatever its declared intentions. ■

Eduard Bernstein

Bernstein became a socialist at the age of 22, joining the Marxist wing of Germany's socialist movement. With the passing of the Anti-Socialist Law in 1878, which banned socialist organizations, he fled to Switzerland and then London. He joined other exiles including Friedrich Engels, with whom he developed a close working relationship.

Bernstein returned to Zurich to become editor of the newspaper of the newly united Social Democratic Party (SPD). After the party was legalized in 1890, he began to argue in the paper for a more moderate, "revisionist" form of socialism. He returned to Germany in 1901 and was elected a member of the Reichstag the following year. His opposition to World War I led him to break with the SPD in 1915, founding a new organization, the USPD. He was re-elected as an SPD member of parliament from 1920 to 1928.

Key works

1896–98 *Problems of Socialism*
1899 *The Prerequisites for Socialism and the Tasks of Social Democracy*

THE DISDAIN OF OUR FORMIDABLE NEIGHBOUR IS THE GREATEST DANGER FOR LATIN AMERICA

JOSÉ MARTÍ (1853–1895)

IN CONTEXT

IDEOLOGY
Anti-imperialism

FOCUS
United States interference

BEFORE
1492 Partly financed by Spain, Christopher Columbus explores the New World.

1803 Venezuela is the first Latin American country to revolt against Spanish rule.

AFTER
1902 Cuba gains formal independence from the US, which retains the Guantánamo Bay naval base.

1959 Cuban dictator General Batista is ousted by Fidel Castro's 26 July Movement.

1973 Chile's elected ruler, Salvador Allende, is overthrown in a CIA-backed coup, and replaced by a military dictatorship or *junta*. By the 1980, *juntas* have seized control across Latin America.

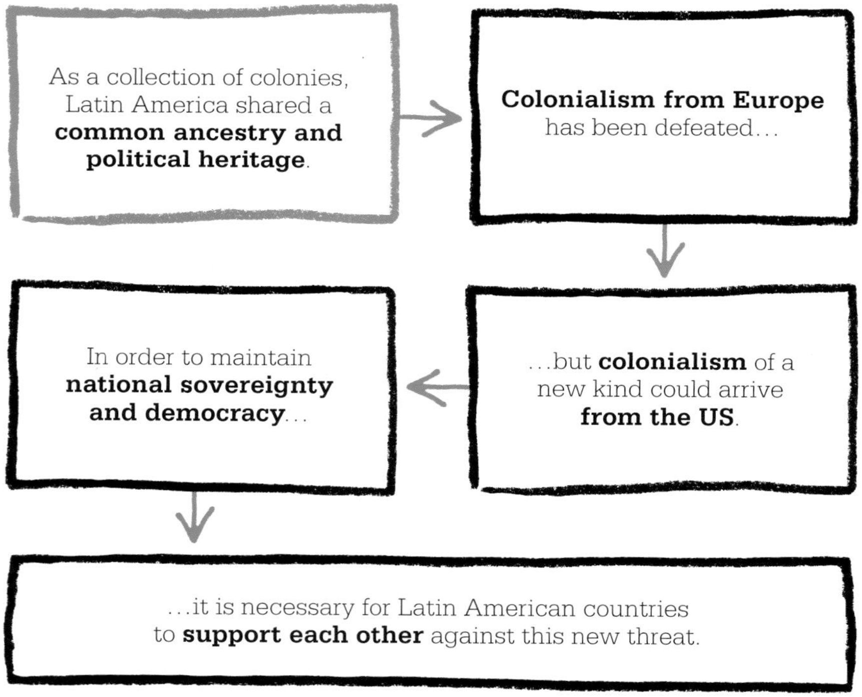

By the 19th century, Spain and Portugal's ability to defend their colonial possessions had weakened. The examples of the French and American Revolutions helped to promote a succession of uprisings throughout colonial Latin America against rule from Europe. By the 1830s, most of these colonies had achieved formal independence. Only Puerto Rico and Cuba remained under direct rule.

José Martí became one of the leaders of the Cuban struggle for independence. But as the fight against the Spanish empire wore on, through a series of uprisings

See also: Simón Bolívar 162–63 ▪ Emiliano Zapata 246 ▪ Smedley D. Butler 247 ▪ Che Guevara 312–13 ▪ Fidel Castro 339

> Rights are to be taken, not requested; seized, not begged for.
> **José Martí**

and wars in the second half of the 19th century, Martí became keenly aware of a far bigger threat to the sovereignty of Latin America.

To the north, the United States had waged its own battle for independence when the Thirteen States declared their freedom from colonial rule in 1776 and won the American War of Independence by 1783. By the end of the Civil War in 1865, the unified republic controlled much of the northern continent, and was looking outwards. In the Monroe Doctrine of 1823, US president James Monroe had affirmed that the United States would remain opposed to European colonialism and would treat any further efforts by the Old World to extend or establish colonies in the Americas as an act of aggression. Critically, the Monroe Doctrine identified both North and South America as falling under the protection of the United States.

A new colonial power

Latin American revolutionaries at first greeted the Monroe Doctrine with enthusiasm. The Venezuelan leader, Simón Bolívar, believed initially they now had a powerful ally in their fight for freedom. But as it consolidated its power, the US increasingly used the Doctrine to assert its control over its own "sphere of influence".

Towards the end of his life, Martí argued for a common Latin American response in defence of their hard-won liberties. He saw a threat to democracy in the form of a new, potentially colonial power to the north. In doing so, he helped articulate a common theme of Latin American anti-imperialism for the next century or more: that the US would pursue its own economic and political interests, whatever the impact on Latin America.

Martí died in 1895. Three years later, the US won control of Cuba from Spain. Since World War II, the US has been blamed for supporting military coups and dictatorships in the region. ■

In 1973, Chile's presidential palace was hit – and its socialist president Salvador Allende killed – in a military coup, one of several in Latin America that have been backed by the US.

José Martí

José Martí was a Cuban journalist, poet, essayist, and revolutionary. Born in Havana, then under Spanish rule, he became active in the movement for Cuban independence with the outbreak of the Ten Years' War against Spain in 1868. Charged with treason in 1869, he was sentenced to six years in prison. On falling ill, he was exiled to Spain, where he was allowed to continue his studies.

On graduating in law, Martí toured the Americas, arguing the case for Latin American independence and unity. He formed the Cuban Revolutionary Party in 1892. During an insurrection against the Spanish in 1895, Martí was killed at the Battle of Dos Ríos on May 19 that year. Cuba finally broke free from Spain in 1898, when the US intervened during the Spanish-American War.

Key works

1891 *Our America* (essay)
1891 *Simple Verses* (from which Cuba's best-known patriotic song, *Guantanamera*, is adapted)
1892 *Patria* newspaper

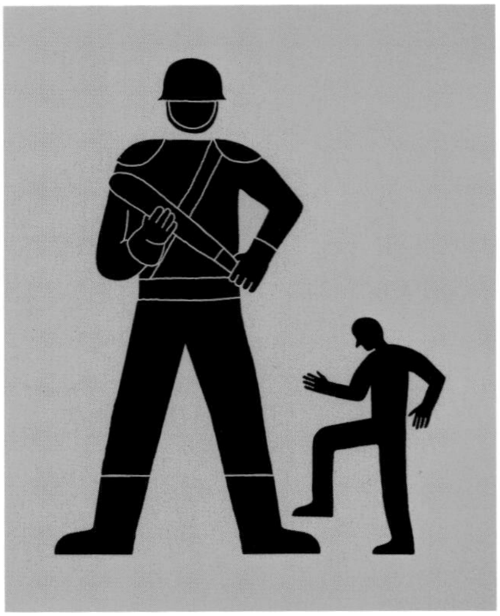

IT IS NECESSARY TO DARE IN ORDER TO SUCCEED

PETER KROPOTKIN (1842–1921)

IN CONTEXT

IDEOLOGY
Anarcho-communism

FOCUS
Political action

BEFORE
1762 Jean-Jacques Rousseau writes *The Social Contract,* stating that "man is born free, and is everywhere in chains".

1840 In *What is Property?,* Pierre-Joseph Proudhon calls himself an anarchist.

1881 Tsar Alexander II is assassinated in St Petersburg.

AFTER
1917 The Bolsheviks seize power in Russia.

1960s Counter-culture movements in Europe and the US squat in empty buildings and form communities.

2011 The Occupy Movement protests against economic inequality by occupying Wall Street during the global economic crisis.

At the end of the 19th century, Tsarist Russia was a hothouse for every new social movement from fascism to radical communism. Peter Kropotkin, who spurned his privileged life as the son of a prince, was a product of his times, advocating the destruction of authority. In *The Conquest of Bread* (1892), Kropotkin argued that the best aspect of humanity – its ability to cooperate – could allow it to do away with all oppressive structures. He saw in the developing labour movement the possibility to overthrow oppressors – from priests to capitalists – and establish a new society based on mutual respect and cooperation. He lay down the principles of what was to become anarcho-communism: belief in a collaborative, egalitarian society, free of the state.

Call to action

Anarchism is a theory of action, and Kropotkin urged those who would listen to always act. Sympathetic to the Bolshevik Revolution of 1917, he denounced its authoritarianism in the subsequent civil war. Establishing a new world did not require fresh rules, but anarchists able to act courageously against all oppression. Compromise and political calculation were alien to anarchism; instead, its adherents must act with moral fervour against a corrupt world. Kropotkin, like other anarchists, helped define the "politics of the deed" – a belief that would recur in radical ideologies over the next century. ■

> In place of the cowardly phrase, 'Obey the law,' our cry, is 'Revolt against all laws!'
> **Peter Kropotkin**

See also: Pierre-Joseph Proudhon 183 ▪ Mikhail Bakunin 184–85 ▪ Henry David Thoreau 186–87 ▪ Karl Marx 188 –93 ▪ Vladimir Lenin 226–33

EITHER WOMEN ARE TO BE KILLED, OR WOMEN ARE TO HAVE THE VOTE

EMMELINE PANKHURST (1858–1928)

IN CONTEXT

IDEOLOGY
Feminism

FOCUS
Civil disobedience

BEFORE
1792 Mary Wollstonecraft publishes *A Vindication of the Rights of Woman*, an early defence of women's equality.

1865 Liberal philosopher John Stuart Mill campaigns successfully for parliament on a platform of women's suffrage.

1893 New Zealand is the first major country to grant women the vote.

AFTER
1990 The Swiss canton of Appenzell Innerhoden is forced to accept women's suffrage (the other cantons had accepted it in 1971).

2005 Women are granted the right to vote and stand for parliament in Kuwait.

By the early 1900s, the right to vote was gaining acceptance around the world, but the right for women to do so lagged behind. New Zealand had been the first major country to grant the vote to women, in 1893, but progress in Europe and North America was achingly slow, hindered by obstinate politicians, conservative public opinion, and often vicious press campaigns.

Emmeline Pankhurst is arrested outside Buckingham Palace in May 1914. The WSPU strongly advocated direct action in pursuit of its goals.

Activist Emmeline Pankhurst, with others, established the Women's Social and Political Union (WSPU) in Britain in 1903. Known as "suffragettes", their militant action and civil disobedience soon included window-smashing, assaults, and arson. In 1913, campaigner Emily Davidson died after throwing herself under the king's horse at the Derby race, and a hunger strike of imprisoned suffragettes was met with force-feeding.

When Pankhurst, speaking later in 1913, said, "either women are to be killed or women are to have the vote", she was laying claim both to the suffragettes' moral authority to act as they saw fit in furthering a just cause, and emphasizing their apparently implacable determination to win it. However, this determination lasted only until World War I in 1914, when the WSPU dropped their campaign in order to support the war effort. Women over the age of 30 were granted the right to vote in Britain at the war's end, with all adult women able to vote from 1928. ■

See also: Mary Wollstonecraft 154–55 ■ John Stuart Mill 174–81 ■ Simone de Beauvoir 284–89 ■ Shirin Ebadi 328

IT IS RIDICULOUS TO DENY THE EXISTENCE OF A JEWISH NATION

THEODOR HERZL (1860–1904)

IN CONTEXT

IDEOLOGY
Zionism

FOCUS
A Jewish state

BEFORE
1783 In *Jerusalem, or On Religious Power and Tolerance*, German philosopher Moses Mendelssohn calls for religious tolerance in a secular state.

1843 German philosopher Bruno Bauer's book *The Jewish Question* states that Jews must give up religion to achieve political emancipation.

AFTER
1933 Adolf Hitler becomes chancellor of Germany, promoting German nationalism and anti-Semitism.

1942 Plans for the Final Solution of the Jewish question are discussed by Nazi leaders at the Wannsee Conference.

1948 The state of Israel is established.

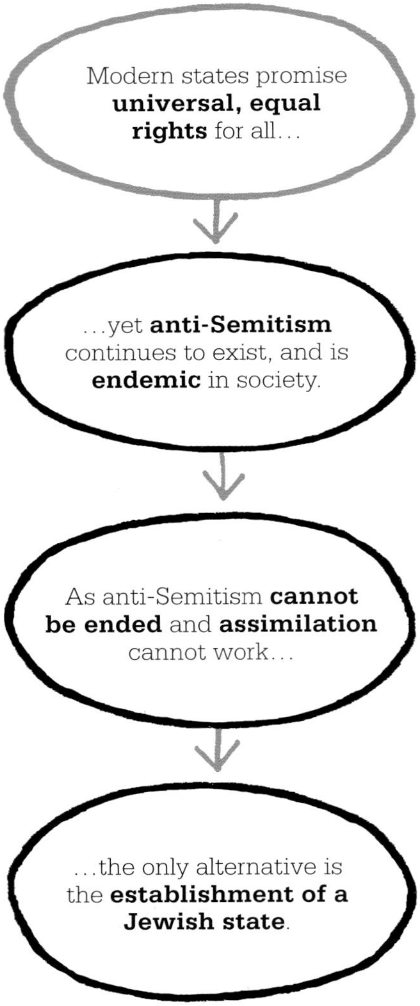

The French Third Republic, founded at the end of a century of revolutions, promised the guarantee of equal legal rights for all its citizens. However, this constitutional equality was put severely to the test. In December 1894, Alfred Dreyfus, a young artillery officer, was convicted of spying for Germany and sentenced to life imprisonment, despite clear evidence that another man had been passing the secrets, and that the evidence against Dreyfus had been fabricated. His trial was covered by a young Jewish journalist, Theodor Herzl, working for an Austrian newspaper.

Dreyfus was also Jewish, and his case exposed deep divisions in French society. His supporters, known as "Dreyfusards", saw anti-Semitism as the central reason for the framing of an innocent man. Their campaign for Dreyfus's release drew in intellectuals such as writer Émile Zola alongside politicians and trade unionists.

However, for the anti-Dreyfusards, his case revealed something quite different: the need for vigilance against France's enemies. Liberty, equality, and

See also: Johann Gottfrield Herder 142–43 ▪ Marcus Garvey 252 ▪ Hannah Arendt 282–83 ▪ Adolf Hitler 337

fraternity were true French values, but not all those who lived in France should be considered French, they claimed. Protests in Dreyfus's defence were met by mobs chanting "Death to the Jews!"

Anti-Semitism had a long and ugly history in Europe, where the official discrimination of Church edicts had mingled with popular prejudice, leading frequently to ethnic cleansing. Jews had been expelled from several countries, and denied full rights elsewhere. By the end of the 19th century, however, inspired by the rational ideals of the Enlightenment, many modern nation-states, including France, had formally ended state-sanctioned discrimination on the grounds of religious belief. Assimilation – the belief that minority groups could integrate fully into wider society – became an increasingly accepted ideal.

Against assimilation

Despite these official changes at state level, the Dreyfus case convinced Herzl that anti-Semitism was endemic in society, and that attempts to defeat it, or for Jews to assimilate, were doomed to fail.

Creating a Jewish homeland where Jews could be united was central to their identity, according to Herzl. He believed it was the only way that Jews could avoid anti-Semitic attitudes.

> We have sincerely tried everywhere to merge with the national communities in which we live, seeking only to preserve the faith of our fathers. It is not permitted us.
> **Theodor Herzl**

Instead, Jews would have to borrow a totally different concept from the Enlightenment – nationalism. Herzl stated that Jews were "one people", and that the diaspora population should be united in a single Jewish state, preserving their rights as Jews in the modern world. He set about campaigning for a Jewish state, urging European powers to assist him in finding a place for it, and encouraging Jews to give funds to the cause. He believed that the new Jewish homeland would need to be outside Europe – either in Argentina or Israel.

Herzl's ideas spread quickly, but met with stiff resistance from those sections of Jewish society that still favoured assimilation. His Zionist movement only really gained ground in the decades after his death. The granting by the British of a homeland for the Jews in Palestine in 1917 helped pave the way, and in the aftermath of the Holocaust, the state of Israel was created in 1948. Alfred Dreyfus was finally pardoned in 1906. ■

Theodor Herzl

Theodor Herzl was born in Pest in the Austro-Hungarian empire to strongly secular Jewish parents. He moved to Vienna aged 18 and began his studies in law. His first political activity was with the German nationalist student fraternity, Albia, from which he later resigned in protest at their anti-Semitism.

After a brief legal career, Herzl turned to journalism, and it was while he was the Paris correspondent for the *Neue Freie Presse* that he began covering the Dreyfus Affair. The virulent and widespread racism the case revealed in French society pushed Herzl to break with his earlier assimilationist beliefs. He became a skilled advocate and organizer for the Zionist cause, publishing *The Jewish State* in 1896 to considerable controversy. A year later, he chaired the First Zionist Congress in Basel, Switzerland, seeing it as a symbolic parliament for the Zionist state. He died from a heart attack, aged 44.

Key works

1896 *The Jewish State*
1902 *The Old New Land*

NOTHING WILL AVAIL TO SAVE A NATION WHOSE WORKERS HAVE DECAYED

BEATRICE WEBB (1858–1943)

IN CONTEXT

IDEOLOGY
Socialism

FOCUS
Social welfare

BEFORE
1848 In *A General View of Positivism*, French philosopher Auguste Comte argues for scientific social analysis.

1869 The English section of the Charity Organization Society is established to promote charitable work among the "deserving poor".

1889 Social reformer Charles Booth finds a third of London's population lives in poverty.

AFTER
1911 The National Insurance Act expands UK insurance for unemployment and illness.

1942 Economist William Beveridge's *Social Insurance and Allied Services* lays the foundations for the welfare state in the UK.

By the late 19th century, with industrial capitalism firmly entrenched in Britain, public concern turned towards its consequences. Industrial towns and cities were home to swathes of people deprived of work, cut loose from society, and living in squalor.

A Royal Commission was established in 1905 to address the problem, but in 1909 its report produced a weak set of proposals. As a member of the commission, pioneering social researcher Beatrice Webb produced a far more radical minority report, arguing for a welfare state that would provide protection against unemployment and illness. She and Sidney Webb, her husband and collaborator, opposed the view that the poor produced their own poverty. They argued that social problems could be solved by benevolent planners, administering society in the best interests of all.

Planned society

Countering those who stressed the superiority of unregulated markets, and a continuing reliance on charity and self-help for the poor, the Webbs offered a new vision of an orderly society. However, like many of their contemporaries, they were eugenicists, believing the "stock" of humanity could also be improved by this kind of benevolent planning. To Webb, the wishes of the poor, and their attempts to alleviate their own conditions, were insignificant. She believed a rational society would emerge, in which the majority would accept the wise rule of the planners. ■

> It is urgently necessary to 'clean up the base of society'.
> **Beatrice Webb**

See also: Eduard Bernstein 202–03 ▪ Jane Addams 211 ▪ John Rawls 298–303 ▪ Michel Foucault 310–11

PROTECTIVE LEGISLATION IN AMERICA IS SHAMEFULLY INADEQUATE

JANE ADDAMS (1860–1935)

IN CONTEXT

IDEOLOGY
Progressive movement

FOCUS
Social reform

BEFORE
1880s Otto von Bismarck, German Chancellor, introduces the first social insurance programmes.

1884 Toynbee Hall is opened in Whitechapel, East London, to provide amenities to the poor. Jane Addams visits in 1887.

AFTER
1912 The US Children's Bureau is established to administer the provision of child welfare.

1931 Jane Addams becomes the first American woman to be awarded the Nobel Peace Prize.

1935 The first national system of social insurance is introduced in the US.

The frontier marking the limit of western settlement in the United States was declared closed by the census of 1890, but not before the notion of America as a society defined by an entrepreneurial "frontier spirit" had taken root. Challenging the myth of boundless growth and opportunity, social reformers pointed instead to the poverty and the absence of meaningful opportunity faced by America's poor and working classes. Radical change was due.

In 1889, Jane Adams, pioneering sociologist and campaigner for women's suffrage, established Hull House in Chicago, the first "settlement house" to provide amenities and welfare services to the city's poor – women and children especially. Relying on donations from wealthy benefactors and on volunteer labour, Addams wanted the House to show how the different classes of society could learn the practical benefits of cooperation. She was convinced that by channelling the energies of the young into productive activity, good habits would be learned early on, and the costs of poverty in crime and disease lessened.

Promoting education as key to opportunity for all, Hull House ran a kindergarten, clubs for older children, and evening classes for adults.

Addams wrote of America lagging far behind other nations' legislation to protect women and children in industry. She viewed direct charitable intervention with individuals as ineffective: only concerted public action, backed up by legislation, could deal with social problems. In this she helped to define social work as an activity concerned with changing society as much as individuals. ■

See also: Beatrice Webb 210 ▪ Max Weber 214–15 ▪ John Rawls 298–303

LAND TO THE TILLERS!

SUN YAT-SEN (1866–1925)

IN CONTEXT

IDEOLOGY
Nationalism

FOCUS
Fair distribution of land

BEFORE
1842 The Treaty of Nanjing grants Britain trade concessions with China and the port of Hong Kong.

1901 The Boxer Rebellion against foreign rule fails, resulting in the capture of Beijing by the Eight Nation Alliance.

AFTER
1925–26 The First Chinese Revolution is defeated by the KMT, leading to a Communist Party retreat – the "Long March".

1932 Japan invades China. The KMT and the Communist Party lead the resistance.

1949 The defeat of Japan is followed by civil war, which is won by the Communist Party.

China had been a single state since the founding of the Qin dynasy in 222 BCE. But in the second half of the 19th century, it was carved up among the major Western powers, who pushed through the "Unequal Treaties". These were a series of agreements that were signed under duress by successive emperors, crippling development and impoverishing the people. The failure of the Chinese empire to defend either itself, or the people it claimed to provide for, provoked a prolonged crisis. As conditions worsened, the regime became deeply unpopular, and successive uprisings became increasingly destructive.

China is led by a **weak and corrupt Imperial Court** and is dominated by foreign powers.

But **respect for China** as a great nation with a great history…

…plus "**Western**" **democracy**…

…plus **economic development** and fair distribution of land…

…will lead to a **modern republican China**.

See also: Ito Hirobumi 195 ▪ José Martí 204–05 ▪ Emiliano Zapata 246 ▪ Mustafa Kemal Atatürk 248–49 ▪ Mao Zedong 260–65

The vast peasantry of China were promised land to work under Sun's Three Principles of the People. Economic progress would come from a fair distribution of land, he believed.

A distinctive form of Chinese nationalism arose against this backdrop of social strife and subjugation by Western powers – and, later, by the Japanese. It stressed the need to learn from the West – transforming China into a modern society, breaking with the failures of the empire and with the perceived backwardness of the peasant rebellions. From the 1880s, Sun Yat-Sen was among those forming nationalist groups and attempting an uprising against Beijing's rule. Unlike many of his contemporaries, he stressed the strengths of Chinese culture, fusing a respect for China's history with an appropriation of "Western" values.

The Three Principles

Sun organized his thought around what became known as the Three Principles of the People: nationalism, democracy, and "the people's livelihood". The last principle referred to economic development, but was understood by Sun to be development on the basis of the fair distribution of China's resources, especially land for its peasantry – "the tillers". A corrupt landlord system would be overthrown, alongside the corrupt emperor system it supported, clearing the way for a modern, republican, and democratic China.

Sun became a uniquely unifying figure among China's revolutionary movements. He founded the republican Kuomintang (KMT), which rapidly came to dominance in the chaotic period after the collapse of the Qing dynasty in 1911. The KMT united with the Communist Party in 1922, but with warlords fighting for territory, and a series of new emperors, it proved impossible to establish a central government. The KMT crushed a communist-led uprising in Shanghai in 1926, after which the two groups separated. Communist victory in the 1949 revolution forced the KMT into exile in Taiwan.

In recent years, communist China has increasingly come to embrace Sun's legacy, citing him as an inspiration behind its move to a market-led economy. ■

> Our society is not free to develop and the common people do not have the means of living.
> **Sun Yat-Sen**

Sun Yat-Sen

Sun Yat-Sen was born in the village of Cuihen in southern China. He moved to Honolulu, Hawaii, aged 13 to continue his education. There, he learned English and read widely. After further study in Hong Kong, Sun converted to Christianity. He became a doctor, but later abandoned his medical practice to concentrate full-time on his revolutionary activity.

Sun became a campaigner for the renewal of China as a modern state. Following a series of failed revolts, he was forced into exile. But in October 1911, a military uprising at Wuchang spread across southern China. Sun Yat-Sen was elected president of the "Provisional Republic" but stepped down in a deal with pro-Qing dynasty forces in the north. In 1912, Sun helped to establish the Kuomintang to continue the fight for a unified republic as the country descended into civil war.

Key works

1922 *The International Development of China*
1927 *San Min Chu I: Three Principles of the People*

THE INDIVIDUAL IS A SINGLE COG IN AN EVER-MOVING MECHANISM

MAX WEBER (1864–1920)

IN CONTEXT

IDEOLOGY
Liberalism

FOCUS
Society

BEFORE
1705 Dutch philosopher Bernard Mandeville writes *The Fable of the Bees*, demonstrating collective institutions arising from individual behaviour.

1884 The final volume of Marx's *Capital* is published, though it is unfinished.

AFTER
1937 American sociologist Talcott Parsons publishes *The Structure of Social Action*, introducing Weber's work to a new international audience.

1976 *Capitalism and Social Theory* by British sociologist Anthony Giddens criticizes Weber's sociology, arguing instead for the primacy of structures in social action.

Capitalism's rise in the 19th century prompted new ways to think about the world. Relations between people were transformed, with traditional ways of life torn up. Scientific and technical knowledge appeared to be advancing relentlessly, and society was seen as an object that could be studied and understood. Max Weber provided a new approach to the study of society – in the new discipline of "sociology". His incomplete work *Economy and Society* is an attempt to describe the functioning of society, as well as a method by which such study can be taken further. One of Weber's methods of study was to use abstract notions such as

An individual's actions are informed by their **view of the world**.

Individuals **operate collectively** in complex ways.

Individual viewpoints coalesce into **collective understandings**, such as religion.

But the **social structures** created by these collective understandings can **constrain individual freedoms**.

The individual is a single cog in an ever-moving mechanism.

See also: Mikhail Bakunin 184–85 ■ Karl Marx 188–93 ■ Georges Sorel 200–01 ■ Beatrice Webb 210

Fire ants live in a complex community where the individual's role is key to the success of the nest. In a similar way, Weber saw the actions of individuals as part of a larger human society.

"ideal-types". Like a caricature of a person, an ideal-type exaggerated key features and reduced the less important ones – but to draw out the underlying truth, rather than to amuse. This approach was key to Weber's method, and allowed him to understand complex parts of society via a simplified version. The role of the sociologist was to construct and analyse ideal-types based on the observation of reality. This stood in contrast to Karl Marx and earlier writers on social issues, who attempted to deduce the operations of society based on its internal logic, rather than through direct observation.

Collective understandings

Society, Weber argued, could only be understood on the basis of its constituent parts – in the first instance, individuals. These individuals operated collectively in ways that were complex, but could be understood by the sociologist. Individuals possessed a capacity to act, and their actions would be informed by their view of the world. These views would emerge as collective understandings. Religion and political systems such as capitalism are examples of these understandings. Weber, in his earlier work *The Protestant Ethic and the Spirit of Capitalism*, claimed that it was the new "spirit" of individualist Protestantism that paved the way for capital accumulation and the creation of a market society. *Economy and Society* develops this idea, distinguishing between types of religious belief, and analysing the ways in which individuals may perform social action using a wide variety of belief structures.

Restraints to action

Once society's collective structures are in place, Weber notes, they may act not as enablers, expanding human freedom, but as constraints. This is why Weber speaks of people as "cogs" in a "machine". The structures people create also restrain their actions, producing further results: Protestants were instructed to work, but also to avoid consuming, and their savings created capitalism. ■

> For sociological purposes, there is no such thing as a collective personality which 'acts'.
> **Max Weber**

Max Weber

Max Weber was born in Erfurt, Germany, and initially studied law at the University of Heidelberg. Working in a time before the discipline of sociology existed, Weber's work covered legal theory, history, and economics. He eventually became an economics professor at Freiburg University. Politically engaged from early in his career, Weber made his name as a thinker in social policy, writing on Polish immigration in the 1890s and joining one of Germany's movements for social reform, the Evangelical Social Congress. After WWI, he co-founded the liberal German Democratic Party.

A tempestuous relationship with his father ended on his father's death in 1897. Weber had a nervous breakdown, and never fully recovered. He was unable to hold a permanent teaching post again, and suffered from insomnia and bouts of depression.

Key works

1905 *The Protestant Ethic and the Spirit of Capitalism*
1922 *Economy and Society*
1927 *General Economic History*

THE CLA
OF IDEO
1910–1945

SH

OGIES

1910
Emiliano Zapata founds the **Liberation Army of the South** (the "Zapatistas") to fight in the Mexican Revolution.

1912
Following the overthrow of the Qing dynasty, Sun Yat-Sen becomes the first president of the **Republic of China**.

1914
World War I begins with the **assasination of Archduke Franz Ferdinand** at Sarajevo in present-day Bosnia.

1917
After the **February Revolution**, Tsar Nicholas II of Russia abdicates; in the **October Revolution**, Lenin establishes a Bolshevik government.

1918
The Armistice ends the fighting in World War I, but the war is formally ended the following year with the signing of the **Treaty of Versailles**.

1922
Benito Mussolini leads his Fascists in the **March on Rome** and becomes prime minister of Italy.

1922
Joseph Stalin becomes general secretary of the **Communist Party of the Soviet Union**.

1923
After leading nationalist forces in the Turkish War of Independence, Mustafa Kemal Atatürk becomes president of the **Republic of Turkey**.

The first half of the 20th century saw the erosion of the old imperial powers and the establishment of new republics. The result was widespread political instability, especially in Europe, which led to the two world wars that dominated the period. In the process of replacing the old European order, a wave of extreme nationalist, authoritarian parties emerged, and in Russia the Bolshevik Revolution of 1917 paved the way for a totalitarian communist dictatorship. Meanwhile, the Great Depression of the early 1930s prompted a move to increased economic and social liberalism in the United States.

By the end of the 1930s, political thinking among the major powers was polarized between the ideologies of fascism, communism, and the social democracy of liberal, free-market capitalism.

World revolutions

The revolutions that sparked this shake-up in political thought did not begin in Europe. In 1910, a decade-long armed struggle known as the Mexican Revolution began, on the fall of the old regime of Porfirio Díaz. In China, the ruling Qing dynasty was overthrown in the Xinhai Revolution of 1911 and replaced with a republic founded by Sun Yat-Sen the following year. But the most influential revolutionary events of the period took place in Russia. Political unrest had led to an unsuccessful revolution in 1905, which was rekindled in 1917 and led to the violent overthrow of Tsar Nicholas II by the Bolsheviks.

The optimism many felt at the end of World War I was short-lived. The formation of the League of Nations, with its hope of ensuring an enduring peace, did little to stem the rising tensions in Europe. Punitive war reparations and post-war economic collapse were a major factor in fostering the appeal of extremist movements.

Dictatorship and resistance

Out of small extremist parties in Italy and Germany arose the Fascist party of Benito Mussolini and the Nazi party of Adolf Hitler. In Spain, in reaction to the formation of a second Spanish Republic, nationalists fought for power under Francisco Franco. And in Russia after the death of Vladimir Lenin in 1924, Joseph Stalin became increasingly

1926 — **Adolf Hitler** sets out his political ideas in *Mein Kampf*.

1930 — Mahatma Gandhi begins a campaign of **civil disobedience** against British rule in India by leading the Dandi Salt March.

1933 — US president Franklin D. Roosevelt begins a programme of **government intervention** known as the New Deal.

1936 — A military coup led by **Francisco Franco** against the Second Spanish Republic triggers the Spanish Civil War.

1937–45 — Mao Zedong rises to prominence as a **communist commander** during the Second Sino-Japanese War.

1939 — German troops **invade Poland**, sparking the outbreak of World War II.

1941 — The United States enters World War II after the Japanese bombing of **Pearl Harbor** in Hawaii.

1945 — **War in Europe** ends as Allied troops capture Berlin, Germany; **Japan surrenders** after the Allies drop two atomic bombs.

autocratic, eliminating opponents and establishing the Soviet Union as an industrial and military power.

While totalitarian regimes grew in strength on continental Europe, Britain faced the break-up of its empire. Independence movements in the colonies threatened British rule, especially in India, with the campaign of non-violent civil disobedience led by Mahatma Gandhi, but also in Africa, where activists such as Jomo Kenyatta of Kenya were mobilizing resistance.

Entering the fray

In the United States, the massive crash on the New York stock market in 1929 ended the boom years of the 1920s and ushered in the Great Depression. In 1933, President Franklin D. Roosevelt introduced the New Deal, which brought a new liberalism to American politics. The United States was keen to remain neutral in Europe's unstable affairs, but Nazi Germany's anti-Semitic policies led to the migration of intellectuals from Europe to America, in particular from the Marxist-inspired Frankfurt School. These migrants brought a fresh thinking that challenged some of Roosevelt's policies.

It was not only Europe that the United States tried to ignore. Asia was also experiencing political turmoil as Japanase militarism sparked the Sino-Japanese War of 1937. As the war turned against China, Mao Zedong rose to prominence as a communist leader.

Britain, too, was reluctant to become involved in any conflict, despite the threat of fascism. Even with the onset of the Spanish Civil War in 1936, with Germany and the Soviet Union supporting opposite sides, Britain kept its distance. But pressure was growing in Britain and the United States to stop appeasing Hitler's territorial demands. After war broke out in 1939, the alliance against Germany grew, with the United States joining after the attack on Pearl Harbor by the Japanese in 1941.

Although Britain, the United States, and the Soviet Union collaborated successfully during World War II, once fascism was defeated, the political lines were redrawn. A standoff soon emerged, with the communist East opposed to the capitalist West, and the rest of Europe struggling to find its place in the middle. The scene was set for the Cold War, which would dominate post-war politics. ■

NON-VIOLENCE IS THE FIRST ARTICLE OF MY FAITH

MAHATMA GANDHI (1869–1948)

IN CONTEXT

IDEOLOGY
Anti-colonial nationalism

FOCUS
Non-violent resistance

BEFORE
5th–6th centuries BCE Jainist teachings stressing non-violence and self-discipline develop in India.

1849 Henry David Thoreau publishes *Civil Disobedience*, defending the morality of conscientious objection to unjust laws.

AFTER
1963 In his "I have a dream" speech in Washington DC, civil rights leader Martin Luther King outlines his vision of black and white people living together in peace.

2011 Peaceful protests in Cairo's Tahrir Square lead to the overthrow of Egyptian president Hosni Mubarak.

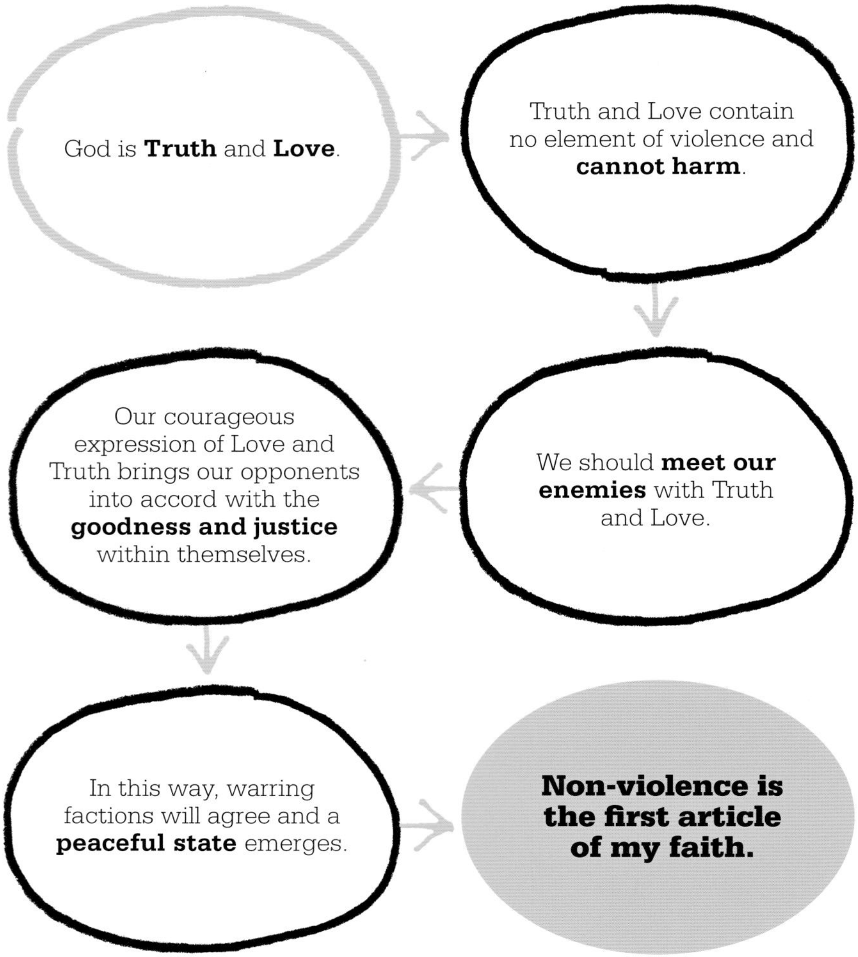

In the worldwide empires that European powers built from the 16th century onwards, it was the example of the imperialists themselves that ultimately gave rise to the nationalist movements that sprang up in opposition to colonial rule. Witnessing the colonizers' strong sense of national identity, based on European ideas about nations and the importance of sovereignty within geographical borders, eventually ignited a desire for nationhood and self-determination in the colonized peoples. However, the lack of economic or military strength led many anti-colonial movements to develop distinctly non-European modes of resistance.

A spiritual weapon

In India, the fight for independence from the UK in the first half of the 20th century was characterized by the political and moral philosophy of its spiritual leader, Mohandas Gandhi, more commonly known by the honorific title "Mahatma", meaning "Great Soul". Although he believed in a strong democratic state, Gandhi held that such a state could never be won, forged, or held by any form of violence. His ethic of radical non-violent resistance and civil disobedience, which he named *satyagraha* ("adherence to truth"), focussed a lens of morality and conscience on the tide of anti-colonial nationalism that was transforming the political landscape of the 20th century. He described this method as a "purely spiritual weapon".

Gandhi believed that the universe was governed by a Supreme Principle, which he called *satya* ("Truth"). For him, this was another name for God, the one God of Love that he believed to be the basis of all the great world religions.

See also: Immanuel Kant 126–29 ▪ Henry David Thoreau 186–87 ▪ Peter Kropotkin 195 ▪ Arne Naess 290–93 ▪ Frantz Fanon 304–05 ▪ Martin Luther King 316–21

Since all human beings were emanations of this divine Being, Gandhi believed that love was the only true principle of relations between humans. Love meant care and respect for others and selfless, lifelong devotion to the cause of "wiping away every tear from every eye". This enjoined *ahimsa*, or the rule of harmlessness, on Gandhi's adherents. Although a Hindu himself, Gandhi drew on many different religious traditions as he developed his moral philosophy, including Jainism and the pacifist Christian teachings of Russian novelist Leo Tolstoy, both of which stressed the importance of not causing hurt to any living creature.

Political ends

Gandhi's ideology was an attempt to work out the rule of love in every area of life. However, he believed that the endurance of suffering, or "turning the other cheek" to abusive treatment at the hands of an individual or a state, as opposed to violent resistance or reprisal, was a means to a political end as well as a spiritual one. This willing sacrifice of the self would operate as a law of truth on human nature to secure the reformation and cooperation of an opponent. It would act as an example to wider society – political friend and foe alike. Home rule for India would be, for Gandhi, the inevitable outcome of a mass revolution of behaviour based on a rich brew of peaceful transcendental principles.

South African activist

Gandhi's first experience of opposing British rule came not in India, but in South Africa. After training as a barrister in London, he worked for 21 years in South Africa – then another British colony – defending the civil rights of migrant Indians. It was during these years that he developed his sense of "Indianness", which he saw as bridging every divide of race, religion, and caste, and which underpinned his later vision of a united Indian nation. In South Africa, he witnessed first-hand the social injustice, racial violence, »

Gandhi was influenced by Jainism, a religion whose central principle is to avoid harming living things. Jain monks wear masks so that they do not inadvertently breathe in insects.

Mahatma Gandhi

Mohandas Karamchand Gandhi was born on 2nd October 1869 to a prominent Hindu family at Porbandar, part of the Bombay Presidency in British India. Gandhi's father was a senior government official and his mother a devout Jain.

Gandhi was married aged just 13. Five years later, his father sent him to London to study law. He was called to the bar in 1891 and set up a law practice in South Africa, defending the civil rights of Indian migrants. While in South Africa, Gandhi embarked upon a strict course in *brahmacharya*, or Hindu self-discipline, beginning a life of asceticism. In 1915, he returned to India, where he took a vow of poverty and founded an ashram. Four years later, he became head of the Indian National Congress. He was killed on his way to prayer by a Hindu extremist who blamed him for the Partition of India and the creation of Pakistan.

Key works

1909 *Hind Swaraj*
1929 *The Story of My Experiments with Truth*

Gandhi believed that the non-violent means used to achieve his end were just as important as the end itself. He used the example of procuring a person's watch to illustrate his point.

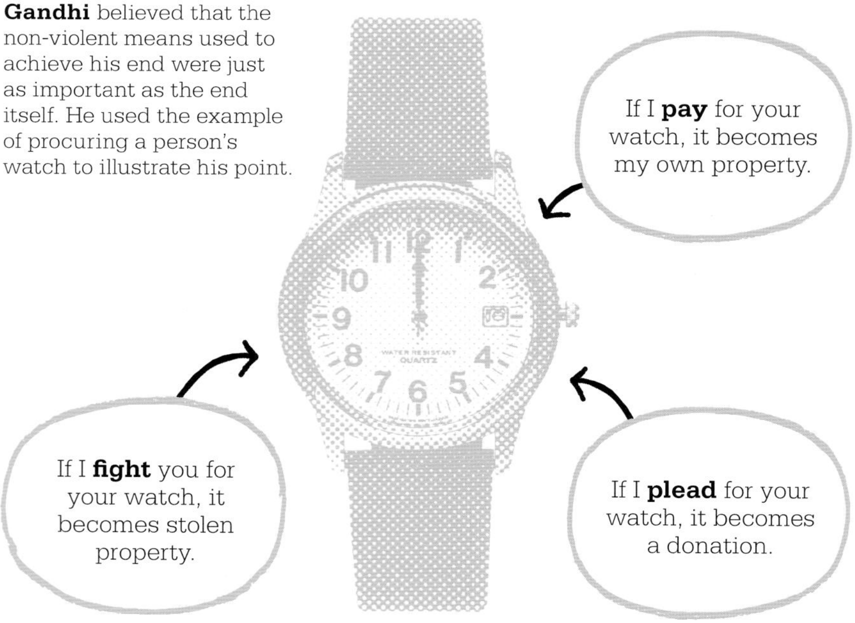

and punitive government exploitation of colonial rule. His response was to develop his pacifist ideals into a practical form of opposition. He proved his gift for leadership in 1906 when he led thousands of poor Indian settlers in a campaign of disobedience against repressive new laws requiring them to register with the state. After seven years of struggle and violent repression, the South African leader, Jan Christiaan Smuts, negotiated a compromise with the protestors, demonstrating the power of non-violent resistance. It might take time, but it would win out in the end, shaming opponents into doing the right thing.

In the years that followed, Gandhi had considerable success in promoting his idea that non-violent resistance was the most effective resistance. He returned to India in 1915 with an international reputation as an Indian nationalist, and soon rose to a position of prominence in the Indian National Congress, the political movement for Indian nationalism. Gandhi advocated the boycott of British-made goods, especially textiles, encouraging all Indians to spin and wear *khadi*, or homespun cloth, in order to reduce dependence on foreign industry and strengthen their own economy. He saw such boycotts as a logical extension of peaceful non-cooperation and urged people to refuse to use British schools and law courts, to resign from government employment, and to eschew British titles and honours. Amid increasing excitement and publicity, he learned to distinguish himself as an astute political showman, understanding the power of the media to influence public opinion.

Thousands joined Gandhi's protest against the tax on salt imposed by the British. They marched to the coast at Dandi in Gujarat in May 1930 to gather salt water and make their own salt.

Public defiance

In 1930, with the British government refusing to respond to Gandhi's congressional resolution calling for Indian dominion status, full independence was unilaterally declared by the Indian National Congress. Soon after, Gandhi launched a new *satyagraha* against the British tax on salt, calling on thousands to join him on the long march to the sea. As the world watched, Gandhi picked up a handful of the salt that lay in great white sheets along the beach, and was promptly arrested. Gandhi was imprisoned, but his act of defiance had publicly demonstrated the unjust nature of British rule in India to commentators around the world. This carefully orchestrated act of non-violent disobedience began to shake the hold of the British empire on India.

> “A religion that takes no account of practical affairs and does not help to solve them is no religion.”
> **Mahatma Gandhi**

Reports of Gandhi's campaigns and imprisonment appeared in newspapers all over the world. German physicist Albert Einstein said of him: "He has invented a completely new and humane means for the liberation war of an oppressed country. The moral influence he had on the consciously thinking human being of the entire civilized world will probably be much more lasting than it seems in our time, with its overestimation of brutal violent forces."

Strict pacifism

However, Gandhi's absolute confidence in his doctrine of non-violence sometimes seemed unbalanced when he applied it to the conflicts unfolding in the wider world, and this earned him criticism from many quarters. "Self-suffering endurance" appeared sometimes to require mass suicide, as shown by his weeping plea to the British Viceroy of India that the British give up arms and oppose the Nazis with spiritual force only. Later, he criticized Jews who had tried to escape the Holocaust or had fought back against German repression saying, "The Jews should have offered themselves to the butcher's knife. They should have thrown themselves into the sea from cliffs. It would have aroused the world and the people of Germany." Criticism also came his way from the left, and British Marxist journalist Rajani Palme Dutt accused him of "using the most religious principles of humanity and love to disguise his support of the property class." Meanwhile, British prime minister Winston Churchill attempted to dismiss him as a "half-naked fakir".

Whatever the limits of their application in other situations, Gandhi's methods were certainly successful in eventually winning independence for India in 1947, although he bitterly opposed the Partition of India into two states split along religious lines – predominantly Hindu India and Muslim Pakistan – which led to the displacement of millions of people. Soon after Partition, Gandhi was assassinated by a Hindu nationalist who accused him of appeasing Muslims.

Today's rapidly industrializing India is a far cry from the rural romanticism and asceticism of Gandhi's political ideals. Meanwhile, the ongoing tension with neighbour Pakistan shows that Gandhi's belief in an Indian identity that transcended religion has ultimately been unfulfilled. The caste system, which Gandhi had steadfastly opposed, also maintains a strong hold on Indian society. However, India remains a secular, democratic state, which still accords with Gandhi's fundamental belief that it is only through peaceful means that a just state can emerge. His example and methods have been taken up by activists around the world, including civil rights leader Martin Luther King, who credited Gandhi as the inspiration for his peaceful resistance to racist laws in the US in the 1950s and 60s. ■

> Christ gave us the goals and Mahatma Gandhi the tactics.
> **Martin Luther King**

Forms of non-violent protest, from blocking roads to boycotting goods, have become popular and powerful methods of civil disobedience in today's political world.

POLITICS BEGIN WHERE THE MASSES ARE

VLADIMIR LENIN (1870–1924)

IN CONTEXT

IDEOLOGY
Communism

FOCUS
Mass revolution

BEFORE
1793 During the Reign of Terror following the French Revolution, thousands are executed as "enemies of the revolution".

1830s French political activist Auguste Blanqui teaches that a small band of expert conspirators can execute a revolutionary seizure of power.

1848 Karl Marx and Friedrich Engels publish the *Communist Manifesto*.

AFTER
1921 The Communist Party of China (CPC) is organized as a Leninist vanguard party.

1927 Stalin reverses Lenin's New Economic Policy and collectivizes agriculture.

At the turn of the 20th century, the Russian empire was a lumbering agrarian colossus that had fallen far behind the industrializing states of western Europe in economic terms. The empire's population comprised many different ethnic groups – including Russians, Ukrainians, Poles, Belorussians, Jews, Finns, and Germans – only 40 per cent of whom spoke Russian. The empire was ruled over by an absolutist, authoritarian tsar, Nicolas II, and a strict social hierarchy was ruthlessly enforced. There was no free press, no freedom of speech or association, no minority rights, and few political rights. Unsurprisingly, in this atmosphere of repression, revolutionary forces were gaining an ever-stronger foothold, and they would finally be carried to victory in the 1917 October Revolution by a political agitator named Vladimir Lenin.

A law of history

During the 19th century, socialism had developed in Europe as a response to the hardship that characterized the lives of the new industrial working class. Unprotected by social institutions or traditions such as unions, workers were particularly at risk of exploitation by their new employers. In response to their suffering, and believing that class conflict holds within it the dynamics of social change, Karl Marx and Friedrich Engels proclaimed that an international revolution against capitalism was inevitable. In the *Communist Manifesto* of 1848, they called for an international merger of the proletariat across Europe.

However, Marx and Engels had not foreseen that as workers in the advanced industrialized societies of western Europe became more secure and began to acquire better living standards, they would aspire to become the bourgeoisie (merchant class), not revolt against it. Socialists began more and more to work through legal and constitutional channels with the aim of winning the vote for working class men and thereby achieving change through the democratic process. Socialist opinion became increasingly divided between those who

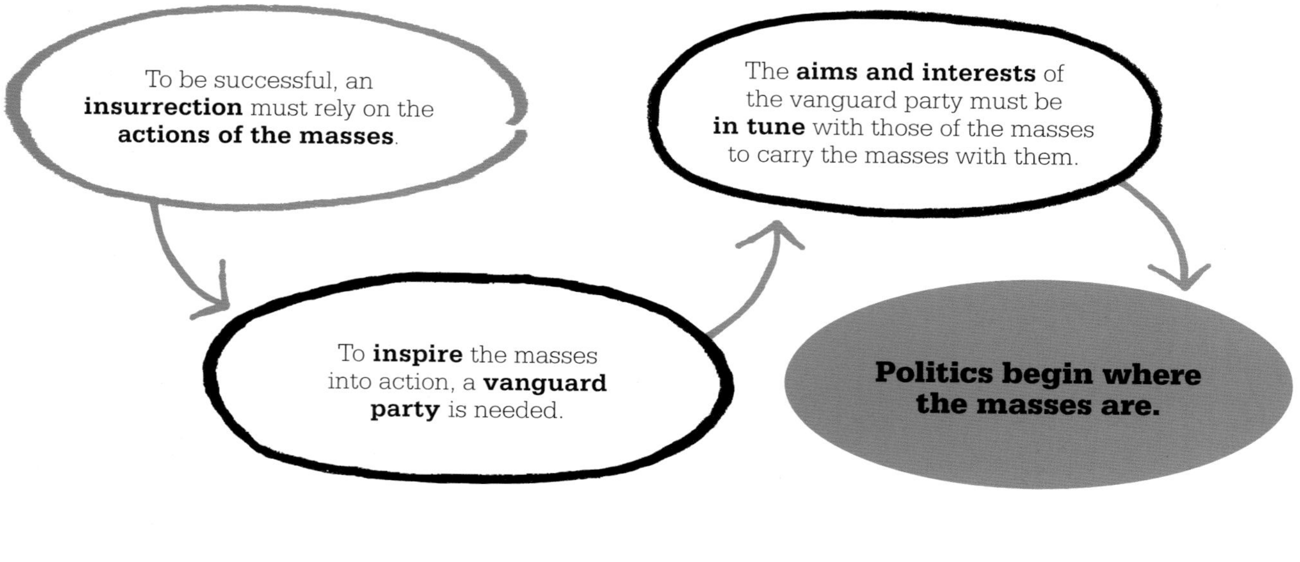

See also: Karl Marx 188–93 ▪ Joseph Stalin 240–41 ▪ Leon Trotsky 242–45 ▪ Mao Zedong 260–65

> We have combined, by a freely adopted decision, for the purpose of fighting the enemy.
> **Vladimir Lenin**

advocated reform through the ballot box and those who sought reform through revolution.

Russian conditions

Russia had come late to industrialization and at the end of the 19th century, its working class had still not won any real concessions from their employers. Unlike the peoples of western Europe, the vast majority of Russia's population had not seen any material benefits from industrialization. In the 1890s, growing numbers of political activists in Russia, including radical young law student Vladimir Lenin, plotted against the increasingly repressive state and its secret police force, and in 1905, a wave of unrest swept the country. This first attempt at a revolution failed to overthrow the tsar, but it did win some concessions to democracy. Russian workers continued to endure harsh conditions, however, and revolutionaries continued to plot the total overthrow of the tsarist regime.

Throughout his career, Lenin strove to translate Marxist theory into practical politics. Analysing Russia's position through a Marxist lens, he saw that the country was moving in sudden leaps from feudalism to capitalism. Lenin viewed the peasant economy as another exploitative plank in the capitalist platform – judging that if it were pulled out, the whole capitalist economy would collapse.

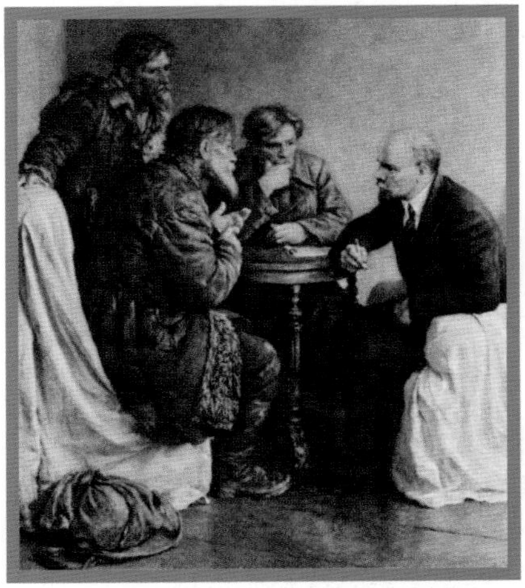

Lenin initially attempted to garner support for the revolution from Russian peasants. He concluded that peasants could not form the revolutionary class because they aspired to own land.

However, as the peasants aspired to own their own land, Lenin realized they would not be the class to bring about a socialist revolution, one of whose central aims was the eventual ending of private ownership. It was clear to Lenin that the driving force of »

Vladimir Lenin

Vladimir Ilich Ulyanov, who later adopted the surname "Lenin", was born in Simbirsk, Russia, now called Ulyanovsk. He received a classical education and showed a gift for Latin and Greek. In 1887, his brother Aleksandr was executed for the attempted assassination of Tsar Alexander III. That year, Lenin enrolled at Kazan University to study law but was expelled for student protests. Exiled to his grandfather's estate, he steeped himself in the works of Karl Marx. He received his law degree and began his real career as a professional revolutionary. He was arrested, jailed, exiled to Siberia, and then travelled through Europe, writing and organizing for the coming revolution. The October Revolution of 1917 effectively made him ruler of all Russia. Lenin survived an assassination attempt in 1918, but never fully regained his health.

Key works

1902 *What Is To Be Done?*
1917 *Imperialism, the Highest Stage of Capitalism*
1917 *The State and Revolution*

the revolution would have to be the burgeoning industrial working class.

Vanguard party

In Marxist analysis, the bourgeoisie is the merchant class – the social class that owns the means of production (such as the factories) – while the proletariat comprises those who have no choice but to live off the sale of their own labour. Within the bourgeoisie were educated individuals, such as Lenin himself, who viewed the exploitation of the proletariat by the bourgeoisie as unjust, and agitated for change. Such "revolutionary bourgeois" individuals had played a leading role in past revolutions, including the French Revolution of 1789. However, the rapid industrialization of Russia was being financed largely by foreign capital, and this meant that the Russian bourgeoisie was a relatively small class. To make matters trickier still, there were few revolutionaries within their number.

Lenin understood that a revolution required leadership and organization, and he championed Engels' and Marx's idea of a "vanguard party" – a group of "resolute individuals" of clear political understanding, mostly recruited from the working class, who would spearhead the revolution. They were to inspire the proletariat to become a "class-for-itself", which would then overthrow bourgeois supremacy and establish a democratic "dictatorship of the proletariat". Lenin drew together his vanguard party under the name of the Bolsheviks; this party would ultimately become the Communist Party of the Soviet Union.

International revolution

Like Marx, Lenin believed that a united proletariat would rise in a great revolutionary wave that would transcend borders and national identities, ethnocentrism, and religion, effectively becoming a borderless, classless state in itself. It would be an international expansion of "democracy for the poor", and would occur alongside a forced suppression of the exploiting and oppressing class, who would be excluded from the new democracy. Lenin saw this transitory phase as an essential part of the shift from democracy to communism – the ultimate revolutionary state envisioned by Marx, which would follow the dictatorship of the proletariat.

Rich bankers flee as the workers advance under the slogan "Long Live the International Socialist Revolution!", a quote from Lenin emphasizing cross-border class allegiances.

A rebellious army, sick of the appalling casualties of World War I, played a crucial role in making the 1917 October Revolution a success. The old regime was discredited by the war.

In this ultimate communist state, class would be transcended and private property abolished.

Lenin declared that his political ideas could take hold "not where there are thousands, but where there are millions. That is where serious politics begin". In order to confront the might and force of the heavily armed imperialist state, millions of disaffected workers, alienated by that state, were needed to participate. Only in their united millions, organized by professional revolutionaries, could they hope to destroy a well-armed and well-financed capitalist regime. Under the tsars, the working classes and peasants had seen their own interests as dependent upon the interests of the owners of production or the landowner, but Lenin the Marxist urged them to see their rights and welfare as dependent only upon their own social class. The masses had been welded together into a single political body by their suffering, and now this was reinforced by constant rhetoric from Lenin's Bolshevik lieutenants. For Lenin, the power of the masses was the only effective revolutionary power.

> Victory will belong only to those who have faith in the people, those who are immersed in the life-giving spring of popular creativity.
> **Vladimir Lenin**

When Lenin delivered his political report to the Extraordinary Seventh Congress of the Russian Communist Party on 6 March 1918, a year after the successful 1917 revolution, he provided them with a review of the revolution that was "a truly Marxist substantiation of all our decisions". His Bolshevik party had seized power from the transitional government the preceding October in what was essentially a bloodless *coup d'etat*. They were the first successful communist revolutionaries in the world. Even though Russia was a poor country within the capitalist finance system, with a relatively weak proletariat, its bourgeois state was even weaker, and the masses of working-class urban workers had been mobilized to dispossess it, resulting in an "easy victory".

One major factor in the success of the revolution had been Russia's role in World War I. By 1917, the war was causing the Russian people intolerable hardship. Even death squads could not stop troop mutinies and desertions, and the "imperialist" war was transformed into civil war between the Bolshevik Red Army and the anti-Bolshevik White Army. Lenin wrote, "In this civil war, the overwhelming majority of the population proved to be on our side, and that is why victory was achieved with such extraordinary ease." Everywhere he saw the fulfilment of Marx's expectation that, as the proletariat learned through harsh experience that there could be no collaboration with the bourgeois state, the "fruit" of mass revolution would "ripen" spontaneously.

In reality, many other factors played a part. As the events of 1917 had played out, the institutions of the old order »

– the local administration, the army, and the Church – lost their authority. Both urban and rural economies collapsed. Russia's forced withdrawal from World War I, and the subsequent civil war, took place against a backdrop of severe shortages, which brought about widespread suffering. Lenin had realized that only a dominant and coercive force could hope to create a new order out of this chaos. The Bolshevik party was the vanguard, but not the main substance of revolutionary power. Thinking in terms of the Marxian categories of the masses and blocks of workers and peasants, Lenin saw the proletarian democracy of the workers' soviets (councils or groups) as the elementary substance of the new "commune" state. These groups united into one under the cry: "All Power to the Soviets!" In October 1917, the world's first socialist state, the Russian Socialist Federative Soviet Republic, was born.

War Communism

Economically, the revolution was followed by three years of War Communism, which saw millions of Russian peasants die of starvation as food produced in the countryside was confiscated and brought to feed Bolshevik armies and cities, and to aid in the civil war against the anti-Bolshevik Whites. Conditions were so harsh that Lenin and the Bolsheviks faced uprisings from the same masses on whose support Lenin had based his politics. Historian David Christian writes that War Communism challenged the ideals of Lenin's new Communist party, as "the government claiming to represent the working class now found itself on the verge of being overthrown by that same working class".

While War Communism was the improvised condition that resulted from a revolution, what replaced it at the end of the civil war was a specific policy proposed by Lenin. The New Economic Policy, which Lenin referred to as state capitalism, allowed some small businesses, such as farms, to sell on their surpluses for personal gain. Large industries and banks remained in the hands of the state. The new policy, which was reviled by many Bolsheviks for diluting socialist economics with capitalist elements, succeeded in increasing agricultural production, as farmers were encouraged to produce larger quantities of food through appeal to their own self-interest. The policy was later replaced by Stalin's policy of forced collectivism in the years after Lenin's death, leading to more widespread famines in the 1930s.

> This struggle must be organized… by people who are professionally engaged in revolutionary activity.
> **Vladimir Lenin**

Proletarian power

The extent to which Lenin's October Revolution was an authentically socialist revolution depends upon the extent to which "the masses" were actually in accord with and represented by the Bolsheviks. Was the suffering proletariat actually self-liberated "from below", or did Bolshevik leaders ride to power on the Marxist narrative of victory for the suffering masses? How real was this new proletarian

During the civil war that followed the revolution, the Bolsheviks fought the anti-revolutionary "White Army". Emergency measures were imposed, testing the support of the masses.

In China's Cultural Revolution, young Red Guards formed a vanguard, rooting out anti-revolutionary attitudes. Lenin believed that vanguards were needed to lead a revolution.

power – the power of the masses – which was brought into being and then constantly defined, explained, and eulogized by Lenin?

A contemporary of Lenin, Nikolay Sukhanov, a socialist activist and critic of the Bolshevik revolution, was sceptical. Sukhanov wrote: "Lenin is an orator of a great power who is capable of simplifying a complicated matter… the one who is pounding, pounding, and pounding people's minds until they lose their will, until he enslaves them."

> Lenin alone could have led Russia into the enchanted quagmire; he alone could have found the way back to the causeway.
> **Winston Churchill**

Labour aristocracy

Many critics have considered that when the Bolsheviks insisted that the dictatorship of the party was synonymous with a true workers' state, they were in reality justifying their dominance over the workers. Lenin excused this dominance through his elitist belief that without the "professional revolutionaries", workers on their own could not rise higher than a "trade union consciousness". By this, he meant that workers would not see beyond alliances with their immediate colleagues at work to a wider class alliance.

Compounding the problem, in Lenin's eyes, was the fact that the concessions won by the working classes in parts of western Europe had not lifted the working class as a whole. Rather, these concessions had created what Lenin called a "labour aristocracy" – a group of workers who had won significant concessions and as a result had become detached from their true class allegiance. For Lenin, the situation required a "revolutionary socialist consciousness" that could grasp Marxist principles of class unification. This could only be provided by a vanguard from within the working class – and the Bolsheviks formed that vanguard party.

Lenin held that the existence of absolute truth was unconditional, and further that Marxism was truth, which left no room for dissent. This absolutism gave Bolshevism an authoritarian, anti-democratic, and elitist nature that would seem to be at odds with a belief in bottom-up democracy. His vanguard-party revolution has since been replicated across the political spectrum, from the right-wing anti-communist Kuomintang Party in Taiwan to the Communist Party of China. Some intellectuals still describe themselves as "Leninists", including Slovenian philosopher Slavoj Zizek, who admires Lenin's desire to apply Marxist theory in practice and his willingness "to dirty his hands" in order to achieve his aims. Contemporary Leninists see globalization as the continuation of the 19th-century imperialism that Lenin opposed, as capitalist interests turn towards poor countries in search of new labour forces to exploit. Their solution to this problem, like Lenin's a century ago, is an international mass workers' movement. ■

THE MASS STRIKE RESULTS FROM SOCIAL CONDITIONS WITH HISTORICAL INEVITABILITY

ROSA LUXEMBURG (1871–1919)

IN CONTEXT

IDEOLOGY
Revolutionary socialism

FOCUS
The mass strike

BEFORE
1826 The first General Strike in the UK is held in response to mine owners attempting to reduce miners' pay.

1848 Karl Marx theorizes in his *Communist Manifesto* that revolution and historical change are the result of class conflict between dominant and subordinate classes.

AFTER
1937–38 Stalin's forcible transformation of the USSR into an industrial power leads to his Great Purge. Hundreds of thousands are executed.

1989 Solidarity, a Polish trade union, defeats the Communist Party with a coalition government led by Lech Walesa.

Inequality and oppression exist in a capitalist society.

↓

The oppressed workers do not need **external leaders**...

↓

...as they will **rise up spontaneously** to throw off their oppressors.

↓

The mass strike results from social conditions with historical inevitability.

The Marxist theorist Rosa Luxemburg articulated the idea of the mass strike in a revolutionary way, emphasizing its organic nature. She identified both political and economic mass strikes as the most important tools in the struggle for workers' power.

Luxemburg's ideas were formed in response to widespread workers' strikes and the Bloody Sunday protest in St Petersburg that mushroomed into the Russian Revolution of 1905.

A social revolution

Karl Marx and Friedrich Engels had imagined that a mass strike of the proletariat would be led by a professional vanguard outside or "above" the working class, while to anarchist theorists, revolution was sparked through extraordinary acts of destruction and propaganda. To Luxemburg, neither idea was the right way to understand or facilitate the mass strike. Rather, she saw many different dynamics working together in a social revolution.

In her work *Dialectic of Spontaneity and Organization*, Luxemburg explained that political organization would develop naturally from within, as workers

See also: Karl Marx 188–93 ▪ Eduard Bernstein 202–03 ▪ Vladimir Lenin 226–33 ▪ Joseph Stalin 240–41 ▪ Leon Trotsky 242–45

Lech Walesa founded Solidarity in Poland in 1980. The independent trade union used mass strikes to improve the lives of workers, and these strikes were the catalyst for political change.

learned by participating in strikes for better wages and later for political ends. Revolution would teach itself to the participating masses. She believed that leaders should be nothing more than the conscious embodiment of the feelings and ambitions of the masses, and that mass strikes would bring about a new form of socialism. The events of 1905 had shown Luxemburg that a general strike could not be decreed by an executive decision, nor could it reliably be fomented by grass roots groups, but that it was a natural phenomenon of the proletariat consciousness. It was an inevitable result of social realities, particularly the hardship of working people forced, in order to survive, to carry out onerous, underpaid work in the new industrial workplaces of Central Europe and Russia.

The workers advance

Luxemburg believed that the pressure of proletarian discontent against the military might and financial control of the state would explode in unsuccessful and successful strikes, culminating in a spontaneous mass strike. This would bring about the workers' objectives and transform the party leadership while advancing the revolution against capitalism. During these developments, workers would advance intellectually, guaranteeing their further progress.

> The mass strike is merely the form of the revolutionary struggle at a given moment.
> **Rosa Luxemburg**

Vladimir Lenin objected that this "revolutionary sponteneity" took away the benefits of the inherent discipline and forward-planning of a revolution led by enlightened commanders. He assigned the leadership role to his Bolshevik party. Luxemburg saw this as conducive to dictatorship and ultimately to "the brutalization of public life". The horrors of Lenin's Red Terror and Stalin's murderous trajectory were to prove her right. ■

Rosa Luxemburg

Born in the Polish town of Zamosc, Rosa Luxemburg was a gifted student and linguist, absorbed by age 16 in socialist politics. She became a German citizen in 1898 and moved to Berlin, where she joined the international labour movement and the Social Democratic Party. She wrote on socialist issues, women's suffrage, and economics, and worked for a workers' revolution. She met Lenin in 1907 at a conference of Russian Social Democrats in London.

After being imprisoned in Breslau in 1916, she formed the Spartakusbund (Spartacus League), an underground political organization. In January 1919, during revolutionary activities in Berlin, Luxemburg was seized by army officers and shot. Her corpse was thrown into the Landwehr Canal and was recovered several months later.

Key works

1904 *Organizational Questions of the Russian Social Democracy*
1906 *The Mass Strike*
1913 *The Accumulation of Capital*
1915 *The Junius Pamphlet*

AN APPEASER IS ONE WHO FEEDS A CROCODILE HOPING IT WILL EAT HIM LAST

WINSTON CHURCHILL (1874–1965)

IN CONTEXT

IDEOLOGY
Conservatism

FOCUS
Non-appeasement

BEFORE
c.350 BCE Statesman and orator Demosthenes criticizes his fellow Athenians for not anticipating Philip of Macedon's imperial goals.

1813 European powers try to settle with Napoleon, but his renewed military campaigns drive a coalition of allies to defeat him at Leipzig.

AFTER
1982 British prime minister Margaret Thatcher refers to Chamberlain when urged to compromise with Argentina during the Falklands War.

2003 US president George Bush and British prime minister Tony Blair invoke the dangers of appeasement in the run-up to the Iraq War.

In the mid-1930s the word "appeasement" had not yet taken on the taint of cowardice and ignominy that later events would give it. Conciliatory policy-making had become the norm after World War I, as European powers sought to ease what Winston Churchill had called "the fearful hatreds and antagonisms which exist in Europe". But as the Great Depression took its toll around the world and Adolf Hitler rose to power in Germany, Churchill and a very few others saw that this policy was becoming dangerous.

Defence expenditure in Britain had been greatly constrained by the economic slump. The need to rearm against Hitler came at a time of extreme financial duress for a nation that was still struggling to recover from the Great War and deploying most of its military resources in the remote outposts of the British empire. The idea of confronting Germany again to contain Hitler was dismissed by conservative prime minister Stanley Baldwin and his successor, fellow conservative Neville Chamberlain. Assuaging the

An appeaser believes he is **not powerful enough** to defeat a tyrant.

↓

Therefore he **makes concessions** in order to avoid going to war.

↓ ↓

His concessions **make him weaker**.

His concessions make **the tyrant stronger**.

See also: Mahatma Gandhi 220–25 ▪ Napoleon Bonaparte 335 ▪ Adolf Hitler 337

Churchill denounced the settlement that Chamberlain negotiated with Hitler at Munich in 1938 as "a total, unmitigated defeat".

dictator's mounting grievances seemed to them the moderate, practical approach.

Churchill's unofficial network of military and government intelligence kept him informed about Nazi aims and movements and the unprepared state of British forces. He warned Parliament about Hitler's intentions in 1933, and continued to raise the alarm in speeches of immense poetic power in the face of what he saw as complacency, only to be mocked as a warmonger and relegated to the back benches of Parliament.

The Munich Agreement

The appeasement mindset in British politics was firmly entrenched, and the British offered no resistance to Hitler's systematic breach of the conditions of the Versailles Treaty they had signed at the end of World War I – including his remilitarization of the Rhineland – or to his legislation against the Jews. Emboldened, Hitler annexed Austria into the Reich in 1938, and in the same year, crudely coerced Chamberlain at Munich to trade Czechoslovakia's Sudetenland for another false promise of peace.

Hitler was bemused by his easy gains. He had planned to "smash" Czechoslovakia with a "shock and awe"-style entry into Prague and instead found her "virtually served up to me on a plate by her friends".

Churchill denounced the Munich Agreement. He contended that to feed the Nazi monster with

> "
> You were given the choice between war and dishonour. You chose dishonour and you will have war.
> **Winston Churchill**
> "

concessions would simply make it more voracious. Other politicians trusted Hitler, and Churchill stood almost alone, among Conservatives at least, in condemning him. He refused at all times to discuss anything at all with Hitler or with his representatives. Radical but reasoned, this non-negotiable defiance of tyranny, to the death if need be, was the core idea that would bring down the Nazis. ■

Winston Churchill

The son of English lord Randolph Churchill and American heiress Jennie Jerome, Sir Winston Leonard Spencer-Churchill once described himself as "an English-Speaking Union". He was educated at Harrow Public School and Sandhurst Military Academy and then served in India with a cavalry commission. During the 1890s, he distinguished himself as a war correspondent covering the Cuban Revolt against Spain, British campaigns in India and the Sudan, and the Boer War in South Africa. His career in the House of Commons, first as a Liberal MP and later as a Conservative, spanned 60 years. He took charge of a government of national unity during World War II, and served one further term as prime minister in 1951. Churchill was a prolific writer and received the Nobel Prize for Literature in 1953, largely for his six-part history of World War II.

Key works

1953 *The Second World War*
1958 *A History of the English Speaking Peoples*
1974 *The Complete Speeches*

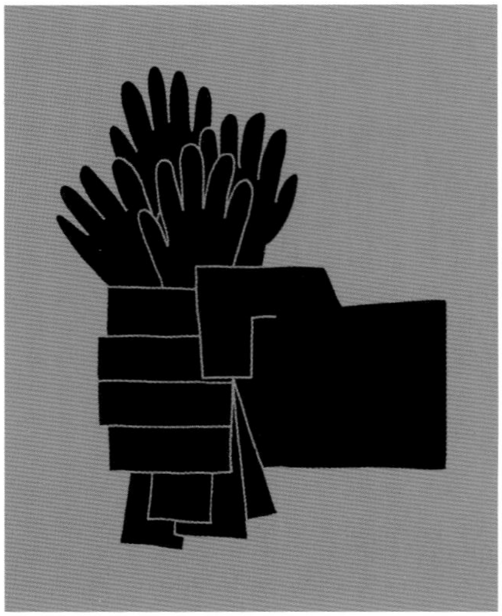

THE FASCIST CONCEPTION OF THE STATE IS ALL-EMBRACING

GIOVANNI GENTILE (1875–1944)

IN CONTEXT

IDEOLOGY
Fascism

FOCUS
Philosophy of the state

BEFORE
27 BCE–476 CE The Roman empire quickly expands from Europe to Africa and Asia.

1770–1831 Georg Hegel develops his philosophy of unity and absolute idealism, later used by Gentile to argue for the all-embracing state.

AFTER
1943–1945 Allied forces invade Italy at the end of World War II, and the fascist regime surrenders.

1940s–1960s Neo-fascist movements become increasingly popular in Latin America.

From 1960s Neo-fascist philosophies become incorporated into many nationalist movements.

When World War I ended in 1918, Italy was in a state of social and political unrest. The country had been forced to concede territory to Yugoslavia and was reeling from heavy losses in the war. At the same time, unemployment was rising as the economy shrank. Mainstream politicians appeared unable to provide answers, and both left- and right-wing groups were growing in popularity among the struggling peasants and workers. The right-wing National Fascist Party, under the political leadership of Benito Mussolini and the philosophical guidance of Giovanni Gentile, used nationalist rhetoric to win over popular support. They advocated a radical new form of social organization based around the fascist state.

Mussolini visited the Exhibition of the Fascist Revolution, Milan, 1932. This vast and striking propaganda event was designed by artists and intellectuals including Gentile to herald a new era.

Unity through collectivism

The guiding principles for the new Italian state are laid out in *The Doctrine of Fascism*, a text that is thought to have been ghostwritten by Gentile for Mussolini. Gentile rejected the idea of individualism and thought the answer to both the people's need for purpose and the state's need for vitality and cohesiveness lay in collectivism.

Gentile describes the fascist conception of the state as an attitude towards life in which individuals and generations are bound together by a higher law and will: specifically, the law and will of the nation. Like communism, fascism sought to promote values beyond materialism, and like Marx,

See also: Georg Hegel 156–59 ▪ Karl Marx 188–93 ▪ Friedrich Nietzsche 196–99 ▪ Vladimir Lenin 226–33 ▪ Joseph Stalin 240–41 ▪ Benito Mussolini 337

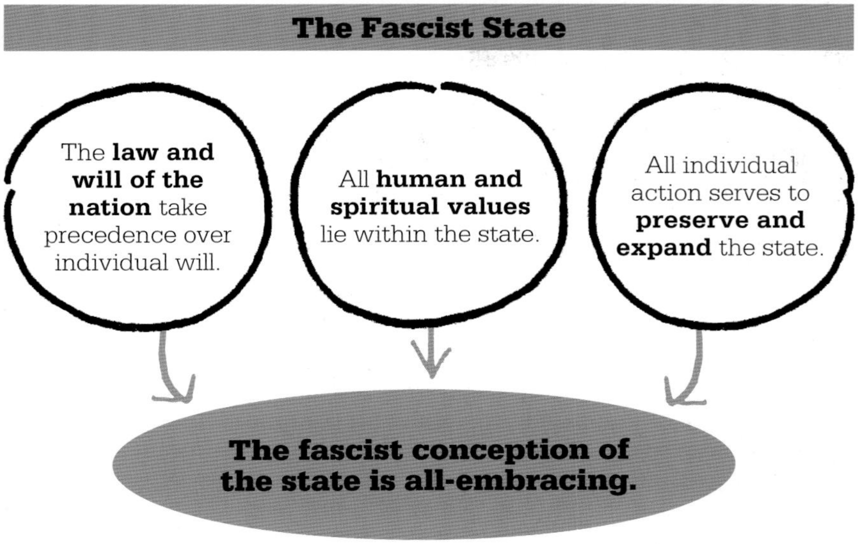

Gentile wanted his philosophy to underlie the new form of the state. However, he did not agree with the Marxist position, which saw society as divided into social classes and historical processes as driven by class struggle. Gentile also opposed the democratic idea of majority rule, which sees the will of the nation as subordinate to the will of the majority. Above all, Gentile's fascist state was defined in opposition to the prevailing doctrines of political and economic liberalism, which at that moment in history had proved itself unable to maintain political stability. He thought that the aspiration for permanent peace was absurd, because it failed to recognize the conflicting interests of different nations that make conflict inevitable.

This new understanding of the state was designed to appeal to a confident and victorious "Italian spirit" that could be traced back to the Roman empire. With Mussolini as "Il Duce" ("The Leader"), the fascist understanding of the state would place Italy back on the world map as a great power. In order to create the new fascist nation, it was necessary to mould all individual wills into one. All forms of civil society outside the state were repressed, and all spheres of life – economic, social, cultural, and religious – became subordinate to the state. The state also aimed to grow through colonial expansion, which was mainly to be achieved through conquests in North Africa.

Gentile was the foremost philosopher of fascism. He became Mussolini's minister of education and chief organizer of cultural politics. In these roles, he played a key role in the construction of an all-embracing fascist Italian state. ■

Giovanni Gentile

Giovanni Gentile was born in Castelvetrano, in western Sicily. After completing high school in Trapani, he received a scholarship to the prestigious Scuola Normale Superiore in Pisa, where he studied philosophy with Donato Jaja, focusing on the idealist tradition in Italy. Gentile later taught at universities in Palermo, Pisa, Rome, Milan, and Naples. During his time in Naples, he co-founded the influential journal *La Critica* with the liberal philosopher Benedetto Croce. Gentile and Croce would later fall out as Croce became increasingly critical of the fascist regime of Benito Mussolini, in which Gentile had become a key figure.

As Minister of Public Education in Mussolini's first cabinet, Gentile implemented the so-called *Riforma Gentile*: a radical reform of the secondary school system that prioritized the study of history and philosophy. He was the main force behind the *Enciclopedia Italiana*, a radical attempt to rewrite Italian history. He later became the fascist regime's leading ideologist. Gentile was made president of The Academy of Italy in 1943, and supported the puppet regime of the Republic of Salò when the Kingdom of Italy fell to the Allies. He was killed the following year by a communist resistance group.

Key works

1897 *Critique of Historical Materialism*
1920 *The Reform of Education*
1928 *The Philosophy of Fascism*

THE WEALTHY FARMERS MUST BE DEPRIVED OF THE SOURCES OF THEIR EXISTENCE

JOSEPH STALIN (1878–1953)

IN CONTEXT

IDEOLOGY
State socialism

FOCUS
Collectivization

BEFORE
1566 In Russia, Ivan the Terrible's efforts to create a centralized state result in peasants fleeing and a drop in food production.

1793–94 The Jacobins institute the Reign of Terror in France.

AFTER
1956 Nikita Krushchev reveals that Stalin executed thousands of loyal communists during the purges.

1962 Alexander Solzhenitsyn's *One Day in the Life of Ivan Denisovich*, telling of life in a Russian labour camp, becomes a worldwide bestseller.

1989 Mikhail Gorbachev introduces *glasnost* (openness), saying "I detest lies".

After the Russian Revolution of 1917, Vladimir Lenin's Bolsheviks set about creating a new socialist system through nationalization, taking privately held assets or enterprises into government ownership. Lenin's successor as leader of the Soviet Union, Joseph Stalin, accelerated this process from 1929, and over five years the economy was rapidly industrialized and collectivized by edict from the centre. In the name of modernizing the Soviet Union's agricultural system, Stalin amalgamated farms under state control as "socialist state property". The class of relatively wealthy farmers known as kulaks were compelled to give up their land and join collective farms. Stalin's police confiscated food and took it to the towns, and the peasants retaliated by burning their crops and killing their animals. A disastrous famine

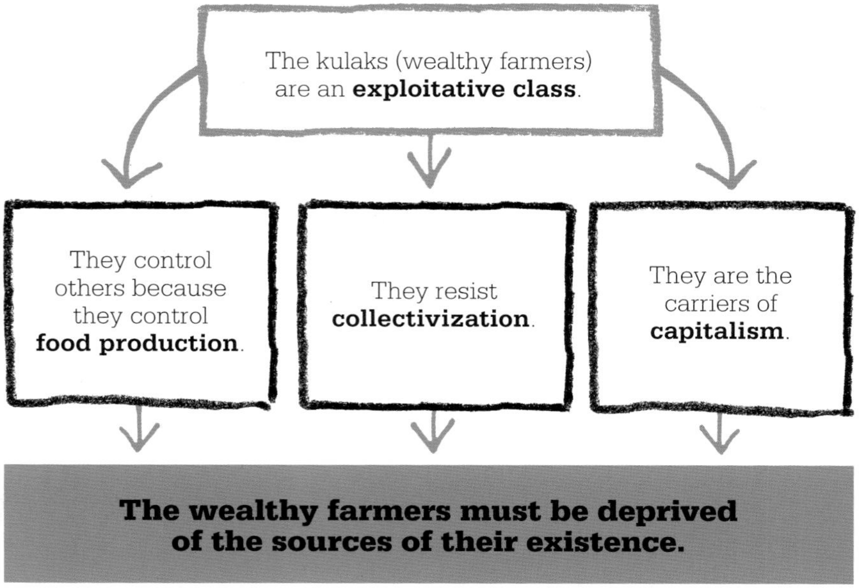

See also: Karl Marx 188–93 ▪ Vladimir Lenin 226–33 ▪ Leon Trotsky 242–45

ensued, and in the area of Ukraine known as the "breadbasket" because of its rich farmland, five million people starved, or were shot or deported. By 1934, seven million kulaks had been "eliminated". Those who survived were now living on state farms run by government officials.

During the collectivization of farming, propaganda posters urged farmers to till every available hectare. However, the forced collectivization led to a disastrous drop in production.

Revolution from above

Stalin reasoned that collectivization was an essential form of class war, forming part of a "revolution from above". This simple conflation gave him the justification he needed to move away from Lenin's policy of using persuasion to organize the peasants into cooperatives. Stalin began by "restricting the tendencies of the kulaks", then moved on to "ousting" them from the countryside, and finally "eliminating" them as an entire class. Lenin had warned that as long as the Soviet Union remained surrounded by capitalist countries, the class struggle would need to continue. Stalin quoted this often as collectivization advanced. He complained that the individual peasant economy "generated capitalism", and that as long as it did, capitalism would remain a feature of the Soviet economy.

Stalin framed the mass-murder of millions of individuals as the "liquidation" of a class, to be carried out by "depriving them of the productive sources of existence". However, when the destruction of private farming was complete, he sustained the terror, claiming that the old "kulak mentality" was lingering, and continued to threaten the communist state.

As the terror of Stalin's regime spread, it was not only the kulaks who would suffer persecution. Opponents of Stalin's rule, real and imagined, were killed, including every single surviving member of Lenin's politburo. Lenin's revolution was transformed into Stalin's dictatorship, and the Bolshevik party, which Lenin had seen as a "vanguard party" inspiring the masses, became a hulking, institutionalized state party that performed the role of the instrument of terror in Stalin's regime. Stalin had begun his persecution with the kulaks, but by the middle of the 1930s, few were safe from the state terror machine. ■

Joseph Stalin

Joseph Stalin was born Ioseb Besarionis dze Jughashvili in the village of Gori, Georgia. He was educated at the local church school, and later expelled from Tiflis Theological Seminary, where he had become a Marxist. As a young man, he was a noted poet.

Stalin's political career took off in 1907 when he attended the 5th Congress of the Russian Social Democratic Labour Party in London with Lenin. Active in the political underground, he was exiled to Siberia several times, and in 1913, he adopted the name Stalin from the Russian word *stal* ("steel"). By the revolution of 1917, he had become a leading figure in the Bolshevik party. Stalin's ruthless actions in the subsequent civil war were an early warning of the terrors that would come when he succeeded Lenin as the leader of the Soviet Union. He had a troubled private life, and both his first son and second wife committed suicide.

Key works

1924 *The Principles of Leninism*
1938 *Dialectical and Historical Materialism*

IF THE END JUSTIFIES THE MEANS, WHAT JUSTIFIES THE END?

LEON TROTSKY (1879–1940)

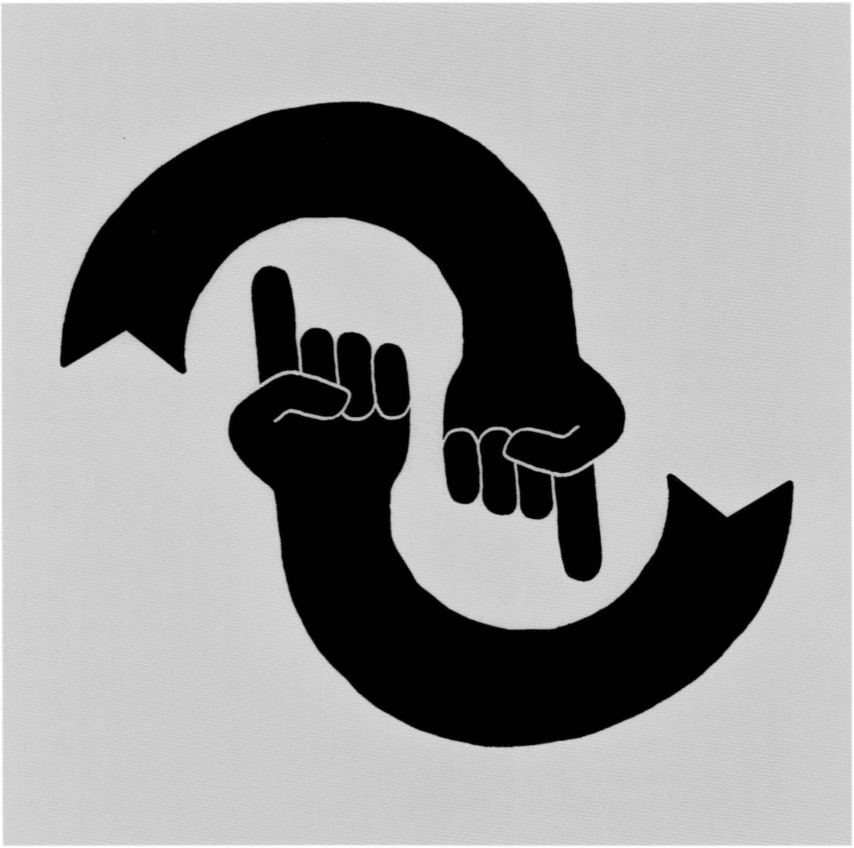

IN CONTEXT

IDEOLOGY
Communism

FOCUS
Permanent revolution

BEFORE
360 BCE Plato describes an ideal state in the *Republic*.

1794 French writer Francois Noel Babeuf proposes a communistic society with no private property and a guaranteed livelihood for all.

AFTER
1932 President Roosevelt promises the American people a New Deal, initiating an era of government intervention and regulation of the economy.

2007 Venezuelan president Hugo Chávez declares himself to be a Trotskyist.

2012 Russian punk band Pussy Riot denounce Vladimir Putin's "totalitarian system".

Throughout his career, Russian revolutionary Leon Trotsky always sought to promote what he saw as a truly Marxist position. He worked closely with Vladimir Lenin to translate Karl Marx's theories into practice as the two men led the Bolshevik Revolution of 1917. According to Marx's theory, the revolution was to be followed by a "dictatorship of the proletariat" as workers took control of the means of production. However, following Lenin's death in 1924, Joseph Stalin's absolutist bureaucracy soon crushed any hope of such a mass movement, imposing a dictatorship of one man instead.

See also: Karl Marx 188–93 ▪ Vladimir Lenin 226–33 ▪ Joseph Stalin 240–41 ▪ Mao Zedong 260–65

If the end justifies the means, what justifies the end?

The end is itself a **means to another end**.

Any end is justified if it is itself a means to achieve the increasing power of **man over nature** and the abolition of the power of **man over man**.

Only actions that ultimately advance this end are **"moral"**.

Trotsky had hoped to safeguard the advances he believed had been made in the revolution through a strategy of "permanent revolution", which would be guaranteed by the ongoing support of an international working class. Marx had warned that socialism in one place could not hope to succeed in isolation from the global proletariat, stating that revolution must continue "until all the more or less propertied classes have been driven from their ruling positions… not only in one country but in all the leading countries of the world". Lenin had insisted that the socialist revolution in Russia could triumph only if supported by workers' movements in one or several other economically advanced countries. Trotsky's followers have since argued that this failure to achieve a critical mass of support internationally was the reason that the Soviet Union fell into Stalin's hands.

Communism under Stalin

Within four years of Lenin's death, the inner party democracy and the soviet democratic system – the cornerstone of Bolshevism – had been dismantled within communist parties across the world. Within the Soviet Union itself, Stalin's doctrine of "Socialism in One Country" removed the wider aspiration for an international workers' revolution.

Dissidents were vilified as Trotskyists and expelled from party ranks. When his Left Opposition faction against Stalin failed, Trotsky was expelled from the Communist Party and exiled from the Soviet Union. By 1937, Stalin had jailed or killed all of the so-called Trotskyists of the Left Opposition, and Trotsky himself was in Mexico, hiding from assassins.

Against morality

Many on the left reacted to Stalin's excesses by moving to the right and rejecting revolutionary Marxism, taking up what Trotsky described as "moralistic" positions that emphasized universal values. The suggestion was that Bolshevism – the centralist system of Lenin and Trotsky – had allowed the crimes of Stalin.

In *Their Morals and Ours*, Trotsky describes this claim as a reactionary spasm of class conflict disguised as morality. One of the main criticisms levelled at Bolshevism was that Lenin's »

Stalin, Lenin, and Trotsky were all leading figures in the Bolshevik Revolution. After Lenin died, Stalin took power and Trotsky was a marked man.

The Allies' fire-bombing of Dresden, Germany, in World War II illustrated Trotsky's contention that liberal capitalist governments will break their own rules of morality during wartime.

belief that "the end justifies the means" had led directly to the "amorality" of treachery, brutality, and mass murder. To these critics, morality protected against such atrocities. Trotsky considered that, whether intended or not, this was simply a defence of capitalism, as he believed that capitalism could not exist "through force alone. It needs the cement of morality."

> We must rid ourselves once and for all of the Quaker-Papist babble about the sanctity of human life.
> **Leon Trotsky**

For Trotsky, there is no such thing as morality if it is conceived as a set of eternal values that are not derived from sensory or material evidence. Hence, any behaviour that is not motivated by the existing social conditions or class conflict is illegitimate and inauthentic. Abstract moral concepts that are not based on empirical evidence are simply tools used by ruling-class institutions to suppress the class struggle. The ruling class imposes "moral" obligations on society that its members do not observe themselves and which serve to perpetuate their power.

Trotsky gives the morality of war as an example: "The most 'humane' governments, which in peaceful times 'detest' war, proclaim during war that the highest duty of their armies is the extermination of the greatest possible number of people." The insistence on the prescribed behavioural norms of religion and philosophy was also a tool of class deception. For Trotsky, to expose this deceit was the revolutionary's first duty.

The new aristocracy

Trotsky was keen to show that the centralizing tendencies of Bolshevism were not the "means" whose "end" was Stalinism. Such centralization was necessary to defeat the Bolsheviks' enemies, but its end was always intended to be a decentralized dictatorship of the proletariat, ruling through the system of soviets. For Trotsky, Stalinism was an "immense bureaucratic reaction" against what he saw as the advances of the 1917 revolution. Stalinism reinstated the worst of absolutist entitlements, "regenerating the fetishism of power" beyond the dreams even of the tsars; it had created a "new aristocracy". Trotsky saw the crimes of Stalin as the consequence of the most brutal class struggle of all – that of "the new aristocracy against the masses that raised it to power". He was scathing of self-declared Marxists who linked Bolshevism with Stalinism by stressing the immorality of both. In Trotsky's eyes, he and his followers had opposed Stalin from the beginning, while his critics had only arrived at their position after Stalin's atrocities had come to light.

> Root out the counter-revolutionaries without mercy, lock up suspicious characters in concentration camps. Shirkers will be shot, regardless of past service.
> **Leon Trotsky**

Critics of Marxism often claim that the idea that "the end justifies the means" is used to justify acts of murder and barbarism, as well as the deception of the masses, purportedly for their own benefit. Trotsky insisted that this was a misunderstanding, stating that "the end justifies the means" simply signifies that there is an acceptable way to do a right thing. For example, if it is permissible to eat fish then it is right to kill and cook them. The moral justification of any action must be linked to its "end" in this way. Killing a mad dog that is threatening a child is a virtue, but killing a dog gratuitously, or perversely for no "end", is a crime.

The ultimate end

So what is the answer to the question "what may we, and what may we not do"? What end justifies the means needed to achieve it? For Trotsky, the end is justified if it "leads to the increasing power of man over nature and to the abolition of the power of man over man". In other words, the end can itself be seen as a means to this ultimate end. But did Trotsky mean that the liberation of the working classes was an end for which any destructiveness was permissible? He will only consider this question in relation to the class struggle, thinking it a meaningless abstraction to do otherwise. Thus, the only meaningful good is that which unites the revolutionary proletariat, strengthening it as a class for the ongoing struggle.

Trotsky's reasoning has been seen by some notable Marxists as dangerous, counter-revolutionary, and false. Harry Haywood, an African-American Marxist-Leninist who was in the Soviet Union during the 1920s and 30s, believed that "Trotsky was doomed to defeat because his ideas were incorrect and failed to conform to objective conditions, as well as the needs and interests of the Soviet people." During the Russian Civil War of 1917–22, Trotsky had centralized command structures in what was known as "War Communism". This centralizing tendency has been criticized by disillusioned former followers as closed to critical reflection, convinced of the absolute rightness of its own analysis, and brooking no dissent. In addition, such structures necessarily restrict power to a small group of leaders, as they are too demanding of workers' time and effort for a wide-based system of mass participation to develop. Writing in the 1940s, US Marxist Paul Mattick asserted that the Russian Revolution had itself been as totalitarian as Stalinism, and that the legacy of Bolshevism, Leninism, and Trotskyism served "as a mere ideology to justify the rise of modified capitalist (state-capitalist) systems… controlled by way of an authoritarian state." ■

Slaughter on a grand scale was perpetrated by Trotsky's Red Army in the Russian Civil War, leading critics to compare Bolshevism to Stalin's purges.

Leon Trotsky

Lev Davidovich Bronshtein was born in 1879 in the small village of Yanovka in what is now Ukraine. Schooled in cosmopolitan Odessa, he was involved in revolutionary activities and took up Marxism after initially opposing it. He was arrested, imprisoned, and exiled to Siberia by the time he was just 18.

In Siberia, he took his prison guard's name, Trotsky, and escaped to London where he met and worked with Lenin on the revolutionary journal *Iskra*. In 1905, he returned to Russia to support the revolution. Arrested and sent back to Siberia, his bravery earned him popularity. He escaped from Siberia again, joining Lenin in the successful revolution of 1917. He led the Red Army during the Russian Civil War and held other key posts, but after Lenin's death, he was forced out of power by Stalin and into exile. He was assassinated on Stalin's orders by Ramón Mercader in Mexico City in 1940.

Key works

1937 *The Stalin School of Falsification*
1938 *Their Morals and Ours*

WE WILL UNITE MEXICANS BY GIVING GUARANTEES TO THE PEASANT AND THE BUSINESSMAN

EMILIANO ZAPATA (1879–1919)

IN CONTEXT

IDEOLOGY
Anarchy

FOCUS
Land reform

BEFORE
1876 Porfirio Díaz takes power in Mexico, reinforcing inequalities in social status and land ownership.

1878 In Russia, a revolutionary party adopts the name "Land and Liberty" – the same slogan will be used by the Zapatistas in the 1990s.

AFTER
1920 A degree of land reform is granted in the south of Mexico as the revolution comes to an end.

1994 The Zapatista Army of National Liberation begins an armed uprising in the southern state of Chiapas, in protest against the Mexican government's mistreatment of indigenous people.

The struggle for land and social rights lay at the core of the Mexican Revolution between 1910 and 1920. A peasant by birth, Emiliano Zapata was a key figure in the revolutionary movement, leading forces in the south. He aimed to resolve the conflict through a mixture of rights, guarantees, and armed struggle.

Zapata's ideas chimed with much of the Mexican anarchist tradition and its core principle of communal land ownership, which was based on indigenous traditions. To ensure Mexico's political and economic development, Zapata wanted to break the monopoly of the *hacendados*, or plantation owners, and unite the country – peasants and businessmen alike – behind an agenda of government reform. Harnessing the nation's resources of labour and production would also secure its independence on the international stage.

Zapata's vision was crystallized in his 1911 Plan of Ayala. This blueprint for reform demanded free elections, an end to the dominance of the *hacendados*, and the transfer of property rights to towns and individual citizens.

The troops who fought for Zapata in the Mexican Revolution were mostly indigenous peasants, and included all-female divisions.

Like most of the leaders in the revolution, Zapata was killed before the end of the conflict. Although land reform was enacted in the 1920s, huge inequalities persisted. Yet Zapata's ideas left an enduring legacy in Mexico, and inspired the recent Zapatista movement among indigenous peasants in Chiapas, which has created a quasi-autonomous state in the south. ■

See also: Pierre-Joseph Proudhon 183 ▪ Peter Kropotkin 206 ▪ Antonio Gramsci 259 ▪ José Carlos Mariátegui 338

WAR IS A RACKET

SMEDLEY D. BUTLER (1881–1940)

IN CONTEXT

IDEOLOGY
Non-interventionism

FOCUS
War profiteering

BEFORE
1898–1934 The "Banana Wars" in Central America and the Caribbean aim to protect US business interests, notably for the United Fruit Company.

1904 The US government funds the new Panama Canal and declares sovereignty over the Panama Canal Zone.

AFTER
1934 US president Franklin D. Roosevelt institutes the Good Neighbor Policy, limiting US intervention in Latin America.

1981 Contra rebels backed by the US oppose the Sandinista government in Nicaragua.

2003 The US-led invasion of Iraq leads to the granting of concessions to US businesses.

Industrialization in the Western world has radically altered the nature of both trade and warfare. The relationship between economic interests and foreign affairs has raised questions about the motives and benefits of armed conflict, leading many people, including Smedley D. Butler, to highlight the role of the military in driving foreign policy.

Butler was a highly decorated US Marine Corps general who served for 34 years in numerous overseas campaigns, particularly in Central America. Drawing on his own experiences, especially during the "Banana Wars", Butler felt that much of his military career had served to secure US business interests overseas, with him acting as "a racketeer, a gangster for capitalism".

> War is conducted for the benefit of the very few, at the expense of the very many.
> **Smedley D. Butler**

Redefining a just war

Concerned that the main benefits of military action were the profits made by industrialists through securing foreign sites for trade and investment, Smedley suggested limiting the justification for war to self-defence and the protection of civil rights.

On retiring from the Marines, Butler voiced his concerns in a series of talks, and in *War is a Racket*, published in 1935, he set out his agenda for limiting the profitability of war and restricting governments' capacity to engage in offensive action overseas.

Although Butler's impact at the time was limited, his views on war profiteering and US foreign policy have remained influential. ■

See also: José Martí 204–05 ▪ Hannah Arendt 282–83 ▪ Noam Chomsky 314–15

SOVEREIGNTY IS NOT GIVEN, IT IS TAKEN

MUSTAFA KEMAL ATATÜRK (1881–1938)

IN CONTEXT

IDEOLOGY
Nationalism

FOCUS
Representative democracy

BEFORE
1453 Mehmed II attacks Constantinople, and the city becomes the capital of the growing Ottoman empire.

1908 The Young Turk Revolution re-establishes the parliament, which the sultan had suspended in 1878.

1918 The Ottoman empire is defeated in World War I.

AFTER
1952 Turkey joins NATO and aligns itself with the West in the Cold War.

1987 Turkey applies for full membership of the European Economic Community.

2011 Turkey's top military command resigns, ceding political control to the prime minister for the first time.

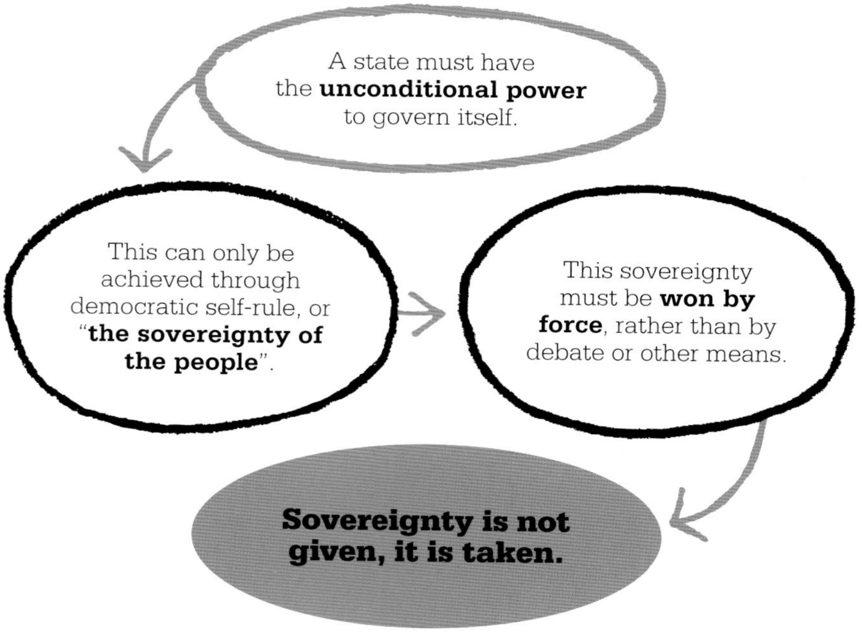

Following the Ottoman empire's defeat in World War I, the 1920 Treaty of Sèvres dispossessed it of its Arab provinces, set up an independent Armenia, made the Kurds self governing, and put Greece in control of western parts of Turkey. A rebel Turkish army, under the command of Mustafa Kemal Atatürk, rose up to challenge the caliphate army of the Ottoman sultan and the occupying forces that were supporting it. The war for Turkish independence had begun.

With the help of Russian Bolshevik weapons and money, Atatürk defeated the foreign occupiers and the sultan fled to Malta on a British battleship. Just three years after the Treaty of Sèvres, the Treaty of Lausanne

See also: Jean-Jacques Rousseau 118–25 ▪ Ito Hirobumi 195 ▪ Sun Yat-Sen 212–13

recognized an independent Turkish state, and Atatürk was elected its first president.

Sovereign will of the people

Atatürk was determined to establish a modern nation-state amid the ruins of the feudal Ottoman empire, which had undergone little industrial development. He believed that a balanced and equitable society, which could deliver the essential guarantees of freedom and justice for individuals, could only be built upon a state's unconditional power to govern itself, or "the sovereignty of the people". This, he insisted, could not be granted or negotiated, but had to be wrested by force.

Sovereignty meant, first of all, democratic self-rule, free from any other authority (including the sultan-caliph), from religious interference in government, and from outside powers. Atatürk's "Kemalist" nationalism saw the Turkish state as a sovereign unity of territory and people that respected the same right to independence in all other nations. Although an alliance with those outside powers, or "civilization", would act as an ongoing support for the new nation, the nation would still have to bring itself into being, politically, culturally, and economically, through revolutionary self-imposed reforms.

This concept of the sovereign power of a people to reform their own state was alien to the bulk of the population. Many in poor rural areas saw Atatürk's programme of modernization as the imposition of the will of a secular urban elite on an illiterate and deeply religious rural culture. Atatürk's ability to harness the support of the armed forces enabled him to shape the new Turkish republic as a secular, Western-looking nation-state, but tensions between rural Islamists and the secularist military and urban elites persist to this day. ■

In accordance with Atatürk's strict secularist ideals, the Muslim hijab, or headscarf, is banned in many Turkish institutions such as universities. This policy is a source of ongoing dispute.

> There is only one power.
> That is national sovereignty.
> There is only one authority.
> That is the presence,
> conscience, and heart
> of the nation.
> **Mustafa Kemal Atatürk**

Mustafa Kemal Atatürk

Mustafa Kemal was born in Salonica, Greece in 1881. He was a distinguished student at military school, excelling in mathematics and literature, and completed his studies in the School of the General Staff in Constantinople. He quickly rose through the ranks and took command of the Seventh Army during World War I, but resigned from the Ottoman army in 1919 to head a resistance movement against the occupying forces.

From an early age, Kemal had taken part in underground opposition groups, and he led Turkey to independence in 1923, becoming the first president of the new, secular state. He was given the name "Atatürk", meaning "Father of the Turks" in 1934 by the Turkish parliament. He died in 1938 of cirrhosis of the liver, after many years of heavy drinking.

Key works

1918 *A Chat with the Chief Commander*
1927 *Nutuk* (transcript of a speech to the Grand National Assembly of Turkey)

EUROPE HAS BEEN LEFT WITHOUT A MORAL CODE

JOSÉ ORTEGA Y GASSET (1883–1955)

IN CONTEXT

IDEOLOGY
Liberalism

FOCUS
Pro-intellectualism

BEFORE
380 BCE Plato advocates rule by philosopher kings.

1917 In Spain, news of the Russian Revolution instills fear in Primo de Rivera's regime, which consolidates its power by control of the masses.

AFTER
1936–1939 The Spanish Civil War results in the deaths of more than 200,000 people.

1979 French philosopher Pierre Bourdieu examines the ways that power and social positioning have an influence on aesthetics.

2002 US historian John Lukacs publishes *At the End of an Age*, arguing that the modern bourgeois age is coming to an end.

Philosopher José Ortega y Gasset first rose to prominence during the 1920s, a period of great social unrest in Spain. The monarchy was losing its authority following unrest in Spanish Morocco, and the dictatorial regime of Miguel Primo de Rivera had deepened divisions between left- and right-wing forces. These divisions would eventually lead to civil war in 1936.

World War I had been a period of economic boom in neutral Spain, which supplied both sides during the conflict. As a result, the country had rapidly industrialized, and the swelling masses of the workers were becoming increasingly powerful. Concessions were won, and a strike in Barcelona in 1919 led to Spain becoming the first country to institute an eight-hour day for all workers.

Rise of the masses

As worker power increased, the question of social class was at the centre of philosophical and sociological debate in Europe, but Ortega y Gasset challenged the idea that social classes are purely a result of an economic divide. Rather, he distinguished between "mass-man" and "noble-man" on the basis of their allegiance to moral codes based on tradition. In his book *The Rise of the Masses*, he explained that "to live as one likes is plebeian; the noble man aspires to order and law". Discipline and service bring nobility, he believed. He saw the accession to power of the masses and their increased tendency towards rebellion – through strikes and other forms of social unrest – as highly problematic, calling it one of "the greatest crises that can afflict people, nations, and civilizations".

To Ortega y Gasset, the threat posed by the masses was linked to a wider demoralization in post-war

> The European stands alone, without any living ghosts by his side.
> **José Ortega y Gasset**

See also: Plato 34–39 ▪ Immanuel Kant 126–29 ▪ Friedrich Nietzsche 196–99 ▪ Michael Oakeshott 276–77

The rise to power in Europe of the **industrial masses**...

...has led to the decline of the **true intellectual** and the rise of the **pseudo-intellectual**.

The pseudo-intellectual has no sense of **tradition, purpose, or morality**.

Europe has been left without a moral code.

Europe, which had lost its sense of purpose in the world. The decline of imperial power, coupled with the devastation of the war, had left Europe no longer believing in itself, despite remaining a strong industrial force.

Pseudo-intellectuals

Ortega y Gasset argued that the rise of the masses is accompanied by the decline of the intellectual. This signals the triumph of the pseudo-intellectual – a vulgar man with no interest in traditions or moral codes, who sees himself as superior. The pseudo-intellectual represents a new force of history: one without a sense of direction.

For Ortega y Gasset, the masses lack purpose and imagination and limit themselves to demands for a share in the fruits of progress without understanding the classical scientific traditions that made progress possible in the first place. The masses are not interested in the principles of civilization or in the establishment of a real sense of public opinion. As such, he views the masses as highly prone to violence. In his eyes, a Europe without real intellectuals, dominated by disinterested masses, is somewhere that risks losing its place and purpose in the world.

Ortega y Gasset's philosophy remains influential today. His followers stress the links between economic class and culture. ■

Following World War I, workers – such as these striking metal workers in France – won significant concessions and began to wield political power.

José Ortega y Gasset

Ortega y Gasset was born in Madrid to a political family with a deep liberal tradition. His mother's family owned the newspaper *El Imparcial*, while his father edited it. He studied philosophy in Spain and continued his education in Germany at Leipzig, Nuremberg, Cologne, Berlin, and Marburg, where he became deeply influenced by the neo-Kantian tradition.

In 1910, Ortega y Gasset became full professor of metaphysics in Madrid. He later founded the magazine *Revista de Occidente*, which published work by some of the most important figures in philosophy at the time. Elected to Congress in 1931 after the fall of the monarchy and de Rivera's dictatorship, he removed himself from politics having served for less than a year. He left Spain at the outbreak of the Civil War and travelled to Buenos Aires, Argentina, only to return to Europe in 1942.

Key works

1930 *The Revolt of the Masses*
1937 *Invertebrate Spain*
1969 *Some Lessons in Metaphysics*

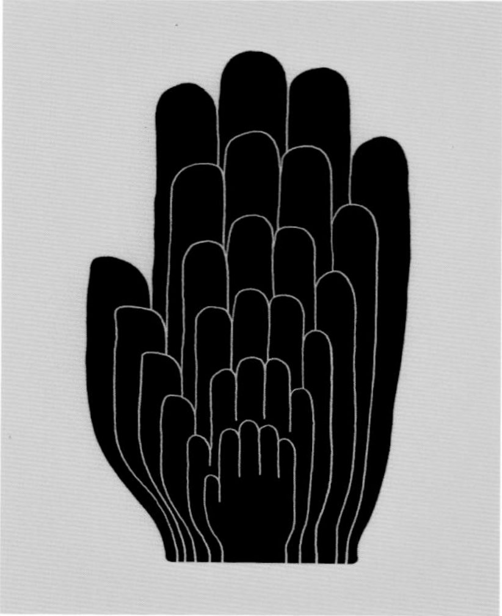

WE ARE 400 MILLION PEOPLE ASKING FOR LIBERTY

MARCUS GARVEY (1887–1940)

IN CONTEXT

IDEOLOGY
Black nationalism

FOCUS
Social activism

BEFORE
16th century The *Maafa*, or African Holocaust, of transatlantic slavery begins.

1865 The 13th Amendment makes slavery illegal throughout the US.

1917 The city of East St Louis explodes in one of the worst race riots in US history.

AFTER
1960s The "Black is Beautiful" movement gathers pace.

1963 Martin Luther King delivers his "I have a dream" speech at a vast civil rights march in Washington, DC.

1965 US Congress passes the Voting Rights Act, outlawing discrimination that prevented African-Americans from exercising their vote.

In the early 20th century, Jamaican activist Marcus Garvey gave black people in the Americas a rousing response to white supremacy. He founded the Universal Negro Improvement Association in 1914, and called for the "400 million" Africans around the world to unite in a commitment to liberate the African continent – and their own lives – from racial oppression. Two years later, he took his campaign to the United States, where he organized businesses to employ African-Americans.

Confident that black people could advance through any cultural, political, or intellectual field they chose, Garvey put race first, individual self-determination next, and black nationhood last. He envisaged a United States of Africa that would preserve the interests of all black people, galvanized by an almost religious sense of racial redemption. The "New Negro" consciousness would borrow from existing intellectual traditions, yet forge its own racial interpretation of international politics. Coining the term "African fundamentalism", Garvey promoted a sense of black selfhood, rooted in the belief that ancient African civilizations that had declined would be regenerated.

> I am the equal of any white man; I want you to feel the same way.
> **Marcus Garvey**

Garvey's radical message – and the mismanagement of his many blacks-only businesses – attracted the ire of rival black leaders and the US government. Yet he was the first to insist on black power, and the first to articulate the African liberation proposition that animates African nationalists to this day. ■

See also: John C. Calhoun 161 ▪ Jomo Kenyatta 258 ▪ Nelson Mandela 294–95 ▪ Malcolm X 308–09 ▪ Martin Luther King 316–21

INDIA CANNOT REALLY BE FREE UNLESS SEPARATED FROM THE BRITISH EMPIRE

MANABENDRA NATH ROY (1887–1954)

IN CONTEXT

IDEOLOGY
Revolutionary socialism

FOCUS
Permanent revolution

BEFORE

1617 The Mughal emperor permits the English East India Company to trade in India.

1776 America's Declaration of Independence asserts people's right to govern themselves.

1858 The Indian Rebellion results in the British Crown assuming direct rule of the Raj.

1921 Mahatma Gandhi is elected leader of the Indian National Congress and urges non-violent civil disobedience.

AFTER

1947 The Indian Independence Act brings the British Raj to an end.

1961 Frantz Fanon's *Wretched of the Earth* analyses the violence of colonialism and the need for armed resistance.

In 1931, after returning to India from a tour of the world's communist governments, Indian activist and political theorist M.N. Roy was charged by the British with "conspiring to deprive the King Emperor of his sovereignty in India", under the notorious Section 121-A of the Penal Code. Tried in prison instead of a court – and allowed no defence statement, witnesses, or jury – Roy was sentenced to 12 years in squalid jails that would ruin his health.

Ironically, in Roy's writings on British sovereignty in India, he had always grounded his arguments on English principles of justice. Accused by the authorities of advocating violence, he held that the use of force was honourable when employed to defend the "pauperized" masses of India against despotism, and was dishonourable when employed to oppress those masses. Over three centuries, the British had acquired "this valuable possession" through the "quiet" transfer of power from the declining Mughal empire to the East India Company – whose administration was backed by a large army – and, ultimately, to the British Crown.

Arguing that the British government in India had not been established for the purpose of advancing the wellbeing of its people, but solely for the benefit of a "plutocratic dictatorship", Roy held that the interests of the Indian people could only be served by an absolute severance from the British, by force if necessary. ■

> Once we have consciously set our feet on the right road, nothing can daunt us.
> **M. N. Roy**

See also: Mahatma Gandhi 220–25 ▪ Paulo Freire 297 ▪ Frantz Fanon 304–07

SOVEREIGN IS HE WHO DECIDES ON THE EXCEPTION

CARL SCHMITT (1888–1985)

IN CONTEXT

IDEOLOGY
Conservatism

FOCUS
Extrajudicial power

BEFORE
1532 In *The Prince*, Niccolò Machiavelli lays out the principles of sovereignty.

1651 Thomas Hobbes's *Leviathan* uses the concept of the social contract to justify the power of the sovereign.

1934 Adolf Hitler comes to power in Germany.

AFTER
2001 John Mearsheimer uses Schmitt's theories to justify "offensive realism", where states are ever-prepared for war.

2001 The Patriot Act in the US establishes a permanent installment of martial law and emergency powers.

Carl Schmitt was a German political theorist and lawyer whose work during the early 20th century established him as a leading critic of liberalism and parliamentary democracy. Schmitt saw the "exception" (*Ernstfall*) – unexpected events – as a quintessential characteristic of political life. For this reason, he disagreed with the liberal idea that the law is the best guarantor of individual liberty. While the law is able to provide a framework through which to manage "normal" states of affair, Schmitt argued that it was not designed to deal with "exceptional" circumstances such as *coups d'etat*, revolutions, or war.

See also: Niccolò Machiavelli 74–81 ▪ Thomas Hobbes 96–103 ▪ Giovanni Gentile 238–39 ▪ José Ortega Y Gasset 250–51 ▪ Adolf Hitler 337

The **political life** of a country always includes exceptional circumstances.

The **judgements** of law courts depend on historical precedents, so can only be applied in **"normal" situations**.

When an **exceptional situation** occurs…

…**one person** must be able to operate above the law, suspending it and taking all steps necessary to **save the state**.

The only person capable of this is the sovereign. Sovereign is he who decides on the exception.

He saw legal theory as too far removed from legal practice and changing social norms. It was unfit to deal with the unexpected turns of history, many of which could threaten the very existence of the state. A president, he argued, is better able to guard a country's constitution than a court, and so should necessarily be above the law. The ruler should be the ultimate law-maker in exceptional situations.

A constant struggle

Schmitt's criticism of liberalism was directly tied to his unique understanding of "the political" as the constant possibility of struggle between both friends and enemies. He anticipated this struggle at both the international level – with feuding nations – and the domestic level – with feuding individuals. Schmitt disagreed with Thomas Hobbes's vision of nature as being a state of "all against all", and its implication that co-existence is impossible without the rule of law. On the other hand, he argued that liberals had done humanity, and the nation-state in particular, a disservice by promoting the possibility of a perpetually peaceful world. He saw World War I as a consequence of liberalism's failure to recognize the possibility of enmity, and blamed liberals for »

Carl Schmitt

Born into a devout Catholic family in Plettenberg, Germany, Carl Schmitt later renounced his faith, although elements of his understanding of the divine remained in his work. He studied law and later taught at several universities. In 1933, he joined the Nazi party and was appointed State Councillor for Prussia. However, in 1936 he was denounced by the SS and expelled from the Nazi party.

Schmitt continued to work as a professor in Berlin, but at the end of World War II, he was interned for two years for his Nazi connections. In 1946 he returned to Plettenberg, where, shunned by the international community, he continued to study law until his death, aged 95.

Key works

1922 *Political Theology: Four Chapters on the Concept of Sovereignty*
1928 *The Concept of the Political*
1932 *Legality and Legitimacy*

> The exception is more interesting than the rule. The rule proves nothing; the exception proves everything.
> **Carl Schmitt**

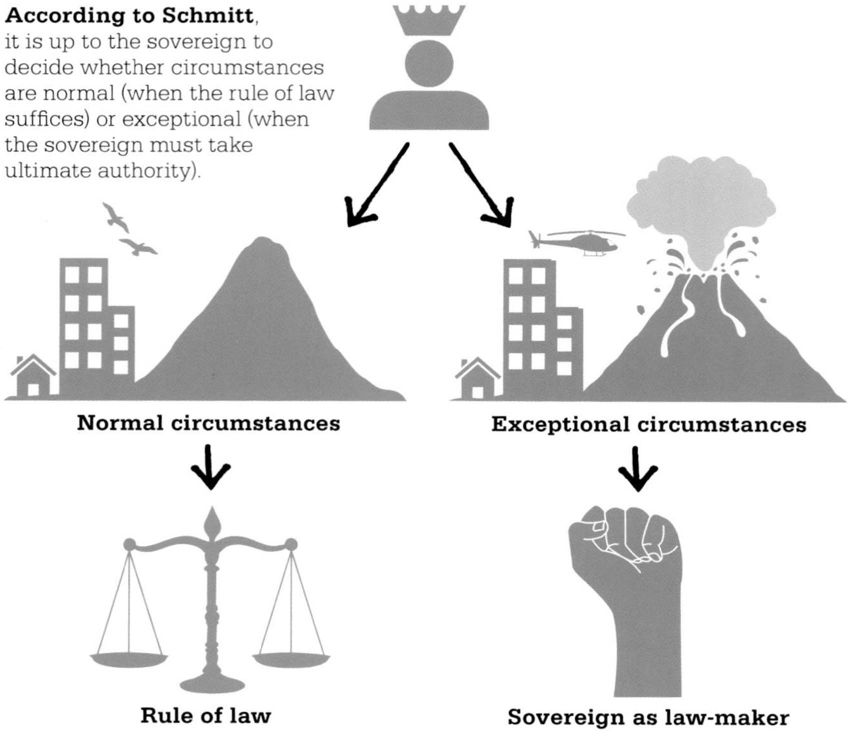

According to Schmitt, it is up to the sovereign to decide whether circumstances are normal (when the rule of law suffices) or exceptional (when the sovereign must take ultimate authority).

both misunderstanding the true nature of politics and being insincere with regards to the true nature of the political. Under an assumption of perpetual peace and friendliness, he said, states are less likely to be prepared for the exceptional, and so risk the lives of their citizens.

Schmitt argued instead that the possibility of enmity always exists alongside the possibility of alliance and neutrality. He envisioned the individual as potentially dangerous; and consequently this provides a constant political danger, with the ever-present possibility of war. Schmitt considered that this constant possibility should be the ultimate guide for the sovereign, who must at all times be prepared for it. The political sphere is necessarily an antagonistic world, not merely an independent domain in which citizens interact, like the realms of civil society or commerce. The law might work adequately through the courts and their associated bureaucracy under normal conditions, but in politics, exceptional conditions – even chaos – can erupt, and the courts are not equipped to make good or rapid judgements under these conditions. Someone must be entitled to suspend the law during exceptional circumstances. Schmitt claimed this was part of the sovereign's role: he or she possesses the ultimate authority to decide when times are "normal" and when they are "exceptional", and as such, can dictate when certain laws are to be applied and when they are not.

By placing life above liberty, Schmitt argued that the legitimacy of the sovereign relies not upon his application of the law, but upon his ability to protect the state and its citizens. Schmitt thought that the true power of a sovereign emerges in exceptional circumstances, when decisions need to be based entirely on new grounds. It is only in these circumstances that the sovereign becomes a true law-maker as opposed to a law-preserver, and is thus able to mobilize the population against a designated enemy. Schmitt concluded that sovereign power, in its full form, requires the exercise of violence, even when not otherwise legitimate under the law.

Defending Hitler

The limits of Schmitt's theory became apparent with his defence of Hitler's policies and rise to power. Schmitt justified "the Night of the Long Knives" – when around 85 of Hitler's political opponents were murdered – as "the highest form of administrative justice". In Schmitt's eyes, Hitler was acting as a true sovereign, taking matters into his own hands under exceptional circumstances that threatened the very existence of the German state. Violence against the left-wing arm of the Nazi party, as well as Jews, was justified in Schmitt's eyes by the supposed threat they posed to the state.

Schmitt's personal support for the Nazi regime strongly suggests that, for him, the survival of the state was more important than the liberty of the individuals within it – and sometimes more important than the lives of the citizens of the state. However, this prioritization of the preservation of the state at all costs fails to take into account the fact that, just like individuals, the state also changes; it is not a monolithic entity whose character is set and forever perfect. It can – and many would say should – be questioned at any point in time.

> The state of exception is not a dictatorship… but a space devoid of law.
> **Giorgio Agamben**

Contemporary exceptions

Schmitt's inability to see the radical effect of his theory, or that genocide is not an acceptable form of violence under any circumstances, led to his being shunned by the academic and intellectual world. However, in the late 20th century, a revival of interest in his work was led by various authors who saw Schmitt's contribution to legal and political philosophy as significant, despite his shortcomings. Schmitt's understanding of the "political", the "friend–enemy distinction", and the "exceptional" was used by these writers to better understand the conditions under which modern states operate and political leaders make decisions.

US philosopher Leo Strauss built on Schmitt's critique of liberalism, arguing that it tended towards extreme relativism and nihilism by completely disregarding the reality "on the ground" – it focuses not on what is, but on what ought to be. Strauss distinguished between two forms of nihilism: a "brutal" nihilism, as expressed by the Nazi and Marxist regimes, which seeks to destroy all previous traditions, history, and moral standards; and a "gentle" nihilism, as expressed in Western liberal democracies, which establishes a value-free and aimless egalitarianism. For Strauss, both are equally dangerous in that they destroy the possibility for human excellence.

Italian political philosopher Giorgio Agamben argues that Schmitt's state of exception is not a state where the law is suspended – hiding somewhere until it can be re-established – but rather a state completely devoid of law, in which the sovereign holds ultimate authority over the lives of citizens. Considering the Nazi concentration camps created during World War II, Agamben argues that the prisoners in these camps lost all human qualities and became "bare life" – they were alive, but stripped of all human and legal rights. He sees the creation of a state of exception as particularly dangerous, because its effects compound in unpredictable ways: the "temporary" suspension of the law is never really "temporary", because it leads to consequences that cannot be undone upon the restoration of the law.

Schmitt's concept of the exception became particularly pertinent after 9/11, when it was used by conservatives and left-wing political thinkers to justify or denounce anti-terrorist measures such as the Patriot Act in the United States. The conservatives used the idea of exceptionality to justify violations of personal liberties such as increased surveillance and longer detention times without trial. Left-wing scholars argued against these very same practices, pointing out the dangers of suspending protections against human rights violations.

The existence of camps such as those at Guantánamo Bay serves to demonstrate the dangers of labelling an event "exceptional" and apportioning it exceptional measures, in particular the re-writing of rules by the executive without any checks in place. More than 10 years later, the state of exception declared after 9/11 remains more or less in place, with worrying consequences that show no signs of abating. ■

Leading Nazis were put on trial at Nuremberg at the end of World War II. Schmitt was investigated for his role as a propagandist for the regime, but eventually escaped trial.

COMMUNISM IS AS BAD AS IMPERIALISM

JOMO KENYATTA (1894–1978)

IN CONTEXT

IDEOLOGY
Post-colonialism

FOCUS
Conservative pan-Africanism

BEFORE

1895 The protectorate of British East Africa emerges from British trading interests in East Africa.

1952–59 Kenya is in a state of emergency during a pro-independence rebellion by the Mau Mau.

1961 In Belgrade in modern-day Serbia, the Non-Aligned Movement is founded for countries wishing to be independent of superpowers.

AFTER

1963 The Organization of African Unity (OAU) is founded to oppose colonialism in Africa.

1968 Britain's last African colonies gain independence.

Jomo Kenyatta was one of the leading figures in Kenya's independence from British colonial rule, becoming its first prime minister and president in the post-colonial era. A political moderate, he pursued a programme of gradual change, rather than dramatic revolution.

External threats

Kenyatta's ideas melded anti-colonialism and anti-communism. He was fiercely opposed to white rule in Africa, and promoted the idea of Kenyan independence through the establishment of the Kenyan African National Union. Pursuing a mixed-market economic programme, Kenya was opened up to foreign investment and developed a foreign policy that was pro-Western and anti-communist.

Post-colonial nations, Kenyatta believed, were in danger of becoming exploited by external forces in order to consolidate the position of other nations on the world stage. To secure genuine independence, it would not be possible to tolerate the external influence that came hand-in-hand with Soviet communism. In this sense, the threats posed by communism could be as restrictive to Kenyan self-determination as colonial rule. ■

Leaders of newly independent East African states – Julius Nyerere of Tanganyika, Milton Obote of Uganda, and Kenyatta – met in Nairobi in 1964 to discuss their post-colonial future.

See also: Manabendra Nath Roy 253 ▪ Nelson Mandela 294–95 ▪ Frantz Fanon 304–07 ▪ Che Guevara 312–13

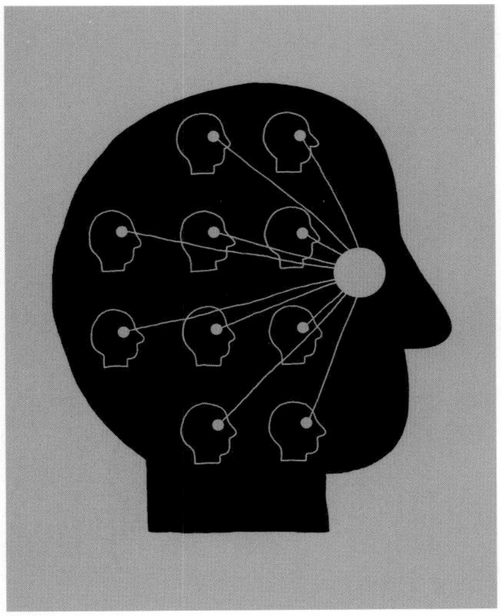

THE STATE MUST BE CONCEIVED OF AS AN "EDUCATOR"

ANTONIO GRAMSCI (1891–1937)

IN CONTEXT

IDEOLOGY
Marxism

FOCUS
Cultural hegemony

BEFORE
1867 Karl Marx completes the first volume of *Capital*, in which he analyses the capitalist system and the ways in which the masses are exploited by the rich.

1929 José Ortega y Gasset laments the demise of the intellectual as the working class grows in power.

AFTER
1980 Michel Foucault describes the ways in which power is distributed across society in institutions such as schools and the family.

1991 The *Lega Nord* (Northern League) is founded on a platform of greater autonomy for the industrialized north of Italy.

Italian Marxist theorist Antonio Gramsci, while exposing the imbalances between the industrialized north and rural south of Italy, identified that the struggle to tackle the dominance of the ruling classes was a cultural battle as much as a revolutionary one.

Gramsci developed the notion of "cultural hegemony", referring to the ideological and cultural control of the working classes that goes beyond coercion to the development of systems of thought – reinforcing the position of the powerful through consent.

The role of intellectuals

For Gramsci, no government, regardless of how powerful it is, can sustain its control by force alone. Legitimacy and popular consent are also required. By viewing the functions of the state as a means of educating and indoctrinating society into subservience, Gramsci radically altered Marxist thought. He saw that in order to tackle the grip of cultural hegemony on society, education was vital. Gramsci had a particular view of the role of intellectuals in this context. He felt that intellectuals could exist at all levels of society, rather than solely as a traditional elite, and that the development of this capacity among the working class was necessary to the success of any attempt to counter the hegemony of the ruling classes. ■

> "A human mass does not 'distinguish' itself, does not become independent… without organizing itself: and there is no organization without intellectuals."
> **Antonio Gramsci**

See also: Karl Marx 188–93 ▪ Vladimir Lenin 226–33 ▪ Rosa Luxemburg 234–35 ▪ Michel Foucault 310–11

POLITICAL POWER GROWS OUT OF THE BARREL OF A GUN

MAO ZEDONG (1893–1976)

IN CONTEXT

IDEOLOGY
Marxism-Leninism

FOCUS
Modernization of China

BEFORE
1912 The Republic of China is established, bringing to an end more than 2,000 years of imperial rule.

1919 The May Fourth Movement politicizes events in China, leading directly to the foundation of the Communist Party of China in 1921.

AFTER
1966–76 Mao's Cultural Revolution, the suppression of supposedly capitalist, traditional, and cultural elements in China, leads to factional strife and huge loss of life.

1977 Deng Xiaoping implements a programme of economic liberalization, leading to rapid growth.

At the beginning of the 20th century, Chinese students and intellectuals, including the young Mao Zedong, began to learn of the socialist ideologies on the rise in Europe, and apply them to China. At the time, Marxism was not as compelling to these young Chinese as Mikhail Bakunin's theory of anarchism and other schools of Utopian socialist thought. Marx had stipulated that a sound capitalist economy was the necessary basis for a socialist revolution, but China was still primarily agrarian and feudal, with no modern industry or urban working class.

Revolutionary inspiration

Before the Russian Revolution in 1917, there was little to encourage disaffected Chinese intellectuals in Marx's conviction that the processes of capitalist production must achieve critical mass before a workers' revolution could succeed. Looking back on the immense changes he had carved out on the Chinese political landscape, Mao would later assert that the Bolshevik uprising struck political thinkers in China like a "thunderbolt". Events in Russia were now a matter of intense interest because of the perceived similarities between the two backward giants. Travelling to Beijing, Mao became the assistant and protégé of the university librarian Li Dazhao, an early Chinese communist who was studying, holding seminars, and writing about the Russian revolutionary movement.

Mao took Marxist and Leninist ideas and adapted them to resolve the problem of a workers' revolution in a land of peasants. Lenin's theory of imperialism envisaged communism spreading through developing countries and gradually surrounding the capitalist West. Mao believed that countries still mired in feudalism would skip the capitalist stage of development and move straight into full socialism. An elite vanguard party with a higher class "consciousness" would instil revolutionary values and a proletarian identity in the peasantry.

Politicization of the people

The excitement generated by the Russian Revolution might have been confined to university

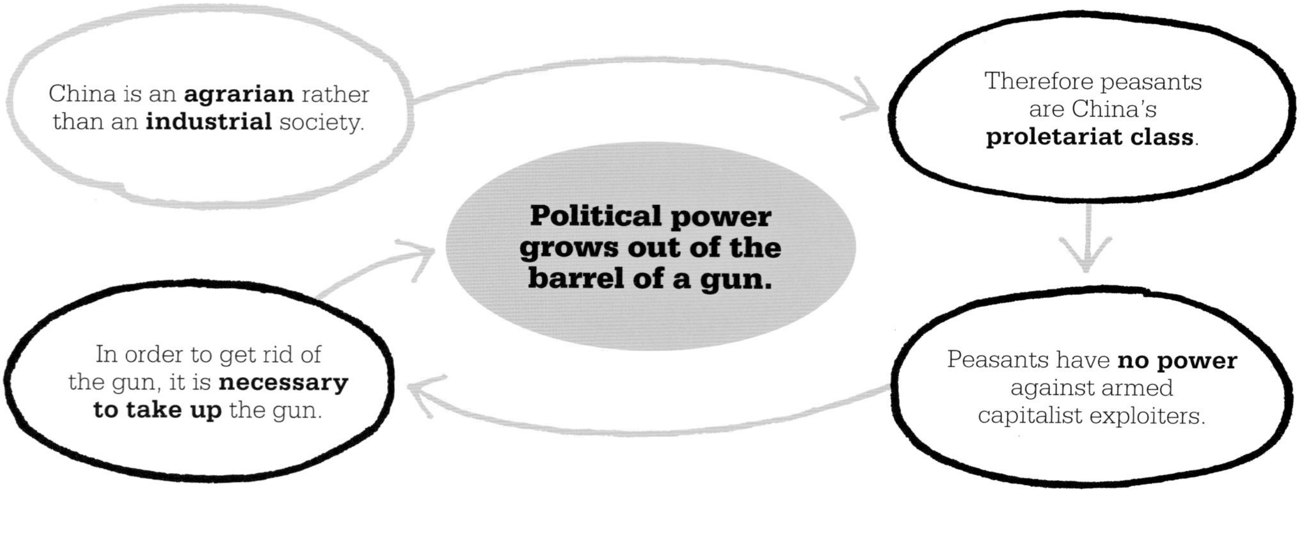

See also: Karl Marx 188–93 ▪ Sun Yat-Sen 212–13 ▪ Vladimir Lenin 226–33 ▪ Joseph Stalin 240–41 ▪ Leon Trotsky 242–45 ▪ Che Guevara 312–13 ▪ Ho Chi Minh 337

Rice farmers and other peasants handed over their land to cooperatives in a collectivization programme that would form a key part of Mao's drive to reform China's rural economy.

discussion groups had it not been for the Western Allies' heedless betrayal of Chinese interests following World War I. More than 140,000 Chinese labourers had been shipped to France to support the war effort of the Triple Entente – Britain, France, and Russia – with the understanding that, among other things, the German protectorate of Shandong on the northeast coast of China would be returned to Chinese hands after the war. Instead, the Allies gave the territory to Japan at the Versailles Peace Conference of 1919.

Students across China protested against their country's "spineless" capitulation. City workers and businessmen in Shanghai joined them, and a coalition of diverse groups united as the May Fourth Movement to force the government to accede to their demands. China's representatives at Versailles refused to sign the peace treaty, but their objections had no effect on the actions of the Allies. The real significance of the May Fourth Movement was that vast numbers of Chinese people began to think about their precarious lives and the vulnerability of their country to threats from the outside world. It was a significant turning point for Chinese political thought, in which Western-style liberal democracy lost much of its appeal, and Marxist-Leninist concepts gained traction.

Mao was one of the radical intellectuals who came to the fore at this time and went on to organize peasants and workers in the Communist Party. He would never forget the lesson of Shandong: to negotiate from a position of weakness was to lose. The ultimate power in politics is the power of armed force. Mao would be ruthless both in seeking armed power and in his willingness to use it.

In 1921, Mao attended the First Congress of the Communist Party of China (CPC) in Shanghai, and in 1923 he was elected to the party's Central Committee. He spent the 1920s organizing labour strikes, studying, and developing his ideas. It became clear to him that in China, it would have to be a rural and not an urban proletariat who would carry out the revolution.

> It is very difficult for the labouring people… to awaken to the importance of having guns in their own hands.
> **Mao Zedong**

Crucible of communism

The CPC shared the ideological outlook of Marxist-Leninism with the Kuonmintang (KMT) – China's nationalist and anti-monarchist party founded by Sun Yat-Sen, with links to Soviet Russia – and both had the overall aim of national unification. However, the Communists' popular movement of peasants and workers was too radical for the KMT, who turned on their CPC allies in 1927, crushing them and suppressing their organizations in the cities. This violent conflict was the crucible from which the doctrine of "Maoism" emerged as a guerrilla-style rural Marxian revolutionary strategy. »

Mao's cult of personality was relentlessly reinforced by mass demonstrations of crowds carrying posters of their leader and copies of his *Little Red Book* of quotations.

> Without an army for the people, there is nothing for the people.
> **Mao Zedong**

In 1934 and 1935, Mao – now the chairman of the Chinese Soviet Republic, a small republic declared in the mountainous region of Jiangxi, southeast China – cemented his position as foremost among Chinese communists during "The Long March". The first of a series of marches, this 9,600-km (6,000-mile) ordeal, lasting over a year, was ostensibly undertaken to repel Japanese invaders, but it also served as a military retreat by the Communists' Red Army to evade the Nationalist forces led by Chiang Kaishek. They crossed 18 mountain ranges and 24 major rivers, and only one-tenth of the original force of 80,000 soldiers and workers who set out from Jiangxi in October 1934 survived the march to reach Shanghai a year later. Mao's supremacy was sealed, and he became leader of the CPC in November 1935. Following Japan's defeat by the Allies in World War II, the resumption of civil war in China, and the eventual surrender of Nationalist forces, the communist People's Republic of China was finally established in 1949, with Mao at the helm.

> Politics is war without bloodshed, while war is politics with bloodshed.
> **Mao Zedong**

The Great Helmsman

In 1938, in his concluding remarks to the Sixth Plenary Session of the Sixth Central Committee of the CPC, Mao expounded on his theory of revolution. He maintained that in a China that was still semi-feudal, the truly revolutionary class was the peasantry, and only military struggle could achieve revolution; demonstrations, protests, and strikes would never be enough. With the peasant-proletariat armed and powerful, Mao – now known as "The Great Helmsman" – did bring about many changes for the good. Among other measures, he banned arranged marriages and promoted the status of women, doubled school attendance, raised literacy, and created universal housing. However, Mao's admiration for Stalin and his infatuation with Marxian language and theories of revolution disguised the many thousands of brutal killings that he and his forces committed on the road to power. There were to be many millions more – some from the violent repression of those deemed opponents of China, and some from neglect. In the space of three decades, Mao forced the country to almost complete self-sufficiency, but at an unspeakable cost in human life, comforts, freedoms, and sanity.

The Five Year Plan launched in 1953 achieved spectacular increases in output, and was followed by the "Great Leap Forward" in 1958. By forcing the

Chinese economy to attempt to catch up with the West through mass-labour projects in agriculture, industry, and infrastructure, Mao brought about one of the worst catastrophes the world has ever known. Between 1958 and 1962, at least 45 million Chinese people – mostly peasants – were tortured, overworked, starved, or beaten to death, a fatality rate only slightly smaller than the entire death toll of World War II.

The atrocities of this period were carefully catalogued in the now-reopened Communist Party archives. These records show that the "truly revolutionary class" – Mao's chosen people in the great struggle for social justice – were in fact treated as faceless, expendable objects by Mao and the Party.

Tractors made in China not only increased output but symbolized Mao's policy of "maintaining independence and relying on our own efforts".

In contrast to Marx's conviction that socialism would be an inevitable development from the material and cultural achievements of capitalism, Mao correlated the poverty he saw in China with a moral purity that he believed would lead to a socialist Utopia. In 1966, the Cultural Revolution was introduced with the aim of cleansing China of "bourgeois" influences. Millions were "re-educated" through forced labour, and thousands executed.

Mao in modern China

The politics that for Mao grew "out of the barrel of a gun" turned out to be the totalitarian politics of terror, brutality, fantasy, and deceit. On his death, the CPC declared that his ideas would remain "a guide to action for a long time to come". However, as society evolves and awareness grows of his horrific crimes, Mao's influence on Chinese thought may finally be cast off. ■

Mao Zedong

The son of a prosperous peasant, Mao Zedong was born in Shaoshan, in Hunan province, central China, in 1893. Mao described his father as a stern disciplinarian who beat his children on any pretext, while his devout Buddhist mother would try to pacify him.

After training as a teacher, Mao travelled to Beijing where he worked in the university library. He studied Marxism and went on to become a founder member of the Chinese Communist Party in 1921. After years of civil and national wars, the Communists were victorious and, under Mao's leadership, founded the People's Republic of China in 1949.

Mao set out to ruthlessly modernize China with his "Great Leap Forward" mass labour programme, and later the Cultural Revolution. Both initiatives failed, resulting in millions of deaths. Mao died on 9 September 1976.

Key works

1937 *On Guerrilla Warfare*
1964 *Little Red Book* or *Quotations from Chairman Mao Zedong*

POST–W
POLITIC
1945–PRESENT

AR
S

1945
Germany surrenders, followed by Japan, bringing World War II to a close. **Europe is partitioned** between East and West.

1945
A Labour government is elected in the UK, ushering in a swathe of reforms that will shape the **modern welfare state**.

1949
Simone de Beauvoir publishes *The Second Sex*, which becomes an important **feminist resource**.

1950–1953
The **Korean War** is fought between Western powers and the communist North Korean and Chinese forces.

1962
The **Cuban missile crisis** brings relations between the USSR and the US to breaking point.

1963
Kenya **declares independence**, following many other former European colonies.

1963
US president John F. Kennedy is **assassinated**.

1963
Martin Luther King leads the **March on Washington for Jobs and Freedom**.

Huge industrial and social changes took place in the years that followed the end of World War II. The scale and industrialization of warfare, the decline of the great colonial powers, and the ideological battles between communism and free-market capitalism all had a profound effect on political thought. A world recovering from human tragedy on such a scale urgently needed to be reinterpreted, and new prescriptions for human development and organization were required.

Across western Europe, a new political consensus emerged, and mixed economies of private and public businesses were developed. At the same time, new demands for civil and human rights emerged across the world in the immediate post-war period, and independence movements gathered support in Europe's colonies.

War and the state

There were many questions for political thinkers that plainly stemmed from the experience of global conflict. World War II had seen an unprecedented expansion of military capacity, with a dramatic impact on the industrial base of the major powers. This new environment provided the platform for a collision of ideas between East and West, and the Korean and Vietnam wars, alongside countless smaller dramas, were in many ways proxies for conflict between the Soviet Union and the United States.

The nuclear bombs that had brought World War II to an end also signalled an era of technological developments in warfare that threatened humanity on a terrifying scale. These developments led many writers to reconsider the ethics of warfare. Theorists such as Michael Walzer explored the moral ramifications of battle, developing the ideas put forward by Thomas Aquinas and Augustine of Hippo.

Other writers, such as Noam Chomsky and Smedley D. Butler, explored the configurations of power at play behind the new military-industrial complex. In recent years, the emergence of global terrorism, and the subsequent conflicts in Iraq and Afghanistan, have thrown these debates into sharp relief.

The period immediately after the war also raised serious questions about the appropriate role of the state. In the post-war

1968
Martin Luther King is assassinated. The **Civil Rights Act** is passed in the USA.

1973
The last US ground forces **withdraw from Vietnam**, amid public discontent and protest.

1979
The Iranian Revolution brings in a series of **fundamentalist laws** instituting authoritarian rule in Iran.

1989
The **Berlin Wall falls**, as part of a series of revolutions across Eastern Europe, marking the collapse of Soviet communism.

1990
Nelson Mandela is **released from prison**, precipitating the fall of apartheid in South Africa.

2001
The 9/11 attacks on the World Trade Center and the Pentagon building in the US precipitate the "**Global War on Terror**".

2003
A US-led coalition **invades Iraq**.

2005
Robert Pape publishes his analysis of **suicide terrorism**, *Dying to Win*, which concludes that it is a "demand-driven phenomenon".

period, European democracies established the foundations of the welfare state, and across Eastern Europe communism took hold. In response, political thinkers began to consider the implications of these developments, particularly in relation to individual liberty. New understandings of freedom and justice were developed by writers such as Friedrich Hayek, John Rawls, and Robert Nozick, and the position of individuals in relation to the state began to be reconsidered.

Feminism and civil rights

From the 1960s onwards, a new, overtly political strand of feminism emerged, inspired by writers such as Simone de Beauvoir, who questioned the position of women in politics and society. Around the same time, the battle for civil rights gathered pace – with the decline of colonialism in Africa and the popular movement against racial discrimination in the United States – driven by thinkers such as Frantz Fanon and inspirational activists including Nelson Mandela and Martin Luther King. Once more, questions of power, and particularly civil and political rights, formed the main preoccupation of political thinkers.

Global concerns

During the 1970s, concern for the environment grew into a political force, boosted by the ideas about "deep ecology" of Arne Naess and coalescing into the green movement. As issues such as climate change and the end of cheap oil increasingly enter the mainstream, green political thinkers look set to become increasingly influential.

In the Islamic world, politicians and thinkers have struggled to agree on the place of Islam in politics. From Maududi's vision of an Islamic state to Shirin Ebadi's consideration of the role of women in Islam, and through the rise of al-Qaeda to the hope offered by the "Arab Spring", this is a dynamic and contested political arena.

The challenges of a globalized world – with industries, cultures, and communication technologies that transcend national boundaries – bring with them fresh sets of political problems. In particular, the financial crisis that erupted in 2007 has led political thinkers to reconsider their positions, seeking new solutions to the new problems. ■

THE CHIEF EVIL IS UNLIMITED GOVERNMENT

FRIEDRICH HAYEK (1899–1992)

IN CONTEXT

IDEOLOGY
Neoliberalism

FOCUS
Free-market economics

BEFORE

1840 Pierre-Joseph Proudhon advocates a naturally ordered society without authority, arguing that capital is analogous to authority.

1922 Austrian economist Ludwig von Mises criticizes centrally planned economies.

1936 John Maynard Keynes argues that the key to escaping economic depression is government spending.

AFTER

1962 US economist Milton Friedman argues that competitive capitalism is essential for political freedom.

1975 British politician Margaret Thatcher hails Hayek as her inspiration.

Free markets respond to individual needs.

So markets must be allowed to **operate freely**...

...and **governments must be limited** to allow order to arise spontaneously in society.

Central planning cannot respond to the changing needs of every individual.

So central planning involves **coercion** and **curtails the freedom** of all...

...and leads to unlimited, **totalitarian government**.

The chief evil is unlimited government.

Austrian-British economist Friedrich Hayek wrote his warning against unlimited government in an appendix called "Why I am not a Conservative" in his 1960 work, *The Constitution of Liberty*. In 1975, newly elected British Conservative party leader Margaret Thatcher threw this book on a table at a meeting with her fellow Conservatives declaring, "This is what we believe".

Thatcher was not the only conservative politician to admire Hayek's ideas, and he has emerged as something of a hero to many politicians on the right. For this reason, it may seem strange that he should have so firmly insisted that he was not a conservative. Indeed, such is the apparent ambiguity of his position that many commentators prefer the term "neoliberal" to describe Hayek and others who, like Thatcher and US president Ronald Reagan, championed the idea of unfettered free markets.

Hayek versus Keynes

The principle of free markets is at the heart of Hayek's insistence that "the chief evil is unlimited government". Hayek first came to public prominence in the 1930s, when he challenged British economist John Maynard Keynes's ideas for dealing with the Great Depression. Keynes argued that the only way to get out of the downward spiral of unemployment and sluggish spending was with large-scale government intervention and public works. Hayek insisted that this would simply bring inflation, and that periodic "busts" were an inevitable – indeed necessary – part of the business cycle.

See also: Immanuel Kant 126–29 ▪ John Stuart Mill 174–81 ▪ Pierre-Joseph Proudhon 183 ▪ Ayn Rand 280–81 ▪ Mikhail Gorbachev 322 ▪ Robert Nozick 326–27

According to Hayek, a free market spontaneously matches the availability of resources to the need for them through supply and demand. The knowledge to make these adjustments deliberately is way beyond the possibility of any individual.

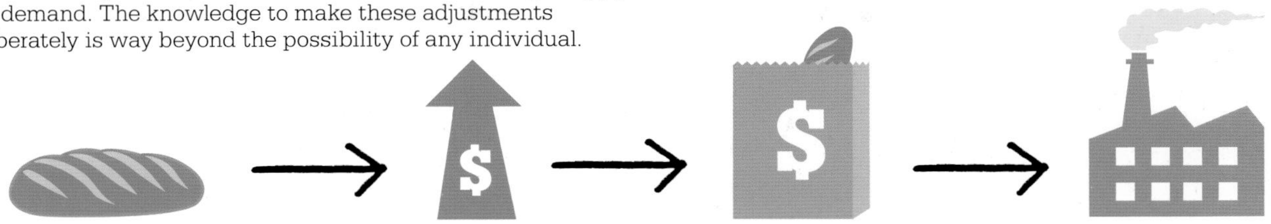

When **demand** for a product is **greater than supply**... → ...its price goes **up**. → Consumers may find it hard to find the goods, and will have to pay a **higher price**. → **More goods** are made to capitalize on profits.

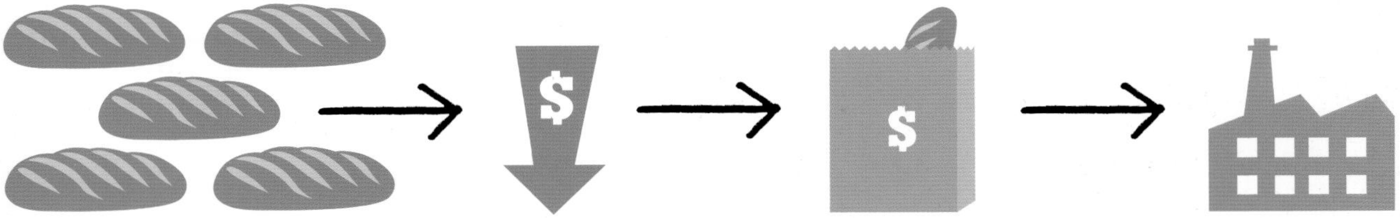

When **supply** of a product is **greater than demand**... → ...its price goes **down**. → Consumers can easily find the goods, and may be able to buy them at **discounted prices**. → Suppliers make **less product**.

Keynes's arguments won over policy-makers at the time, but Hayek continued to develop his ideas. He argued that central planning is doomed to failure because the planners can never have all the information required to account for the changing needs of every individual. It is simply a delusion to imagine that planners might have the omniscience to cater for so many disparate needs.

The gap in the planning is data, and this is where free markets come in. Individuals have a knowledge of resources and the need for them that a central planner can never hope to have. Hayek contended that the free market reveals this knowledge perfectly and continually. It does so through the operation of prices, which vary to signal the balance between supply and demand. If prices rise, you know that goods must be in short supply; if they fall, goods must be oversupplied. The market also gives people an incentive to respond to this knowledge, boosting production of goods in short supply to take advantage of the extra profits on offer. Hayek viewed this price mechanism not as a deliberate human invention, but as an example of order in human society that emerges spontaneously, like language.

Loss of freedom

Over time, Hayek began to feel that the gap between the planned economy and the free market was not simply a matter of bad economics but a fundamental issue of political freedom. Planning economies means controlling people's lives. And so, in 1944, as World War II raged on, he wrote his famous book *The Road to Serfdom* to warn the people of his adopted country, Britain, away from the dangers of socialism.

In *The Road to Serfdom*, Hayek argues that government control of our economic lives amounts to totalitarianism, and makes us all »

> A claim for equality of material position can be met only by a government with totalitarian powers.
> **Friedrich Hayek**

> Economic control is not merely control of a sector of human life which can be separated from the rest, it is the control of the means for all our ends.
> **Friedrich Hayek**

serfs. He believed that there was no fundamental difference in outcome between socialist central control of the economy and the fascism of the Nazis, however different the intentions behind the policies. For Hayek, to put any economic master plan into action, even one intended to benefit everyone, so many key policy issues must be delegated to unelected technocrats that such a programme will be inherently undemocratic. Moreover, a comprehensive economic plan leaves no room for individual choice in any aspect of life.

Government needs limits

It is in *The Constitution of Liberty* that Hayek's arguments about the link between free markets and political freedom are most fully developed. Despite his assertion that free markets must be the prime mechanism to give order to society, he is by no means against government. Government's central role, Hayek asserts, should be to maintain the "rule of law", with as little intervention in people's lives as possible. It is a "civil association" that simply provides a framework within which individuals can follow their own projects.

The foundations of law are common rules of conduct that predate government and arise spontaneously. "A judge," he writes, "is in this sense an institution of a spontaneous order." This is where Hayek's claim that he is not a conservative comes in. He argues that conservatives are frightened of democracy, and blame the evils of the times on its rise, because they are wary of change. But Hayek has no problem with democracy or change – the problem is a government that is not properly kept under control and limited. He asserts that "nobody is qualified to wield unlimited power" – and that, he implies, includes "the people". Yet, "the powers which modern democracy possesses," he concedes, "would be even more intolerable in the hands of some small elite."

Hayek is critical of laws intended to remedy a particular fault and believes that government use of coercion in society should be kept to a minimum. He is even more critical of the notion of "social justice". The market, he says, is a game in which "there is no point in calling the outcome just or unjust". He concludes from this that "social justice is an empty phrase with no determinable content". For Hayek, any attempt to redistribute wealth – for instance, by raising taxes to pay for the provision of social welfare – is a threat to freedom. All that is needed is a basic safety net to provide "protection against acts of desperation by the needy".

For a long time, Hayek's ideas had only a few disciples, and Keynesian economics dominated the policies of Western governments in the post-war years. Many countries established welfare states despite Hayek's warnings against it. But the oil shortage and economic downturn of the 1970s persuaded some to look again at Hayek's ideas, and in 1974, to the surprise of many, he was awarded the Nobel Prize for Economics.

In post-war Europe, the ideas of John Maynard Keynes won out over those of Hayek. Key industries such as the railways were run by state-owned companies.

Ronald Reagan and Margaret Thatcher both enthusiastically embraced Hayek's message that government should be shrunk, cutting taxes and state-provided services.

From this point on, Hayek's ideas became the rallying point for those who championed unregulated free markets as the route to economic prosperity and individual liberty. In the 1980s, Reagan and Thatcher pursued policies intended to roll back the welfare state, reducing taxation and cutting regulations. Many of the leaders of the revolutions against communist rule in eastern Europe were also inspired by Hayek's thinking.

Shock policies

Hayek's claim to be a liberal has been criticized by many, including former British Liberal Party leader David Steel, who argued that liberty is possible only with "social justice and an equitable distribution of wealth and power, which in turn require a degree of active government intervention". More damning still from a liberal point of view is the association of Hayek's ideas with what Canadian journalist Naomi Klein describes as the "shock doctrine". In this, people are persuaded to accept, "for their own ultimate good", a range of extreme free-market measures – such as rapid deregulation, the selling of state industries, and high unemployment – by being put in a state of shock, either through economic hardship or brutal government policies.

Hayek's free-market ideology became associated with a number of brutal military dictatorships in South America, such as that of General Augusto Pinochet in Chile – apparently just the kind of totalitarian regime Hayek was arguing against. Hayek was himself personally associated with these regimes, though he always insisted that he was only giving economic advice.

Hayek remains a highly controversial figure, championed by free marketeers and many politicians on the right as a defender of liberty, and despised by many on the left, who feel his ideas lie behind a shift towards hardline capitalism around the world that has brought misery to many and dramatically increased the gap between rich and poor. ■

> A government big enough to give you everything you want is strong enough to take everything you have.
> **Gerald Ford**

Friedrich Hayek

Born in Vienna in 1899, Friedrich August von Hayek entered the University of Vienna just after World War I, when it was one of the three best places in the world to study economics. Though enrolled as a law student, he was fascinated by economics and psychology, and the poverty of post-war Vienna urged him to a socialist solution. Then in 1922, after reading Ludwig von Mises's *Socialism*, a devastating critique of central planning, Hayek enrolled in Mises's economics class. In 1931, he moved to the London School of Economics to lecture on Mises's theory of business cycles, and began his sparring with Keynes on the causes of the Depression. In 1947, with Mises, he founded the Mont Pèlerin Society of libertarians. Three years later, he joined the Chicago school of free-market economists, along with Milton Friedman. By his death in 1992, Hayek's ideas had become highly influential.

Key works

1944 *The Road to Serfdom*
1960 *The Constitution of Liberty*

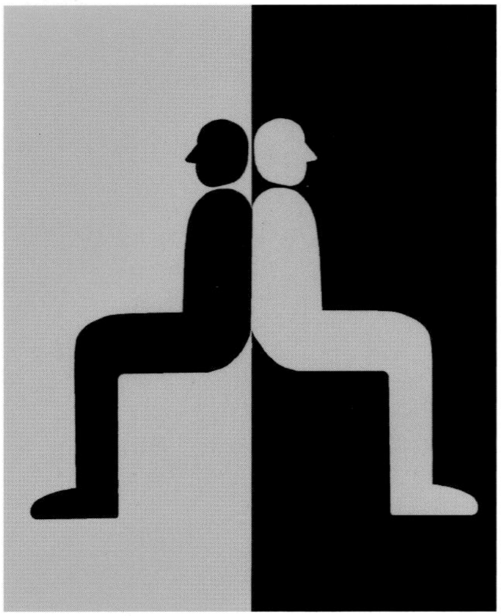

PARLIAMENTARY GOVERNMENT AND RATIONALIST POLITICS DO NOT BELONG TO THE SAME SYSTEM

MICHAEL OAKESHOTT (1901–1990)

IN CONTEXT

IDEOLOGY
Conservatism

FOCUS
Practical experience

BEFORE
1532 Machiavelli's *The Prince* analyses the usually violent means by which men seize, retain, and lose political power.

1689 Britain's Bill of Rights limits the monarchy's powers.

1848 Marx and Engels publish *the Communist Manifesto*, which Oakeshott believes is used unthinkingly as a "rulebook" for political action.

AFTER
1975 In Cambodia, Pol Pot proclaims "Year Zero", erasing history. His Maoist regime kills 2 million people in 3 years.

1997 China's principle of "One Country, Two Systems" allows for Hong Kong's free-market economy after Britain returns the territory to China.

Parliamentary institutions grew out of the **practical art of governing**.

↓

They have existed for generations and govern based **on experience and history**.

↓

Rationalist politics is based on **ideology and abstract notions**.

↓

It engages in **destruction** and the **creation of a new order**.

↓

Parliamentary government and rationalist politics do not belong to the same system.

The political extremism that engulfed much of the world in the 20th century, with the rise of Hitler in Germany, Stalin in Russia, and Mao in China, stirred Michael Oakeshott's career-long investigation into the nature of political ideologies and their impact on the lives of nations. He considered that Marxist and fascist leaders had seized on the thought of political theorists like "an infection", with disastrous consequences for millions. Oakeshott named this contagious disease "rationalism".

Tracing the emergence of British parliamentary institutions to the "least rationalistic period

See also: Niccolò Machiavelli 74–81 ▪ Thomas Hobbes 96–103 ▪ Edmund Burke 130–33 ▪ Georg Hegel 156–59 ▪ Karl Marx 188–93

of politics – the Middle Ages", Oakeshott explained that in Britain, parliament had not developed following a rationalist or ideological order. Rather, the imperative to limit political power and protect against tyranny acted as a deterrent, stabilizing Britain against the rationalist absolutisms that gripped Europe.

Fixed beliefs

Oakeshott saw rationalism in politics as a fog obscuring the real-life, day-to-day practicalities that all politicians and parties must address. The rationalist's actions are a response to his fixed theoretical beliefs rather than to objective or "practical" experience. He must memorize a rulebook, such as Marx and Engels's *Communist Manifesto*, before he can navigate the waters in which he finds himself, and so he is constantly detached from reality, operating through an ideological fog of abstract theories.

Oakeshott likened political life to a ship on rough seas. Predicting exactly how the waves will form is impossible, so negotiating the storms requires experience.

> In political activity, then, men sail on a boundless and bottomless sea.
> **Michael Oakeshott**

Oakeshott declared that "men sail a boundless and bottomless sea" – meaning that the world is hard to fathom and that attempts to make sense of society's behaviour inevitably distort and simplify the facts. He was wary of ideologies, seeing them as abstract, fixed beliefs that cannot explain what is inexplicable. Allergic to uncertainty, they convert complex situations into simple formulae. The rationalist politician's impulse is to act from within the "authority of his own reason" – the only authority he recognizes. He acts as though he understands the world and can see how it should be changed. It is very dangerous in politics, Oakeshott believed, to act according to an artificial ideology rather than real experience of government. Practical knowledge is the best guide and ideology is false knowledge.

Although Oakeshott was known as a conservative theorist, and his thinking has been appropriated by elements of modern-day conservatism, this is an ideological label that he did not recognize, and he did not pledge public support for conservative political parties. ■

Michael Oakeshott

Michael Oakeshott was born in London in 1901 to a civil servant and a former nurse. He studied history at the University of Cambridge, graduating in 1925. He remained in academia for the next half century, barring his covert role in World War II when he served with British intelligence as part of the "Phantom" reconnaissance unit in Belgium and France.

Oakeshott taught at both Cambridge and Oxford universities, after which he moved to the London School of Economics and was made Professor of Political Science. He published widely on the philosophy of history, religion, aesthetics, and law as well as politics. His influence on Conservative party politics in Britain led prime minister Margaret Thatcher to put him forward for a knighthood, which he declined, not seeing his work as party-political in nature. He retired in 1968, and died in 1990.

Key works

1933 *Experience and Its Modes*
1962 *Rationalism in Politics and Other Essays*
1975 *On Human Conduct*

THE OBJECTIVE OF THE ISLAMIC JIHAD IS TO ELIMINATE THE RULE OF AN UN-ISLAMIC SYSTEM

ABUL ALA MAUDUDI (1903–1979)

IN CONTEXT

IDEOLOGY
Islamic fundamentalism

APPROACH
Jihad

BEFORE
622–632 CE The first Muslim commonwealth, in Medina under Muhammad, unites separate tribes under the umbrella of faith.

1906 The All-India Muslim League is founded by Aga Khan III.

AFTER
1979 In Pakistan, General Zia ul-Haq puts some of Maududi's ideas into practice as Islamic Sharia-based criminal punishments become law.

1988 Osama bin Laden forms al-Qaeda, calling for a global *jihad* and the imposition of Sharia law across the world.

1990 The Cairo Declaration on Human Rights in Islam cites Sharia law as its sole source.

Islam is **not just a religion**, it is a **revolutionary programme** of life.

↓

Muslims must **carry out** its revolutionary programme.

↓

Jihad is the **revolutionary struggle** that the Islamic party uses to achieve its goal.

↓

Islam's purpose is an Islamic state, and the destruction of states that oppose this.

The genesis of the global Islamic revival in the 20th century has often been traced to the rejection of European colonialism and Western decadence in Africa and Asia. However, it was also linked to internal issues of communal politics, Muslim identity, the dynamics of power in a multi-ethnic, multi-faith society, and – in India – the question of nationalism. The political party Jama'at-i-Islami, founded by Maulana Abul Ala Maududi in 1941, became a revolutionary force at the vanguard of the Muslim reawakening in India. Addressing what he saw as a deep intellectual uncertainty and political anxiety among Indian Muslims after the

See also: Muhammad 56–57 ▪ Karl Marx 188–93 ▪ Theodor Herzl 208–09 ▪ Mahatma Gandhi 220–25 ▪ Ali Shariati 323 ▪ Shirin Ebadi 328

rule of the British Raj, Maududi formulated a fresh perspective on Islam designed to reverse the decline in Muslim political power by forging a new universal ideological brotherhood.

The Islamic state

Always more of a scholar and a *mujaddid* (reformer) than a practical, hands-on politician, Maududi remained detached from specific political and social issues. Instead, he concentrated on communicating his vision of the ideal Islamic state. Every element of this state would be informed "from above" by the laws of *din* (religion), not by secular Western principles of democratic governance. The Islamic state would therefore be innately democratic because it directly reflected the will of Allah.

This holy community could come into being only if its citizens were converted from ignorance and error to an uncompromising and purer understanding of Islam as a whole way of life. Maududi had studied European socialists, who saw their "base" as the masses of the working class in every country. Maududi saw the world population of Muslims as his "base" in the same way. If united ideologically, Muslims would eventually be politically indivisible, rendering secular nation-states irrelevant. The Islamic *jihad* (holy war) was not only a struggle to evolve spiritually, it was also a political struggle to impose an all-encompassing Islamic ideology. This would focus on Islamic control of state resources, so that finally the kingdom of God would be established on Earth.

In 1947, on the Partition of India and Pakistan on religious lines, the British Raj was dissolved. Although his party did not back Partition, criticizing its leaders' policies as insufficiently Islamic, Maududi moved to Pakistan, determined to make it an Islamic state.

Criticism of the approach

Western critics of Maududi's call for an Islamic world order claim that Islam sees its own history as a long descent from ideal beginnings, rather than as an evolutionary advance of civilization and reason. Meanwhile, the fundamentalist Muslims in Maududi's slipstream see the ongoing interference of Western countries in the internal politics of the Middle East as the continuation of colonial domination, and believe that only Islamic government ruling through Sharia law (canonical law based on the teachings of the *Quran*), as interpreted by Muslim clerics, can govern mankind. ▪

The Islamic revolution in Iran, led by Ruhollah Khomeini, ushered in the world's first Islamic republic in 1979. A state run on Islamic religious lines was Maududi's lifelong goal.

Abul Ala Maududi

Born in Aurangabad, India, the reformer, political philosopher, and theologian Maulana Abul Ala Maududi belonged to the Chisti tradition, a mystic Sufi Islamic order. He was educated at home by his religious father. Later, he began to earn his living as a journalist. In 1928, he published *Towards Understanding Islam* (*Risala al Dinyat*), earning him a reputation as an Islamic thinker and writer. Initially he supported Gandhi's Indian nationalism, but quickly began to urge India's Muslims to recognize Islam as their only identity.

In 1941, Maududi moved to Pakistan, where he advocated an Islamic state. He was arrested and sentenced to death in 1953 for inciting a riot, but the sentence was commuted. He died in New York in 1979.

Key works

1928 *Towards Understanding Islam*
1948 *Islamic Way of Life*
1972 *The Meaning of the Quran*

> Islam does not intend to confine its rule to a single state or a handful of countries. The aim of Islam is to bring about a universal revolution.
> **Abul Ala Maududi**

THERE IS NOTHING TO TAKE A MAN'S FREEDOM AWAY FROM HIM, SAVE OTHER MEN

AYN RAND (1905–1982)

IN CONTEXT

IDEOLOGY
Objectivism

FOCUS
Individual liberty

BEFORE
1917 The young Ayn Rand witnesses the October Revolution in Russia.

1930s Fascism rises across Europe as a series of authoritarian states centralize state power.

AFTER
1980s Conservative, free-market governments – in the UK under Margaret Thatcher, and in the US under Ronald Reagan – achieve electoral success.

2009 The Tea Party movement begins in the US, with a right-wing, conservative, tax-reducing agenda.

Late 2000s Renewed interest in Rand's works follows the global financial crisis.

During the mid-20th century, the twin forces of fascism and communism led many in the West to question the ethics of state involvement in the lives of individuals.

Russian-American philosopher and novelist Ayn Rand believed in a form of ethical individualism, which held that the pursuit of self-interest was morally right. For Rand, any attempt to control the actions of others through regulation corrupted the capacity of individuals to work freely as productive members of society. In other words, it was important to preserve the freedom of a man from interference by other men. In particular, Rand felt that the state's monopoly on the legal use of force was immoral, because it undermined the practical use of

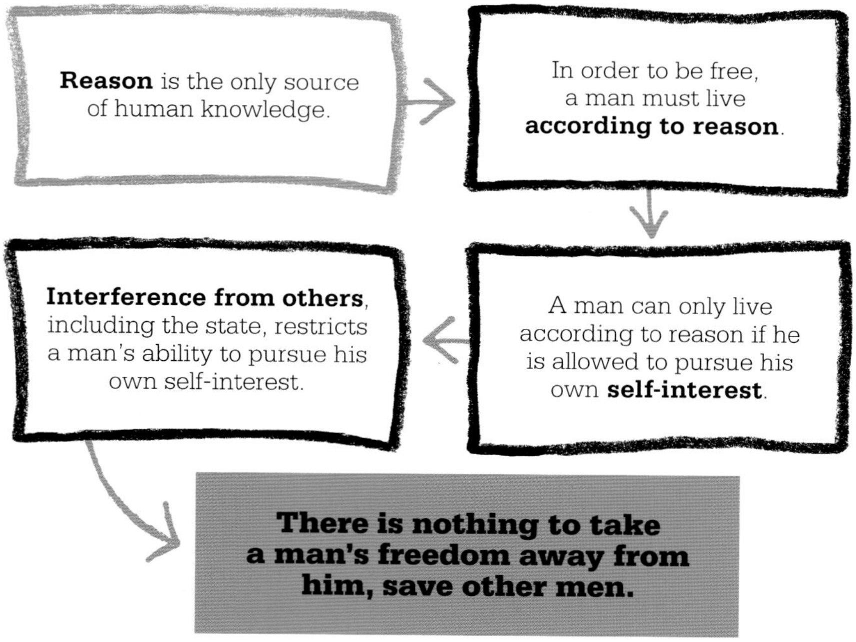

See also: Aristotle 40–43 ▪ Friedrich Nietzsche 196–99 ▪ Friedrich Hayek 270–75 ▪ Robert Nozick 326–27

> Man – every man – is an end in himself, not the means to the ends of others.
> **Ayn Rand**

reason by individuals. For this reason, she condemned taxation, as well as state regulation of business and most other areas of public life.

Objectivism

Rand's main contribution to political thought is a doctrine she called objectivism. She intended this to be a practical "philosophy for living on Earth" that provided a set of principles governing all aspects of life, including politics, economics, art, and relationships.

Atlas supports the world on his shoulders in this sculpture at the Rockefeller Center, New York. Rand believed that businessmen supported the nation state in the same way.

Objectivism is built on the idea that reason and rationality are the only absolutes in human life, and that as a result, any form of "just knowing" based on faith and instinct, such as religion, could not provide an adequate basis for existence. To Rand, unfettered capitalism was the only system of social organization that was compatible with the rational nature of human beings, and collective state action served only to limit the capabilities of humanity.

Her most influential work, *Atlas Shrugged*, articulates this belief clearly. A novel set in a United States that is crippled by government intervention and corrupt businessmen, its heroes are the industrialists and entrepreneurs whose productivity underpins society and whose cooperation sustains civilization.

Today, Rand's ideas resonate in libertarian and conservative movements that advocate a shrinking of the state. Others point out problems such as a lack of provision for the protection of the weak from the exploitation of the powerful. ■

Ayn Rand

Ayn Rand was born Alisa Zinov'yvena Rosenbaum in St Petersburg, Russia. The Bolshevik Revolution of 1917 resulted in her family losing their business and enduring a period of extreme hardship. She completed her education in Russia, studying philosophy, history, and cinema, before leaving for the US.

Rand worked as a screenwriter in Hollywood before becoming an author in the 1930s. Her novel *The Fountainhead* appeared in 1943 and won her fame, but it was her last work of fiction, *Atlas Shrugged*, that proved to be her most enduring legacy. Rand wrote more non-fiction and lectured on philosophy, promoting objectivism and its application to modern life. Rand's work has grown in influence since her death and has been cited as providing a philosophical underpinning to modern right-libertarian and conservative politics.

Key works

1943 *The Fountainhead*
1957 *Atlas Shrugged*
1964 *The Virtue of Selfishness*

EVERY KNOWN AND ESTABLISHED FACT CAN BE DENIED

HANNAH ARENDT (1906–1975)

IN CONTEXT

IDEOLOGY
Anti-totalitarianism

FOCUS
Truth and myth

BEFORE
1882 French historian Ernest Renan claims that national identity depends upon a selective and distorted memory of past events.

1960 Hans-Georg Gadamer publishes *Truth and Method* focusing on the importance of collective truth creation.

AFTER
1992 British historian Eric Hobsbawn states that "no serious historian can be a committed political nationalist".

1995 British philosopher David Miller argues that myths serve a valuable social integrative function, despite being untrue.

1998 Jürgen Habermas criticizes Arendt's stance in *Truth and Justification*.

The German political philosopher Hannah Arendt wrote about the nature of politics at a particularly tumultuous time: she lived through the rise and fall of the Nazi regime, the Vietnam War, student riots in Paris, and the assassinations of US president John F. Kennedy and Martin Luther King. As a Jew living in Germany, who later moved to occupied France, and then Chicago, New York, and Berkeley in the US, Arendt experienced these events first-hand. Her political philosophy was informed by these events and their portrayal to the general public.

In her 1967 essay *Truth and Politics*, Arendt is particularly concerned with the way that historical facts often become distorted when politicized – they are used as tools in order to justify particular political decisions. This distortion of historical facts was not new in the political domain, where lies have always played an important part in foreign diplomacy and security. However, what was new about the political lies of the 1960s onwards was their significantly wider scope. Arendt notices that they went far beyond simply keeping state secrets to encompassing an entire collective reality in which facts known to everyone are targeted and slowly erased, while a different version of historical "reality" is constructed to replace them.

This mass manipulation of facts and opinions, Arendt notes, is no longer restricted to totalitarian regimes, where oppression is pervasive and evident, and people may be on guard against continual propaganda, but increasingly takes place in liberal democracies such as the US, where doctored reports and purposeful misinformation

During the war in Vietnam, the US government supplied misinformation to the public – distorting the facts in the way that Arendt describes – in order to justify their involvement.

See also: Ibn Khaldun 72–73 ▪ Karl Marx 188–93 ▪ José Ortega y Gasset 250–51 ▪ Michel Foucault 310–11 ▪ Noam Chomsky 314–15

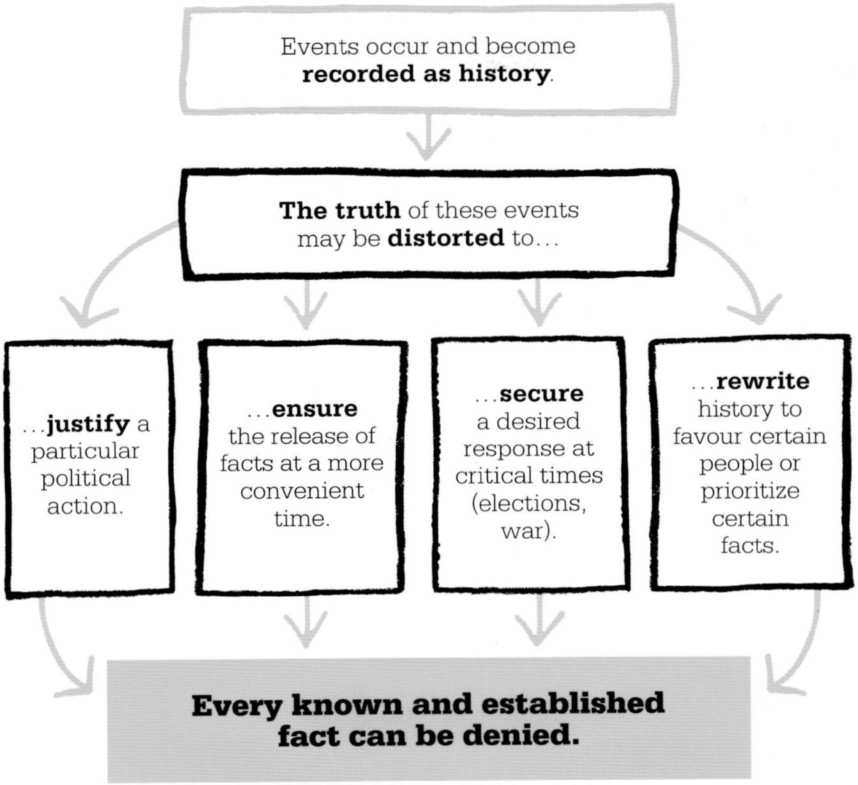

serve to justify violent political interventions such as the Vietnam War of 1954–75. In free countries, she claims, unwelcome historical truths are often transmuted into mere opinion, losing their factual status. For example, it is as though the policies of France and the Vatican during World War II "were not a matter of historical record but a matter of opinion".

An alternative reality

The rewriting of contemporary history under the very eyes of those who witnessed it, through the denial or neglect of every known and established fact, leads not only to the creation of a more flattering reality to fit specific political needs, but also to the establishment of an entirely substitute reality that no longer has anything to do with factual truth. This, Arendt argues, is particularly dangerous – the substitute reality that justified mass killings under the Nazi regime is a good example. What is at stake, Arendt says, is "common and factual reality itself".

Contemporary followers of Arendt point to the 2003 invasion of Iraq by the US and its allies as an example of this phenomenon. Arendt's arguments might also be used by Julian Assange, founder of WikiLeaks, to justify the release of secret documents that contradict the official version of events given by governments around the world. ▪

Hannah Arendt

Hannah Arendt was born in Linden, Germany, in 1906, to a family of secular Jews. She grew up in Königsberg and Berlin and studied philosophy at the University of Marburg with philosopher Martin Heidegger, with whom she developed a strong intellectual and romantic relationship, later soured by Heidegger's support for the Nazi party.

Arendt was prohibited from taking up a teaching position at a German university due to her Jewish heritage, and during the Nazi regime, she fled to Paris and later the US, where she became part of a lively intellectual circle. She published many highly influential books and essays, and taught at the University of California, Berkeley, the University of Chicago, the New School, Princeton (where she became the first female lecturer), and Yale. She died in 1975 of a heart attack.

Key works

1951 *The Origins of Totalitarianism*
1958 *The Human Condition*
1962 *On Revolution*

WHAT IS A WOMAN?

SIMONE DE BEAUVOIR (1908–1986)

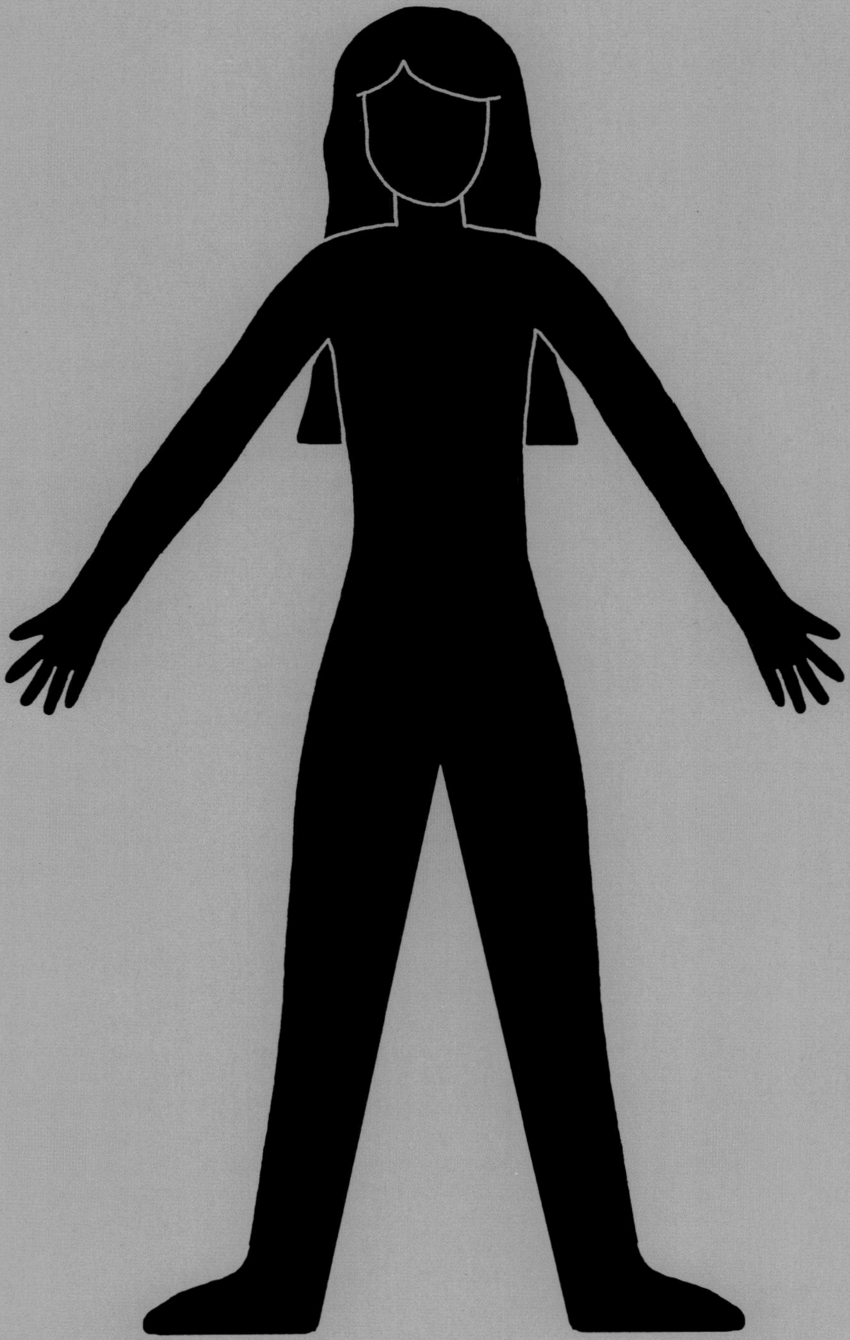

IN CONTEXT

IDEOLOGY
Existentialist feminism

FOCUS
Freedom of choice

BEFORE
1791 Olympe de Gouges writes the *Declaration of the Rights of Woman and the Female Citizen*.

1892 Eugénie Potonié-Pierre and Léonie Rouzade found the Federation of French Feminist Societies.

1944 Women finally win the right to vote in France.

AFTER
1963 Betty Friedan publishes *The Feminine Mystique*, bringing many of de Beauvoir's ideas to a wider audience.

1970 In *The Female Eunuch*, Australian writer Germaine Greer examines the limits placed on women's lives in consumer societies.

Across the world, women are on lower incomes than men, are frequently deprived of legal and political rights, and are subject to various forms of cultural oppression. In this context, feminist interpretations of political problems have provided an important contribution to political theory and inspired generations of political thinkers.

Throughout the 19th century, the concept of feminism had been growing in force, but there were deep conceptual divides between the various feminist groups. Some supported the concept of "equality through difference", accepting that there are inherent differences between men and women, and that these differences constitute the strength of their positions in society. Others held the view that women should not be treated differently from men at all, and focused first and foremost on universal suffrage as their main goal, viewing equal political rights as the key battle. This battle for rights has since become known as "first-wave feminism", to distinguish it from the "second-wave feminism" movement that had wider political aims and gathered pace around the world in the 1960s. This new movement considered women's experience of discrimination in the home and the workplace, and the often subtle manifestations of unconsciously held prejudices that could not necessarily be fixed merely through changes in the law. It took much of its intellectual inspiration from the work of French philosopher Simone de Beauvoir.

> He is the Subject,
> he is the Absolute.
> She is the Other.
> **Simone de Beauvoir**

Transcending feminism

Although she is sometimes described as the "mother of the modern women's movement", at

Simone de Beauvoir

Simone Lucie-Ernestine-Marie-Bertrand de Beauvoir was born in Paris in 1908. The daughter of a wealthy family, she was educated privately and went on to study philosophy at the Sorbonne. While she was at university, she met Jean-Paul Sartre, who would go on to become her life-long companion and philosophical counterpart.

De Beauvoir openly declared her atheism when she was a teenager. Her rejection of institutions such as religion later led her to refuse to marry Sartre. Her work was inspired both by her own personal experiences in Paris, and by wider political issues such as the international growth of communism. Her interest in the latter led to several books on the subject. She also wrote a number of novels.

After Sartre's death in 1980, de Beauvoir's own health deteriorated. She died six years later, and was buried in the same grave.

Key works

1943 *She Came To Stay*
1949 *The Second Sex*
1954 *The Mandarins*

See also: Mary Wollstonecraft 154–55 ▪ Georg Hegel 156–59 ▪ John Stuart Mill 174–81 ▪ Emmeline Pankhurst 207 ▪ Shirin Ebadi 328

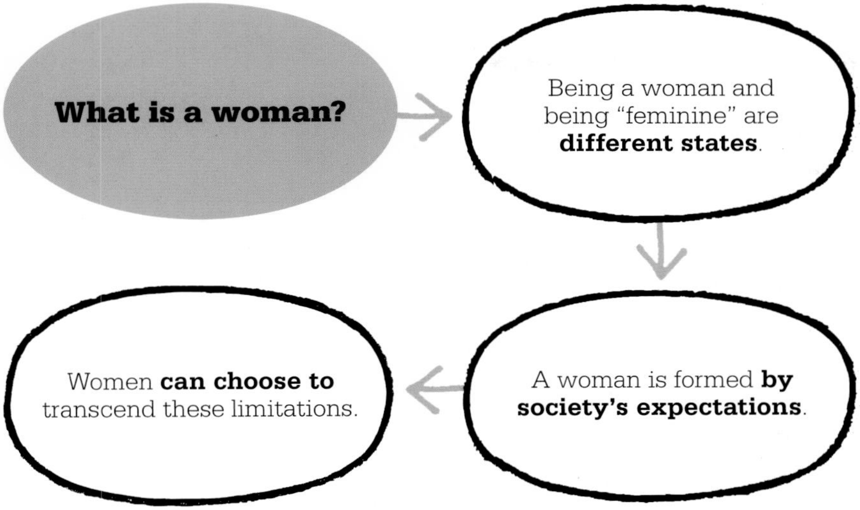

the time of writing her seminal work *The Second Sex* in 1949, de Beauvoir did not view herself primarily as a "feminist". She held ambitions to transcend this definition, which she felt often became bogged down in its own arguments. Instead, she took a more subjective approach to the concept of difference, combining feminist arguments with her existentialist philosophical outlook. However, de Beauvoir was later to join the second-wave feminist movement, and was still active in support of its arguments in the 1970s, examining the wider condition of women in society in a series of novels.

De Beauvoir realized that when she made an effort to define herself, the first phrase that came to her mind was "I am a woman". Her need to examine this involuntary definition – and its deeper meaning – formed the basis of her work. For de Beauvoir, it is important to differentiate between the state of being female, and that of being a woman, and her work eventually alights on the definition "a human being in the feminine condition". She rejects the theory of the "eternal feminine" – a mysterious essence of femininity – which can be used to justify inequality. In *The Second Sex*, she points out that the very fact that she is asking the question "What is a woman?" is significant, and highlights the inherent "Otherness" of women in society in relation to men. She was one of the first writers to fully define the concept of "sexism" in society: the prejudices and assumptions that are made about women. She also asks whether women are born, or whether they are created by society's preconceptions, including educational expectations and religious structures, as well as historical precedents. She examines how women are represented in psychoanalysis, history, and biology, and draws on a variety of sources – literary, academic, and anecdotal – to demonstrate the effects on women of these assumptions.

De Beauvoir's approach in answering the question "What is a woman?" is guided by her involvement with existentialism, »

A woman's traditional role as wife, homemaker, and mother traps her, according to de Beauvoir, in a place where she is cut off from other women and defined by her husband.

De Beauvoir maintained a long-term relationship with Jean-Paul Sartre, but the two never married. She saw their open relationship as an example of freedom of choice for a woman.

which is essentially concerned with the discovery of the self through the freedom of personal choice within society. De Beauvoir sees women's freedom in this regard as peculiarly restricted. This philosophical direction was reinforced by her relationship with Jean-Paul Sartre, who she met at the Sorbonne in 1929. He was a leading existentialist thinker, and they were to maintain a long and fruitful intellectual dialogue, as well as a complex and lasting personal relationship.

De Beauvoir's position is also informed by her left-wing political convictions. She describes women's struggles as part of the class struggle, and recognizes that her own start in life as a member of the bourgeoisie meant that opportunities were open to her that were not available to women from the lower classes. Ultimately, she wanted such freedom of opportunity for all women – indeed all people – regardless of class. De Beauvoir draws parallels between a woman's physical confinement – in a "kitchen or a boudoir" – and the intellectual boundaries imposed on her. She suggests that these limitations lead women to accept mediocrity and discourage them from pushing themselves to achieve more. De Beauvoir calls this state "immanence". By this, she means that women are limited by, and to, their own direct experience of the world. She contrasts this position with men's "transcendence", which allows them access to any position in life that they might choose to take, regardless of the limits of their own direct experience. In this way, men are "Subjects" who define themselves, while women are "Others", who are defined by men.

> What a curse to be a woman! And yet the very worst curse when one is a woman is, in fact, not to understand that it is one.
> **Søren Kierkegaard**

De Beauvoir questions why women generally accept this position of "Other", seeking to account for their submissiveness to masculine assumptions. She clearly states that immanence is not a "moral fault" on the part of women. She also acknowledges what she sees as the inherent contradiction facing women: the impossibility of choosing between herself – as a woman – as fundamentally different from a man, and herself as a totally equal member of the human race.

Freedom to choose

Many aspects of *The Second Sex* were highly controversial, including de Beauvoir's frank discussion of lesbianism and her open contempt for marriage, both of which resonated deeply with her own life. She refused to marry Sartre on the principle that she did not want their relationship to be restrained by a masculine institution. For her, marriage lay at the heart of women's subjection to men, binding them in a submissive position in society and isolating them from other members of their sex. She believed that only where women remained autonomous might they be able to rise together against their oppression. She felt that if girls were conditioned to find "a pal, a friend, a partner", rather than "a demigod", they could enter a relationship on a far more equal footing.

Central to de Beauvoir's thesis is the concept, rooted in existentialism, that women can "choose" to change

> In human society nothing is natural and woman, like much else, is a product elaborated by civilization.
> **Simone de Beauvoir**

their position in society: "If woman discovers herself as the inessential, and never turns into the essential, it is because she does not bring about this transformation herself." In other words, only women could liberate themselves – they could not be liberated by men. Taking responsibility for difficult choices was a core idea in de Beauvoir's existentialism. Her own choice of relationship in the 1920s was a difficult one, involving a complete rejection of the values of her own upbringing, and a disregard for social norms.

Some of those who read *The Second Sex* believed de Beauvoir was saying that women should become like men – that they should eschew the "femininity" that had been enforced on them, and with it their essential differences from men. However, her main thesis was that collaboration between men and women would eradicate the conflicts inherent in the accepted position of man as Subject and woman as Object. She explored this possibility in her relationship with Sartre, and attempted to embody in her own life many of the qualities she championed in her writing.

De Beauvoir has been accused of being against motherhood, in the same way that she was against marriage. In truth, she was not anti-motherhood, but she did feel that society did not provide women with the choices to allow them to continue to work, or to have children out of wedlock. She saw how women might use maternity as a refuge – giving them a clear purpose in life – but end up feeling imprisoned by it. Above all, she stressed the importance of the existence of real choices, and of choosing honestly.

Reshaping feminist politics

It is now widely acknowledged that the first translation of *The Second Sex* into English failed to accurately interpret either the language or the concepts of de Beauvoir's writing, leading many outside France to misunderstand her position. De Beauvoir herself declared in the 1980s, having been unaware for 30 years of the shortcomings of the translation, that she wished another one would be made. A revised version of the book was finally published in 2009.

The popularity of *The Second Sex* around the world – despite the shortcomings of the original English translation – led to it becoming a major influence on feminist thinking. De Beauvoir's analysis of women's role in society, and its political consequences for both men and women, struck a chord across the Western world, and was the starting point for the radical second-wave feminist movement. In 1963, US author Betty Friedan took up de Beauvoir's argument that women's potential was being wasted in patriarchal societies. This argument was to form the basis for feminist political thought throughout the 1960s and 70s. ■

De Beauvoir believed that men had the accepted position "Subject" within society, while women were classed as "Other".

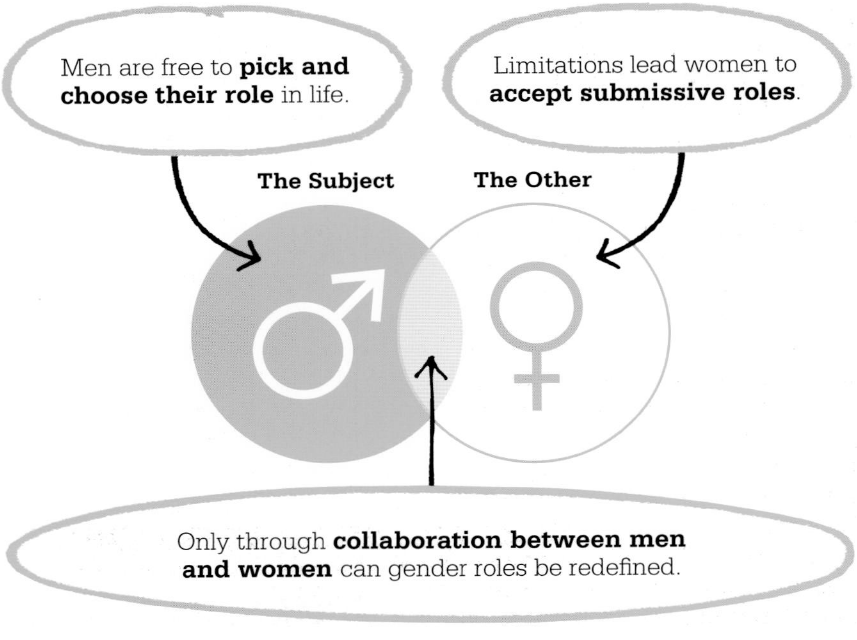

NO NATURAL OBJECT IS SOLELY A RESOURCE

ARNE NAESS (1912–2009)

IN CONTEXT

IDEOLOGY
Radical environmentalism

APPROACH
Deep ecology

BEFORE
1949 Aldo Leopold's "Land Ethic" essay, calling for a new ethic in conservation, is posthumously published.

1962 Rachel Carson writes *Silent Spring*, a key factor in the birth of the environmental movement.

AFTER
1992 The first Earth Summit is held in Rio, Brazil, signalling an acknowledgment of environmental issues on a global scale.

1998 The "Red/Green" coalition takes power in Germany, the first time an environmental party is elected to national government.

In recent decades, the economic, social, and political challenges of climate change have provided an imperative for the development of new political ideas. Environmentalism as a political project began in earnest in the 1960s, and has now entered the mainstream of political life. As a field of inquiry, the green movement has developed a variety of offshoots and avenues of thought.

The first environmentalists

Environmentalism has well-established roots. In the 19th century, thinkers such as the English critics John Ruskin and William Morris were concerned

See also: John Locke 104–09 ▪ Henry David Thoreau 186–87 ▪ Karl Marx 188–93

Mankind forms one part of a **fragile ecosystem**.

Human action is **causing irreparable damage** to the ecosystem.

Shallow ecology holds that current economic and social structures can be adapted to **solve environmental problems**.

Deep ecology holds that profound social and political change is needed to **avert an environmental crisis**.

with the growth of industrialization and its subsequent impact on the natural world. But it was not until after World War I that a scientific understanding of the extent of the damage humans were causing to the environment began to develop. In 1962, American marine biologist Rachel Carson published her book *Silent Spring*, an account of the environmental problems caused by the use of industrial pesticides. Carson's work suggested that the unregulated use of pesticides such as DDT had a dramatic effect on the natural world. Carson also included an account of the effects of pesticides on humans, placing mankind within the ecosystem rather than thinking of man as separate from nature.

Carson's book provided the catalyst for the emergence of the environmental movement in mainstream politics. Arne Naess, a Norwegian philosopher and ecologist, credited *Silent Spring* with providing the inspiration for his work, which focused on the philosophical underpinnings for environmentalism. Naess was a philosopher of some renown at the University of Oslo, and was primarily known for his work on »

> Earth does not belong to humans.
> **Arne Naess**

Arne Naess

Arne Naess was born near Oslo, Norway, in 1912. After training in philosophy, he became the youngest ever professor of philosophy at the University of Oslo at the age of 27. He maintained a significant academic career, working particularly in the areas of language and semantics. In 1969, he resigned from his position to devote himself to the study of ethical ecology, and the promotion of practical responses to environmental problems. Retreating to write in near-solitude, he produced nearly 400 articles and numerous books.

Outside of his work, Naess was passionate about mountaineering. By the age of 19, he had built a considerable reputation as a climber, and he lived for a number of years in a remote mountain cabin in rural Norway, where he wrote most of his later work.

Key works

1973 *The Shallow and the Deep, Long-Range Ecology Movement: A Summary*
1989 *Ecology, Community and Lifestyle: Outline of an Ecosophy*

The Industrial Revolution changed people's thinking about the environment. It was seen as a resource to be exploited, an attitude that Naess thought could lead to the destruction of mankind.

language. From the 1970s, however, he embarked on a period of sustained work on environmental and ecological issues, having resigned his position at the university in 1969 and devoted himself to this new avenue of thought. Naess became a practical philosopher of environmental ethics, developing new responses to the ecological problems that were being identified. In particular, he proposed new ways of conceiving the position of human beings in relation to nature.

Fundamental to Naess's thought was the notion that the Earth is not simply a resource to be used by humans. Humans should consider themselves as part of a complex, interdependent system, rather than consumers of natural goods, and should develop compassion for non-humans. To fail to understand this point was to risk destroying the natural world through narrow-minded, selfish ambition.

Early in his career as an environmentalist, Naess outlined his vision of a framework for ecological thought that would provide solutions to society's problems. He called this framework "Ecosophy T", the T representing Tvergastein, Naess's mountain home. Ecosophy T was based on the idea that people should accept that all living things – whether human, animal, or vegetable – have an equal right to life. By understanding oneself as part of an interconnected whole, the implications of any action on the environment become apparent. Where the consequences of human activity are unknown, inaction is the only ethical option.

Deep ecology

Later in his career, Naess developed the contrasting notions of "shallow" and "deep" ecology to expose the inadequacies of much existing thinking on the subject. For Naess, shallow ecology was the belief that environmental problems could be solved by capitalism, industry, and human-led intervention. This line of thinking holds that the structures of society provide a suitable starting point for the solution of environmental problems, and imagines environmental issues in a human-centric way. Shallow ecology was not without value, but Naess believed it had a tendency to focus on superficial solutions to environmental problems. This view of ecology, for Naess, imagined mankind as a superior being within the ecosystem and did not acknowledge the need for wider social reform. The broader social, philosophical, and political roots of these problems were left unsolved, as the primary concern was with the narrow interests of humans, rather than nature in its entirety.

In contrast, deep ecology says that, without dramatic reform of human behaviour, irreparable environmental damage will be brought upon the planet. The fast pace of human progress and social change has tilted the delicate balance of nature, with the result that not only is the natural world being damaged, but mankind – as part of the environment – is ushering itself towards destruction.

> "The supporters of shallow ecology think that reforming human relations towards nature can be done within the existing structure of society."
> **Arne Naess**

Resolving environmental issues within current political, economic, and social systems is doomed to failure, according to Naess. What is needed is a new way of looking at the world around us, seeing mankind as a part of the ecological system.

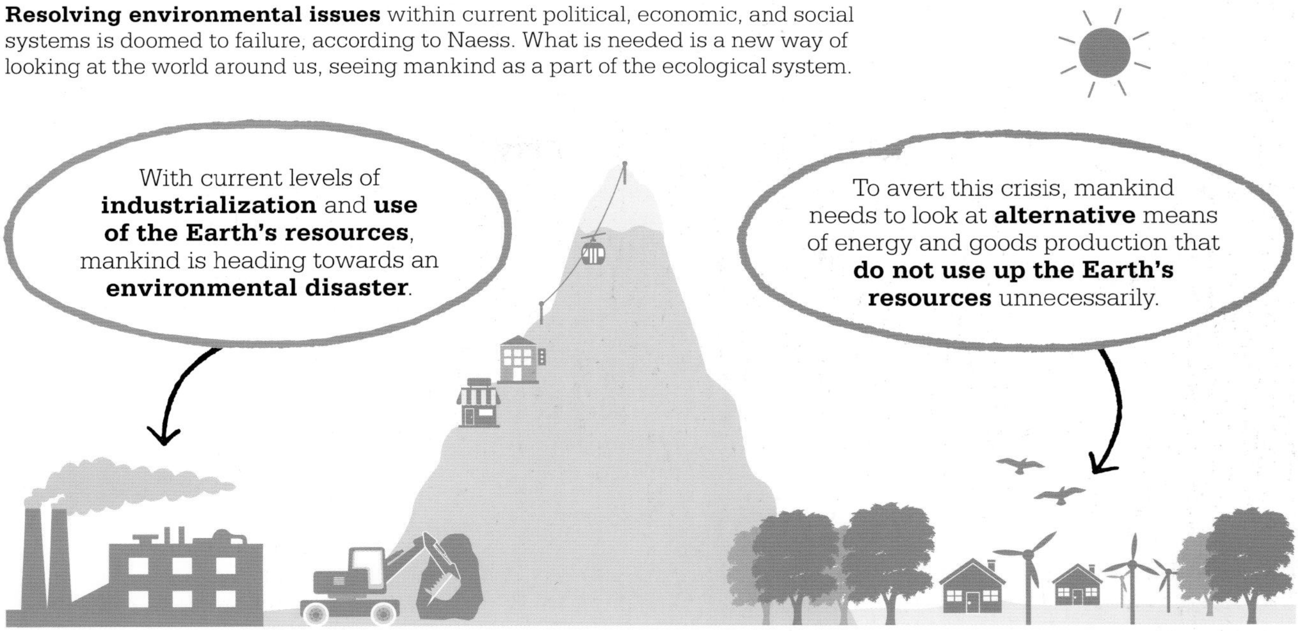

Naess proposes that, in order to understand that nature has an intrinsic value quite separate from human beings, a spiritual realization must take place, requiring an understanding of the importance and connection of all life. Human beings must understand that they only inhabit, rather than own, the Earth, and that only resources that satisfy vital means must be used.

Direct action

Naess combined his engagement in environmental thought with a commitment to direct action. He once chained himself to rocks near the Mardalsfossen, a waterfall in a Norwegian fjord, in a successful protest against the proposed site of a dam. For Naess, the realization that accompanied a deep ecological viewpoint must be used to promote a more ethical and responsible approach to nature. He was in favour of reducing consumerism and the standards of material living in developed countries as part of a broad-reaching programme of reform. However, Naess disagreed with fundamentalist approaches to environmentalism, believing that humans could use some of the resources provided by nature in order to maintain a stable society.

Naess's influence

Despite his preference for gradual change, and his disdain for fundamentalism, Naess's ideas have been adopted by activists with more radical perspectives. Earth First!, an international environmental advocacy group that engages in direct action, has adapted Naess's ideas to support their own understanding of deep ecology. In their version of the philosophy, deep ecology can be used to justify political action that includes civil disobedience and sabotage.

As awareness of environmental issues grows, Naess's ideas are gaining ever-greater resonance at a political level. Environmental issues show no respect for the boundaries of national governments, and generate a complex set of questions for theorists and practitioners alike. The green movement has entered the political mainstream, both through formal political parties and advocacy groups such as Greenpeace and Friends of the Earth. Naess's work has an important place in providing a philosophical underpinning to these developments. His ideas have attracted controversy, and criticism has come from many quarters, including the accusation that they are disconnected from the reality of socio-economic factors and given to a certain mysticism. Despite these criticisms, the political questions raised by the environmental movement, and the place of deep ecological perspectives within them, remain significant and seem sure to grow in importance in the future. ■

WE ARE NOT ANTI-WHITE, WE ARE AGAINST WHITE SUPREMACY

NELSON MANDELA (1918–)

IN CONTEXT

IDEOLOGY
Racial equality

FOCUS
Civil disobedience

BEFORE
1948 The Afrikaaner-dominated National Party is elected to power, marking the start of apartheid in South Africa.

1961 Frantz Fanon writes *The Wretched of the Earth*, outlining the process of armed struggle against an oppressor.

1963 Martin Luther King delivers his "I have a dream" speech in Washington, DC.

AFTER
1993 The Nobel Peace Prize is awarded to Mandela for his work towards reconciliation in South Africa.

1994 In the country's first free and multi-racial elections, Mandela is voted the first black president of South Africa.

Apartheid is an unjust form of **racial segregation**.

↓

We must protest against this **injustice and inequality**.

↓

It is a fight by **all South Africans** for change.

↓

We are not anti-white, we are against white supremacy.

The fight against apartheid in South Africa was one of the defining political battles of the late-20th century. From 1948, the election of the apartheid National Party spelled the beginning of a period of oppression by the white minority. Nelson Mandela was at the forefront of the resistance, organizing public protest and mobilizing support through his involvement in the African National Congress (ANC) party. This grew in response to the legislation implemented by the new government and, by the 1950s, a popular movement was taking part in the resistance to apartheid, drawing its inspiration from civil rights leaders such as Mahatma Gandhi and Martin Luther King.

For freedom

The strategy pursued by the ANC was intended to make effective government impossible, through a mixture of civil disobedience, the massed withdrawal of labour, and public protest. By the mid-1950s the ANC and other groups within the anti-apartheid movement had articulated their demands in the Freedom Charter. This enshrined the values of democracy,

See also: Mahatma Gandhi 220–25 ▪ Marcus Garvey 252 ▪ Frantz Fanon 304–07 ▪ Martin Luther King 316–21

participation, and freedom of movement and expression, which were the mainstays of the protesters' demands. However, it was treated by the government as an act of treason.

From protest to violence

The effect of this dissent on the apartheid regime was gradual, but telling. By the 1950s, although the democratic process was still closed to most non-whites, a number of political parties had begun to promote some form of democratic rights – albeit only partial – for black people in South Africa.

This was significant as, by gaining the support of some of the politically active white minority, the anti-apartheid movement was able to demonstrate that it was not mobilizing along racial lines. This fitted Mandela's view of the struggle, which was inclusive in its vision of a new South Africa. He emphasized that the primary motivation for the protest was to combat racial injustice and white supremacy, rather than to attack the white minority themselves.

The battle to end apartheid was not an attack on South Africa's white minority, Mandela asserted, it was against injustice and as such was a more inclusive call for change.

> I have fought against white domination, and I have fought against black domination. I have cherished the ideal of a democratic and free society.
> **Nelson Mandela**

Despite the well-organized and active approach of the ANC, dramatic reform was still not forthcoming, and demands for a full extension of voting rights were not met. Instead, as the intensity of protest escalated, the government's response became ever more violent, culminating in the Sharpeville Massacre in 1960, when police shot dead 69 people who were protesting against laws that required black people to carry pass books.

However, the struggle against apartheid was not wholly peaceful itself. Like other revolutionary figures, Mandela had come to the conclusion that the only way to combat the apartheid system was through armed struggle. In 1961, Mandela, with other leaders of the ANC, established *Umkhonto we Sizwe*, the armed wing of the ANC, an act which contributed to his later imprisonment. Despite this, his belief in civil protest and the principle of inclusion gained worldwide support, culminating in Mandela's eventual release and the fall of apartheid. ■

Nelson Mandela

Nelson Rolihlahla Mandela was born in the Transkei, South Africa, in 1918. His father was advisor to the chief of the Tembu tribe. Mandela moved to Johannesburg as a young man and studied law. He joined the African National Congress (ANC) party in 1944 and became involved in active resistance against the apartheid regime's policies from 1948. In 1961, he helped establish the ANC's military wing, *Umkhonto we Sizwe*, partly in response to the Sharpeville Massacre a year earlier. In 1964, he received a sentence of life imprisonment, remaining incarcerated until 1990, and spending 18 years on Robben Island.

On his release from prison, Mandela became the figurehead of the dismantling of apartheid, winning the Nobel Peace Prize in 1993 and becoming president of South Africa in 1994. Since stepping down in 1999, he has been involved with a number of causes, including work to tackle the AIDS pandemic.

Key works

1965 *No Easy Walk to Freedom*
1994 *Long Walk to Freedom*

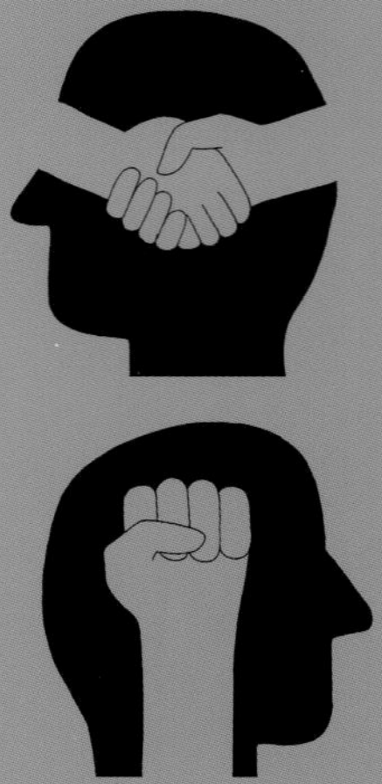

ONLY THE WEAK-MINDED BELIEVE THAT POLITICS IS A PLACE OF COLLABORATION

GIANFRANCO MIGLIO (1918–2001)

IN CONTEXT

IDEOLOGY
Federalism

FOCUS
De-unification

BEFORE
1532 Niccolò Machiavelli's *The Prince* predicts the eventual unification of Italy.

1870 The unification of Italy is completed with the Capture of Rome by the Italian army of King Victor Emmanuel II.

AFTER
1993 US political scientist Robert Putnam publishes *Making Democracy Work*, which examines the divisions in political and civic life across Italy.

1994 The separatist party Lega Nord participates in Italian national government for the first time.

Italian politics has a history of confrontation. Historically, Italy was a divided nation, ruled by a loose coalition of city-states until the unification of the country was completed in 1870. Between the industrial north and the rural south, a long history of inequity and dispute exists, with many in the north feeling that unification had brought economic benefits to the south but disadvantage to their own region.

Gianfranco Miglio was an Italian academic and politician whose work examined the structures of power in political life. Drawing his inspiration from Max Weber and Carl Schmitt, Miglio argued against the centralization of political resources across Italy on the basis that this form of collaboration had harmed the interests and identity of the north.

Northern separatism

Miglio believed that collaboration was not a desirable feature of politics, nor was it possible in the political marketplace. The differing interests of Italy's various regions would not be resolved through compromise and discussion, but through the dominance of the more powerful groupings. Miglio's ideas eventually led him into a political career, and in the 1990s he was elected to the national senate as a radical member of the separatist party Lega Nord ("Northern League"), founded in 1991. ■

Car manufacturers such as Fiat have contributed to northern Italy's wealth. In Miglio's view, it was unfair that such wealth should subsidize the poorer south.

See also: Niccolò Machiavelli 74–81 ▪ Max Weber 214–15 ▪ Carl Schmitt 254–57

DURING THE INITIAL STAGE OF THE STRUGGLE, THE OPPRESSED TEND TO BECOME OPPRESSORS

PAULO FREIRE (1921–1997)

IN CONTEXT

IDEOLOGY
Radicalism

FOCUS
Critical education

BEFORE
1929–34 Antonio Gramsci writes his *Prison Notebooks*, outlining his development of Marxist thought.

1930s Brazil suffers extreme poverty during the Great Depression.

AFTER
1960s While professor of history and philosophy of education at the University of Recife, Brazil, Freire develops a programme to deal with mass illiteracy.

1970s Freire works with the World Council of Churches, spending nearly a decade advising on education reform in a number of countries across the world.

Political writers have often attempted to understand the struggle against political oppression. Thinkers such as Karl Marx and Antonio Gramsci framed oppression in terms of two groups of actors – the oppressors and those who are oppressed.

Brazilian educator Paulo Freire's work revisited this relationship, concentrating on the conditions needed to break the cycle of oppression. He believed that the act of oppression dehumanizes both parties and that, once liberated, there is a danger of individuals repeating the injustice they have experienced. In effect, the oppressed themselves might become oppressors.

Genuine liberation

This line of thinking held that it would take more than just a shift in roles to end oppression and begin the genuine process of liberation. Freire believed that through education, humanity could be restored, and that a reform of education could produce a class of people who would rethink their lives. In this way, oppressors would stop viewing others as an abstract grouping and would understand their position as individuals who are subject to injustice.

Freire saw education as a political act in which students and teachers needed to reflect on their positions and appreciate the environment in which education takes place. His work has influenced many political theorists. ■

> The greatest humanistic and historical task of the oppressed is to liberate themselves and their oppressors as well.
> **Paulo Freire**

See also: Georg Hegel 156–59 ■ Karl Marx 188–93 ■ Antonio Gramsci 259

JUSTICE IS THE FIRST VIRTUE OF SOCIAL INSTITUTIONS

JOHN RAWLS (1921–2002)

IN CONTEXT

IDEOLOGY
Liberalism

FOCUS
Social justice

BEFORE
1762 Jean-Jacques Rousseau's treatise *Of The Social Contract* discusses the legitimacy of authority.

1935 American economist Frank Knight's essay *Economic Theory and Nationalism* lays the basis for Rawls's understanding of the deliberative procedure.

AFTER
1974 Robert Nozick publishes a critique of Rawls's *A Theory of Justice* under the title *Anarchy, State, and Utopia*.

1995 Gerald Cohen publishes a Marxist critique of Rawls.

2009 Amartya Sen publishes *The Idea of Justice*, which he dedicates to Rawls.

The key to a fair society is a **just social contract** between the state and individuals.

For a social contract to be just, the **needs of all individuals** party to it must be **treated equally**.

To ensure equal treatment, **social institutions must be just**: they must be accessible to all and redistribute where necessary.

Only **just institutions** can produce a **fair society**.

Justice is the first virtue of social institutions.

American philosopher John Rawls's life-long preoccupation with ideas to do with justice, fairness, and inequality were shaped by his experience of growing up in racially segregated Baltimore and in the US Army. Rawls was concerned with identifying a general framework of moral principles within which it is possible to make individual moral judgments. For Rawls, these general moral principles could only be justified and agreed upon through the use of commonly accepted procedures for reaching decisions. Such procedures are key to the process of democracy – Rawls thought that it was the process of debate and deliberation before an election, rather than the act of voting itself, that gives democracy its true worth.

The inequality of wealth

Rawls attempted to show that principles of justice cannot be based solely on an individual's moral framework. Rather, they are based on the way the individual's sense of morality is expressed and preserved in social institutions – such as the education system, the healthcare system, the tax collection system, and the electoral system. Rawls was particularly concerned with the process by which wealth inequalities translated into different levels of political influence, with the result that the structure of social and political institutions was inherently biased in favour of wealthy individuals and corporations.

Writing at the time of the Vietnam War, which he considered an unjust war, Rawls argued that civil disobedience needs to be

See also: John Locke 104–09 ▪ Jean-Jacques Rousseau 118–25 ▪ Immanuel Kant 126–29 ▪ John Stuart Mill 174–81 ▪ Karl Marx 188–93 ▪ Robert Nozick 326–27

Principles of justice must be based on more than just individual morality, according to Rawls. The entire framework of society must be taken into account when formulating a system of justice.

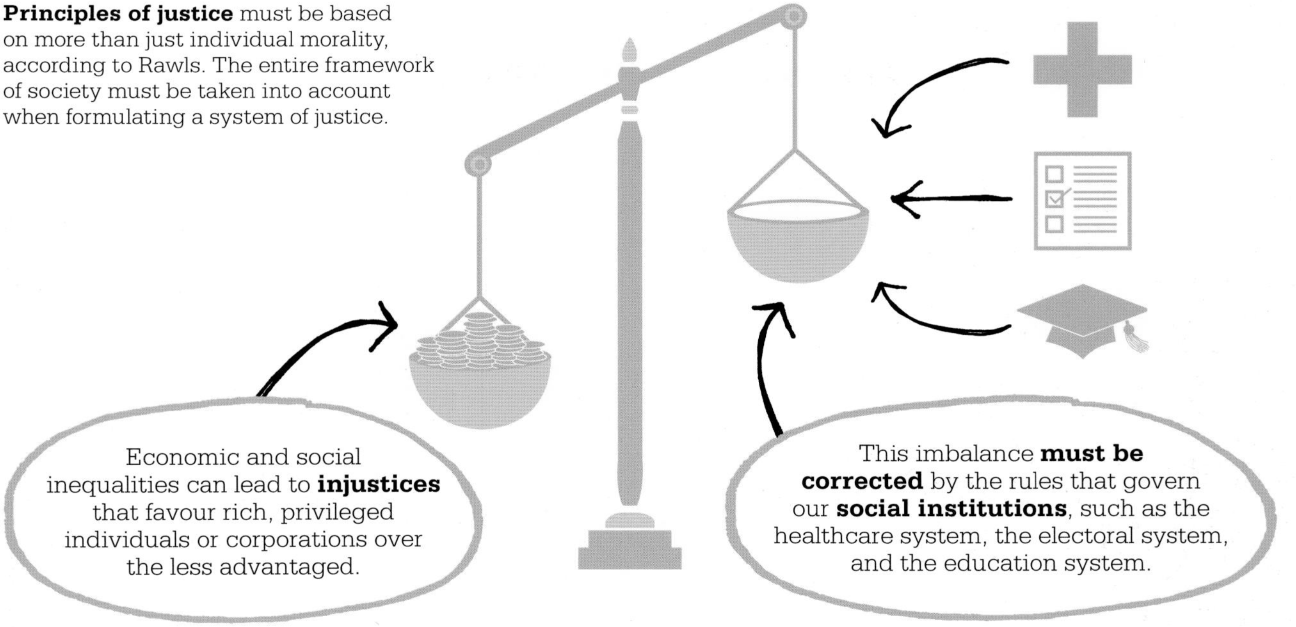

understood as the necessary action of a just minority appealing to the conscience of the majority. He argued against the US government's policies of conscription, which allowed wealthy students to dodge the draft while poorer students were often taken into the army because of one failed grade. The translation of economic inequalities into discriminatory institutions such as conscription was deeply troubling to him, particularly when those institutions were the very bodies that purported to implement or act on behalf of justice.

> In justice as fairness, the concept of right is prior to that of the good.
> **John Rawls**

Principles of justice

To Rawls, for justice to exist, it has to be considered "fair" according to certain principles of equality. In his theory of justice-as-fairness, Rawls develops two main principles of justice. The first is that everyone has an equal claim to basic liberties. The second is that "social and economic inequalities are to be arranged so that they are both reasonably expected to be to everyone's advantage, and attached to positions and offices open to all". The first principle – the principle of liberty – takes priority over the second principle – the principle of difference. He justifies this by arguing that, as economic conditions improve due to civilization's advancement, questions of liberty become more important. There are few, if any, instances where it is to an individual's or a group's advantage to accept a lesser liberty for the sake of greater material means.

Rawls identifies certain social and economic privileges as "threat advantages". He calls these "de facto political power, or wealth, or native endowments", and they allow certain people to take more than a just share, much as a school bully might take lunch money from other students by virtue of being bigger than them. Inequality – and the advantages based on this inequality – could not lie at the basis of any principle or theory of justice. Since inequalities are part of the reality of any society, Rawls concludes that "the arbitrariness » of the world must be corrected for by adjusting the circumstances of the initial contractual situation". By "contractual situation", he means a social contract between individuals – both with each other and with all the institutions of the state, even including the family. However, this social contract involves agreements between individuals on an unequal footing. Since the state has an equal responsibility towards each citizen, justice can only be secured if this inequality is corrected at its root.

For Rawls, social institutions are key to making this correction – by ensuring that all individuals have equal access to them, and by developing a redistribution mechanism that makes everyone better off. Rawls considers liberalism and liberal democracies to be the political systems best suited to ensuring that this redistribution is done fairly. He believed that communist systems focus too much on complete equality without considering whether that equality produces the most good for everyone. He thought that a capitalist system with strong social institutions is more likely to secure a fair system of justice. Where capitalism would produce unfair outcomes left on its own, social institutions imbued with a strong sense of justice can correct it.

Multicultural society

Rawls sees a further role for just institutions in binding society together. He believes that one of the most important lessons of modernity is that it is possible to live together under common rules without necessarily sharing a common moral code – as long as all individuals share a moral commitment to the structure of society. If people agree that the structure of society is fair, they will be satisfied, despite living among people who might possess significantly different moral codes. This, for Rawls, is the basis of pluralist, multicultural societies, and social institutions are key to ensuring fairness in such complex social systems.

The veil of ignorance

Rawls argues that, initially, the principles underpinning redistribution need to be decided behind what he calls "a veil of ignorance". He imagines a situation in which the structure of an ideal society is being decided, but none of those deciding on that structure knows what their place in the society will be. The "veil of ignorance" means that nobody knows the social position, personal doctrine, or intellectual or physical attributes they themselves will have. They might belong to any gender, sexual orientation, race, or class. In this way, the veil of ignorance ensures that everyone – independent of social position and individual characteristics – is granted justice: those deciding on their circumstances must, after all, be happy to put themselves in their position. Rawls assumed that, from behind the veil of ignorance, the social contract would necessarily be constructed to help the least well-off members of society, since everyone is ultimately afraid of becoming poor and will want to construct social institutions that protect against this.

Rawls accepts that differences in society are likely to persist, but argues that a fair principle of justice would offer the greatest benefit to the least advantaged members of society. Other scholars, including Indian theorist Amartya

> "Envy tends to make everyone worse off."
> **John Rawls**

For Rawls, equal access for all to institutions such as public libraries is essential for a fair society, allowing everyone the same life chances regardless of their place in society.

Sen and Canadian Marxist Gerald Cohen, have questioned Rawls's belief in the potential of a liberal capitalist regime to ensure these principles are adhered to. They also question the benefit of the "veil of ignorance" in modern societies, where inequalities are deeply embedded in social institutions. A veil of ignorance is only of value, many argue, if you are in the position of starting from scratch.

Criticisms of Rawls

Sen believes that Rawls makes a false distinction between political and economic rights. For Sen, inequalities and deprivation are largely a result of the absence of an entitlement to some goods, rather than the absence of the goods themselves. He uses the example of the Bengal famine of 1943, which was caused by a rise in food prices brought about by urbanization, rather than an actual lack of food. The goods – in this case food – do not represent an advantage in themselves. Instead, the advantage is defined by the relationship between people and goods – those who could afford food at the higher price versus those who could not. Sen further argues that the social contract in Rawls's definition is flawed, since it assumes that the contract only occurs at an interpersonal level. He argues that the social contract is instead negotiated through the interests of a number of groups not directly party to the contract, such as foreigners, future generations, and even nature itself.

Intrinsic inequality

Gerald Cohen questions the trust Rawls places in liberalism. Cohen argues that liberalism's obsession with self-interest maximization is not compatible with the egalitarian intentions of the redistributive state policy that Rawls argues for. He sees inequality as intrinsic to capitalism, and not simply a result of an unfair state-redistribution system. Capitalism and liberalism, for Cohen, can never provide the "fair" solution that Rawls was looking for.

Despite these criticisms, Rawls's *Theory of Justice* remains one of the most influential contemporary works of political theory, and is still the bestselling book published by Harvard University Press. His ideas have spurred a series of debates on the restructuring of the modern welfare system, both in the US and across the world. Many of his former students, including Sen, are at the core of these debates. In recognition of his contribution to social and political theory, Rawls was presented with the National Humanities Medal in 1999 by US President Bill Clinton, who stated that his work had helped to revive faith in democracy itself. ■

The Bengal famine was caused by unequal economic relations between people. Rawls's system, centred on political rather than economic structures, appears not to explain such disasters.

John Rawls

Rawls was born in Baltimore, USA, the son of prominent lawyer William Lee Rawls and Anna Abell Stump Rawls, president of the Baltimore League of Women Voters. His childhood was marked by the loss of his two brothers to contagious illnesses, which he had unknowingly passed on to them. A shy man with a stutter, Rawls studied philosophy at Princeton University. After completing his BA, he enlisted in the US Army and served in the Pacific, touring New Guinea, the Philippines, and occupied Japan. He then returned to Princeton, earning his PhD in 1950 with a thesis on moral principles for individual moral judgments. Rawls spent a year at the University of Oxford, UK, where he established close relations with legal philosopher H.L.A. Hart and political theorist Isaiah Berlin. Over a long career, Rawls trained many leading figures in political philosophy.

Key works

1971 *A Theory of Justice*
1999 *The Law of Peoples*
2001 *Justice as Fairness: A Restatement*

COLONIALISM IS VIOLENCE IN ITS NATURAL STATE

FRANTZ FANON (1925–1961)

IN CONTEXT

IDEOLOGY
Anti-colonialism

FOCUS
Decolonization

BEFORE
1813 Simón Bolívar is called "The Liberator" when Caracas in Venezuela is taken from the Spanish.

1947 Gandhi's non-violent protests eventually achieve independence for India from British rule.

1954 The Algerian War of Independence against French colonial rule begins.

AFTER
1964 At a meeting of the UN, Che Guevara argues that Latin America has yet to obtain true independence.

1965 Malcolm X speaks of obtaining rights for black people "by any means necessary".

By the middle of the 20th century, European colonialism was in fast decline. Exhausted by two world wars and challenged by the social changes that accompanied industrialization, the grip of many colonial powers on their territories had loosened.

Grassroots movements demanding independence emerged with growing speed in the post-war era. The UK's hold over Kenya was shaken by the growth of the Kenyan African National Union, while India secured independence in 1947 after a long struggle. In South Africa, the fight against colonial rule was entrenched in

See also: Simón Bolívar 162–63 ▪ Mahatma Gandhi 220–25 ▪ Manabendra Nath Roy 253 ▪ Jomo Kenyatta 258 ▪ Nelson Mandela 294–95 ▪ Paulo Freire 297 ▪ Malcolm X 308–09

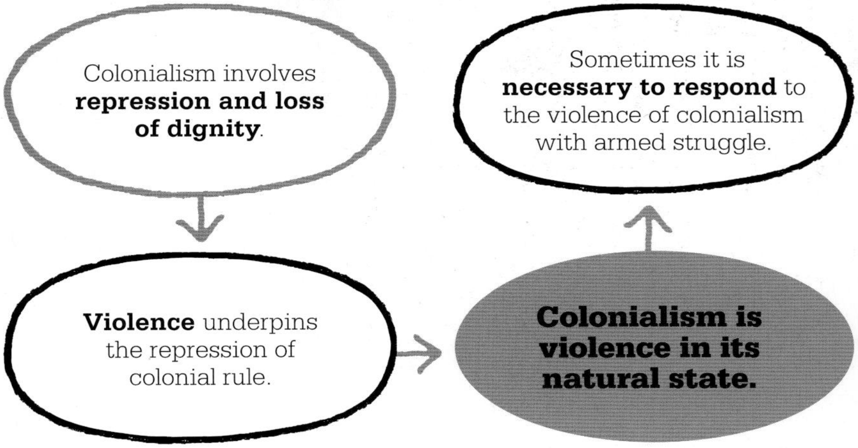

the far longer battle against apartheid oppression. Yet questions began to emerge about exactly what form post-colonial nations should take, and how best to deal with the legacy of violence and repression left behind by years of colonial rule.

Post-colonial thinking

Frantz Fanon was a French-Algerian thinker whose work deals with the effects of colonialism, and the response of oppressed peoples to the end of European rule. Drawing on the earlier perspectives of Marx and Hegel, Fanon takes an idiosyncratic approach to the analysis of racism and colonialism. His writing is concerned as much with language and culture as with politics, and frequently explores the relations between these different areas of enquiry, showing how language and culture are shaped by racism and other prejudices. Perhaps the most influential theorist of decolonization – the process of emancipation from colonial oppression – Fanon has had a major impact on anti-imperialist thinking, and his work inspires activists and politicians to this day.

Fanon examined the impact and legacy of colonialism. His view of colonialism was closely tied up with white domination, and linked with a strong egalitarianism, rejecting the human oppression and loss of dignity that colonial rule entails. In part, this reflects Fanon's role as a participant in the fight against oppression. In his book *A Dying Colonialism*, he puts forward an eyewitness view of the Algerian struggle for independence from French colonial rule, detailing the course of the armed conflict and the way it led to the emergence of an independent nation. The strategy and ideology of the armed anti-colonial struggle are presented in their entirety, and he carries out a detailed analysis of the tactics used by both sides.

> What matters is not to know the world but to change it.
> **Frantz Fanon**

The Algerian War raged from 1954–1962 as French colonial forces tried to quell the Algerian independence movement. Fanon became a passionate spokesman for the Algerian cause.

Framework of oppression

Fundamentally, however, Fanon's contribution was theoretical rather than practical, exposing the structures of oppression at work within colonial systems. He examined the hierarchies of ethnicity that provided the backbone of colonial oppression, showing how they ensure not only a strictly ordered system of privilege, but also an expression of difference that is cultural as well as political. In Algeria – and in other countries, such as Haiti – a post-colonial political order »

The Mau Mau uprising against colonial rule in Kenya was violently suppressed by British forces, causing divisions among the majority Kikuyu, some of whom fought for the British.

was created with the explicit intention of avoiding this kind of domination.

Fanon's vision of decolonization has an ambivalent relationship with violence. Famously, his work *The Wretched of the Earth* is introduced by Jean-Paul Sartre in a preface that emphasizes the position of violence in the struggle against colonialism. Sartre presents the piece as a call to arms, suggesting that the "mad impulse to murder" is an expression of the "collective unconsciousness" of the oppressed, brought about as a direct response to years of tyranny. As a result of this, it would be easy to read Fanon's work as a clarion call to armed revolution.

Colonial racism

However, concentrating on the revolutionary aspect of Fanon's work does a disservice to the complexity of his thought. For him, the violence of colonialism lay on the part of the oppressors.

> The settler keeps alive in the native an anger which he deprives of an outlet; the native is trapped in the tight links of colonialism.
> **Frantz Fanon**

Colonialism was indeed violence in its natural state, but a violence that manifested itself in a number of different ways. It might be expressed in brute force, but also within the stereotypes and social divisions associated with the racist worldview that Fanon identified as defining colonial life. The dominance of white culture under colonial rule meant that any forms of identity other than those of white Europeans were viewed negatively. Divisions existed between colonizers and the people they ruled on the basis of the presumed inferiority of their culture.

Fanon believed that violence was part and parcel of colonial rule, and his work is a damning indictment of the violence meted out by colonial powers. He argues that the legitimacy of colonial oppression is supported only by military might, and this violence – as its solitary foundation – is focused on the colonized as a means of ensuring their acquiescence. Oppressed peoples face a stark choice between accepting a life of subjugation and confronting such persecution.

Any response to colonialism needed to be developed in opposition to the assumptions of colonial rule, but also independently of it, in order to shape new identities and values that were not defined by Europe. Armed struggle and violent revolution might be necessary, but it would be doomed to failure unless a genuine decolonization could take place.

Towards decolonization

The Wretched of the Earth remains Fanon's most significant publication, and provides a theoretical framework for the emergence of individuals and nations from the indignity of colonial rule. Exploring in depth the assumptions of cultural superiority identified elsewhere in his work, Fanon develops an understanding of white cultural oppression through a forensic analysis of the way it functioned: forcing the white minority's values onto the whole of society. Nevertheless, he prescribes an inclusive approach to the difficult process of decolonization. Fanon's ideas are based on the dignity and value of all people, irrespective of their race or

> I am not the slave of the slavery that dehumanized my ancestors.
> **Frantz Fanon**

background. He stresses that all races and classes can potentially be involved in – and benefit from – decolonization. Moreover, for Fanon, any attempt at reform based on negotiations between a privileged elite leading the decolonization process and colonial rulers would simply reproduce the injustices of the previous regime. Such an attempt would be rooted in assumptions of privilege and, more significantly, would fail, because there is a tendency of oppressed peoples to mimic the behaviour and attitudes of the ruling elites. This phenomenon is particularly prevalent in the middle and upper classes, who are able – through their education and relative wealth – to present themselves as culturally similar to the colonialists.

By contrast, a genuine transition from colonialism would involve the masses, and represent a sustained move towards the creation of a national identity. A successful decolonization movement would develop a national consciousness, generating new approaches to art and literature in order to articulate a culture that was simultaneously in resistance to, and separate from, the tyranny of colonial power.

Fanon's influence

These ideas about the violence of colonialism, and the importance of identity in shaping the future political and social direction of a nation, have had a direct impact on the way activists and revolutionary leaders treat the struggle against colonial power – *The Wretched of the Earth* is, in essence, a blueprint for armed revolution. Beyond this, Fanon's role in shaping the understanding of colonialism's workings and effects has left a lasting legacy. His insightful perspectives on the racist underpinnings of colonialism, and, in particular, his theories concerning the conditions for a successful decolonization, have been hugely influential in the study of poverty and the phenomenon of globalization. ■

12 Pages 12 Pages

Le Petit Journal

HEBDOMADAIRE
61, rue Lafayette, Paris

illustré

PRIX : 0 fr. 30
9 Décembre 1923

La Voix Mystérieuse

Les concerts par T. S. F. ne ravissent pas seulement les mélomanes de France. Les ondes sonores s'étendent maintenant au delà des mers et des saharas. C'est vraiment une musique céleste que les nègres du Centre-Africain écoutent avec un effarement presque comique, sous le regard amusé des Européens.

In France, colonizers were portrayed as civilized Europeans bringing order to savage natives. Such racist attitudes were used to justify the use of oppression and violence.

Frantz Fanon

Frantz Fanon was born in Martinique in 1925 to a comfortably well-off family. After fighting for the Free French Army during World War II he studied medicine and psychiatry in Lyon. Here he encountered the racist attitudes that were to inspire much of his early work.

On completing his studies, he moved to Algeria to work as a psychiatrist, and became a leading activist and spokesman for the revolution. He trained nurses for the National Liberation Front, and published his accounts of the revolution in sympathetic journals. Fanon worked to support the rebels until he was expelled from the country. He was appointed ambassador to Ghana by the provisional government towards the end of the struggle, but fell ill soon afterwards. Fanon died of leukaemia in 1961 at the age of just 35, managing to complete *The Wretched of the Earth* shortly before his death.

Key works

1952 *Black Skin, White Masks*
1959 *A Dying Colonialism*
1961 *The Wretched of the Earth*

THE BALLOT OR THE BULLET

MALCOLM X (1925–1965)

IN CONTEXT

IDEOLOGY
Civil rights and equality

FOCUS
Self-determination

BEFORE
1947 The British are forced to leave India as a result of Mahatma Gandhi's campaign for independence.

1955 Black American Rosa Parks refuses to give up her seat in the "white section" of a bus, sparking Martin Luther King to organize direct action.

AFTER
1965 The assassination of Malcolm X leads to the formation of the Black Panther Party for Self-Defense, a militant black power movement.

1965 The Voting Rights Act is passed in the USA, restoring equal voting rights to all US citizens and overturning an earlier law that required citizens to pass a literacy test.

Black Americans should **participate in elections**.

↓

Black voters should only vote for candidates who promise to **stand up for their rights**.

↓

However, politicians often **renege on promises** made during elections when they assume office.

↓

If politicians **do not deliver** the equality they promise in elections, black Americans should **turn to violence** to achieve their aims.

↓

The ballot or the bullet.

The civil rights movement in post-war America was a focal point for the long-running struggle to establish social and political equality across society. The means by which this should be achieved, however, was far from certain. Civil rights leaders such as Martin Luther King took inspiration from the non-violent protest of Mahatma Gandhi in India, and built a similar movement that began to gain sympathy from all areas of society. However, the slow pace of change and the continued oppression of black people in America led many to contest this approach.

Malcolm X was one of the leading figures in the Nation of Islam, an organization that advocated ideas of racial separatism and black nationalism. In this capacity, he articulated a view of the civil rights struggle that was very different from the mainstream represented by King. Rather than concentrate on non-violence, Malcolm believed the struggle for equality was closely bound up with people's ability to determine their lives for themselves, and therefore any attempt to restrict those rights should be met with direct action and, if necessary, force.

See also: José Martí 204–05 ▪ Emmeline Pankhurst 207 ▪ Emiliano Zapata 246 ▪ Marcus Garvey 252 ▪ Mao Zedong 260–65 ▪ Nelson Mandela 294–95 ▪ Che Guevara 312–13 ▪ Martin Luther King 316–21

> We want freedom by any means necessary. We want justice by any means necessary. We want equality by any means necessary.
> **Malcolm X**

The Nation of Islam forbade its members from taking part in the political process, but when Malcolm left the Nation in 1964 to start his own organization, he advocated political participation and demanded equal voting rights. He envisaged the development of a black voting bloc, which could be used to demand genuine change at election time and direct the actions of white politicians to ensure greater social and political equality. Despite this, Malcolm remained sceptical about the likelihood that the extension of voting rights would promote real change in America. In particular, he was concerned about the disparity between the words of politicians during election campaigns and their actions once in government.

The year of action

In 1964, Malcolm delivered a speech in Detroit that contained a stern warning to politicians: if formal politics did not adequately recognize black people's needs, they would be forced to take matters into their own hands, and violence would follow. "The young generation," he said, "are dissatisfied, and in their frustrations they want action." They were no longer ready to accept second-class status, and didn't care whether the odds were against them. He said that black Americans had "listened to the trickery, and the lies, and the false promises of the white man now for too long." Unless the political system became genuinely more responsive to the demands of black voters, there would be little alternative but to use not votes but guns; not the ballot, but a bullet.

African-Americans carry a coffin and a "Here Lies Jim Crow" sign down a street to demonstrate against the "Jim Crow" segregation laws of 1944, which legitimized anti-black racism.

Despite his high profile at the time, Malcolm X left few written words. However, his ideas continue to shape the civil rights agenda, with their focus on empowerment and reconnecting black Americans with their African heritage. ■

Malcolm X

Malcolm X was born Malcolm Little in Omaha, Nebraska in 1925. In the early part of his life, he experienced racism directed at his family, and in particular his father, a Baptist lay-preacher. His father's death in 1931 precipitated the break up of the family. Malcolm's mother was committed to a mental institution and he was taken into foster care. He fell into petty crime and was imprisoned for burglary in 1946.

During his imprisonment, Malcolm experienced a religious and social awakening, converting to Islam and becoming involved with the Nation of Islam (NOI). On his release, he took the name Malcolm X and rose to become one of the public faces of black nationalism in America. In 1964, he left the NOI and became a Sunni Muslim, completing his Hajj to Mecca and speaking publicly in Africa, Europe, and the US. In 1965 he was assassinated by three members of the Nation of Islam.

Key work

1964 *The Autobiography of Malcolm X* (with Alex Haley)

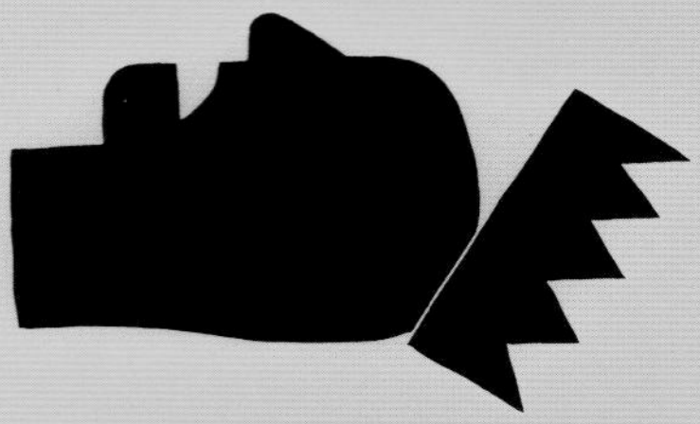

WE NEED TO "CUT OFF THE KING'S HEAD"

MICHEL FOUCAULT (1926–1984)

IN CONTEXT

IDEOLOGY
Structuralism

FOCUS
Power

BEFORE

1532 Machiavelli publishes *The Prince*, which analyses the cynical use of power by individuals and the state.

1651 Thomas Hobbes completes his magnum opus, *Leviathan*, a comment on the role of the sovereign and man's corrupt state of nature.

AFTER

1990s Green theorists use Foucault's ideas to explain how ecological policies can be developed by governments alongside experts.

2009 Australian academic Elaine Jeffreys uses Foucault's theories to analyse power structures in China, emphasizing the rational nature of Chinese society.

Political thought has long been concerned with how best to define and locate the source of power in society. Many of the most significant political works have imagined a powerful state as the centre of legitimate political authority. Machiavelli, in *The Prince*, viewed the crude expression of power as justified in the interests of government. Hobbes, in *Leviathan*, saw a powerful monarch as the antidote to the corrupt spirit of mankind. These and other thinkers set the template for much modern political scholarship, and the analysis of state power has remained the dominant form of political analysis.

For French philosopher Michel Foucault, power – rather than being centred on the state – was diffused across a great many "micro-sites" throughout society. Foucault criticized mainstream political philosophy for its reliance on notions of formal authority, and its insistence on analysing an entity called "the state". For Foucault, the state was simply the expression of the structures and configuration of power in society, rather than a single entity that exerts dominance over individuals. This view of the state as a "practice" rather than a "thing in itself" meant that a true understanding of the structure and distribution of power in society could only be reached through a broader analysis.

Foucault's analysis concerned the nature of sovereignty. He wanted to get away from what he considered to be a mistaken idea – that political theory should involve understanding the power wielded by an individual sovereign, who passes laws and punishes those who break them. Foucault believed that the nature of government changed between

> Power is not an institution, and not a structure; neither is it a certain strength we are endowed with.
> **Michel Foucault**

See also: Niccolò Machiavelli 74–81 ▪ Karl Marx 188–93 ▪ Paulo Freire 297 ▪ Noam Chomsky 314–15

The **nature** of society has **changed**.

→ **Power** no longer resides only **within the state** or with one single **authority figure**.

→ Power also exists in **"micro-sites"** across society, such as schools, workplaces, and families.

→ The power of the state can **no longer be separated** from power in society.

→ **To understand the workings of power, we need to "cut off the King's head" in political theory.**

the 16th century – when the problems of politics related to how a sovereign monarch could obtain and maintain power – and the present day, when the power of the state cannot be disconnected from any other form of power in society. He suggested that political theorists needed to "cut off the King's head" and develop an approach to understanding power that reflected this change.

Governmentality

Foucault developed these thoughts in lectures at the Collège de France in Paris, where he proposed the concept of "governmentality". This approach viewed government as an art involving a range of techniques of control and discipline. These might take place in a variety of contexts, such as within the family, at school, or in the workplace. By broadening his understanding of power away from the hierarchical structures of sovereignty, Foucault highlighted different kinds of power in society, such as knowledge and the collection of statistics. He elaborated on this analysis of power in many of his works, looking at areas such as language, punishment, and sexuality. ■

The school classroom is a "micro-site" of political power, according to Foucault. Micro-sites exercise this power within society, away from the traditional structures of government.

Michel Foucault

Foucault was born in Poitiers, France, to a wealthy family. Academically gifted, he soon established a reputation as a philosopher. In 1969, he became the first Head of the Philosophy Department at the newly created University of Paris VIII, itself created in response to the 1968 student unrest in France. He gained notoriety by embracing student activism, even engaging in running battles with police. In 1970, he was elected to the prestigious Collège de France as professor of the History of Systems of Thought, a position he held until his death.

Foucault engaged in activism in his later career, which was spent mainly in the US. He published widely throughout his life, and became a major figure in a variety of fields across philosophy and the social sciences. He died of an AIDS-related illness in 1984.

Key works

1963 *The Birth of the Clinic*
1969 *The Archaeology of Knowledge*
1975 *Discipline and Punish*
1976–1984 *The History of Sexuality*

LIBERATORS DO NOT EXIST. THE PEOPLE LIBERATE THEMSELVES

CHE GUEVARA (1928–1967)

IN CONTEXT

IDEOLOGY
Revolutionary socialism

FOCUS
Guerrilla warfare

BEFORE
1762 Jean-Jacques Rousseau opens *The Social Contract* with: "Man is born free, yet everywhere he is in chains".

1848 Political theorists Karl Marx and Friedrich Engels publish the *Communist Manifesto*.

1917 Revolutions in Russia depose the tsar and his family and establish a communist Bolshevik government.

AFTER
1967 French political philosopher Régis Debray formalizes the tactics of guerrilla warfare as "focalism".

1979 The Somoza dictatorship in Nicaragua is overthrown through the use of guerrilla warfare tactics.

Because of his participation in revolutions in Cuba, Congo-Kinshasa, and Bolivia, Guevara is popularly seen as a "man of action" rather than a political theorist, but his adoption of guerrilla tactics was a major contribution to the development of revolutionary socialism. Having seen first-hand the oppression and poverty throughout South America under dictatorships backed by the US, he believed the salvation of the continent could only come about through anti-capitalist revolution, as advocated by Karl Marx.

However, Guevara's practical interpretation of revolution was more political and militant than Marx's economic analysis, which was intended to be used against the capitalist states of Europe. The tyrannical regimes of South America made European states seem relatively benign, and Guevara realized that the only

The forces of the people can put in place the conditions that make **revolution** possible.

Militant groups always have an advantage when in a **rural setting**.

Guerrilla groups launching attacks from rural areas can mobilize unrest to create a **popular front** against a regime.

Liberators do not exist. The people liberate themselves.

See also: Karl Marx 188–93 ▪ Vladimir Lenin 226–33 ▪ Leon Trotsky 242–45 ▪ Antonio Gramsci 259 ▪ Mao Zedong 260–65 ▪ Fidel Castro 339

An army of the people led the Cuban Revolution to victory over the state military. The tenets of guerrilla warfare outlined by Guevara were key to the revolution's success.

way to achieve their overthrow was through armed struggle. Rather than waiting for the arrival of conditions that would allow for a successful revolution, Guevara believed that these conditions could be created through a strategy of guerrilla warfare, which would inspire the people to rebellion.

Power to the people

In his *Reminiscences of the Cuban Revolutionary War* and *Guerrilla Warfare*, Guevara explains how the success of the 1956 Cuban Revolution was dependent on the mobilization of a popular front. Rather than seeing the revolution in terms of a liberator bringing freedom to the people, he saw it as a grass-roots movement to topple an oppressive regime, with the people liberating themselves. The starting point for this kind of revolution, he believed, was not in industrialized towns and cities, but in rural areas where small groups of armed rebels could have maximum effect against a regime's forces. This insurrection would then provide a focus for discontent, and support for the rebellion would develop into a popular front, providing the impetus necessary for a full-scale revolution.

After his success in Cuba, Guevara expressed his support for the armed struggles in China, Vietnam, and Algeria, and later fought in the unsuccessful revolutions in Congo-Kinshasa and Bolivia. Guevara's guerrilla warfare was key to his *foco* ("focus") theory of revolution, and his ideas later inspired many other movements to adopt the tactics, including South Africa's ANC in their fight against apartheid, and Islamist movements such as the Taliban in Afghanistan.

Guevara was also recognized as an able statesman. While a minister in the Cuban socialist government, he helped establish Cuba as a leading player among international socialist states, and instituted policies in industry, education, and finance that he believed would continue the liberation of the Cuban people by eradicating the egotism and greed associated with capitalist society. He left a legacy of writings, including his personal diaries, that continue to influence socialist thinking today. ▪

> If you tremble with indignation at every injustice, then you are a comrade of mine.
> **Che Guevara**

Che Guevara

Ernesto Guevara, better known by the nickname Che ("friend"), was born in Rosario, Argentina. He studied medicine at the University of Buenos Aires, but took time out to make two motorcycle journeys around Latin America. The poverty, disease, and appalling working conditions he saw on his travels helped to consolidate his political views.

After graduating in 1953, Guevara made a further trip across Latin America, when he witnessed the overthrow of the democratic Guatemalan government by US-backed forces. In Mexico in 1954, he was introduced to Fidel Castro, with whom he led the rebels during the successful Cuban Revolution. In 1965, he left Cuba to aid guerrillas in Congo-Kinshasa, and the next year he fought in Bolivia. He was captured by CIA-backed troops on 8 October 1967 and, against the wishes of the US government, was executed the next day.

Key works

1952 *The Motorcycle Diaries*
1961 *Guerrilla Warfare*
1963 *Reminiscences of the Cuban Revolutionary War*

EVERYBODY HAS TO MAKE SURE THAT THE RICH FOLK ARE HAPPY

NOAM CHOMSKY (1928–)

IN CONTEXT

IDEOLOGY
Libertarian socialism

FOCUS
Power and control

BEFORE

1850s Karl Marx argues that one societal class holds complete political and economic power.

1920s German sociologist Max Weber claims that bureaucrats form elites that manage societies.

1956 In *The Power Elite*, US sociologist Charles W. Mills claims that important policies come from big business, the military, and a few politicians.

AFTER

1985 Czech playwright Václav Havel publishes his essay "The Power of the Powerless".

1986 British sociologist Michael Mann claims that societies are made up of overlapping power networks.

Dominant institutions in society, such as the media and banks, are controlled by a **wealthy minority**.

↓

This minority runs the institutions in a way that **favours its interests**.

↓

Any **attempts at reform** lead to a drying up of investment, which **ruins the economy**.

↓

To keep the economy healthy, everyone, even the poor, must **support** a system that is run in the **interests of the rich**.

↓

Everybody has to make sure that the rich folk are happy.

One question that continues to fascinate political thinkers and politicians is: where is power concentrated in society? Many different types of people and social institutions are involved in shaping human progress and organization, and over time a dense network of power relations has established itself across the globe. However, does this mean that power is diffused throughout society, or has it instead become concentrated in the hands of a few privileged individuals who make up an elite?

US linguist and political philosopher Noam Chomsky's view is that in most countries a wealthy minority controls the key social and political institutions, such as the mass media and the financial system, ensuring that the functioning of modern society favours a powerful elite. In turn, this means that dissent and meaningful change are nearly impossible, as the dominant institutional structures in society – from newspapers to banks – focus on maintaining their positions to their mutual benefit. Not only are social elites advantaged by their wealth and position, but they are

See also: Plato 34–39 ▪ Karl Marx 188–93 ▪ Friedrich Hayek 270–75 ▪ Paulo Freire 297 ▪ Michel Foucault 310–11

> Power is increasingly concentrated in unaccountable institutions.
> **Noam Chomsky**

also at the pinnacle of a society that is structured to favour them still further.

Any attempt at widespread reform would, in Chomsky's view, result in one of two outcomes: a military coup, which would restore power to the hands of private individuals; or (more likely) the drying up of investment capital, which would have serious consequences for the economy. The latter outcome ensures that all members of society, no matter how humble, have a stake in supporting the privileged position of the very wealthy. Everybody has to make sure that the rich folk are happy, to ensure the health of the economy.

Keeping profits up

This concentration of power is structural, rather than a conspiracy carried out by a small number of individuals. The economic interests of large corporations, the government, and investors ensure that public decisions are made by groups whose interdependence means that radical change is not possible. Instead, a mutually supporting network of institutions work to ensure the maintenance of a stable economic system, which is said to be beneficial to all. However, Chomsky notes that many of the "benefits" of this system are "good for profits, not for people, which means that it's good for the economy in the technical sense". Chomsky also considers the wealthiest countries of the world to be elites that threaten the security and resources of smaller, less-developed nations. However, he points out that while the principles of imperial domination have changed little, the capacity to implement them has declined as power becomes more broadly distributed in a diversifying world. ■

Large banks such as France's Societe Generale display their wealth in their expensive head offices. According to Chomsky, the whole of society is run to keep such rich organizations happy.

Noam Chomsky

Avram Noam Chomsky was born in Philadelphia, USA. After graduate study at the University of Pennsylvania, and a period as a Junior Fellow at Harvard University, he began work at MIT, where he has remained for more than 50 years. During this time he has forged a career that has been notable both for its significant contribution in the field of linguistics, and a willingness to engage with questions of broad political significance. Chomsky published an article criticizing fascism at the age of 12, and has been a political activist ever since, concerning himself particularly with questions of power and the global influence of the USA. Often controversial, his work has had a significant influence in a wide range of fields, and he has won many prestigious awards. He has authored over 100 books and has lectured widely around the world.

Key works

1978 *Human Rights and American Foreign Policy*
1988 *Manufacturing Consent*
1992 *Deterring Democracy*

NOTHING IN THE WORLD IS MORE DANGEROUS THAN SINCERE IGNORANCE

MARTIN LUTHER KING (1929–1968)

IN CONTEXT

IDEOLOGY
Social justice

APPROACH
Civil disobedience

BEFORE
1876–1965 The Jim Crow laws are implemented, legalizing a series of discriminatory practices in the southern states of the US.

1954 Brown versus Board of Education, a case adjudicated by the US Supreme Court, mandates the desegregation of public schools on the grounds that segregation is unconstitutional.

AFTER
1964–68 In the US, a series of laws are passed banning discriminatory practices and restoring voting rights.

1973 US ground forces are withdrawn from Vietnam, amid waves of anti-war protest on the home front.

By the 1960s, the battle for civil rights in the United States was reaching its final stages. Since the reconstruction following the Civil War a century earlier, the southern states of the US had been pursuing a policy of disenfranchisement and segregation of black Americans, through overt, legal means. This was codified in the so-called "Jim Crow" laws – a set of local and regional statutes that effectively stripped the black population of many basic rights. The struggle to win civil rights for black people had been ongoing since the end of the Civil War, but in the mid-1950s, it had developed into a broad movement based on mass protest and civil disobedience.

Struggle against ignorance

At the forefront of the movement was Dr Martin Luther King, a civil rights activist who worked with the National Association for the Advancement of Colored People (NAACP). Inspired by the success of civil rights leaders elsewhere, and in particular by the non-violent protests against British rule in India led by Mahatma Gandhi, King became perhaps the most significant figure to emerge from the struggle. In 1957, with other religious leaders, King had established the Southern Christian Leadership Conference (SCLC), a coalition of black churches that broadened the reach of the organizations involved in the movement. For the first time, this had generated momentum on a national scale.

Like many others in the civil rights movement, King characterized the struggle as one of enlightenment against ignorance. The long-standing beliefs of racial

> Freedom is never voluntarily given by the oppressor; it must be demanded by the oppressed.
> **Martin Luther King**

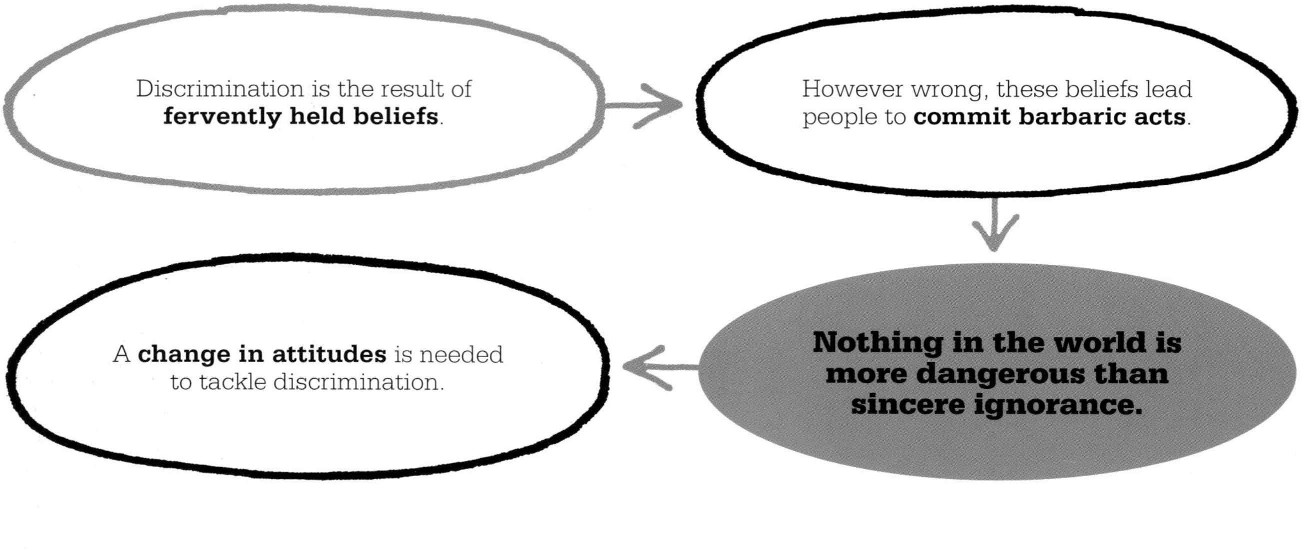

See also: Henry David Thoreau 186–87 ▪ Mahatma Gandhi 220–25 ▪ Nelson Mandela 294–95 ▪ Frantz Fanon 304–07 ▪ Malcolm X 308–09

superiority and entitlement that dominated the government of the southern states of the US had given rise to a political system that excluded black people and many other minorities. King felt that this position was fervently believed in by those in power, and that this "sincere ignorance" was at the root of the problems of inequality. Therefore, any attempt to deal with the problem solely through political means would be doomed to failure. Direct action would be needed to reform politics and win equality of participation and access in democratic life. At the same time, the movement for civil rights would also have to tackle the underlying attitudes of the majority towards minorities in order to achieve lasting change.

Non-violent protest

In contrast to other leaders within the civil rights movement, such as Malcolm X and Stokely Carmichael, King was committed to non-violence as one of the fundamental principles of the struggle for equality. The utmost moral strength was required to adhere to non-violence in the face of extreme provocation, but Gandhi had shown what was possible. Gandhi believed that the moral purpose of the protesters would be eroded, and public sympathy lost, if resistance became violent. As a result, King took great pains to ensure that his involvement in the civil rights movement did not promote violence, going so far as to cancel speeches and protests when he felt that they might result in violent action on the part of the activists. At the same time, King pursued a fearless confrontation of intimidation and violence when it was visited on civil rights activists. He frequently led demonstrations from the front, was injured more than once, and was jailed on numerous occasions. Images of the brutality of the police towards civil rights activists became one of the most effective means of garnering nationwide support for the cause.

King's adherence to non-violence also inspired his opposition to the Vietnam War. In 1967, he delivered his celebrated "Beyond Vietnam" speech, which spoke out against the ethics of conflict in Vietnam, branding it as American adventurism, and taking issue with the resources lavished upon the military. In part, King felt that the war was morally corrupt as it consumed vast amounts of the federal budget, which could otherwise be spent on relieving the problems of poverty. Instead, as he saw it, the war was in fact compounding the suffering of poor people in Vietnam.

The difference of opinion between those advocating non-violence and those prepared to use violence in the struggle for civil rights is a major area of debate in »

> Nonviolence means avoiding not only external physical violence but also internal violence of spirit. You not only refuse to shoot a man, but you refuse to hate him.
> **Martin Luther King**

Nine black students challenged the segregation at Little Rock's whites-only Central High School in 1957. They were refused entry, and federal troops were sent in to ensure their safety.

Non-violent civil disobedience took many forms during the fight for civil rights, such as refusing to sit in the "colored" section at the back of public buses.

the discussion of civil disobedience to this day. In his "Letter from Birmingham Jail", King articulated his strategy for confronting the ignorance of racism in the US, stating that "non-violent direct action seeks to create such a crisis and foster such a tension that a community, which has constantly refused to negotiate, is forced to confront the issue". However, critics within the movement felt that the pace of change was too slow, and that there was a moral imperative to respond to violence and intimidation in kind.

Against all inequality

King's vision for the civil rights movement developed as the 1960s progressed, and he broadened his focus to include inequality more generally, proposing to tackle economic, as well as racial, injustice. In 1968, he began the "Poor People's Campaign", focusing on income, housing, and poverty, and demanding that the federal government invest heavily in dealing with the problems of poverty. Specifically, the campaign promoted a minimum income guarantee, an expansion in social housing, and a commitment on the part of the state to full employment. The campaign was intended from the outset to unite all racial groups, focusing on the common problems of poverty and hardship. However, King died before it began and, despite a widely publicized march and series of protests, the movement did not match the success of the campaigns for civil rights.

The link between racism and poverty had long been a theme of the civil rights movement, and formed a part of much of the activism in which King was involved. The 1963 "March on Washington for Jobs and Freedom" had the fight against racism at its core, but also demanded the extension of economic rights.

> Discrimination is a hellhound that gnaws at Negroes in every waking moment of their lives to remind them that the lie of their inferiority is accepted as truth.
> **Martin Luther King**

King's stand against the Vietnam War had explicitly criticized US involvement in the conflict as distracting attention and financial support from the battle against poverty. Beyond these specific campaigns, a commitment to an extension of social welfare was a consistent theme throughout much of the activism King had pursued with the SCLC.

King believed that solving the problems of poverty meant tackling another facet of the ignorance he had identified in the fight for racial equality. In his final book, *Where Do We Go From Here: Chaos or Community?*, he argued for the need for change in attitudes towards poor people. Part of the problem of poverty, he felt, lay in stereotyping the poor as idle. He suggested that prevailing attitudes had meant that "economic status was considered the measure of the individual's abilities and talents" and that "the absence of worldly goods indicated a want of industrious habits and moral fibre". In order to tackle poverty, this underlying attitude needed to be challenged.

King's legacy

King remains one of the most influential civil rights leaders of the modern era. His oratory is timeless and has passed into the modern vernacular, and his work has inspired the activists who followed him in the US and worldwide. Perhaps the most concrete measure of his influence, however, is in the reform of civil rights that occurred as a result of the movement he helped to lead. The Voting Rights Act introduced in 1965 and the Civil Rights Act of 1968 signalled the end of the Jim Crow laws, and removed overt discrimination from the southern states. The last great injustice he tackled, however – the problem of poverty – remains unsolved. ■

> When an individual is protesting society's refusal to acknowledge his dignity as a human being, his very act of protest confers dignity on him.
> **Bayard Rustin**

King knew he was a target for assassination, but this did not stop him from leading the civil rights movement from the front. The Civil Rights Act was passed just days after his death.

Martin Luther King

Born in Atlanta, Georgia, Martin Luther King Jr was educated at Boston University. By 1954, he had become a pastor and a senior figure within the National Association for the Advancement of Colored People (NAACP). In this capacity, he became a leader in the civil rights movement, organizing protests across the south, including the 1955 boycott of the Montgomery bus system. In 1963, he was arrested during a protest in Birmingham, Alabama, and jailed for more than two weeks.

On his release, King led the March on Washington and delivered his iconic "I have a Dream" speech. He was awarded the Nobel Peace Prize in 1964 and led the popular pressure for the repeal of the Jim Crow laws. King was assassinated in Memphis, Tennessee, in March 1968, while on a visit in support of striking sanitation workers.

Key works

1963 *Why We Can't Wait*
1963 *Letter from Birmingham Jail*
1967 *Where Do We Go From Here: Chaos or Community?*

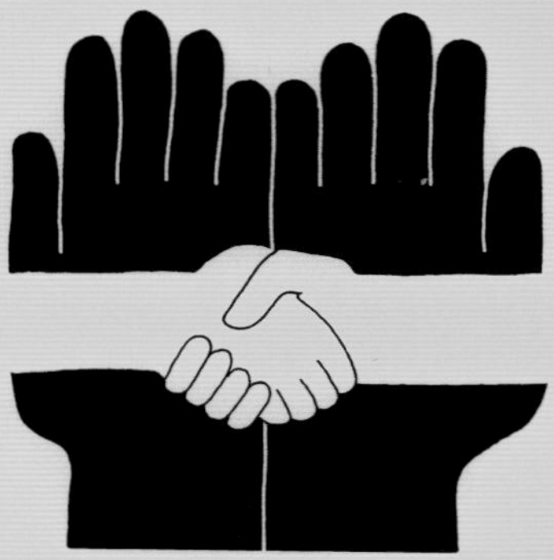

PERESTROIKA UNITES SOCIALISM WITH DEMOCRACY

MIKHAIL GORBACHEV (1931–)

IN CONTEXT

IDEOLOGY
Leninism

FOCUS
Perestroika

BEFORE
1909 Lenin publishes *Materialism and Empiriocriticism*, which becomes an obligatory subject in all institutions of higher education in the Soviet Union.

1941 Stalin becomes the premier of the Soviet Union, ruling with a strong hand.

AFTER
1991 The USSR is officially dissolved, dividing up into 15 independent sovereign states. This marks the end of the Cold War.

1991–1999 Boris Yeltsin becomes the first president of the Russian Federation and begins to transform the country's centralized economy into a market economy.

Mikhail Gorbachev, Secretary General of the Communist Party of the Soviet Union, planned reforms designed to boost the stalled Russian economy of the 1980s. Gorbachev argued that this stagnation was a result of an unfair distribution of social wealth, inflexible structures that stopped the masses from using their full creativity, and the overbearing authority of the state.

His programme comprised two main components. *Perestroika* (restructuring) involved a rethinking of the principles of democratic centralism, a shift to scientific methods, and the equal implementation of universal principles of social justice. *Glasnost* (openness) meant increased transparency in social and political spheres, and freedom of speech.

Gorbachev stated that such democratization did not signal an abandonment of socialism. The true spirit of Lenin, he claimed, did not see socialism as a rigid theoretical scheme, but rather as a constantly changing process. Gorbachev argued that socialism and democracy were in fact indivisible, although his understanding of democracy refers only to the freedom of the working masses to rise to power.

Unfortunately, Gorbachev's economic reforms resulted in a deep economic downturn, and his social reforms precipitated the break-up of the Soviet state. ■

Gorbachev's democratic agenda included a determination to negotiate an end to the Cold War with US president Ronald Reagan.

See also: Karl Marx 188–93 ▪ Vladimir Lenin 226–33 ▪ Leon Trotsky 242–45 ▪ Antonio Gramsci 259 ▪ Mao Zedong 260–65

THE INTELLECTUALS ERRONEOUSLY FOUGHT ISLAM

ALI SHARIATI (1933–1977)

IN CONTEXT

IDEOLOGY
Islamism

FOCUS
Islamic independence

BEFORE
1941 Soviet and British forces invade Iran to secure access to oil.

1962 Jalal Al-e-Ahmad publishes his book *Occidentosis: A Plague from the West* – a critique of Western civilization.

AFTER
1978 The Iranian Revolution brings Ayatollah Ruhollah Khomeini to power.

1980 Encouraged by Western powers, Iraq invades Iran, starting an eight-year war and causing devastation on both sides.

2005 Mahmoud Ahmadinejad becomes president of Iran, taking a religious hard line and reversing previous reforms.

Influenced by Islamic puritanism, as well as Marxism and post-colonial thinkers, Iranian philosopher Ali Shariati advocated Islamic thought and beliefs as pillars of Islamic society, while promoting independence from Western domination.

Shariati sought to defend Islam from misconceptions. For him, these misunderstandings were largely the result of an unhealthy divide between the educated class and the masses in Iran. He distinguishes between intellectuals and enlightened people. The latter, he argues, do not require a university degree, but rather an awareness of traditions, religion, and the needs of the people.

Anti-intellectual

In their attempt to apply European models of development and modernity to Iran, intellectuals fail to recognize that conditions in Iran are different from those in Europe. Intellectuals fail to acknowledge the Islamic spirit that dominates and sustains Iranian culture, and often blame religion for a failure to acknowledge material concerns. The emancipation of Iran is only possible by recognizing the country's Islamic roots and the creation of an egalitarian social system that adheres to religious norms. While the masses may need more self-awareness, intellectuals need more "faith". Shariati's views were not a rejection of modernity – to him, Islam was a fundamental tool for Iran to come to grips with the modern world. ■

> There is no prophecy which is as advanced, powerful, and conscious as the prophecy of Muhammad.
> **Ali Shariati**

See also: Muhammad 56–57 ▪ Mahatma Gandhi 220–25 ▪ Mustafa Kemal Atatürk 248–49 ▪ Abul Ala Maududi 278–79

THE HELLISHNESS OF WAR DRIVES US TO BREAK WITH EVERY RESTRAINT

MICHAEL WALZER (1935–)

IN CONTEXT

IDEOLOGY
Communitarianism

FOCUS
Just war theory

BEFORE
1274 Thomas Aquinas sets out the moral principles of a just war in *Summa Theologica*.

14th–15th centuries Scholars at the School of Salamanca conclude that war is just only when it is waged to prevent an even greater evil.

1965 The US begins a ground war in Vietnam. The US's eventual defeat, coupled with domestic opposition, leads to a reappraisal in the US of the moral boundaries of war.

AFTER
1990 US president George Bush invokes just war theory prior to the First Gulf War.

2001 US-led forces invade Afghanistan following the 9/11 terrorist attacks.

The **ethics of warfare** have come under pressure due to the **changing nature of conflict**, such as…

…**guerrilla warfare**.

…**complex inter-relations** between states.

…**military industrialization**, especially use of nuclear weapons.

To cope with these changes, the **concept of a just war** must be reappraised.

A reappraisal shows that **war remains necessary** in certain circumstances, but subject to restraints.

However, war is so hellish that **any restraint may be broken** if it hastens the end of the war.

The hellishness of war drives us to break with every restraint.

See also: Sun Tzu 28–31 ▪ Augustine of Hippo 54–55 ▪ Thomas Aquinas 62–69 ▪ Niccolò Machiavelli 74–81 ▪ Smedley D. Butler 247 ▪ Robert Nozick 326–27

When is war justified? What conduct is permissible on the battlefield? Questions like these have troubled political thinkers for as long as people have waged war. Augustine of Hippo provided an early examination of the conditions for just warfare, suggesting that defence of oneself, or others in need, was not only a moral justification for warfare, but an imperative. Later, in his *Summa Theologica*, Thomas Aquinas put forward the basis of modern just war theory, suggesting that war cannot be fought for personal gain and must be waged by a legitimate body, and that the overriding motive must be to secure peace.

However, recent rapid advances in military industrialization, complex inter-relations between states, and the emergence of guerrilla warfare all challenge the solidity of the ethical underpinning to armed conflict.

The use of nuclear weapons in war profoundly affected Walzer's ideas. The immense destructive capabilities of these weapons led him to urge a reassessment of the ethics of warfare.

Michael Walzer is a US political philosopher regarded as one of the most eminent just war theorists of the last century. His work has reinvigorated just war theory and provided the impetus for a new set of responses to the complexities of conflict. For Walzer, war is, in certain circumstances, necessary, but the conditions for warfare and its conduct are subject to strong moral constraints and ethics.

However, Walzer believes that a just and necessary war may need to be fought to the full extent of the means available, however horrific that might seem. For instance, if the killing of civilians is judged likely to hasten the end of the war, it might be justified. He believes that those waging war should be subject to moral restraints, but that those restraints cannot be absolute.

Just and unjust wars

Walzer's *Just and Unjust Wars* argues for the maintenance of a strong ethical base, while holding that warfare is sometimes necessary, but rejects moral absolutism – the idea that some acts are never morally permissible.

Walzer suggests that in modern conflicts, the muddied dynamics of the battlefield and the complex ethics involved provide challenges to ethical thinking. He gives the Allied bombing of Dresden in World War II as an example of a very difficult case to judge. Nuclear weapons, in particular, trouble Walzer, who suggests that they shift the boundaries of morality so drastically that it is now difficult to make a moral framework for warfare. However, as a last resort, even the most extreme measures might be justified. ■

Michael Walzer

Michael Walzer was born in New York and attended Brandeis University, Boston and the University of Cambridge in the UK before completing his doctorate at Harvard in 1961. He went on to teach a course at Harvard in the 1970s in tandem with Robert Nozick, which provided the genesis for two influential books: Nozick's *Anarchy, State and Utopia*, and Walzer's *Spheres of Justice*. He was made emeritus professor at the Institute of Advanced Study at Princeton University in 2007.

Walzer's work has been influential in a number of areas, including just war theory, but also taking in equality, liberalism, and justice. As a supporter of self-governing communities, he has been concerned with civil society and the role of the welfare state. A leading public intellectual, his work on just warfare has influenced many contemporary politicians and military leaders.

Key works

1977 *Just and Unjust Wars*
1983 *Spheres of Justice*
2001 *War and Justice*

NO STATE MORE EXTENSIVE THAN THE MINIMAL STATE CAN BE JUSTIFIED

ROBERT NOZICK (1938–2002)

IN CONTEXT

IDEOLOGY
Liberalism

FOCUS
Libertarian rights

BEFORE
1689 John Locke writes two treatises on government outlining a social contract.

1944 In *The Road to Serfdom*, Friedrich Hayek condemns government control through central planning.

1971 John Rawls's book *A Theory of Justice* argues for the state to correct inequalities in society.

AFTER
1983 Michael Walzer looks at how society distributes "social goods" such as education and work in *Spheres of Justice*.

1995 Canadian theorist Gerald Cohen publishes a Marxist critique of Rawls and Nozick titled *Self-ownership, Freedom, and Equality*.

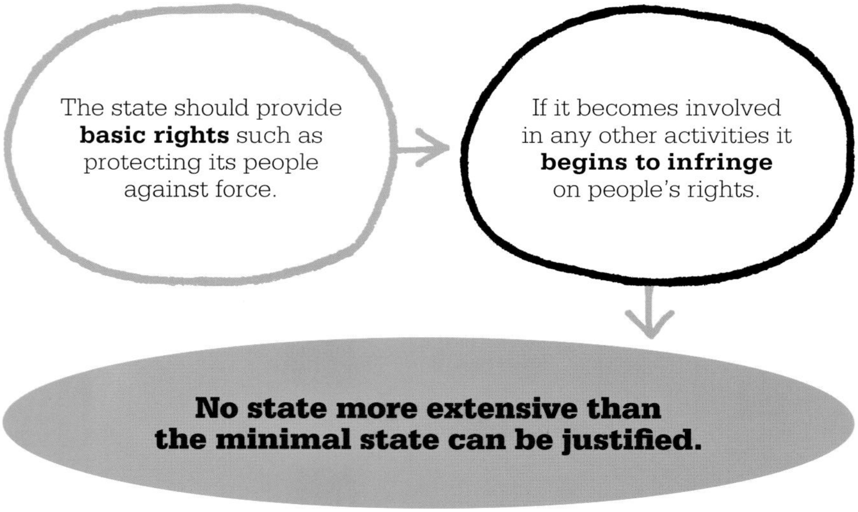

The position of individual rights in an era of strong states and extensive public institutions has proved a fertile ground for political theory. Prominent in the debate has been philosopher Robert Nozick, whose work was in part a response to the ideas of John Locke and John Rawls.

Locke, writing his *Second Treatise on Government* in 1689, provided the foundations of the theory of the modern state by suggesting that people held individual rights, but that some form of state was needed to enforce them. From this came the notion of the social contract, outlined by Jean-Jacques Rousseau, whereby individuals give up some of their freedom in order to have protection from the state.

Rawls's influential 1971 book *A Theory of Justice* built on this idea by proposing a variant of the social contract, which he believed reconciled it with the ideas of liberty and equality that were explored in Locke's work. Rawls suggests a framework that allows

See also: John Locke 104–09 ▪ Immanuel Kant 126–29 ▪ Henry David Thoreau 186–87 ▪ John Rawls 298–303 ▪ Michael Walzer 324–25

> Individuals have rights and there are things no person or group may do to them.
> **Robert Nozick**

individuals to collectively agree on an idea of justice that is based on fairness and equality rather than personal self-interest, laying a foundation for social democracy. Nozick drew on Locke and Kant to argue that there were dangers in the forms of cooperation that lay in Rawls's argument. He revived the idea of libertarianism, which holds that the reach of the state should be as limited as possible.

The result of Nozick's argument was the notion that any form of state other than the minimal was incompatible with individual rights, and therefore unjustifiable. Where the state became involved in any activity other than the most basic – "protection against force, theft, fraud, enforcement of contracts, and so on" – then it would infringe the rights that Rawls sought to preserve.

Anarchy, State, and Utopia

Nozick's most vivid description of this view was in his book *Anarchy, State, and Utopia*, which argued for a minimal state and provided a series of direct responses to the claims made by Rawls. The book was developed from a course taught by Nozick at Harvard with the political theorist Michael Walzer, which took the form of a debate between the two. Later, Walzer became one of the most significant critics of the arguments made in the book.

Perhaps the most famous conclusion reached in *Anarchy, State, and Utopia* was the idea that taxation, as employed by modern states to redistribute income and fund public agencies, was morally indefensible. In Nozick's view, it amounts to a form of forced labour, where a proportion of a person's work compulsorily benefits others. Indeed, Nozick went as far as to imagine this as a form of slavery, where every member of society had some claim of ownership to an individual's labour.

Anarchy, State, and Utopia proved hugely influential and helped define the modern boundaries of the debate between libertarian thought and liberalism. Often read alongside *A Theory of Justice*, it ranks as one of the most important works of political philosophy in the modern era. ▪

Taxation is described as a form of slavery by Nozick, in the sense that members of society can demand a portion of an individual's labour, making it into a forced employment.

Robert Nozick

Born in New York in 1938, Robert Nozick was the son of a Jewish entrepreneur. He pursued an academic career, training at Columbia, Oxford, and Princeton universities.

Initially drawn to the ideas of the Left, his reading of Friedrich Hayek, Ayn Rand, and other free-market thinkers during his graduate studies moved his standpoint towards libertarianism. His career was spent mostly at Harvard, where he established himself as one of the leading figures in libertarian thought. Famously, he is said to have only ever taught the same course twice.

Nozick's most significant work of political theory was his first, *Anarchy, State, and Utopia*, though he wrote on a variety of subjects throughout his career, and did not restrict himself to political philosophy. In later life he rejected extreme libertarianism, and suggested limits on inheritances.

Key works

1974 *Anarchy, State, and Utopia*
1981 *Philosophical Explanations*
1993 *The Nature of Rationality*

NO ISLAMIC LAW SAYS VIOLATE WOMEN'S RIGHTS

SHIRIN EBADI (1947–)

IN CONTEXT

IDEOLOGY
Islam

FOCUS
Human rights activism

BEFORE

1953 A CIA-backed coup overthrows the democratically elected Iranian prime minister, Mohammad Mosaddeq.

1979 The Islamic revolution, led by Ayatollah Khomeini, removes an autocratic monarchy and inaugurates an Islamic republic that brings in a series of repressive laws.

AFTER

2006 Peaceful demonstrations for women's rights are broken up in Tehran, Iran, and several demonstrators are sentenced to prison terms and corporal punishment.

2011 The "Arab Spring" brings rapid social and political change to a number of states in North Africa and the Middle East, though not to Iran.

The position of human rights in Islamic states raises issues that have serious implications for political thought. The roles women take in public life, in particular, have been curtailed by the rise of fundamentalism, with gender discrimination pursued through a number of retrograde laws. The correct response to these problems, and especially the role of Western powers, has been much debated by Islamic thinkers.

Shirin Ebadi is a Nobel Prize-winning human rights activist. A practising judge prior to the Iranian Revolution in 1979, she was forced to cease legal work as the result of a series of laws enacted by the new regime, which restricted the rights of women. Despite this, Ebadi sees women's rights as entirely compatible with Islam, and suggests that the previously strong position of women in Iranian society points to the regime as the problem, rather than Islamic law.

The role of Western nations and values in promoting human rights in this environment is hotly contested. Ebadi argues strongly against Western intervention in Iran, suggesting that, despite the regime's poor human rights record, gender discrimination, and a lack of democracy, any involvement by foreign powers would be undesirable and unhelpful – and would simply make matters worse. Instead, she believes change must come from within, and points to the relatively strong women's movement in Iran compared with other Islamic states. ■

Iranian women protested in 1979 against new laws requiring them to cover up in public. Ebadi believes that the oppression of the regime can only be reversed by Iranians themselves.

See also: Emmeline Pankhurst 207 ▪ Abul Ala Maududi 278–79 ▪ Simone de Beauvoir 284–89 ▪ Ali Shariati 323

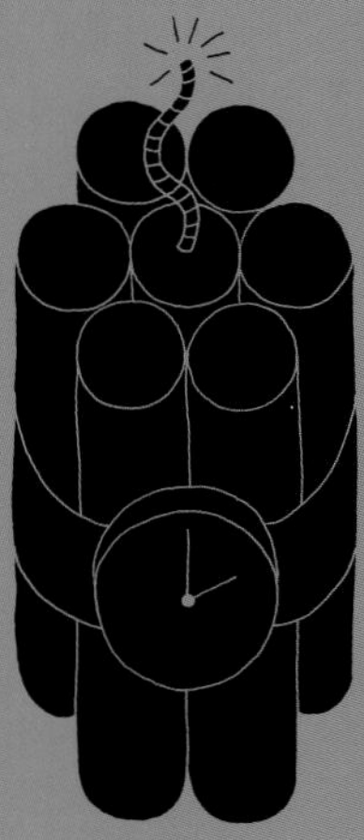

SUICIDE TERRORISM IS MAINLY A RESPONSE TO FOREIGN OCCUPATION

ROBERT PAPE (1960–)

IN CONTEXT

IDEOLOGY
War studies

FOCUS
Empirical political science

BEFORE

1881 Russian tsar Alexander II is killed by a suicide bomber.

1983 In Lebanon, two suicide bomb attacks on US and French barracks in Beirut are claimed by the Islamic Jihad.

2001 The 9/11 attacks by al-Qaeda are followed by US-led occupations of Iraq and Afghanistan.

AFTER

2005 A series of suicide bomb attacks on buses and trains across London kills 52 people.

2009 Sri Lanka's civil war ends after 26 years, during which time the Tamil Tigers carried out 273 suicide attacks.

2011 The US withdraws its military presence from Iraq.

Suicide terrorism has widely been believed to be an expression of religious fundamentalism, fuelled by a ready supply of willing martyrs. American political scientist Robert Pape has compiled evidence to suggest that suicide terrorism is in fact a secular tactic rather than a religious one, and forms part of a broader campaign to remove an occupying force from the area perceived by the perpetrators to be their homeland.

> There is little connection between suicide terrorism and Islamic fundamentalism, or any one of the world's religions.
> **Robert Pape**

A strategic response

Pape's 2005 publication *Dying to Win* analyses all known instances of suicide terrorism between 1980 and 2003: a total of 315 attacks. He found that the attacks were not explained by individual motives and beliefs, and discovered little correlation between religion and suicide terrorism. He proposed instead a "causal logic of suicide terrorism", which suggests that such actions are a strategic response to foreign occupation by a democratic power. Pape's research found that every terrorist campaign, and more than 95 per cent of all suicide bombings, had the objective of national liberation at their heart.

The corollary of this argument is that the use of military force by foreign powers to subjugate or reform societies will serve only to promote a larger number of suicide terrorists than would otherwise be the case. As Pape argues, suicide terrorism is not the result of an existing supply of fanatics, but is a "demand-driven phenomenon". ■

See also: Abul Ala Maududi 278–79 ▪ Frantz Fanon 304–07 ▪ Ali Shariati 323 ▪ Michael Walzer 324–25

DIRECTO

RY

DIRECTORY

The most important ideas of political thought and some of the most prominent political thinkers have been presented in this book, but inevitably there has not been space to include all who have shaped the political thinking of the world throughout the ages. This directory, although by no means exhaustive, gives some information on a selection of those figures who have not been dealt with elsewhere, including their achievements and the ideas for which they are best known. It also gives links to other pages in the book that discuss the ideas, movements, and thinkers they have been associated with or that have influenced their thinking, and others that they have inspired.

DARIUS THE GREAT
c.550–486 BCE

Darius I seized the Persian crown in 522 BCE. He put down rebellions that had previously toppled his predecessor, Cyrus the Great, and expanded the empire into central Asia, northeast Africa, Greece, and the Balkan region. To administer this huge empire, he divided it into provinces overseen by satraps, who also administered the system of taxation. The satraps were based in regional capitals such as Persepolis and Susa, which were the sites of massive construction projects.
To unify the empire, Darius also introduced a universal currency, the *daric*, and made Aramaic the official language.
See also: Alexander the Great 332

MENCIUS
c.372–289 BCE

Also known as Mengzi, the Chinese philosopher Mencius is believed to have studied with one of Confucius's grandsons, and his interpretation of Confucianism did much to establish it as a model of government during the Warring States period. Unlike Confucius, he stressed the essential goodness of human nature, which could be corrupted by society, and advocated education to improve public morals. He was also less respectful of rulers, believing that they should be overthrown by the people if they ruled unjustly.
See also: Confucius 20–27 ▪ Mozi 32–33 ▪ Han Fei Tzu 48

ALEXANDER THE GREAT
c.356–323 BCE

The son of King Philip II of Macedon, Alexander was born at the height of the classical period of Greek history, and is believed to have been tutored by Aristotle as a youth. After the death of his father, he succeeded to the throne and embarked on a campaign of expansion. He successfully invaded Asia Minor, and from there conquered the remainder of the Persian empire of Darius III, eventually extending his power as far as northern India. In the process, he introduced Greek culture and institutions into Africa and Asia, where many Hellenistic cities were founded, modelled on the classical Greek city-states.
See also: Aristotle 40–43 ▪ Chanakya 44–47

GENGHIS KHAN
1162–1227

Born into a ruling clan in northern Mongolia, Temujin gained the title Genghis Khan (meaning "the Emperor Genghis") on founding the Mongol empire. Before he came to power, the people of Central Asia belonged to several different clans, and were largely nomadic. Genghis Khan brought the clans together as one nation and led a series of military campaigns, expanding his empire into China. Under his rule as Great Khan, the empire was divided into khanates ruled by members of his family, and continued to expand as far as central Europe. Seen by those he conquered as cruel, he nevertheless created an empire that respected the cultural diversity of its people.
See also: Sun Tzu 28–31 ▪ Chanakya 44–47

BARTOLOMÉ DE LAS CASAS
1484–1566

The Spanish priest and historian Bartolomé de las Casas emigrated to Hispaniola in 1502. He initially worked a plantation there and owned slaves. He remained a priest, however, and participated in the conquest of Cuba as chaplain, but was so appalled by the atrocities perpetrated against the local Taíno people that he became an advocate of the Indian people. He entered a monastery in Santo Domingo as a Dominican friar, and travelled throughout Central America, eventually becoming bishop of Chiapas in Mexico and "Protector of the Indians", before returning to Spain in 1547. His writings on the cruelty of the colonization of the Americas can be seen as an early proposal of universal human rights.
See also: Francisco de Vitoria 86–87 ▪ Nelson Mandela 294–95 ▪ Martin Luther King 316–21

AKBAR THE GREAT
1542–1605

The third Mughal emperor in India, Akbar not only extended the empire to cover most of central and northern India, but also introduced a culture of religious tolerance to an ethnically diverse population, and instigated a reorganization of its government. Rather than divide his empire into autonomous regions under separate rulers, regions were administered by military governors under the rule of a central government. This central government was divided into different departments dealing with separate issues, such as revenue, the judiciary, and the military. In this way, Akbar unified the disparate regions into a prosperous and peaceful whole.
See also: Chanakya 44–47 ▪ Mahatma Gandhi 220–25 ▪ Manabendra Nath Roy 253

TOKUGAWA IEYASU
1543–1616

Japanese military leader and statesman Tokugawa Ieyasu was the son of the ruler of Mikawa province. He was born during a period of prolonged civil conflict. Ieyasu inherited his father's position, as well as his alliance with neighbouring ruler Toyotomi Hideyoshi. Despite promises to honour the alliance after Hideyoshi's death, Ieyasu defeated the Toyotomi clan and established his government in Edo, modern Tokyo. Tokugawa Ieyasu was made a shogun (military governor) by the nominal emperor Go-Yozei in 1603, effectively making him ruler of all Japan and founder of the Tokugawa dynasty. By distributing land among regional leaders and imposing strict regulations on their rule, he maintained a power base and brought stability to the country.
See also: Sun Tzu 28–31 ▪ Niccolò Machiavelli 74–81 ▪ Ito Hirobumi 195

OLIVER CROMWELL
1599–1658

Previously a relatively unimportant member of parliament, Cromwell came to prominence during the English Civil War. He proved an able military leader of the Parliamentarian forces in their defeat of the Royalists. He was then one of the signatories of King Charles I's death warrant. Cromwell's participation in the removal of the monarch was motivated by religion as much as politics, as was his subsequent occupation of Catholic Ireland. He rose to political power during the brief Commonwealth of England, and was made Lord Protector of England, Wales, Scotland, and Ireland in 1653. Seen by some as a ruthless anti-Catholic dictator, Cromwell is also regarded as the bringer of liberty at the time of a decadent monarchy, replacing it with the foundations of parliamentary democracy.
See also: Barons of King John 60–61 ▪ John Lilburne 333

JOHN LILBURNE
1614–1657

English politician John Lilburne devoted his life to fighting for what he called his "freeborn rights", as opposed to rights granted by law. He was imprisoned for printing illegal pamphlets in the 1630s, and enlisted in the Parliamentarian army at the start of the English Civil War. He resigned from the army in 1645 because he felt it was not fighting for liberty as he understood it. Although associated with the Levellers, a movement campaigning for equal property rights, Lilburne argued for equality of human rights, and inspired the Levellers' pamphlet *An Agreement of the People*. He was tried for high treason in 1649 but was freed in response to public opinion and sent into exile. On his return to England in 1653, he was tried again and imprisoned until his death in 1657.
See also: Thomas Paine 134–39 ▪ Oliver Cromwell 333

SAMUEL VON PUFENDORF
1632–1694

The son of a Lutheran pastor in Saxony, Germany, Samuel von Pufendorf originally studied theology in Leipzig, but decided to move to Jena to study law. Here he discovered the works of Grotius and Hobbes, and their theories of natural law. He built a reputation for his ideas on universal law, and was appointed the first professor of law and nations at the University of Heidelberg, where he expanded on his theories of natural law, paving the way for Rousseau's conception of the social contract. He also proposed a system of international law independent of religion. He later moved to Sweden as historian to the royal court, and developed a theory of Church government that stressed the distinction between the laws of the Church and the laws of the state.
See also: Hugo Grotius 94–95 ▪ Thomas Hobbes 96–103 ▪ Jean-Jacques Rousseau 118–25

JUANA INÉS DE LA CRUZ
1651–1695

Juana Inés de Asbaje y Ramírez de Santillana was born near Mexico City, the illegitimate daughter of Isabella Ramirez and a Spanish captain. At a very early age, she learned to read and write, and showed a great interest in her grandfather's library when sent to live with him in 1660. At the time, studying was an exclusively male preserve, and she pleaded with her family to disguise her as a boy in order to go to university, but in the end taught herself the classics. In 1669, she entered the Convent of the Order of St Jerome, where she remained until her death. She wrote numerous poems and, in response to criticism of her writing from the Church authorities, a stout defence of women's right to education, the "Reply to Sister Philotea". She argued that society was damaged by keeping women ignorant, asking "how much injury might have been avoided… if our aged women had been learned?" She was censured by the Church for her comments.
See also: Mary Wollstonecraft 154–55 ▪ Emmeline Pankhurst 207 ▪ Simone de Beauvoir 284–89 ▪ Shirin Ebadi 328

GEORGE WASHINGTON
1732–1799

Commander-in-chief of the Continental Army in the American War of Independence, Washington was one of the Founding Fathers of the United States and the country's first president. He was not a member of a political party, warning against the divisiveness of partisan politics. During his two terms of office, he introduced measures designed to unify the country as a republic ruled by federal government. As well as promoting a sense of nationalism, he took practical steps to improve the prosperity of the republic and promote trade – he brought in a fair tax system to clear the national debt, while in foreign affairs he advocated neutrality to avoid becoming involved in European wars. Many of the conventions of US government, such as the inaugural address and the custom of a two-term presidency, were established by Washington.
See also: Benjamin Franklin 112–13 ▪ Thomas Paine 134–39 ▪ Thomas Jefferson 140–41

JOSEPH DE MAISTRE
1753–1826

Joseph-Marie, comte de Maistre, emerged as a major figure in the conservative backlash that followed the French Revolution. He saw the revolution as the result of atheist Enlightenment thinking, and argued that the Reign of Terror that followed it was an inevitable consequence of rejecting Christianity. He fled to Switzerland and later Italy and Sardinia to escape the revolution. He believed that rationally justified systems of government were doomed to end in violence, and the only stable form of government was a divinely sanctioned monarchy, with the pope as ultimate authority.
See also: Thomas Aquinas 62–69 ▪ Edmund Burke 130–33

NIKOLAI MORDVINOV
1754–1845

An officer in the Russian Navy who had also served in the British Royal Navy, Nikolai Mordvinov came to the attention of Emperor Paul and was promoted to admiral and later navy minister, a position in which he had influence over military policy. He was an advocate of liberalism at a time when the Russian government was resolutely autocratic. A fervent Anglophile, Mordvinov particularly admired British political liberalism and used his influence to argue for its replacement of serfdom, which he felt was holding back Russia's economic development. He believed that this could be achieved without the need for revolution.
See also: John Stuart Mill 174–81 ▪ Peter Kropotkin 206

MAXIMILIEN ROBESPIERRE
1758–1794

A leading figure in the French Revolution, Robespierre was seen by his supporters as an incorruptible upholder of the principles of the revolution, but is remembered as a ruthless dictator. He studied law in Paris, where he first came across the revolutionary writings of Jean-Jacques Rousseau. Practising law in Arras, he became involved in politics and rose to membership of the Constituent Assembly. Here, he argued for equal rights and the establishment of a French Republic. After the execution of Louis XVI, he presided over the Committee of Public Safety, which sought to eradicate the threat of counter-revolution through a Reign of Terror, but was himself arrested and executed.
See also: Montesquieu 110–11 ▪ Jean-Jacques Rousseau 118–25 ▪ Gracchus Babeuf 335

GRACCHUS BABEUF
1760–1797

François-Noël Babeuf had little formal education. He became a writer and journalist and, after the beginning of the French Revolution, published propaganda under the pen-names "Tribune" and "Gracchus" Babeuf, in honour of the Roman reformers and tribunes, the Gracchus brothers. His views proved too radical even for the revolutionary authorities. The publication of his journal *Le Tribun du Peuple* in support of the ideals of the Reign of Terror gained him a following known as the Society of Equals. Evidence from infiltrators into his organization led to accusations of conspiracy and the arrest and execution of Babeuf and many of his fellow agitators.
See also: Jean-Jacques Rousseau 118–25 ▪ Maximilien Robespierre 335

JOHANN FICHTE
1762–1814

Primarily known as a philosopher, Fichte is also regarded as a seminal figure in political nationalism in Germany. After the French Revolution, France annexed many of the western states of Germany and introduced ideas of liberty and civil rights, but this provoked a patriotic reaction. Fichte urged the German people to come together in their shared heritage and language to oppose the French influence and, more controversially, to remove the threat he believed came from the Jewish "state within a state". As well as his openly anti-Semitic ideas, he believed that women should be denied civil rights. The most extreme of his proposals were echoed in Hitler's National Socialism movement.
See also: Johann Gottfried Herder 142–43 ▪ Georg Hegel 156–59 ▪ Adolf Hitler 337

NAPOLEON BONAPARTE
1769–1821

A Corsican of noble Italian extraction, Napoleon studied at a military academy in France and served in the French army, despite remaining a Corsican nationalist. His republican sentiments earned him a place in the republican forces near the end of the French Revolution. After a *coup d'état*, he made himself First Consul of the Republic, and instituted the Napoleonic Code. This established a meritocratic government by outlawing privilege by birth, and introduced measures to ensure religious emancipation – especially to Jews and Protestants. He also signed a concordat with Pope Pius VII restoring some of the Catholic Church's status. He proclaimed himself emperor in 1804 and embarked on a series of wars that would eventually lead to his downfall. He abdicated and went into exile on Elba in 1813, but soon returned to power, only to be defeated by the British at Waterloo in 1815. He was imprisoned on St Helena island until his death.
See also: Friedrich Nietzsche 196–99 ▪ Maximilien Robespierre 335

ROBERT OWEN
1771–1817

Owen came from a humble Welsh family and moved to Manchester, England, as a teenager in search of work. He made his name in the textile trade and became the manager of a cotton mill aged 19. He outlined his ideas for social reform in his book *A New View of Society.* His Utopian socialist philosophy was based on improvements in the workers' environment, such as housing, social welfare, and education. He established cooperative communities at New Lanark in Scotland and elsewhere in Britain, as well as one in New Harmony, Indiana, US. A pioneer of the cooperative movement, his new communities were an inspiration to social reform movements in Britain.
See also: Thomas Paine 134–39 ▪ Jeremy Bentham 144–49 ▪ Karl Marx 188–93 ▪ Beatrice Webb 210

CHARLES FOURIER
1772–1837

Born in Besançon, France, the son of a businessman, Fourier travelled widely in Europe and had a variety of jobs before settling on a career as a writer. Unlike other socialist thinkers of the revolutionary period, he believed that the problems of society were caused by poverty rather than inequality, and developed a form of libertarian socialism. He was also an early advocate of women's rights. In place of trade and competition, which he considered an evil practice operated by Jews, he proposed a system of cooperation. Fourier's Utopian ideas were to be achieved in communities he called "phalanxes" housed in apartment complexes. Workers would be paid according to their contribution, with higher pay for unpopular jobs. His ideas were taken up in the Paris Commune, which briefly ruled Paris in 1871, and phalanxes were set up in several places in the US.
See also: Mary Wollstonecraft 154–55 ▪ Robert Owen 335

GIUSEPPE GARIBALDI
1807–1882

A leading figure in the Italian *Risorgimiento* – the movement towards the unification of Italy in the 19th century – Garibaldi led a guerrilla force famed for their red shirts, which conquered Sicily and Naples. He also fought campaigns in South America during a period of exile from Italy, and spent time in the United States. His exploits led to renown on both sides of the Atlantic, and his popularity did much to hasten Italian unification. A republican who was strongly opposed to political power for the papacy, Garibaldi nonetheless supported the establishment of a monarchy for the sake of unification, and helped to create the Kingdom of Italy under the Sardinian king Victor Emanuel II, which was established in 1861. The Papal states joined the kingdom in 1870, completing the *Risorgimiento*. Garibaldi was a supporter of the idea of a European federation, which he hoped would be led by a newly unified Germany.
See also: Giuseppe Mazzini 172–73

NASER AL-DIN SHAH QUAJAR
1831–1896

The fourth shah of the Qajar dynasty, Naser al-Din came to the throne of Iran in 1848 and began his reign as a reformer influenced by European ideas. As well as improving the infrastructure of the country – building roads and setting up postal and telegraph services – he opened Western-style schools, introduced measures to reduce the power of the clergy, and was sympathetic to the idea of establishing a Jewish state. He toured Europe in 1873 and again in 1878, and was especially impressed with the British political system. As his reign progressed, however, he became increasingly dictatorial, persecuting minorities and giving concessions to European traders while lining his own pockets. Seen as being in thrall to foreign interests, he became increasingly unpopular with the growing Iranian nationalist movement and was assassinated in 1896.
See also: Theodor Herzl 208–09 ▪ Mustafa Kemal Atatürk 248–49

OSWALD SPENGLER
1880–1936

German historian Oswald Spengler made his name with *The Decline of the West*, which, although finished in 1914, was not published until after World War I. In it, he describes his theory that all civilizations face ultimate decay, an idea reinforced by the decline of Germany in the 1920s. Another book, *Prussiandom and Socialism*, advocated a new nationalist movement of authoritarian socialism. He was, however, not a supporter of Nazism, and openly criticized Hitler's ideas of racial superiority, warning of a world war that could bring an end to Western civilization.
See also: Ibn Khaldun 72–73 ▪ Adolf Hitler 337

RICHARD TAWNEY
1880–1962

The English social and economic historian Richard Tawney was a fierce critic of the acquisitiveness of capitalist society. He was the author of the classic historical analysis *Religion and the Rise of Capitalism*, and also wrote several books of social criticism, in which he developed his ideas of Christian socialism and an egalitarian society. A reformist socialist and member of the Independent Labour Party, he worked alongside Sidney and Beatrice Webb campaigning for reforms in industry and education. He was a staunch advocate of adult education and was actively involved in the Workers' Educational Association, becoming its president in 1928.
See also: Beatrice Webb 210 ▪ Robert Owen 335

FRANKLIN D. ROOSEVELT
1882–1945

The 32nd president of the United States, Roosevelt was elected to office in 1932 during the worst period of the Great Depression. He immediately instituted a programme of legislation known as the New Deal to promote economic growth, reduce unemployment, and regulate the financial institutions. At the same time, he introduced social reforms aimed at improving civil rights. His expansion of government social programmes and intervention in the financial markets set the standard for American liberal politics in the 20th century. His policies improved the economy and lifted the public mood, and with the advent of World War II, he cemented his popularity by taking the country from its isolationist stance to become a leading player in world affairs.
See also: Winston Churchill 236–37 ▪ Joseph Stalin 240–41

BENITO MUSSOLINI
1883–1945

As a young man, Mussolini left Italy for Switzerland, where he became a socialist activist and later a political journalist. He was also a fervent Italian nationalist, and was expelled from the Italian Socialist Party for his support of intervention in World War I. After service in the Italian army, he renounced the orthodox socialist notion of a proletarian revolution and developed a blend of nationalist and socialist ideas in the Fascist Manifesto in 1921. He led his National Fascist Party in a coup d'état, the "March on Rome", in 1922, and became prime minister of a coalition government the following year. Within a few years, he had assumed dictatorial power, using the title Il Duce ("The Leader"). He began a programme of public works and economic reforms. In World War II he sided with Hitler's Germany. After the Allied invasion of Italy, he was imprisoned, then freed by German special forces. Eventually, he was caught by Italian partisans and executed in 1945.
See also: Giovanni Gentile 238–39 ▪ Adolf Hitler 337

ADOLF HITLER
1889–1945

Although born in Austria, Adolf Hitler moved to Germany as a young man and quickly became a fierce German nationalist. After serving in World War I, he joined the fledgling German Workers' Party – which was later transformed into the Nazi Party – becoming its leader in 1921. He was imprisoned in 1923 after he staged an unsuccessful *coup d'état*, the Munich Beer Hall Putsch. While in jail, Hitler wrote the memoir *Mein Kampf* ("My Struggle"). Freed the following year, he used his ideas of German nationalism, racial superiority, anti-Semitism, and anti-communism to whip up support, and was elected chancellor in 1933. He quickly established a dictatorial rule, replacing the Weimar Republic with the Third Reich, and proceeded to rearm Germany in preparation for seizing territory for the German people. His invasion of Poland in 1939 marked the start of World War II, during which he expanded the Reich across Europe, but he was eventually defeated in 1945. He committed suicide in his bunker as Allied forces closed in during the Battle of Berlin.
See also: Joseph Stalin 240–41 ▪ Benito Mussolini 337

HO CHI MINH
1890–1969

Ho Chi Minh was born Nguyen Sinh Cung in French Indochina (present-day Vietnam), and educated at the French lycée in Hue. He worked for a while as a teacher before taking a job on a ship and travelling to the US, and then worked in menial jobs in London and Paris. While in France, he learned about communism and campaigned for the replacement of French rule in Vietnam with a nationalist government. He spent some years in the Soviet Union and China and was imprisoned by the British in Hong Kong. He returned to Vietnam in 1941 to lead the independence movement, using his assumed name of Ho Chi Minh. He successfully prevented occupation of the country by the Japanese in World War II, establishing the communist Democratic Republic of Vietnam (North Vietnam) in 1945 with himself as president and prime minister, but continued to fight for a united Vietnam until ill health forced his retirement in 1955. He died in 1969, before the Vietnam War had come to an end, and remained a figurehead for the communist People's Army and Viet Cong against South Vietnam and the US-led forces.
See also: Karl Marx 188–93 ▪ Mao Zedong 260–65 ▪ Che Guevara 312–13 ▪ Fidel Castro 339

JOSÉ CARLOS MARIÁTEGUI
1894–1930

Peruvian journalist Mariátegui left school at age 14 to work as an errand boy at a newspaper, and learned his trade at the dailies *La Prensa* and *El Tiempo*. In 1918 he set up his own left-wing paper, *La Razón*, and in 1920 was forced to leave the country for his support of socialist activists. He toured Europe, and was living in Italy and involved in socialist politics when Mussolini seized power. Mariátegui blamed the rise of fascism on the weakness of the left. He returned to Peru in 1923 and began to write about the situation in his home country in the light of his experiences in Italy. He allied himself with the American Popular Revolutionary Alliance and founded the magazine *Amauta*. A co-founder of the Communist Party of Peru in 1928, he wrote the Marxist analysis *Seven Interpretative Essays on Peruvian Reality*, arguing for a return to the collectivism of the indigenous Peruvian people. His ideas remained influential in Peru after his early death in 1930, and were the inspiration for both the Shining Path and Túpac Revolutionary movements in the late 20th century.
See also: Simón Bolívar 162–63 ▪ Karl Marx 188–93 ▪ Che Guevara 312–13 ▪ Benito Mussolini 337

HERBERT MARCUSE
1898–1979

One of a number of German intellectuals who emigrated to the US in the 1930s, Marcuse studied philosophy and became associated with the Frankfurt School of Social Research, with which he maintained ties even after becoming a US citizen in 1940. In his books *One-Dimensional Man* and *Eros and Civilization*, he presented a Marxist-inspired philosophy stressing the alienation of modern society. His interpretation of Marxism was tailored for US society, with less emphasis on class struggle. He was a critic of Soviet communism, which he believed had the same dehumanizing effect as capitalism. Popular with minority groups and students in the US, his ideas earned him the status of "Father of the New Left" in the 1960s and 70s.
See also: Jean-Jacques Rousseau 118–25 ▪ Karl Marx 188–93 ▪ Friedrich Nietzsche 196–99

LÉOPOLD SÉDAR SENGHOR
1906–2001

Born in French West Africa, Senghor won a scholarship to study in France, where he graduated and became a professor at the universities of Tours and Paris. He was actively involved in the resistance during the Nazi occupation of France. With other African émigrés, including Aimé Césaire and Léon Damas, he developed the concept of *négritude*, asserting the positive values of African culture as opposed to the racist colonial attitudes prevalent in Europe. After World War II, he returned to Africa to continue his academic career, and became increasingly involved in politics. He was elected the first president of Senegal when the country achieved independence in 1960. He adopted a distinctly African socialist stance based on *négritude* rather than the Marxism of many post-colonial states, and maintained ties with France and the West.
See also: Mahatma Gandhi 220–25 ▪ Marcus Garvey 252 ▪ Martin Luther King 316–21

MIHAILO MARKOVIC
1923–2010

Born in Belgrade in what was then Yugoslavia, the Serbian philosopher Mihailo Markovic was a prominent member of the Marxist humanist movement known as the Praxis School. After fighting as a partisan in World War II, he made his name in the Communist Party of Yugoslavia with his fierce criticism of Soviet Stalinism, advocating a return to Marxist principles. He studied in Belgrade and London, and as a respected academic became a focus for the Praxis movement in the 1960s, calling for freedom of speech and a thoroughly Marxist social critique. In 1986, Markovic was a co-author of the SANU Memorandum, which outlined the position of Serbian nationalists, and as a member of the Socialist Party of Serbia was a supporter of Serbian nationalist leader Slobodan Miloševic.
See also: Karl Marx 188–93 ▪ Herbert Marcuse 338

JEAN-FRANCOIS LYOTARD
1924–1998

A leading figure in the French postmodernist philosophical movement, Lyotard studied at the Sorbonne in Paris and was a co-founder of the International College of Philosophy. Like many socialists in the 1950s, he was disillusioned by the excesses of Stalin's Soviet Russia, and joined the *Socialisme ou Barbarie* organization, which had been set up in 1949 to oppose Stalin from a Marxist perspective. Later, he turned to other Marxist groups. He took part in the student and worker protests of May 1968 in Paris, but was disappointed by the lack of response from political thinkers. In 1974, Lyotard renounced his belief in Marxist revolution in his book *Libidinal Economy*. This and many of his political writings provided a postmodernist analysis of Marx and capitalism – and the work of Sigmund Freud – in terms of the politics of desire.

See also: Karl Marx 188–93 ■ Herbert Marcuse 338

FIDEL CASTRO
1926–

A figurehead of anti-imperialist politics, Castro first became involved in Cuban politics while a law student in Havana, which he left to fight in rebellions against right-wing governments in Colombia and the Dominican Republic. In 1959, with his brother Raúl and friend Che Guevara, he led the movement to overthrow the US-backed dictatorship of Fulgencio Batista in Cuba. As prime minister of the new Republic of Cuba, he established a one-party Marxist-Leninist state. Despite US attempts to overthrow and even assassinate him, he became president in 1976. Rather than aligning Cuba too closely with the Soviet Union, Castro took an internationalist stance as a member of the Non-Aligned Movement, which advocated an anti-imperialist middle way between the West and East during the Cold War. After the fall of the Soviet Union, he took Cuba into an alliance with other Latin American countries and passed measures to open the country up to foreign investment before retiring due to ill-health in 2008 and passing the presidency to his brother Raúl.

See also: Karl Marx 188–93 ■ Vladimir Lenin 226–33 ■ Che Guevara 312–13

JÜRGEN HABERMAS
1929–

The German philosopher and sociologist Jürgen Habermas is known for his analyses of modern capitalist society and democracy from a broadly Marxist perspective. He emphasizes the rationalism of Marxist analysis, which he regards as a continuation of Enlightenment thinking. Influenced by his experiences during World War II, and particularly the subsequent Nuremberg trials, he sought to find a new political philosophy for post-war Germany. He studied at the Frankfurt School of Social Research, but disagreed with the institute's anti-modernist stance. He later became director of the Institute for Social Research in Frankfurt. A prolific writer, Habermas has argued for a truly democratic socialism, and has been a frequent critic of postmodernism.

See also: Karl Marx 188–93 ■ Max Weber 214–15

DAVID GAUTHIER
1932–

Born in Toronto, Canada, Gauthier studied philosophy at the Univeristy of Toronto, at Harvard, and at Oxford, then worked as a professor in Toronto until 1980, when he moved to the University of Pittsburgh. His main field of interest is in moral philosophy, and in particular the political theories of Hobbes and Rousseau. In numerous articles and books, Gauthier has developed a libertarian political philosophy based on rational Enlightenment moral theory. In his best-known book, *Morals by Agreement*, he applies modern theories about decision-making – such as games theory – to the idea of the social contract, and examines the moral basis for political and economic decision-making.

See also: Thomas Hobbes 96–103 ■ Jean-Jacques Rousseau 118–25

ERNESTO LACLAU
1935–

The political theorist Ernesto Laclau was a socialist activist in his native Argentina and a member of the Socialist Party of the National Left until he was encouraged to follow an academic career in England in 1969. He studied at Essex University, where he is still professor of Political Theory. Laclau describes his stance as post-Marxist. He applies elements of thought derived from French philosophers, including Jean-Francois Lyotard and Jacques Derrida, and the psychoanalytic theory of Jacques Lacan, to an essentially Marxist political philosophy. However, he rejects Marxist ideas of class struggle and economic determinism in favour of a "radical plural democracy".

See also: Karl Marx 188–93 ■ Antonio Gramsci 259 ■ Jean-Francois Lyotard 338

GLOSSARY

Absolutism The principle of complete and unrestricted power in government. Also known as totalism or **totalitarianism**.

Agrarianism A political philosophy that values rural society and the farmer as superior to urban society and the paid worker, and sees farming as a way of life that can shape social values.

Anarchism The abolition of government authority, through violent means if necessary, and the adoption of a society that is based on voluntary cooperation.

Apartheid Meaning "separation" in Afrikaans, a policy of racial discrimination introduced in South Africa following the National Party's election victory in 1948.

Apparatchik A member of the **communist** party machine. It has come to be used as a derogatory description of a political zealot.

Autocracy A community or state in which unlimited authority is exercised by a single individual.

Bipartisan An approach to a situation or issue agreed by political parties that are normally in opposition to one another.

Bolshevik Meaning "majority" in Russian, a faction of the Marxist Russian Social Democratic Labour Party (RSDLP) that split from the Menshevik faction in 1903, becoming the Communist Party of the Soviet Union after 1917.

Bourgeoisie In Marxism, the class that owns the means of production and whose income derives from that ownership rather than paid work.

Capitalism An economic system characterized by market forces, with private investment in, and ownership of, a country's means of production and distribution.

Collectivism A political theory that advocates collective, rather than individual, control over social and economic institutions, especially the means of production.

Colonialism The claim of a state to sovereignty over new territories. It is characterized by an unequal power relation between the colonists who run the territories and their indigenous population.

Common law The law of the land, derived from neither the statute books nor the **constitution**, but from court law reports.

Communism An ideology that advocates the elimination of private property in favour of communal ownership, based on the 1848 political manifesto of Karl Marx and Friedrich Engels.

Conservatism A political position that opposes radical changes in society. Conservatives may advocate a wide range of policies, including the preservation of economic liberty, enterprise, free markets, private property, the privatization of business, and reduced government action.

Constitutionalism A system of government that adheres to a constitution – a written collection of the fundamental principles and laws of a nation.

Confucianism A system based on the teachings of Confucius, which stresses hierarchy and loyalty, but also the possibility of individual development and improvement.

Democracy A form of government in which supreme power is vested in the people or exercised by their elected representatives.

Dependency theory The notion that rich countries in the northern hemisphere have created a neocolonial relationship with those in the southern hemisphere, in which the less developed countries are dependent and disadvantaged.

Despot A ruler with **absolute** power who typically exercises it tyrannically and abusively.

Dictator An **absolute** ruler, especially one who assumes complete control without the free consent of the people, and who may exercise power oppressively.

Direct democracy Government by the people in fact, rather than merely in principle – citizens vote on every issue affecting them – as practised in ancient Athens.

Divine right of kings A doctrine that holds that a monarch derives legitimacy from God, and is not subject to any earthly authority.

Dystopia A theoretical society characterized by a wretched, dysfunctional state. See **Utopia**.

Economic structuralism The belief that the conduct of world politics is based on the way that the world is organized economically.

Ecosophy In **green politics**, the ecological philosophy of Arne Naess, propounding ecological harmony or equilibrium.

Egalitarianism A philosophy that advocates social, political, and economic equality.

Elitism The belief that society should be governed by an elite group of individuals.

Enlightenment, The Also known as the Age of Reason, a period of intellectual advances in the 18th century that involved a questioning of religious understandings of the world and the application of reason.

Extremism Any political theory that favours uncompromising policies or actions.

Fabian Society A British movement that advocated that **socialism** should be introduced incrementally via education and gradual legislative changes.

Fascism A **nationalist** ideology typified by strong leadership, stress on a collective identity, and the use of violence or warfare to further the interests of the state. The term derives from the Italian *fascio* – a tied bundle of sticks – referring to collective identity, and was first applied to Mussolini's regime.

Federalism A system of government in which powers are divided between central government and smaller states or provinces.

Feudal system A medieval political system that consisted of small geographical units – such as principalities or dukedoms – ruled by the nobility, where the peasant population lived in a state of bondage to their ruler.

Fourth estate A theoretical institution consisting of the press and other forms of media. The term derives from the first three "estates" – classes of people – recognized by the French legislative assembly until the late 18th century: the Church, the nobility, and townsmen.

Fundamentalism The strict adherence to and belief in religious principles.

Glasnost Meaning "openness" in Russian, a policy introduced in the Soviet Union by Mikhail Gorbachev that committed the government to greater accountability and scrutiny.

Green politics An ideology centred around building an ecologically sustainable society.

Habeas corpus The right of an individual detained under accusation to appear before a court of law to have their guilt or innocence examined.

Imperialism The policy of extending the dominion of a nation through direct intervention in the affairs of other countries, and seizure of territory and subjugation of peoples in building an empire.

Isolationism A policy of withdrawing a nation from military alliances, international agreements, and sometimes even international trade.

Junta A clique, faction, or cabal, often military in nature, that takes power after the overthrow of a government.

Just war theory A doctrine of military ethics comprising *Jus ad bellum* – Latin for "right to war" – the need for a moral and legal basis for war, and *Jus in bello* – Latin for "justice in war" – the need for the moral conduct of warfare.

Kleptocracy Political and governmental corruption in which politicians, bureaucrats, and their protected friends exercise power for their own material benefit. From the Greek for "rule by thieves".

Leftism, left wing Ideology of the political "left". It is characterized by an interventionist approach to social welfare and an internationalist worldview. The concept originated in 18th-century France, when nobility who sought to improve the peasants' conditions sat to the left of the king.

Legalism A **utilitiarian** political philosophy adopted in China during the Warring States period, which stressed the importance of maintaining law and order using harsh punishment if necessary.

Liberalism A political ideology that stresses the rights and freedoms of individuals. Liberals may adopt a broad range of policies, including the defence of free trade, freedom of speech, and freedom of religious association.

Liberalism, classic A philosophy originating in the 18th century that advocates the rights of the individual over those of the state or Church, opposing **absolutism** and the **divine right of kings**.

Libertarianism The advocacy of liberty and free will. It can be found on both the political **left** and **right** and incorporates beliefs including self-reliance, reason, and non-interference by the state in economic and personal affairs.

Machiavellian Cunning, cynical, and opportunist political activity. From Niccolò Machiavelli, a 16th-century Florentine political theorist.

Maoism A form of **Marxism-Leninism** derived from the teachings of Mao Zedong. Its central tenet is that the **agrarian** peasantry can take the place of the **proletariat** in supporting revolution.

Marxism-Leninism An ideology based on the theories of Karl Marx and Vladimir Lenin that calls for the creation of an international **communist** society.

Marxian socialism A phase of economic development that Marx believed was an essential stage in the transition from a **capitalist** to a **communist** state.

Marxism The philosophy underpinning the writings of Karl Marx, proposing that the economic order of society determines the political and social relationships within it.

Meritocracy The belief that rulers should be selected on the basis of ability, rather than wealth or birth.

Moral absolutism A philosophy based on the notion that morality should be the absolute guide of human action, particularly in regard to international law.

Multilateralism The cooperation of multiple countries working together in international relations. The opposite of **unilateralism**.

Nationalism Loyalty and devotion to the home nation, and the political belief that its interests should be pursued as the primary goal of political policy.

Natural law The concept that positive and just laws rest upon a "higher law" – originally defined by Thomas Aquinas as reflecting God's eternal law that guides the universe – which is attested to by common sense in most people.

Négritude An ideological position of solidarity based on shared black-African identity, developed by French intellectuals in the 1930s in reaction to the racism of French **colonialism**.

Oligarchy A form of government in which power is held by a small group and exercised in their own interest, usually to the detriment of the general population.

Pacifism The opposition to and campaign against war and violence as a means of resolving dispute, usually based on religious or moral grounds. The term was coined by French peace campaigner Émile Arnaud (1864–1921).

Partisan An absolute supporter of a particular political leader, party, or cause who typically exhibits unquestioning allegiance.

Perestroika Political, bureaucratic, or economic restructuring of a system or organization. From the Russian for "reconstruct", it was first coined by Mikhail Gorbachev to describe reforms to the **communist** system in the former Soviet Union.

Pluralism The belief in a society in which members of diverse social or racial groups are able to express their traditional cultures or special interests freely and alongside one another.

Plutocracy A government that is controlled or greatly influenced by the wealthy in society.

Popular sovereignty The theory that sovereign political authority is vested in and equally shared by the citizens of a state, who grant the exercising of this authority to the state, its government, and political leaders, but do not surrender ultimate **sovereignty**.

Progressivism The doctrine of moderate political progress towards better conditions in government and society.

Proletariat In **Marxist** theory, the workers of a nation who own no property and must sell their labour to earn a living. Marx believed that it was inevitable that the proletariat would rise up and overthrow their **capitalist** masters, instituting a **communist** system under which they would exercise political and economic control.

Radicalism The advocacy of extreme forms of change to achieve political means. Also refers to beliefs that constitute a considerable departure from traditional or established beliefs.

Reactionism A political orientation opposing radical social change, instead favouring a return to a former political or social order.

Realpolitik Pragmatic, realistic politics, rather than that governed by moral or ethical objectives. Realpolitik may involve a loose approach to civil liberties.

Republicanism The belief that a republic – a state with no monarch, in which power resides with the people and is exercised by their elected representatives – is the best form of government.

Rightism, right wing The ideology of the political "right", loosely defined as favouring **conservative**, pro-market attitudes, a preference for individual rights over interventionist government, a strict approach to law and order, and **nationalism**.

Segregationism The belief in the necessity to separate different races, classes, or ethnic groups from each other.

Sharia law The body of divine law in Islam that governs the religious and secular life of Muslims. Some Muslims argue that Sharia is the only legitimate basis for law.

Social contract An actual or theoretical agreement between individuals to form an organized society, or between individuals and a ruler or government to define the limits, rights, and duties of each. Theorists including Thomas Hobbes and John Locke defined the social contract as the means by which individuals were protected by a governing power, and kept from the **state of nature**.

Social democracy A reformist political movement advocating a gradual transition from **capitalism** to **socialism** by peaceful, **democratic** means. Typical tenets include the right of all citizens to education, healthcare, workers' compensation, and freedom from discrimination.

Socialism An ideology and method of government that advocates state ownership and regulation of industry, and central control over the allocation of resources, rather than allowing these to be determined by market forces.

Sovereignty Supreme power as exercised by an autonomous state or ruler, free from any external influence or control. Usually used to refer to a nation's right to self-determination in internal affairs and international relations with other countries.

State of nature In **social contract** theory, the hypothetical condition that existed prior to the emergence of organized government. According to Jean-Jacques Rousseau, this condition was one of idyllic harmony between man and nature, whereas Thomas Hobbes depicts it as a **dystopian** state of man in constant conflict with his fellow man.

Suffrage The right to vote in elections or referenda. Universal suffrage refers to the right to vote of citizens regardless of their gender, race, social status, or wealth, while women's suffrage describes the right of women to vote on the same basis as men, as campaigned for in the early 20th century by activists such as the "suffragettes".

Syndicalism An early 20th-century ideology that emerged as an alternative to **capitalism** and **socialism**. Especially popular in France and Spain, it advocated the seizure of a nation's means of production – and the overthrow of its government – in a general strike by workers' unions, and the organization of production through a federation of local syndicates.

Theocracy A political system that is organized, governed, and led by a priesthood, or even a proclaimed "living god", usually according to religious doctrine or perceived divine intervention.

Totalitarianism A regime that subordinates the rights of the individual in favour of the interests of the state, through control of political and economic affairs and prescription of the attitudes, values, and beliefs of the population.

Unilateralism Any action conducted in a one-sided manner. In politics, it often describes countries conducting foreign affairs in an individualistic manner, with minimal consultation with other nations, even allies. The opposite of **multilateralism**.

Utilitarianism A branch of social philosophy developed by Jeremy Bentham, which holds that the best policy at any given juncture is one that affords the greatest happiness to the greatest number of people.

Utopia An ideally perfect place. In politics, "Utopian" is applied to any system that aims to create an ideal society. From the Greek meaning "no place", the word was first used in Thomas More's fictional work *Utopia* (1516). See **dystopia**.

INDEX

Numbers in **bold** refer to a person's main entry.

D

E

F

S

T

ACKNOWLEDGMENTS

Dorling Kindersley and Tall Tree Ltd would like to thank Sarah Tomley for contents planning, Alison Sturgeon and Gaurav Joshi for editorial assistance, Debra Wolter for proofreading, and Chris Bernstein for the index.

PICTURE CREDITS

The publisher would like to thank the following for their kind permission to reproduce their photographs:

(Key: a-above; b-below/bottom; c-centre; f-far; l-left; r-right; t-top)

23 Dreamstime.com: Rene Drouyer (tr). **25 Getty Images:** Yann Layma / The Image Bank (br). **26 Wikimedia Commons:** http://de.wikipedia.org/w/index.php?title=Datei:Palastexamen-SongDynastie.jpg&filetimestamp=20061104233014 (bl). **27 Getty Images:** Peter Gridley / Photographer's Choice RF (tr). **29 Corbis:** Danny Lehman (cra). **31 Dreamstime.com:** Ron Sumners (tl). **Getty Images:** Chinese School / The Bridgeman Art Library (bl). **33 Getty Images:** Lintao Zhang / Getty Images News (cla). **37 Getty Images:** G. DAGLI ORTI / De Agostini (br). **39 Corbis:** Bettmann (bl). **Getty Images:** FPG / Taxi (tr). **41 Wikipedia:** Jastrow(2006) / National Museum of Rome. Inv. 8575 (tr). **42 Corbis:** Aristidis Vafeiadakis / ZUMA Press (bl). **45 Dreamstime.com:** Basphoto (br). **47 Corbis:** Richard & Gloria Maschmeyer / Design Pics (tr). **49 Getty Images:** Ken Scicluna / AWL Images (crb). **55 Getty Images:** Sandro Botticelli / The Bridgeman Art Library (bl); French School / The Bridgeman Art Library (cr). **57 Getty Images:** Muhannad Fala'ah / Stringer / Getty Images News (tr). **59 Corbis:** Michael S. Yamashita (tr). **61 Dreamstime.com:** Juergen Schonnop (bl). **Getty Images:** Danita Delimont (tr). **65 Corbis:** Alinari Archives (tr); Heritage Images (bl). **66 Getty Images:** Fabrice Coffrini / AFP (tr). **67 Dreamstime.com:** Newlight (cra); Paul Prescott (cla). **68 Corbis:** Hulton-Deutsch Collection (tl). **69 Corbis:** Wally McNamee (bl). **Wikimedia Commons:** Wilfried Huss/http://en.wikipedia.org/wiki/File:Flag_of_the_United_Nations.svg (tr). **70 Corbis:** Stefano Bianchetti (cr). **78 Corbis: (tl). 80 Corbis:** Bettmann (tl). **81 Corbis:** Bettmann (tr). **Getty Images:** James L. Stanfield / National Geographic (bl). **87 Corbis:** Bettmann (bl); Ken Welsh / Design Pics (tr). **89 Getty Images:** French School / The Bridgeman Art Library (br). **91 Alamy Images:** Prisma Archivo (tr). **Getty Images:** Juergen Richter / LOOK (cla). **93 Corbis:** Bettmann (cla). **Wikimedia Commons:** Jean-Jacques Boissard/http://en.wikipedia.org/wiki/File:JohannesAlthusius.png (bl). **95 Corbis:** The Gallery Collection (bl). **Dreamstime.com:** Georgios Kollidas (tr). **98 Dreamstime.com:** Georgios Kollidas (bl). **99 Library Of Congress, Washington, D.C.:** http://www.loc.gov/exhibits/world/images/s37.jpg (cla). **100 Corbis:** The Print Collector (bl). **102 Corbis:** Bettmann (tl). **Fotolia:** Andreja Donko (br); Vladimir Melnikov (cb). **103 Corbis:** Alfredo Dagli Orti / The Art Archive (bl). **106 Getty Images:** Hulton Archive (bl). **107 Corbis:** The Print Collector (br). **108 Getty Images:** Hulton Archive / Stringer / Hulton Royals Collection (bl). **109 Corbis:** The Gallery Collection (br). **111 Corbis:** (bl); Rick Maiman / Sygma (cr). **113 Corbis:** Doug Wilson (clb). **Dreamstime.com:** Georgios Kollidas (tr). **121 Corbis:** Alinari Archives (br). **124 Getty Images:** Time & Life Pictures (bl). **SuperStock:** Peter Willi (tl). **125 Corbis:** Stefano Bianchetti (tl). **127 Getty Images:** The Bridgeman Art Library (br). **129 Corbis:** Michael Nicholson (bl). **Getty Images:** Mario Tama / Getty Images News (cr). **131 Getty Images:** James Gillray / The Bridgeman Art Library (cra). **133 Corbis:** Hulton-Deutsch Collection (tr). **Getty Images:** Imagno / Hulton Archive (tl). **137 The Bridgeman Art Library:** Fitzwilliam Museum, University of Cambridge, UK (br). **138 Corbis:** Owen Franken (tl). **139 Corbis:** Bettmann (bl). **Getty Images:** Universal Images Group (tr). **141 Getty Images:** Hulton Archive (tr). **143 Corbis:** Bettmann (bl); Lebrecht Music & Arts (cr). **148 Corbis:** Andrew Holbrooke (bl). **Getty Images:** Mansell / Contributor / Time & Life Pictures (tr). **149 Getty Images:** Apic / Contributor / Hulton Archive (tr); Peter Macdiarmid / Contributor / Hulton Archive (bl). **151 Corbis:** Bettmann (br). **153 Corbis:** (bl); Martin Van Lokven / Foto Natura / Minden Pictures (tr). **155 Getty Images:** Fine Art Photographic / Hulton Archive (cb); John Keenan / The Bridgeman Art Library (tr). **157 Getty Images:** Universal Images Group (tr). **158 Alamy Images:** The Art Gallery Collection (b). **159 Getty Images:** Samuel N. Fox / Archive Photos (crb). **160 Getty Images:** Hulton Archive / Hulton Royals Collection (cra). **163 Corbis:** Sergio Alvarez / Demotix (cb); Christie's Images (tr). **164 Getty Images:** SuperStock (cb). **171 Corbis:** Bettmann (bl, tr). **173 Corbis:** Bettmann (bl); Alfredo Dagli Orti / The Art Archive (tr). **177 Corbis:** Nazima Kowall (tr). **179 Corbis:** Bodo Marks (bl). **180 Corbis:** Jeremy Horner (clb). **181 Corbis:** Bettmann (tr). **185 Corbis:** Hulton-Deutsch Collection (tr). **Dreamstime.com:** Regina Pryanichnikova (bc). **187 Corbis:** adoc-photos (tr); Bettmann (bl). **192 Corbis:** Swim Ink 2, LLC (tr). **193 Corbis:** Bettmann (tr). **Getty Images:** Time & Life Pictures (clb). **194 Corbis:**

Philippe Giraud / Goodlook (cr). **197 Wikimedia Commons:** F. Hartmann/ http://en.wikipedia.org/wiki/ File:Nietzsche187a.jpg (tr). **198 Corbis:** Heidi & Hans-Juergen Koch / Minden Pictures (bl). **201 Getty Images:** Steve Eason / Stringer / Hulton Archive (cr); Roger Viollet (bl). **203 Getty Images:** CHRISTOF STACHE / AFP (clb); UniversalImagesGroup / Universal Images Group (tr). **205 Corbis:** Bettmann (cr, bl). **207 Corbis:** Hulton-Deutsch Collection (cb). **209 Corbis:** Bettmann (tr). **Getty Images:** Paul Chesley / Stone (clb). **211 Getty Images:** Fotosearch / Archive Photos (cr). **213 Corbis:** Adam Woolfitt (cla). **Library Of Congress, Washington, D.C.:** LC-USZ62-5972 (tr). **215 Corbis:** Mark Moffett / Minden Pictures (cla). **Getty Images:** German / The Bridgeman Art Library (tr). **223 Corbis:** Hulton-Deutsch Collection (bl); Frederic Soltan / Sygma (cr). **224 Getty Images:** Hulton Archive / Stringer / Archive Photos (clb). **225 Corbis:** David Osuna / Demotix (br). **229 Corbis:** Bettmann (tr); Hulton-Deutsch Collection (bl). **230 Corbis:** (bl). **231 Corbis:** Hulton-Deutsch Collection (tr). **232 Corbis:** Bettmann (bl). **233 Corbis:** Bettmann (tl). **235 Alamy Images:** The Art Archive (bl). **Corbis:** Bettmann (cla). **237 Corbis:** Bettmann (cla). **Library Of Congress, Washington, D.C.:** LC-USW33-019093-C (bl). **238 Alamy Images:** tci / MARKA (cb). **241 Corbis:** Bettmann (bl). **Getty Images:** Buyenlarge / Archive Photos (ca). **243 Getty Images:** Keystone-France / Gamma-Keystone (br). **244 Corbis:** Hulton-Deutsch Collection (tl). **245 Corbis:** Underwood & Underwood (bl). **Wikimedia Commons:** The Russian Bolshevik Revolution (free pdf from Archive.org)/http://en.wikipedia.org/wiki/File:Lev_Trotsky.jpg (tr). **246 Corbis:** (cra). **249 Corbis:** Bettmann (bl); Tolga Bozoglu / epa (cl). **251 Corbis:** Bettmann (tr). **Getty Images:** Alinari Archives / Alinari (cb). **257 Getty Images:** (br). **258 Corbis:** Bettmann (cb). **263 Getty Images:** Imagno / Hulton Archive (cra). **264 Getty Images:** Hulton Archive / Archive Photos (tr). **265 Corbis:** Roman Soumar (tr). **Getty Images:** Keystone-France / Gamma-Keystone (bl). **274 Corbis:** Martin Jones; Ecoscene (bl). **275 Corbis:** Wally McNamee (tl). **Getty Images:** Apic / Hulton Archive (bl). **277 Corbis:** (bl). **279 Corbis:** Michel Setboun (cra). **281 Corbis:** Atlantide Phototravel (tr); Oscar White (bl). **282 Corbis:** Bettmann (bc). **283 Getty Images:** Apic / Hulton Archive (tr). **286 Corbis:** Hulton-Deutsch Collection (bl). **287 Corbis:** Blue Lantern Studio (br). **288 Corbis:** Gianni Giansanti / Sygma (tl). **291 Getty Images:** ERLEND AAS / AFP (tr). **292 Corbis:** Stapleton Collection (tl). **295 Corbis:** Hulton-Deutsch Collection (clb); Stephane Ruet / Sygma (tr). **296 Corbis:** Bettmann (cr). **302 Dreamstime.com:** Marcio Silva (bl). **303 Getty Images:** AFP / Stringer / AFP (tr); Frederic REGLAIN / Gamma-Rapho (bl). **305 Corbis:** Raymond Darolle / Europress / Sygma (cra). **306 Getty Images:** Topical Press Agency / Hulton Archive (tr). **307 Getty Images:** AFP (bl); Leemage / Universal Images Group (tr). **309 Corbis:** (cra). **Library Of Congress, Washington, D.C.:** LC-USZ62-115058 (bl). **311 Corbis:** Bettmann (tr); Wolfgang Flamisch (cb). **313 Corbis:** epa (cla). **Getty Images:** Joseph Scherschel / Time & Life Pictures (tr). **315 Corbis:** Christopher Felver (bl). **Getty Images:** Bloomberg (cra). **319 Wikimedia Commons:** US Army/ http://en.wikipedia.org/wiki/File:101st_Airborne_at_Little_Rock_Central_High.jpg (br). **320 Corbis:** Bettmann (tr). **321 Corbis:** Flip Schulke (bl). **Library Of Congress, Washington, D.C.:** LC-USZ62-126559 (tr). **322 Corbis:** Bettmann (cb). **325 Corbis:** Najlah Feanny / CORBIS SABA (tr). **Getty Images:** AFP (clb). **327 Corbis:** Pascal Deloche / Godong (cb). **Getty Images:** Martha Holmes / TIME & LIFE Images (tr). **328 Corbis:** Bettmann (cra)

For more information see:
www.dkimages.co.uk